Searching for Woody Guthrie

Searching for Woody Guthrie

A Personal Exploration of the Folk Singer, His Music, and His Politics

Ron Briley

Charles K. Wolfe Music Series / Ted Olson, Series Editor
The University of Tennessee Press / Knoxville

The Charles K. Wolfe Music Series was launched in honor of the late Charles K. Wolfe (1943–2006), whose pioneering work in the study of American vernacular music brought a deepened understanding of a wide range of American music to a worldwide audience. In recognition of Dr. Wolfe's approach to music scholarship, the series will include books that investigate genres of folk and popular music as broadly as possible.

Copyright © 2020 by The University of Tennessee Press / Knoxville.
All Rights Reserved.
First Edition.

Frontispiece: Woody Guthrie, 1942.
Courtesy of the Woody Guthrie Archives.

Library of Congress Cataloging-in-Publication Data
Names: Briley, Ron, 1949– author.
Title: Searching for Woody Guthrie: a personal exploration
of the folk singer, his music, and his politics / Ron Briley.
Description: First edition. | Knoxville: The University of Tennessee Press, [2020] |
Series: Charles K. Wolfe music series | Includes bibliographical references and index. |
Identifiers: LCCN 2019013800 (print) | LCCN 2019015782 (ebook) |
ISBN 9781621905349 (pdf) | ISBN 9781621905332 (pbk.)
Subjects: LCSH: Guthrie, Woody, 1912–1967—Criticism and interpretation. |
Music—Political aspects—United States—History—20th century.
Classification: LCC ML410.G978 (ebook) | LCC ML410.G978 B75 2020 (print) |
DDC 782.42162/130092 [B] —dc23
LC record available at https://lccn.loc.gov/2019013800

Designed and typeset
by Nathan Moehlmann,
Goosepen Studio & Press

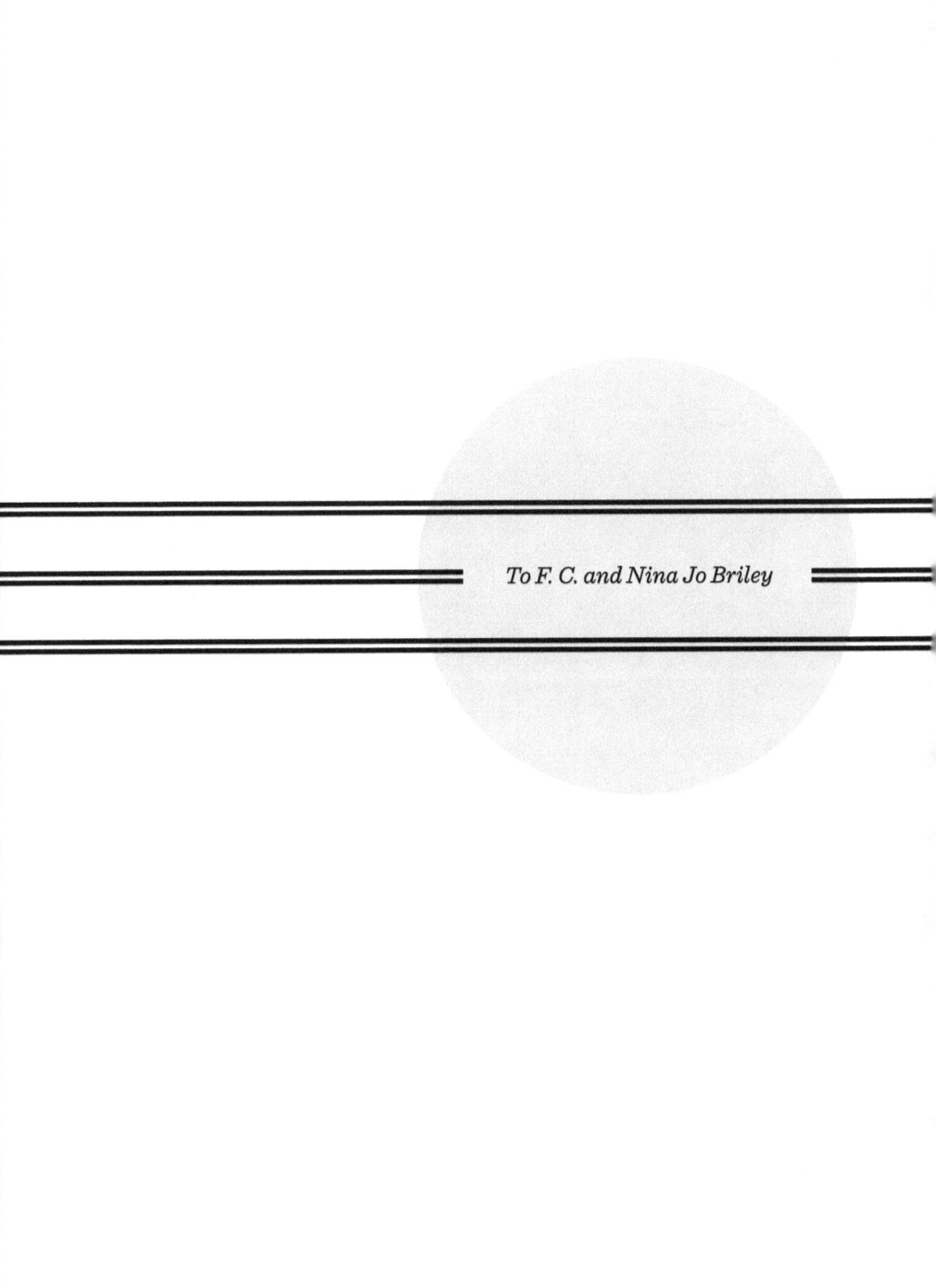
To F. C. and Nina Jo Briley

Contents

Foreword *Ted Olson* — xi

Introduction
My Search for Woody Guthrie — 1

Chapter One
De-radicalizing Woody: Hal Ashby's *Bound for Glory* (1976) — 21

Chapter Two
Woody in California:
The *People's Daily World* and Indigenous Radicalism — 43

Chapter Three
Woody in New York City:
"Woody Sez" and the *Daily Worker* — 59

Chapter Four
Woody and the Bonneville Power Administration:
Twenty-six Songs in Thirty Days — 77

Chapter Five
Woody and World War II: The Struggle against Fascism — 91

Chapter Six
Woody and Postwar Disillusionment: The Korean War — 109

Chapter Seven
Woody and Jesus: The Working-Class
Carpenter and Christian Socialism — 129

Chapter Eight
Primitive Rebels: Woody and the Outlaw Tradition —— 153

Chapter Nine
"I'm Sticking to the Union": Woody and Labor —— 165

Chapter Ten
Woody and Race: Taking on Jim Crow —— 179

Chapter Eleven
Woody and the Women's Question:
Advocate for Equality and Sexual Libertine —— 199

Chapter Twelve
Woody's Songs: *Dust Bowl Ballads*, 1940 —— 219

Chapter Thirteen
Woody's Songs: *Struggle*, 1946 —— 237

Chapter Fourteen
Woody's Songs: *Ballads of Sacco & Vanzetti*, 1946 and 1947 —— 257

Chapter Fifteen
Woody's Children: Arlo Guthrie,
Bob Dylan, and Bruce Springsteen —— 275

Conclusion
Woody Guthrie and Our Times —— 299

Notes —— 311
Bibliography —— 349
Index —— 367

Illustrations

Following page 141

Harris Drug Store in Pampa, Texas
Author at Harris Drug Store
Message Board from Woody Guthrie Folk Music Center
Author outside Harris Drugs
Author and Wife Kathleen at Woody Guthrie Folk Music Center
Poster from *Bound for Glory*
Woody Guthrie, 1942
Okemah Welcome Sign
Okemah Water Tower
Woody Guthrie Statue
Arlo Guthrie Concert in Okemah for Woodyfest Centennial
Commemorative Brick in Okemah Honoring
    Woody Guthrie and the Union Idea
Author and Daughter Pam at Woodyfest Centennial
Bandstand at Woodyfest 2012

Foreword

In Okemah, Oklahoma, just off W. Broadway St., between S. 4th and S. 3rd Streets, stands a statue commemorating that town's most famous citizen, Woody Guthrie. The statue depicts Guthrie holding a low-slung guitar while gazing off into space, perhaps contemplating the topic of, or some words for, his next song. On a nearby plaque is an inscription, proclaiming Okemah as "Nestled in the Oklahoma Hills and the Birthplace on July 14, 1912 of Woody Guthrie, the renowned poet and folk singer. The hometown that influenced songs such as the American classic 'This Land Is Your Land' and scores of other songs, poems, and books, including his autobiographical novel *Bound for Glory*, is designated a literary landmark by Friends of Libraries U.S.A." The statue and plaque were placed there to celebrate Guthrie as Okemah's *genius loci*, and it is undeniable that his formative experiences in Oklahoma, and then in the nearby Texas Panhandle, remained the psychic wellspring from which Guthrie drew inspiration throughout his life.

Guthrie's fate, though, transported him far from Okemah — to Los Angeles, to Washington State, to New York City, and to many places in-between and beyond — and most Americans consider him more of a national bard than strictly a regional or local one. To be sure, Guthrie's life, tragically shortened though it was by Huntington's disease, was broadly impactful. He influenced — and in some ways transformed — American culture through his songs (he was, of course, a brilliant, versatile songwriter), his other writings, and his bold social consciousness. Many people from disparate places — compelled by Guthrie's example to live more fully and deeply and to pursue and practice social justice — have found themselves "searching for Woody Guthrie." Those who have heard and heeded Guthrie's charismatic call have included well-known culture-shapers like Pete Seeger, Ramblin'

Jack Elliot, Bob Dylan, Bruce Springsteen, and Billy Bragg, but there have been countless others whose connections to Woody, while less documented, have been no less vital, no less real. One person from the latter group, West Texas-native Ron Briley, decided to write this book and retrace his steps during his own quest to learn lessons from the Okemah legend.

To Briley, Guthrie was a local hero — a fellow seeker from the Southern Plains who crafted a meaningful and morally upright life in a complex world. As this book eloquently reflects, Briley became an insightful interpreter of Guthrie. Additionally, and uniquely among the many works devoted to understanding Guthrie, *Searching for Woody Guthrie* takes an avowedly personal approach to its subject, conveying Briley's assessment of how Guthrie's life and work might serve to affirm the lived experience of Briley and his own family and community. He hopes that his place-based interpretation of Guthrie will hold value to others who may not have a Southern Plains background. As his main motivation in writing *Searching for Woody Guthrie*, Briley offers, "It is my hope that this examination of Woody's legacy, through the lens of the Briley family, will encourage readers to fight for and realize his vision of our common humanity."

Ted Olson
East Tennessee State University

Introduction

My Search for Woody Guthrie

I will always treasure the letter I received from my father when I became the first member of my family to enter college. It began with the greeting, "Deer Sun." Tears rolled down my cheeks as I recognized my opportunity, which had been denied to him. This book represents an endeavor to come to some understanding of my journey from a poor West Texas background to a family of my own and a teaching career of forty years in a prep school. My guide for this odyssey is Woody Guthrie who shared a similar rural background before leaving Oklahoma and the Texas Panhandle for the greener pastures of Los Angeles and New York City. Woody's life and work are an inspiration and represent a model of how one may grow and change without losing respect for the common folk of America and the world. My search for Woody Guthrie has provided me with guidance for understanding the past and bringing about a better tomorrow. It is my hope that this examination of Woody's legacy, through the lens of the Briley family, will encourage readers to fight for and realize his vision of our common humanity.

Folk singer Woodrow Wilson Guthrie, who became a political and cultural radical during the Great Depression and Second World War, was appropriately born in 1912 on July 14th — Bastille Day. This French-national holiday commemorates the beginnings of the French Revolution and the political desire to implement a degree of social, political, and economic equality into the modern world. As a cultural figure, Woody Guthrie played a crucial role in the struggle for social justice within the United States. Nevertheless, this was not a role into which Woody was necessarily born in Okemah, Oklahoma. His father, Charley was a local land speculator. Like the progressive New Jersey Governor Woodrow Wilson (nominated in 1912 for the Presidency by the Democratic Party), Charley was opposed to the Socialist Party. In the early twentieth century, this party had gained a following in both Oklahoman and American politics. The fortunes of the Guthrie family, however, were decimated by poor investments and a series of fires that destroyed the family home, as well as killing Woody's older sister, Clara, and seriously injuring Charley. Many Okemah residents associated the fires with the increasingly erratic behavior of Woody's mother Nora, who was institutionalized after being diagnosed with Huntington's chorea — a degenerative disease of the central nervous system, better known today as simply Huntington's disease. This hereditary disease eventually impacted her son, Woody.

Following his mother's institutionalization, Woody attempted to survive on his own but finally joined his father and siblings who were living with relatives in the Texas Panhandle community of Pampa, a former oil boom town. Woody married a local girl, Mary Jennings, and began to start a family. Economic prospects were poor during the 1930s as the dust bowl enveloped Pampa and the Texas Panhandle. Woody, who never had much of an interest in farming, tried to make ends meet by playing music, painting signs, and telling fortunes. As the wind and dust swept through Pampa, Woody decided to join the trek of the Oklahoman and Texan migrants toward California. During his tenure in California, from 1937 to 1940, Woody discovered that he could earn money with his music. His observations regarding the exploitation of his fellow dust bowl migrants radicalized the folk singer, however, and he was unwilling to abandon his critique of capitalism to embrace a lucrative and traditional commercial musical career.

Woody arrived in New York City in early 1940, and the authenticity of Woody's music was enthusiastically embraced by musicologists such as Alan Lomax. Again, Woody rejected political compromise and turned his back on a potentially lucrative radio contract. He returned to California before working briefly for the Bonneville Power Administration in Oregon where he publicizied Franklin Roosevelt's New Deal public power project with songs such as "Roll On, Columbia," "The Grand Coulee Dam," and "Pastures of Plenty." Woody split with Mary before once again heading toward New York City. Here, he joined Pete Seeger and the Almanac Singers, whose music supported union organization and antiwar themes until Hitler's invasion of the Soviet Union on June 22, 1941. Woody also fell in love with a dancer, Marjorie Greenblatt Mazia, whom he eventually married. During the Second World War, Woody threw himself into the antifascist crusade, running about New York City with the phrase "this machine kills fascists" printed on his guitar. He also served with the United States Merchant Marine, but he was still briefly drafted into the Army as the war ended.

The post–World War II era was a difficult time for Woody as the war against fascism failed to usher in the millennium of peace and egalitarianism the folk singer had envisioned. Instead, the Cold War and McCarthyism limited reform and change. On a personal level, Woody and Marjorie's daughter Cathy perished in yet another fire shortly after her fourth birthday in February 1947. A devastated Woody sought to lose himself in raising his and Marjorie's other three children, including Arlo — who has maintained his father's musical legacy. Nevertheless, Woody's behavior was increasingly erratic. He deserted Marjorie and his family, eventually marrying Anneke Van Kirk Marshall, who was about half his age. The marriage failed, and Woody checked into the hospital, assuming he was suffering from alcoholism. Instead, he was diagnosed with Huntington's disease, which had plagued his mother. Slowly losing control over his emotions and muscles, Woody was institutionalized from 1954 until his death on October 3, 1967. Marjorie, who had remarried, took care of Woody in these final years and formed the Guthrie Children's Trust to organize the folk singer's finances. While the shadow of McCarthyism loomed over artists such as Pete Seeger, who was blacklisted during the 1950s, Woody Guthrie's voice was silenced by disease, but his music never died.

The folk revival of the early 1960s, along with the Civil Rights Movement and the protest music of the counterculture and antiwar movements, led to renewed interest in Woody's life and music. While many school children in the 1950s and early 1960s sang some of the verses of Woody's "This Land Is Your Land" as a patriotic tribute to American exceptionalism, Seeger and Arlo Guthrie made sure that Woody's more radical verses questioning private property were not forgotten. In a similar fashion, the young folk singer Bob Dylan modeled his early career and persona on the protest music of Woody Guthrie. While Dylan's songs have drifted from the political messages of his early career, Woody's sense of rebellion continues to influence the work of Bruce Springsteen in compositions such as "The Ghost of Tom Joad." Musical artists such as Billy Bragg and Wilco have plumbed the Guthrie Archives, providing fresh musical takes on Woody's lyrics with the *Mermaid Avenue* albums. Tom Morello with Rage Against the Machine and Audioslave, as well as in his solo career as the Nightwatchman, has kept the radical aspects of Woody's music alive and well into the twenty-first century; and numerous artists celebrated Woody's centennial in 2012. Also, every summer in mid-July, Woody is remembered in his hometown of Okemah with Woodyfest. In fact, the better world envisioned in Woody's music continues to inspire and offer hope during our turbulent present — just as it did for common people during the Great Depression and World War II.

With a geographical and economic background somewhat like that of Woody — although lacking any type of musical talent — I have found Guthrie's music, life, and struggle to be an inspiration. Sometimes despairing of progressive change in the world, I play

Woody's songs, and I find my faith in the people and democracy restored. I am then also convinced to renew my commitment to the struggle for social justice to which Woody dedicated his life. In my search for Woody Guthrie, I have found meaning for my own life and that of my parents, especially my father, who embraced the work ethic of Benjamin Franklin's self-made man. But in the final analysis the American dream eluded my family.

I was born in 1949, near the end of the post-World War II baby boom and was brought up in the small Texas Panhandle farming community of Childress — about ninety miles southwest of Woody's adopted home of Pampa. My parents were products of the depression and World War II. My mother's family was slightly more affluent than my father's parents; my mother graduated from high school and the Leach family owned a modest home where they raised chickens and maintained a large garden to help feed the family. My maternal grandfather worked for the Fort Worth and Denver Railroad, but to make ends meet the family still labored in the Texas cotton fields during the summer and fall.

The economic circumstances for my father's family were even more difficult. In fact, the Guthrie family of Okemah was far more prosperous than the Briley clan of Childress. My father, F. C. Briley was only semi-literate. He had to drop out of school during his early primary schooling to help support the family. Unable to pay their rent on a small piece of farm land during the depression, my father's family, along with Woody Guthrie and migrants from Oklahoma and the Texas Panhandle, fled the plains. Unlike Woody and migrant families, such as John Steinbeck's fictional Joads, the Briley family headed to Idaho rather than California. In Idaho, they picked up a rather eccentric son-in-law and harvested potatoes. In fact, family tradition, which is probably not true, insists that my Grandpa Briley, who was illiterate, was elected sheriff of a small Idaho town. He was very popular because he could not write a ticket and thus let off everyone accused of a minor infraction with only a verbal warning. The family failed to find the American dream in Idaho and during the Second World War returned to Childress.

My father was drafted into the Army during the war and was stationed in Europe — as far as I know this was the only time he ever left the United States. Following military service, my father once again returned to Childress where he married my mother. It was the second marriage for both, a fact my brother and I discovered only after my father died. My father did not want his wife to work outside the home, but she eventually was forced, out of economic necessity, to enter the workforce and found a job keeping books for a local dry-cleaning business. F. C. Briley was the hardest working man I ever observed, but with a lack of formal education or vocational skills such as a plumber, carpenter, or electrician, it was difficult for him to support a family of four. He worked as a laborer for the railroad, but he was often laid off and unemployed. During those times, he found work as a used car and insurance salesman, in addition to agricultural labor and odd jobs. He would often go door to door, inquiring whether people had any work. I sometimes accompanied him and was often embarrassed when we knocked at the homes of school classmates. But honest labor never bothered my father.

After living in rental homes, we were finally able to purchase a small two-bedroom and one-bath home, although making the modest monthly house payment was often a source of family stress. During the 1950s and early 1960s, my mother attempted to feed a family of four on only twenty dollars a week, and while we never starved, as a young boy I often went to bed hungry after the small dinner — what we called supper — portions. We had one extra change of school clothes, and my father thought bathing more than once a week was an extravagance we could not afford.

Unlike Charley Guthrie, my father said little about politics, but it was obvious that he was a supporter of his union and programs such as Social Security. I was also taught to respect the racial mores of Jim Crow and the American South. Woody was brought up on similar racial convictions — evidently Charley Guthrie once participated in an Okemah lynching — before becoming a vocal opponent of racial discrimination and segregation. While my parents would never embrace the violence and hatred of the Klan, they were quite uncomfortable with the Civil Rights Movement and manifestations of racial equality. One incident from my childhood that stands out in my mind occurred when we had a black man do some labor at our house with my father. When the black laborer asked my mother for a drink of water, she, without thinking, offered him some tap water in my favorite glass — a *Flintstones'* drinking cup that had been a peanut butter jar. After the black man finished the drink and left, my mother walked over to the trash and shattered the glass. As I started to cry, she explained, "You just can't wash it out." My challenging of such racial assumptions later caused considerable duress within my family. I found it somewhat ironic, as well as hopeful, that in her final years my mother's primary caretaker was a black woman with whom she found some comfort and friendship.

My parents also sought solace in the religious fundamentalism that characterized Oklahoma and the Texas Panhandle in which Woody and I grew up. Woody reconciled his politics and faith in Jesus by appealing to Christian socialism and the notion of the Nazarene as a working-class carpenter who drove the money changers out of the temple and fed the people by dividing the fishes and loaves. This type of social message in Christianity seemed to escape my family. They believed that the poor would suffer in this life, but if, like St. Paul stated, one obeyed the masters, it would be possible to inherit the kingdom of God in the next life. Essentially, this was the type of religious obedience that the white slave owners attempted to instill in their African slaves. A source of considerable disappointment for my mother was my questioning of religious fundamentalism which she attributed to the devil and to advanced education. However, the Assembly of God denomination, in which I was raised, also nourished Elvis Presley and the Everly Brothers, providing some incredible music during my youth. Songs such as "I'll Fly Away" are still in my head today, and the rhythm demonstrates the gospel roots of rock and roll. The pastors were usually fine guitarists and musicians, but this musical interest did not extend into our home.

The type of social gatherings that Woody describes — his family and friends sitting around strumming guitars and singing religious and folk tunes — was not part of my family history. As rather stoic fundamentalists, they were always afraid that somehow all of this singing might lead to such dangerous activities as dancing and drinking. Instead, the Briley family tended to spend their evenings in front of the television set. As I matured, I found little interest in the Westerns and situation comedies on the tube, so I began to seek an escape through reading. In addition to wanting an alternative to the banality of television, reading provided some distraction from my labors in the cotton fields. Woody may have spent more time singing about picking cotton as a cultural worker rather than laboring in the fields, but I still regard my work picking and chopping cotton in the fields of West Texas during the heat of July and August as some of the most difficult experiences in my life. In fact, when I got a job working in the local cemetery as part of Lyndon Johnson's Neighborhood Youth Corps, I found digging graves preferable to picking cotton.

About the only book in our home was the Bible which I read numerous times before beginning to devour the shelves of the Childress County Library. My parents did not quite know what to make of this passion for the written word. My father even burned some of my library books as he blamed them for my poor eye sight and my tendency to strike out during Little League games. However, my love for books did not necessarily translate into educational achievements in the classroom. There was no assumption on the part of either my parents or teachers, who inspired little enthusiasm for learning, that I was college material. Everyone, including myself, just seemed to be going through the motions, and during my high school years far greater emphasis was placed upon football than academics. Accordingly, I paid little attention to class assignments and simply read during my math and science classes. The teachers did not really seem to mind, as long as I was quiet and did not disrupt classroom activities. My reading extended from popular science fiction and adventure books, such as the Hardy Boys and Tarzan, to classics of American and world literature. However, I always fashioned myself as something of a rebel by never reading the books assigned by my English teachers. I even read *War and Peace* for pleasure, and when I looked at my Algebra II final — a course that I failed three times during high school — and recognized that it would be impossible for me to work any of the problems, I decided to turn the test booklet over and write a review of Tolstoy's classic on the back. I doubt that the composition provided much insight into Russian literature. My Algebra teacher was incensed and took me to the principal's office where I received the usual corporal punishment of a "paddling." When I complained that I was probably the first person to be paddled for a bad review, the principal gave me another "three licks" for my insolence. Much like Woody, I believe that the only useful skill I obtained from my high school education was learning to type.

Following my graduation from high school in 1967, my attitude toward education was altered by the Vietnam War, and my search for the ghost and legacy of Woody Guthrie commenced. I had no plans for college and assumed that I might get a job pumping gas or cutting weeds for the state highway department as I had few marketable skills. Everything changed one day when my father came in the door and announced that he had just heard the "damnedst" thing, "If you went to one of them there colleges, you didn't have to go to Vietnam." While my father was hardly a critic of American foreign policy in Southeast Asia, his combat experience during the Second World War in Europe convinced him that that he did not want his son to endure similar conditions in Vietnam. Thus, I enrolled at West Texas State University in nearby Canyon — an institution generous in accepting many poorly educated youths from the high schools of the Texas Panhandle.

Although severely lacking academic skills, I fell in love with a world of books and ideas of which I had only dreamed. Finances remained a problem as I was soon married with a child on the way, but it was possible to stay in school with student loans, several work study jobs, and some savings from high school cotton picking, newspaper routes, and grave digging. I threw myself into the studies. My transition to the educational demands of the university was mentored by a history professor, Peter Petersen, without whose assistance I never would have been able to stay in school. It was also the late 1960s, and I was not immune, even on a rather conservative college campus, from the winds of social, political, and cultural change sweeping the nation. I grew my hair long, but with my family, work, and academic responsibilities, I was not part of the countercultural drug scene. Nevertheless, I was inspired by the antiwar and civil rights movements, finding some time for political activities such as the small campus chapter of Students for a Democratic Society (SDS). As a history major, I was becoming increasingly radicalized in my political beliefs. I recognized in my own family's poverty, despite a strong work ethic, that the American working class was exploited by capitalistic corporations who perverted the American dream of social mobility. I also discovered that there was a rich heritage of dissent and radicalism in the American past. While studying the impact of groups such as the Socialist Party, Industrial Workers of the World (IWW), Congress for Industrial Organization (CIO), Student Non-Violent Coordinating Committee (SNCC), and Black Panthers, I encountered the life and legacy of Woody Guthrie.

I was, of course, familiar with Woody as the composer of "This Land Is Your Land" — minus the radical verses which were not taught in school. However, I was unaware of the extent to which Woody was involved in the radicalism and protests in the 1930s by farmworkers, artists, unionists, socialists, communists, antifascists, and common working people during the Great Depression. The history of protest and dissent in the United States remains hidden from most Americans and may in part explain the increasing frustration and anger of Americans with their political system. And while this history was important to my understanding of the American experience, I tended to ignore cultural history and emphasized politics — following the more traditional path of professional historians. Thus, music about the trials and tribulations of Woody's people and mine often found its way on to my turntable in those record-playing days, but Woody's cultural insights rarely found their way into my teaching and writing. My master's thesis at West Texas State University focused upon political mavericks from the Midwest who comprised the Senate Farm Bloc during the 1920s. I decided to continue my investigation of this topic as I pursued a doctorate in history at the University of New

Mexico beginning in the fall of 1972. Under the tutelage of a rather conservative professor, Gerald D. Nash, I was, nevertheless, able to continue with the leftist political leanings of my research.

Guthrie remained in the background as I concentrated upon the exploits of figures such as Senator Smith Wildman Brookhart of Iowa. When my graduate assistantship expired after three years, economic expediency led me to accept a job teaching junior high school history at a Catholic school in Albuquerque. Although I was not really a good fit for a Catholic school, I enjoyed the students and even taught a few of Woody's songs. Concluding that I could not follow a career in Catholic education, I prepared to borrow additional money to pursue the travel and archival research that would allow me to complete my dissertation. My career and pursuit of Woody changed, however, when an Albuquerque prep school offered me a position teaching American history. From my own educational background, I certainly had no understanding of what a college preparatory school entailed. Fortunately, Sandia Prep was a small, struggling independent school without the elitist trappings one usually associates with private education, and the school proved to be an excellent match for me. The plan was to teach for one year at Sandia Prep, earn some money, and to complete my dissertation before assuming a teaching career at the university level. However, I stayed for thirty-eight years and even spent twenty-six years of that period serving as assistant head of the school in addition to pursuing my teaching duties. And as it turns out, the Sandia Prep environment offered me the opportunity to resume my search for Woody Guthrie.

Sandia Prep School encouraged innovation in teaching and research that made it possible for me to follow new scholarly areas of interest. I had lost enthusiasm in the narrow pursuit of political history and completing a dissertation. It seemed to me that teaching and researching from a base in the school might allow me the freedom to pursue new concerns within cultural and social history. Accordingly, I began to consider research possibilities in the fields of sport, film, and music history. This meant that I would not finish my dissertation on the Senate Farm Bloc, for which I have some regret, but the positive aspects of this career decision more than outweighed the reservations. I joined the North American Society for Sport History and published several articles and books on baseball as a reflection of American society and values. In addition, I delved into film history with my research and writing, developing courses on American History Through Film and World Cinema. Along with incorporating sport history into my American history classes, I found music also invigorated students and the study of history. Thus, Woody found his way into my high school history curriculum. Although I have no musical talent, every year there was a student with a guitar who could help me lead the class in singing Woody's music. But it was also important to develop the historical and cultural context in which Woody lived and worked. In addition to examining depression-era photographs of Dorothea Lange and the Farm Securities Administration, we read John Steinbeck's *The Grapes of Wrath* and listened to Woody's composition "Tom Joad." Another important component of the class was investigating, sometimes employing my personal history and story, the contemporary struggles of working-class Americans to find a place in the so-called global economy.

Following a paper and presentation on Woody's politics which I prepared for a National Endowment for the Humanities Summer Seminar for Teachers on Intellectuals and Communism held at Emory University in the early 1990s, I began an academic search for Woody. My early research resulted in several presentations at academic conferences and publications in scholarly journals, but the highlight of my research was being selected in 2006 as a Guthrie Fellow — which does sound a little pretentious for Woody — to study at the Woody Guthrie Archives in New York City. I used the fellowship stipend to sublease an efficiency apartment and spent much of the summer at the archives which were then located on West 57th Street, in what were the old offices of Woody's business manager Harold Leventhal. The archives have since relocated to Tulsa, Oklahoma where, appropriately, Bob Dylan's papers will also be stored. The Guthrie Archives include a plethora of sources such as Woody's voluminous notebooks, drawings, correspondence, and hundreds of song lyrics. It is a treasure trove of material for anyone interested in Guthrie, and my research into the Guthrie Archives will be an essential source for this book and my search for Woody Guthrie. I was also fortunate to participate in conferences commemorating Woody's centennial at Penn State University and the University of Southern California in 2012. The event in Los Angeles was especially noteworthy as it included a concert at the Staples Center in which artists such as Jackson Browne, Graham Nash, Kris Kristofferson, and Tom Morello appeared. I also was able to attend the 2012 Woodyfest in Okemah that featured a concert by Arlo Guthrie.

My travels and explorations in search of Woody have led me from the dusty streets of Childress, where in the early 1950s I experienced the waning days of the dust bowl, to the busy sidewalks of New York City. This search for Woody Guthrie has helped me learn a great deal about myself and remain connected to my working-class origins. Woody was no saint, especially when it came to family obligations, but he was consistently committed to the larger struggle of the common people to achieve economic and social justice. This represents a progressive model to which we might all aspire.

This book length study of my search for the meaning of Woody's life and work for us today has taken longer than expected, and its completion has had to wait until my retirement from teaching and school administration. I hope that readers will find the delayed manuscript worthy of Woody, as well as their valuable time. My search for Woody Guthrie is a thematic rather than biographical work as there are at least three excellent biographies of Woody available, as well as his autobiographical novel, *Bound for Glory* (1943). In 1980, journalist Joe Klein made extensive use of the Guthrie Archives to publish both an entertaining and informative biography of the folk singer. Klein's work, however, included no endnotes to support his research or guide other Guthrie scholars. Ed Cray's 2004 biography, *Ramblin' Man*, improved on Klein's work by carefully noting archival sources. Some critics, however, believe that both Klein and Cray were derelict in not placing greater emphasis upon Woody's social activism and radical politics. Thus, Will Kaufman, a professor of American literature and culture at the University of Central Lancashire, England, completed *Woody Guthrie: American Radical* for the University of Illinois Press in 2011. In his introduction to the volume, Kaufman writes, "Woody Guthrie spent his productive life on the warpath — against poverty, political oppression, censorship, capitalism, fascism, racism, and, ultimately, war itself. His commitment to radical struggle forced him to face head-on — and sometimes celebrate — the violence inevitable to the tearing down and reconstruction of an oppressive system, whether fascism in Europe or capitalism at home."[1] My own research on Woody and investigation of the Guthrie Archives led me to concur with Kaufman that Woody fits well into the oft ignored tradition of indigenous, American radicalism. Nonetheless, this is not a conclusion with which all admirers of Guthrie's life and work would agree. For example, Woody's daughter Nora Guthrie, who has played a significant role in keeping Woody's music and biography alive with the archives, insisted in a phone interview with me that her father could best be characterized as an independent thinker who resisted the ideological constraints of a narrow and deterministic philosophy such as communism. She concluded that Woody's experiences convinced him to trust in the instinctive wisdom of the common people and the power of love rather than ideological constructs.[2] Nevertheless, my research on Woody finds more evidence for indigenous radicalism. But I would agree with Nora that Woody never lost his faith in the common working people of America, and this populist faith provides hope for the nation and world. The struggles of people like F. C. Briley have meaning and are well articulated in the songs of Woody Guthrie.

Nevertheless, many seek to dismiss Woody's politics by alleging that he was a member of the Communist Party. While Woody was a vocal critic of capitalism, who entertained for Communist Party gatherings and was sympathetic to the party's struggles against racism and fascism, it is, indeed, difficult to conceive of Woody as exhibiting the type of discipline demanded by the party hierarchy. Instead, Woody was an advocate of "commonism" that included elements of communism, Christianity, socialism, progressivism, Jeffersonian agrarianism, and populism; he avoided ideological straitjackets, as

Nora Guthrie suggested. Nevertheless, Woody remained a radical who was a consistent critic of the profit motive. This fact has always concerned some conservatives who are alarmed that school children sing an anthem such as "This Land Is Your Land" composed by an anti-capitalist. There has been, therefore, an effort to de-radicalize Woody by ignoring the verses of "This Land Is Your Land" that question private property.

Chapter one focuses upon one of the more interesting attempts to mainstream Woody. In 1976, director Hal Ashby released a biopic of Woody, *Bound for Glory*, with David Carradine in the title role. Ashby was best known for films such as *Harold and Maude* (1971), *The Last Detail* (1973), and *Shampoo* (1975), featuring antiestablishment themes, and the director appeared to be a good choice for the Guthrie film. *Bound for Glory*, however, takes a more conservative approach to its subject. The film focuses upon Woody in California during the period of his radicalization from 1937 until 1940, when he left the state. Ashby demonstrates how Woody became politically aware of the power his music had to illuminate the plight of the Okie migrants in California. The film fails, however, to develop Woody's more radical ties with the Communist Party during this period, when he even wrote columns for the *People's Daily World* — the West Coast publication of the party. The film ends with Woody celebrating his individualism rather than collectivism after rejecting a radio contract that would have silenced his political voice. As Woody rides a freight train toward New York City, "This Land Is Your Land" is played, providing a positive and optimistic spin that Woody and the American people are moving forward while putting the despair of the depression behind them.

It is a perfect theme for the bicentennial and goes along well with another film from that same year, *Rocky*, extolling the common man. Hollywood and America sought to escape the pessimism of the early 1970s and films such as *Chinatown* (1974). This process of glossing over America's more radical past culminated in 1980 with the election of Ronald Reagan and his slogan of "it's morning in America again." In reality, the gap between rich and poor in America was about to become a chasm.

My research into Woody, however, suggests that the more conservative approach of Ashby's film fails to capture the real Woody Guthrie. The next section of the book concentrates chronologically upon five key periods in Woody's life story. Chapter two examines some of the same ground plowed by Ashby's film, but in this case Woody's time in California and his political ideas will be analyzed through a close reading of his "Woody Sez" columns for the *People's Daily World*. Chapter three follows Woody to New York City where he continued his "Woody Sez" columns for the *Daily Worker*, America's leading communist newspaper. These columns will be employed to develop Woody's growing political consciousness and it's influence on his music and persona, which were touted by the leftist New York City intelligentsia. Woody, however, balked at the compromises commercial success in New York would entail, and he abandoned his promising radio career.

Desperately in need of money to support his family, Woody found brief employment in the Pacific Northwest with the Bonneville Power Administration. Publicizing the public power ideology of the New Deal, Woody demonstrated his belief that a government of the people could improve the lot of the common citizens by building dams and providing cheap electricity while irrigation and resettlement programs were creating pastures of plenty. It is fair, however, to say that Woody tended to ignore the impact of dam construction upon the indigenous, Native American population and the environment. The sojourn in the Pacific Northwest, covered in chapter four, occupies only a short span of Woody's life, but it is important to the understanding of his political beliefs. With his marriage to Mary deteriorating, Woody deposited his family in Texas, while he returned to New York City. Here, he fell in love with and eventually married Marjorie Greenblatt Mazia. Chapter five makes extensive use of Woody's letters to Marjorie while he was serving in the Merchant Marine to develop his belief that the antifascist struggle would defeat capitalist exploitation and Jim Crow, both globally and domestically. Marjorie was then pregnant with the couple's first child, whom Woody insisted upon calling Railroad Pete; but he embraced the birth and name of Cathy Guthrie when Railroad

Pete proved to be a girl. In his letters and diary entries, Woody envisioned the dawn of a new era for his people. However, the folk singer was later disillusioned and depressed by Cathy's death, the Cold War, McCarthyism, the dissolution of his marriage to Marjorie, and his diagnosis with Huntington's disease. Chapter six develops this period by focusing upon Woody's opposition to the Korean War, portrayed in a series of songs denouncing the conflict as a war of imperialist aggression by the United States. These songs, which were unpublished but remain in the Guthrie Archives, reflect Woody's political disillusionment during the Cold War and also suggest that his health was beginning to negatively impact the quality of his song writing.

Following this chronological examination of key periods in Woody's life, the search for Woody Guthrie continues with five chapters devoted to analyzing his ideas on topics of particular importance to his life and political philosophy, establishing his radical credentials and allegiance to "commonism." Chapter seven concentrates upon the admiration Woody always expressed for Jesus of Nazareth and his message of love. Woody had little use for organized religion, but his belief in the Christian socialism preached by Jesus was a consistent element of Woody's thought; the Oklahoman perceived no essential conflict between his admiration for Jesus and his sympathy with elements of Marxist thought, as both fit into his belief in "commonism." Woody's music also contained numerous examples of his identification with outlaws such as Billy the Kid, Jesse James, Belle Starr, Pretty Boy Floyd, and even Tom Joad. In Woody's eyes, these outlaws fought outside the law as a champion of the common people, who were often cheated out of their homes and livelihood by the legal establishment. These outlaw ballads, discussed in chapter eight, fit well into historian E. J. Hobsbawm's argument that outlaws with primarily rural origins were primitive rebels who fought against modernization and capitalist exploitation of small farmers and agricultural laborers. While Woody's roots in Texas and Oklahoma were agrarian, his life and career in New York City brought him into contact with the labor movement.

Chapter nine will examine Woody's support for unionism with a special emphasis upon his association with the Almanac Singers, and their efforts on behalf of CIO organizing before the Second World War. Woody's disappointment with the postwar reaction against the labor movement, which employed the Red Scare to discredit organized labor, is also examined in this chapter. Although Woody was brought up in a racist environment, chapter ten demonstrates Woody's considerable growth in his ideas of race as he became a vocal critic of Jim Crow in the postwar period. While his music would be incorporated into the Civil Rights Movement, health concerns made it impossible for Woody himself to be part of that crusade to reform America.

Chapter eleven raises some questions regarding Woody's sometimes contradictory views on sexuality and gender equality. In much of his writing and songs, such as "Union Maid," Woody exhibits considerable belief in and support for gender equality. He was capable of expressing beautiful sentiments of love and devotion toward women, as his wartime letters to Marjorie well document. On the other hand, he could be a "womanizer" who pursued other women while he was married and demonstrated irresponsibility in deserting his family on numerous occasions. His letters and journal entries are often quite sexually explicit, and these writings sometimes seem to reflect a sexual libertine whose desires could not be circumscribed by such traditional concepts and institutions as monogamy and marriage. Woody's focus upon sexuality may also be a reflection of his Huntington's disease, which causes obsessive behavior. Nevertheless, there seemed to be a gap between Woody's behavior and his philosophical ideas when it came to questions of political and social equality for women.

The next section of the search for Woody Guthrie deals directly with Woody's music and recordings, again re-enforcing themes of indigenous radicalism in Woody's life and work. Chapter twelve considers what is undoubtedly Woody's best-known record, *Dust Bowl Ballads*, originally recorded in 1940 and released by RCA Victor. The songs, such as "Do Re Mi," "Dusty Old Dust," and "Blowin' Down the Road," were acclaimed by musicologists such as Alan Lomax from the Library of Congress as representing the authentic response of the people in the Great Plains to the travails of the dust bowl. Chapters thirteen and fourteen allow readers to examine the political focus of Woody's music by considering the songs he recorded for Moe Asch, the founder of Folkways Records and a key figure in promoting Woody's music in 1946 and 1947. Woody's belief that the political struggles of the common people must continue in the postwar period is evident in the 1946 album *Struggle*, recorded for Asch. The album includes such historical songs as "1913 Massacre" and "Ludlow Massacre." In 1947, Woody also accepted a commission from Asch to compose a series of songs on the anarchists Sacco and Vanzetti, whose executions in Massachusetts during the 1920s took place amid a xenophobic reaction to new immigration from Southern and Eastern Europe. *Struggle*, the subject of chapter thirteen, and *Ballads of Sacco and Vanzetti*, examined in chapter fourteen, did not receive wide release until 1976 and 1996 respectively — when their political messages of the historical struggle for economic, political, and social justice in America resonated well with Americans, including this author, who had participated in the political upheavals of the late 1960s and early 1970s.

Woody's music continues to resonate in contemporary America, and chapter fifteen concentrates upon a group of musicians who have kept Woody's life and legacy alive. Included in the analysis for this chapter will be the work of such artists as Woody's son Arlo, Bob Dylan, and Bruce Springsteen. The final chapter circles back to my original search for Woody Guthrie and his legacy for today. Although my family was not the type to sit around the campfire or living room and enthusiastically sing folk tunes, the music of Woody always resonates when I think of my family. They probably would have been a little stoic for Woody, but they were his kind of people — hard working, dependable, humble, God-fearing, compassionate, neighborly, and simply good people. They were poor and reluctant to consult doctors and dentists because they were too expensive — contributing to my poor teeth and the early deaths of many of my relatives. Housing was modest, and our diet was poor. I remember my family receiving tubs of lard when Texas did not participate in the federal food stamp program. Clothing was often used or handed down from other family members.

Yet the music of Woody provides such common people with a sense of dignity and pride for which I am appreciative. With this search for Woody Guthrie, I have been able to rediscover my roots and regain inspiration for waging the contemporary struggle to achieve Woody's dream of "commonism."

Chapter One

De-radicalizing Woody: Hal Ashby's *Bound for Glory* (1976)

Politics are a central point of reference in my search for Woody Guthrie. Woody not only described the life of the common working people such as my family, but he also asked important questions such as why so many hard-working people lived in poverty. Woody did not buy into the mythology of the American dream. He had seen how many common people, such as my parents, labored their entire lives with few material comforts to show for their efforts, while others inherited property and lived a life of luxury with the revenue from investments. To Woody, the reason for such vast discrepancies in wealth was quite simple: it was human greed. He denounced throughout his life the profit systems created to satisfy this greed. However, he struggled with how to redress this evil. Woody was certainly sympathetic to the ideas of communism, but he was hardly a revolutionary or ideologue who advocated for the violent overthrow of the capitalist system. Instead, Woody championed a common-sense approach to the sharing of resources that combined elements of communism with the teachings of Jesus to form what the folk singer called pure ol' "commonism."

In July 2003, Woody was featured on the cover of the *Nation* magazine as an American radical, who, according to Jack Newfield, embodied "individualism, anti-authoritarianism, talent, egalitarianism, artistic freedom, fearless independence and affinity for the common man." Writing in the same edition, folk singer Steve Earle concluded that Guthrie's life and work symbolized "everything a people's revolution is supposed to be about: that working people have dignity, intelligence and value above and beyond the market's demand for their labor."[1] It is these values which led Woody to a close affiliation with, if perhaps not actual membership in, the Communist Party. To understand Woody's attraction to communism, it is not necessary to study ideology or dialectical materialism. Unlike many intellectuals who were attracted to serving an ideology that embraced the train of history, Woody perceived communism as common sense. Woody's politics were eclectic as he combined elements of agrarian Jeffersonianism, Marxism, populism, and Christian socialism. The folk singer failed to see any fundamental contradiction between Marx and Jesus. Communism, according to Woody, was simply common sense since it required the sharing of God's resources as called for in the Bible. In the spring of 1941, he wrote in one of his voluminous journals, "When there shall be no want among you, because you'll own everything in common. When the Rich will give their goods into the poor. I believe in this way. I just can't believe in any other way. This is the Christian way and it is already on a big part of the earth and it will come. To own everything in common. That's what the Bible says. Common means to all of us. This is pure old 'commonism.' "[2]

Woody's "commonism" seemed to capture the story of the Briley family who labored so hard with little to show for their efforts. In fact, my father, after doing extensive physical labor on a railroad wrecking crew, suffered a massive coronary in his forties and eventually died from heart disease. My perception was that he simply worked himself to death in pursuit of the legal tender, while others lived off investments, interest, and inheritance. As I studied American history, the rich legacy of indigenous radicalism upon which Woody drew for inspiration was increasingly apparent. The struggles of the IWW, socialists under the leadership of Eugene V. Debs, communists fighting Jim Crow during the 1930s, and the work of Christian radicals such as Dorothy Day were an inspiration for me, as they were to Woody and his "commonism."

Although I had considerable family, school, and work responsibilities, I threw myself into the political struggles of the 1960s. Canyon, Texas was hardly an epicenter for protest, nevertheless I joined Students for a Democratic Society and was active in the anti-Vietnam War movement. I even briefly joined the Communist Party — probably in an effort to shock friends and family. But my primary reasons for joining were perhaps similar to Woody's, as was the extent of my participation. We both acknowledged the party's goals of a more equitable society but were less sure about the means to achieve these ends and were not willing to engage in the hard work of party organizing and discipline. My relatives were not really pleased with my radical opinions. Our family tensions sometimes reflected the discourse one found on the popular CBS television show *All in the Family*. My father was similar to Archie Bunker in that he did not approve of the Civil Rights Movement, but he continued to vote Democratic, including for George McGovern in 1972, because the party favored the working people and unions.

I have grown somewhat more pragmatic and tolerant in my political views over time. However, I have nothing to recant regarding my views from the 1960s. Although I was certainly a little intolerant and impatient in my youth, I believe that my fundamental views on issues of race, war, and poverty were sound then, as they are today. Woody's "commonism" of American socialism, communism, and the Christian social gospel made a great deal of sense in the 1960s and continue to resonate with me in the search for Woody Guthrie's America.

But there have been efforts to de-radicalize Woody and the anti-capitalist American traditions upon which he often drew for inspiration. This chapter will focus upon the efforts to tame Woody and his "commonism" in the 1976 Hal Ashby film *Bound for Glory*. Ashby's film tempers Woody's communist past. The folk singer is presented as a bicentennial hero like Rocky Balboa, with whom he shared the silver screen in 1976. While attempting to make Woody more acceptable to the mainstream, *Bound for Glory* distorts the historical Woody and the story of indigenous, American radicalism and anti-capitalism embodied in his philosophy of "commonism." It puts us off on the wrong road in our search for Woody Guthrie.

Bound for Glory, director Hal Ashby's 1976 cinematic tribute to Woody Guthrie, concludes with the folk singer departing California for the greener pastures of New York City in early 1940. As he rides a freight train, Woody, portrayed by David Carradine, sings "This Land Is Your Land," which he actually wrote sometime in February 1940 while living in New York City. Under Ashby's direction and Haskell Wexler's cinematography, the film's conclusion becomes a bicentennial tribute to the resilient spirit of the American people. Film viewers, however, would certainly not surmise that Woody penned his anthem in angry response to the narrow American exceptionalism of Irving Berlin's "God Bless America." As Bryan K. Garman suggests in *A Race of Singers*, the problem with Ashby's film is that "it depicted Guthrie as a romantic individualist." Garman argues, "The most important thing about the filmic Guthrie is not that he fought for social and economic justice but that he celebrated the American landscape and inspired all people to take pride in themselves and their individual accomplishments."[3]

This individualistic rendering of Woody completely obscures his collectivist and radical politics, which were fostered in California during the late 1930s. Although the film depicts Woody being beaten and cursed as a "red" or communist for his endeavors to help farmworkers organize, his actual activities with the party are downplayed. For example, the film leaves out the fact that Woody wrote a column for the communist *People's Daily World*. Ed Robbin, who helped recruit Woody for entertaining at various party functions, is also missing from the film. Instead of Robbin, Woody's political education is entrusted to the fictional union organizer and entertainer Ozark Bule (Ronny Cox) who comes off more as a liberal New Dealer than a radical. In addition, Woody eventually leaves Los Angeles radio station KFVD in the film because the station's operator Frank Burke is attempting to censor Woody's music. Thus, the separation becomes about free speech, while in reality the progressive Burke was upset that Woody was following the Communist Party line in supporting the August 1939 Nazi-Soviet Non-aggression Pact. While there is considerable debate over whether Woody ever formally joined the party, the film downplays any communist associations in favor of a more deradicalized Woody. Ashby's film, however, was hardly the first attempt to make Woody more palatable to the American mainstream.

Although Woody had written "This Land Is Your Land" in 1940, he did not get around to recording the song for Moe Asch until 1944. This recording included the radical fifth and sixth verses attacking capitalism and the creation of private property because these concepts deny many Americans their natural rights and opportunities. However, when Asch released the song in 1951 as part of a Guthrie's children's song collection, *Songs to Grow On*, the radical verses were missing. And as Woody dropped from public view in the 1950s because he was suffering from Huntington's disease, this more innocuous version of "This Land Is Your Land" entered the public realm and nation's classrooms. The sanitized version celebrated American exceptionalism in a similar fashion to Irving Berlin's "God Bless America." In his history of Woody's song, Robert Santelli notes this conservative trend by observing, "For some teachers in American schools, 'This Land Is Your Land' was the perfect musical counterpoint to the evil Communist empire that by 1957, with Sputnik successfully sent into space by the Russians, seriously threatened American supremacy in things like science and math. 'This Land Is Your Land' became a musical testament to the natural virtues of the Promised Land, this place where the wheat fields waved and the redwood forests stood strong and mighty, just like America."[4]

This rendering of "This Land Is Your Land" obscured Woody's original intentions for the song. Woody was upset with the jingoistic simplicity of Berlin's "God Bless America" as interpreted by Kate Smith. Settling into a cold room at the Hanover House near the New York Public Library in February 1940, Woody penned a response — which he initially called "God Blessed America"— to the ubiquitous Berlin and Smith collaboration. Although he shared with Berlin an admiration for the natural beauty of America, Woody questioned an economic system that failed to bless all Americans. Seeking to explain Woody's perspective, biographer Ed Cray writes, "For weeks the sometimes dust bowl refugee and ever restless Okie had listened to the jukeboxes and Kate Smith booming out the saccharine 'God Bless America.' Maybe the almighty had or would sometime in the future, but so far He had missed the America Guthrie knew; the sharecroppers, the boomers, the kids living in ditches alongside California rural roads. There was something too pat, too smug about Irving Berlin's patriotic plea."[5] In Woody's original song, with radical verses questioning private property and exposing the existence of poverty amid America's pastures of plenty, the Oklahoman dispenses with the self-congratulatory tone of Berlin's American exceptionalism and implores the nation to reach its promise and assure its gifts are available to all people. According to Guthrie scholar Robert Santelli, the Oklahoma folk singer perceived "God Bless America" as a "sonic elixir, a numbing narcotic that placed the nation's destiny in a God that hadn't yet figured out what to do with the nation and given people the idea that little, if anything, was wrong with the country."[6] Because of the perspectives he gained from roaming the country during the depression, Woody begged to differ with Berlin's musical celebration of American exceptionalism.

During the turbulent 1960s, Pete Seeger made it his mission to restore his friend's radical verses in public performances and sing-alongs of "This Land Is Your Land." In addition, Seeger argued that in the tradition of folk music new verses should be added to maintain the relevancy of Woody's vision in the continuing struggle for freedom and equality. Seeger's quest to keep the spirit of Woody's anthem true to its original purpose was also embraced by Bruce Springsteen, who often includes "This Land Is Your Land" in his epic concert performances. Introducing the Guthrie standard before a concert audience in Paris, Springsteen remarked, "This is an old song about an old dream. It's hard to think about what to say about the song, because it's sung a whole lot in the States and it's been misinterpreted a whole lot. It was written as a fighting song and it was written, I feel, as a question everybody has to ask themselves about the land they live in every day."[7] Despite the best efforts of artists such as Seeger and Springsteen, Guthrie scholar Mark Allan Jackson concludes, "Considering the song's heavy use in the past decades as a nationalistic jingle, a concentrated effort is still needed to push the song in a direction more keeping with its creator's intentions, especially since Guthrie never had a chance to perform the song after its rise — or explain his intentions in writing it."[8]

Thus, when Hollywood announced intentions to produce a Guthrie film project in the 1970s there was considerable speculation as to whether Woody's radicalism would be acknowledged or obscured by a populist shroud emphasizing the American dream. After all, a cinematic version of his autobiographical novel was a pet project for Woody. He loved the movies as many of his "Woody Sez" columns attest. In fact, he even claimed that he never read Steinbeck's *Grapes of Wrath*, and that his epic "Tom Joad" song was based upon a screening of John Ford's 1941 cinematic adaptation of the novel. Thus, in 1946 Woody agreed to give Popular Front critic and film director Irving Lerner an option on *Bound for Glory*; the folk singer even envisioned portraying himself in the title role. However, with the emergence of the Red Scare and post-World War II Hollywood blacklist, Lerner was unable to secure studio support for Woody's film project.[9]

But the idea for a film based upon Woody's memoir refused to die, even as Woody's health deteriorated. Woody's manager, Harold Leventhal (who ironically began his career in the music business with Irving Berlin), was placed in charge of the Guthrie Children's Trust and served as a virtual father figure to Woody's son Arlo.[10] The folk-music manager was always looking for ways to enhance the Guthrie family's finances and was also interested in getting into the film industry. He helped Arlo secure the deal that resulted in the film version of his song "Alice's Restaurant" (1969). He also actively pursued an appropriate film script for Woody's autobiography. After rejecting numerous scripts, Leventhal and his co-producer Robert F. Blumofe, a former production chief at United Artists, finally selected a script from a young writer, Robert Getchell. Getchell's script for *Alice Doesn't Live Here Anymore* (1974) was nominated for an Academy Award. Blumofe told Joseph McBride of *Film Comment*, "All the previous writers had been Woody's contemporaries. I thought a young writer would be better. The other scripts tended to cover too much of Woody's life. They were too busy detailing events. One of the keys to our approach in this picture is that we made up our minds when we started that we would not have any misconceptions that we were putting a legend on the screen—so we damn well better show who he was, where he came from, and what he stood for."[11]

Responding to the concern that it was too ambitious to place all of Woody's life in the picture, Getchell's script concentrated upon the years from 1936 to 1940. Although much of the book focuses upon Woody's years in Okemah, the film adaptation begins with Woody suffering through the dust bowl in Pampa and then follows him on his trek to California. The film concludes as Woody hops a freight train and departs California for New York City. This was an important period in Woody's life as the dust bowl and his activities in California radicalized him, and he began to devote his life and music to improving the lot of the common people. Subjected to the Red Scare while managing the Weavers in the 1950s, Leventhal wanted a commercial film that would find a large audience and avoid controversy. Thus, in the Getchell script, Woody is transformed into a champion of the people, but issues of his communist affiliations are not explored.

With an acceptable script in place, Leventhal and Blumofe were able to get United Artists to commit, with a hefty budget of $10 million for the picture. With this funding the producers were able to secure the services of acclaimed cinematographer Haskell Wexler and director Hal Ashby, who was coming off the commercially lucrative and critically admired *Shampoo* starring Warren Beatty. With his working-class background, lack of pretense, and troubled personal life, Ashby appeared to be an excellent choice to direct a biographical film on the life of Woody Guthrie.

Ashby was born September 2, 1929, in Ogden, Utah. His parents divorced when he was six years of age, and his father ostensibly committed suicide in 1942. Five years later, Ashby fathered his first child and was married for the first of five times. Drifting in terms of a career, Ashby learned that editing was the best way to get into the film industry. He displayed a strong work ethic and dedication to his trade and gained an excellent reputation for film editing, working with such notable directors as George Stevens, William Wyler, Tony Richardson, and Norman Jewison. In 1968, Ashby won an Academy Award for Best Editing for Jewison's *In the Heat of the Night*. The next year he directed his first film, *The Landlord* with Lee Grant and Beau Bridges. In 1971, Ashby released *Harold and Maude* which was initially a failure at the box office but later proved to be one of the most popular cult films of all time and established the director's reputation with a young, countercultural audience. *The Last Detail* (1973), controversial for the profanity of its sailor protagonists, gained Oscar nominations for actors Jack Nicholson and Randy Quaid. *Shampoo* (1975) proved to be one of the greatest commercial successes in the history of Columbia Pictures and garnered tremendous influence for Ashby in the film industry. After *Bound for Glory*, Ashby released *Coming Home* (1978) and *Being There* (1979), which cemented his reputation for making films that enjoyed both commercial and critical success. Ashby's career, however, slumped during the 1980s when he directed flops such as *Second Hand Hearts* (1981), *Lookin' To Get Out* (1982), *The Slugger's Wife* (1984), and *8 Million Ways to Die* (1986). Rumors persisted that Ashby's rapid decline was due to drug abuse, but biographer Nick Dawson argues that the director was really a perfectionist and workaholic rather than a hippie. However, the stress from overworking and a turbulent relationship with the Lorimar production company contributed to his premature death from pancreatic cancer on December 27, 1988.[12]

During his brief but successful run as a director, Ashby earned an excellent reputation for eliciting strong performances from his actors. Once Ashby signed on to direct the Woody Guthire film, there was considerable speculation about who might depict Woody. Major stars such as Jack Nicholson, Robert De Niro, and Dustin Hoffman were considered for the role, but other contractual obligations eliminated them. Then Ashby considered casting a musician in the title role. Bob Dylan was sent a copy of the script. He allegedly replied that he was not interested in portraying Woody, the hero of his youth, but the rock poet indicated that he was willing to direct the picture.[13] Ashby crossed Dylan off his list. He then apparently settled on musician Tim Buckley, until Buckley died from a drug overdose shortly before production was to begin on *Bound for Glory*. Arlo Guthrie expressed interest in playing his father and had some acting experience in *Alice's Restaurant*. Ashby rejected this interesting idea, concluding that the strain of playing his father would simply be too much for such a relatively inexperienced actor.[14]

Instead, Ashby's thoughts kept returning to David Carradine, perhaps best known for his starring role in the television series *Kung Fu* (1972–1975). He auditioned for the role by playing the guitar and singing some of Woody's songs. Although he was eager to portray Woody, Carradine was initially rejected for simply being too tall (over six feet) to play the diminutive folk singer. But Ashby eventually reconsidered, concluding that Carradine embodied the spirit of Woody. Thus, it was also determined that Carradine would not attempt to do an exact impression of Woody, but rather give a spiritually faithful performance. Leventhal was troubled at first with the casting decision, but Woody's former manager finally recognized that they were designing a portrayal of Woody, not producing a documentary. Marjorie was also present on the set for some of the filming and announced her satisfaction with Carradine's performance. She asserted, "I'm enough of a believer in change to respect the fact that David has to be David. I like what my young kids said about him — he has 'Woody's vibes.' If he has that, I can't complain, can I? I told David, 'We don't need another Woody, we need you.'"[15] Most critics seemed to agree with Marjorie as Carradine generally received positive reviews for his performance.

While Carradine was not to provide an imitation of Woody, the producers, director Ashby, and cinematographer Wexler spared no expense in attempting to document the depression-era historical context of the picture. When Woody's communist friend Ed Robbin was invited by Leventhal to visit the set, he was impressed with the film's authenticity, commenting, "The people, the extras sitting around and rambling up and down the streets in their resurrected thirties clothing, looked as battered and dusty as I remembered them when they filled the roads and the skid rows of Los Angeles. The kids were barefoot, dirty, and ran in packs."[16] The look of the film also plays homage to John Ford's *The Grapes of Wrath* — Wexler used color to improve upon the cinematography style of Greg Toland. There was even a family connection to *The Grapes of Wrath*, as David's father, classic character actor John Carradine, portrayed Preacher Casy in the Ford film. Wexler's cinematography and careful documentation of Hoovervilles and a Texas dust storm earned him an Academy Award, yet some critics considered the attention to detail and beautiful photography to almost be a distraction. For example, film reviewer Roger Ebert complained, "The beauty is sometimes achieved at the cost of tone. Scene after scene unfolds at such a measured pace, with such calculation and understatement, that finally we seem to be watching a travelogue set during the Depression. The film has a grave dignity, which is good, but it often seems to lack life, which would be better."[17]

Not only is the film being perhaps too beautiful for a depiction of the depression, but *Bound for Glory* is also problematic in the way it presents Woody's politics. While Ashby recognized that the filmmakers were depicting a crucial period in Woody's life when the folk singer began to develop a radical political consciousness, the film's focus remains on the personal rather than the political — as is commonplace in Hollywood. Ashby told film critic David Sterritt that he did not see the film as particularly political. The director argued, "It's about learning processes and character, so young people will probably identify with it faster because that's where you are at a certain stage of your life. But older people are drawn to the movie too, if they've been through any part of that '30s experience."[18] Ashby also acknowledged that the Woody portrayed in *Bound for Glory* was far from a saint, and, as exemplified by the abandonment of his family to live on the road, Woody seemed often to love people on a more abstract level than in the flesh. Accordingly, Aljean Harmetz of the *New York Times* observed that his own multiple failed marriages made Ashby feel a certain personal connection to Woody. Harmetz concluded, "Of all Ashby's films, *Bound for Glory* — with its raw Southwestern hero and its uneasy questions about love — is closest to his own life. There is even a scene — in which David Carradine, hitchhiking to California, sleeps all night at the edge of the highway — which comes not from Guthrie's past but from Ashby's."[19]

The failure of *Bound for Glory* to more directly address Woody's radical politics was overlooked by most commentators, but Joseph McBride observed that while he was visiting the set, one person involved with the production (who did not want his name used) told the critic that the film was guilty of "romanticizing" Woody's politics. The source told McBride that an earlier version of the script was far more honest in its treatment of Woody's radicalism, contending, "The political stuff in the script now is just a word here and there. It's like Tom Joad in *The Grapes of Wrath* talking about 'the people.' I guess that's all they think the public can take. But Woody was a red — a maverick red."[20] In his piece on *Bound for Glory* for *Cineaste*, Jeff Green makes the film's political orientation the focal point of his review. Green also laments that in employing only small excerpts from his music, the radical thrust of Woody's songs are thwarted in Ashby's film (although Leonard Rosenman garnered an Oscar for Best Adaptation Score). The director, apparently, did not want the film to become a musical biography picture. Green writes, "The film refuses to look seriously at Woody's radical politics; it fails to do justice to his music; and it depicts the human suffering of the 1930s just a bit too artfully. *Bound for Glory* offers us an impressionistic sketch of Woody Guthrie's life during the Depression, but doesn't show us the stark, terrifying pictures Woody painted in his songs." Green observes that *Bound for Glory* neglects to develop the historical context of the Popular Front in which Woody made common cause with communist organizers. Thus, the film concentrates upon the heroic individual and ignores "the dialectic between its hero and the people."[21]

The film begins in 1936 with Woody and his young family in Pampa struggling to survive during the dust bowl, omitting the large segment of his autobiography that Woody devotes to growing up in Okemah. Woody attempts to support his family by telling fortunes, playing music, and painting signs. But Woody is no businessman. He does not get paid when he paints a sign according to his artistic tastes rather than as the business proprietor contracted. Woody ends up giving away his paint brushes to a young man, who has escaped from a mental institution, so that he may draw the pictures inside his head. Wexler does an excellent job of depicting how a dust storm engulfs Pampa — we see the family soaking towels in bowls of water to place over their faces as the inside of the house is enveloped by dust. (Growing up in the Panhandle in the 1950s, I did the same thing with my family when waiting out a dust storm.) As the film progresses, Woody seems to love his wife Mary (Melinda Dillon) and their children, but he is clearly growing restless with his situation. One day, he simply leaves a note on the icebox stating that he is joining the exodus to California and will send for Mary when he finds work. This lack of responsibility, in both the film and real life, certainly demonstrates that Woody was hardly a saint, and there was often a gap between how he treated women in the abstract and personally — a trait that will be developed in a later chapter.[22]

As Woody hitchhikes and rides the rails across the country, he begins to receive an education on how the poor and destitute are treated in depression-era America. Although there is a degree of comradery among the men riding the freight trains, there is also a sense of frustration and fights often break out between desperate men. Woody finds himself traveling with and learning about the plight of black men, such as Slim Snedeger (Ju-Tu Cumbuka) — a theme of racial integration that is also emphasized in the book. However, some of Woody's journal entries from his arrival in California do suggest that he was not always so racially enlightened and that he carried with him some of the racial baggage from his father and the racist environment in which he was raised. Although his understanding of and opposition to Jim Crow became an important aspect of Woody's world view, this growth in consciousness was not something that he was taught in Oklahoma and Texas and will be addressed in a later chapter. He is also introduced to the violence of the railroad hired guns who seek to stop the unemployed from hopping freights. The railroad "goons" arrest trespassers as vagrants, while those with money are forced to purchase tickets with funds they need for survival and to keep from starving. In a more extreme case, one of the unemployed is shot and killed as he attempts to board a freight train. This violent treatment of migrants on the road and in California led Woody to write the song "Vigilante Man."

The film also presents Woody as a man opposed to charity and who offers to work for his bowl of chili. Providing a negative commentary on organized religion, Ashby stages a scene in which Woody approaches the minister of a church and volunteers to work in exchange for food. The minister explains that he currently has no chores for Woody. Further, to simply provide him with food would undermine Woody's sense of personal independence and responsibility, rendering him dependent on charity. Thus, Woody is left starving. The reverend displays no sense of Christian charity and seems to reflect the philosophy of rugged individualism with which President Herbert Hoover originally responded to the Great Depression.

In fact, it is in the terrible conditions of a California Hooverville that Woody finds some sense of community with Luther Johnson (Randy Quaid) and his family. The migrant workers at the camp are entertained by union organizer Ozark Bule (Ronny Cox), and Woody joins in with the singing. He escapes with Ozark when they are attacked by men with clubs recruited by the farm owners. A friendship develops between Ozark and Woody who roam the countryside outside Los Angeles attempting to get farmworkers to unionize. While they are accused of being "reds," there is no suggestion in the Ashby film that Ozark is a communist or that Woody wrote a column for the *People's Daily World* or entertained for Communist Party gatherings. Ozark gets Woody a job with a radio station performing with Memphis Sue (also played by Melinda Dillon in an interesting bit of casting). The show becomes popular as the radio audience, many of them migrants from Oklahoma and Texas, love the folk music and Woody's humorous commentaries. Radio station manager Locke (John Lehne), however, is concerned that Woody's commentaries criticizing the growers will outrage sponsors, and he urges Woody to follow a program of scripted songs. It should be noted that while characters such as Memphis Sue and Locke tend to represent real-life personalities such as Maxine Crissman and Frank Burke, the film employs fictional names for all characters except Woody and his family.

Meanwhile, Woody begins a relationship with Pauline (Gail Strickland), a woman he met while she was serving at a soup kitchen. In exchange for his bowl of chili, Woody paints her a sign and wrangles an invitation to her home for dinner. He is initially upset that she is wealthy, but he finally confesses that she was the first rich person to really recognize and look at him. They commence a sexual liaison, but Woody eventually informs Pauline that he is married and is now earning enough money to send for his family in Texas. Woody leaves Pauline in another example of his rather cavalier attitude toward women.

When Mary and his girls arrive in California, they are delighted with the home Woody has rented for them. Woody, however, is troubled by Locke's demands that the singer provide a set list for his radio program. Mary urges him to compromise for the sake of the family, and he is prepared to follow her advice until he runs into Luther Johnson, who has been beaten for attempting to organize the farmworkers. Johnson urges Woody to keep singing his songs and making commentaries that encourage the workers to fight for their rights. Woody quits his job at the radio station and heads out on the road again, where he, in turn, is beaten for his organizing efforts with the workers. He eventually returns home to a disappointed Mary, who takes the girls and goes back to Texas.

Woody, nevertheless, makes one last attempt at compromise. His agent finds Woody an even more lucrative gig at a Los Angeles club enthusiastic about marketing his country persona. As he looks around the wealthy surroundings, a rather disgusted Woody asks for directions to the bathroom. Instead, he walks out the front door of the hotel and is done with the audition. As Ozark chases after him, Woody explains that he is on his way to New York City. The film then concludes with some beautiful pastoral shots of Woody riding the rails and singing as "This Land Is Your Land" plays in the background. The conclusion, as Garman argues, seems to suggest that Woody and the American people have put the depression behind them and are bound for glory — a popular theme during the bicentennial and after the travails of the late 1960s and early 1970s.

Nevertheless, the response to the expensive and rather long film — nearly two and one-half hours — was mixed. It was nominated for six Academy Awards, including Best Picture, and garnered Oscars for cinematography and musical adaptation. *Bound for Glory*, however, did not resonate as well at the box office as Leventhal and Ashby anticipated. Its celebration of the common man seemed to fit well with the patriotic theme of 1976, but another film from that year, *Rocky*, appeared to better reflect the contemporary mood. Perhaps rather than being bound for glory, it was enough for American workers in 1976 simply to go the distance, as Rocky did when he battled Apollo Creed for fifteen rounds. *Rocky* also tackled the troubling subject of race relations, while *Bound for Glory*, despite Woody's earlier black traveling companions, was essentially a white film that overlooked themes of race and multiculturalism. And *Rocky* was certainly not about encouraging union organization during a troubled time for American labor.[23]

Conflicting critical reviews reflect the lukewarm audience response to *Bound for Glory*, although Carradine's performance in the title role generally received accolades. For example, Vincent Canby of the *New York Times* touted Carradine for displaying "the right look and manner," but the critic believed the screenplay failed to match "with dramatic conviction the intensity and drive of its largely mysterious central character." Richard Schickel of *Time*, however, found Ashby's film to be boring and criticized Wexler's camera work, which others attested was the centerpiece of the film. Schickel described Carradine as an attractive performer, but the reviewer concluded that a weak script made his Guthrie "all guileless sweetness." Taking Wexler to task, Schickel asserted, "Diffusion filters give a falsely nostalgic pastoral glow to landscapes forever fixed in the hard-edged photos made of the '30s by the likes of Walker Evans. Soft photography makes the movie seem sentimental even on those few occasions when it is trying not to be."[24]

Other reviews were far more positive and accord with the film's presence on the list of Oscar contenders. Writing in *Saturday Review*, Judith Crist praised Leventhal, Ashby, and Getchell "for providing not only an overwhelming encounter with a human being of extraordinary quality but also a touching re-creation of a time in our history that has touched us all." Joseph McBride, reviewing Ashby's film for *Film Comment*, was also enthusiastic, praising *Bound for Glory* as "a majestic film, the most ambitious film made in the United States since *The Godfather Part II*, and one of those rare pictures which are made with the lavish resources, meticulous care, and concern for epic breadth that characterize the way the great Hollywood movies used to be made." David Sterritt of the *Christian Science Monitor* joined the chorus of praise for the film, finding Ashby's direction and Carradine's acting noteworthy. But he expressed some reservations regarding Wexler's cinematography, observing, "Paradoxically, the film's most striking asset is also its most dangerous liability. Haskell Wexler's cinematography has never been famous for restraint, and in *Bound for Glory* its fabulous images overshadow every other consideration." Other critics, however, found Wexler's work to be the strongest element of the film. Frank Rich argued that Wexler brilliantly "captured the texture of depression America," while John Simon argued that *Bound for Glory* "could easily be dismissed as a much lesser *Grapes of Wrath* with music if it weren't for the bitter lyricism of Wexler's camera."[25]

Almost none of the reviews, with a few notable exceptions, mentioned the politics of the film which were downplayed in an effort to de-radicalize Woody and have him fit into an optimistic bicentennial mood, such as that embodied by white working-class hero Rocky Balboa. Nevertheless, Stanley Kauffmann of the *New Republic* criticized *Bound for Glory* for not providing a more realistic look at the political turmoil of the 1930s. Kauffmann argues that the Getchell script was nothing more than "'populist corn' cooked in 'warmed-over Steinbeck sauce' with cardboard figures of the greedy rich and sympathetic common people." The critic concluded, "Politics is never mentioned; we just get a kind of abstract cartoon of Noble Workers vs. Nasty Boss as the backdrop of the action."[26] Thus, Ashby's film failed to capture the radical politics that motivated Woody's songs and actions.

The iconoclastic Pauline Kael, however, perceived *Bound for Glory* as some type of leftist propaganda, littering her review with contempt for Woody and his ideas — essentially labeling him as a fake. Describing Woody's autobiography, Kael asserted, "It was the deep-seated conviction of a man who saw himself as the voice of the downtrodden — as the embodiment of the masses moving into a bright future, on a train bound for glory." Kael argued that in California Woody tried to become Tom Joad, and in the process he transformed into "a living rhetorical device." His anecdotes began to promote the brotherhood of man in a dialect "as patronizing as Steinbeck's." Kael concluded, "Woody Guthrie had a storyteller's gift, the gift of a true folk artist, but he violated it with the rhetoric of a politician. He became a pitchman-troubadour." And Kael makes it clear that she perceived Woody as a pitchman for communism, out to deceive the common people that the folk singer claimed to love. Kael described Ashby's film as exhibiting "the same brand of sanctifying horse manure that Guthrie did. You stop believing, and start wondering if the poor people wouldn't prefer nonpolitical folk music or even frivolous pop, rather than the songs of the dispossessed which the radicals think are good for them." Kael finished her polemical review by noting that Ashby "didn't go all soft on Woody Guthrie the man but on his own warm, spacey sentiments about what Guthrie stood for and about the period itself. This movie is about what a lot of people want to think their roots are. It's filled out with woozy generalities about Woody Guthrie as a man who fought the good fight against greed, and about his radicalization being the same thing as his finding himself as an artist."[27] From Kael's caustic perspective, those who continue to believe in the ideas expressed by Woody's songs are hypocrites who are slumming and only want to briefly identify with the common people while sentimentalizing poverty. As someone who grew up picking cotton in the Texas Panhandle and tasting dust in the beans and cornbread he ate in the cotton fields, it is difficult not to find the views expressed by Kael to be patronizing at best. Perhaps it would have been beneficial for the *New Yorker* critic to spend a little time in the cotton fields.

While Kael condemned *Bound for Glory* for providing sentimental coverage for Woody's embracing of communism and radicalism, James Green in *Cineaste* faults Ashby's film for not depicting the Popular Front politics of the depression era. Rather than the red-baiting anticommunism of Kael's review, Green expresses the view that Americans after the experience of the Vietnam War should have been able to more openly discuss communism without resorting to the demonization of American radicals and communists. Thus, Green laments that Ashby did not more openly embrace Woody's ties with the Communist Party and Popular Front. He concludes, "In fact, Guthrie's political education advanced not through union organizing but through participation in the Communist Party's Popular Front activities in California and later in New York."[28] Despite the protests of Kael, Ashby's *Bound for Glory*, accordingly, does to a great extent de-radicalize Woody as Bryan Garman suggested. Ignoring the radical verses of "This Land Is Your Land" also made Woody more palatable to the American mainstream — obscuring the real Woody Guthrie.

While Ashby's film does significantly downplay Woody's radicalism and communist ties, it certainly projects a favorable treatment of Woody to which Kael objected. The cinematography of Wexler and direction of Ashby also tried to provide film audiences with an authentic recreation of the depression. Of course, this effort to visually reconstruct the dissolution of the 1930s proved to be quite expensive for the filmmakers, and one wonders what Woody would have made of the elaborate sets. Proud of how Ashby and Wexler were getting the look of the 1930s accurately depicted, Leventhal invited Woody's old friend and communist organizer Ed Robbin to visit the film shoot. At lunch, Robbin noted the huge meal that was prepared for the extras, cast, and crew involved with the production and observed, "Mountains of food for people play-acting a time of struggle and hunger. It took me back to the days in the thirties when ranchers, trying to push prices up, sprayed great hills of oranges with gasoline and burned them and poured milk into the ditches of Los Angeles County while children of the Depression refugees went hungry." This observation led Robbin to speculate about what Woody might make of the film spectacle depicting the depression and his life. Robbin concluded, "I decided he probably would have walked off the set and gone to join one of Cesar Chavez's picket lines where workers are still fighting for a decent life."[29] This commentary by Robbin somewhat reflects the conclusion of the film when Woody rejects the commercial compromise of becoming a nightclub performer in Los Angeles. In conjecturing that Woody would have supported the organizing efforts of California farmworkers and Cesar Chavez, Robbin demonstrates that Woody's political activism on behalf of progressive causes remains a model for today.

Efforts to de-radicalize Woody by dismissing his more radical lyrics or ignoring his connections to the Popular Front and Communist Party may have softened Woody's image a bit, but they have not completely obscured the indigenous radicalism of his life and music. As long as we can read, hear, and play Woody's songs, his themes celebrating "commonism" will remain with us. While I was somewhat disappointed, along with Bryan Garman, that Ashby's film downplayed Woody's radicalism, I was still pleased to see Woody's life make it to the screen, encouraging viewers to sing his songs, read his autobiography, and find out more about the champion of "commonism." The film also convinced me that to better understand Woody's politics, I would have to expand my research into his California experience, which transformed his world view. Today the states of Oklahoma and Texas are bastions of conservatism, although this does appear to be slowly changing. But historian Roxanne Dunbar-Ortiz reminds us of another time in the 1930s when things were different, writing, "I could not help but think of another time, a time when the people I came from almost became a revolutionary force, a time when white supremacy nearly was shed, and the KKK was considered to be a tool of the enemy, when militarism was reviled and internationalism was embraced."[30] This is the progressive view that Woody embraced during his tenure in California and that will be explored in the next chapter through Woody's columns for the *People's Daily World*. It is a vision of a more egalitarian America that is essential to the search for Woody Guthrie.

Chapter Two

Woody in California: The *People's Daily World* and Indigenous Radicalism

The time that Woody Guthrie spent in California from 1937 to 1940 is crucial to understanding the radical political transformation of the migrant from Texas and Oklahoma. The dust bowl drove Woody from his home in Pampa, and his experience riding the rails and observing how the dust bowl migrants were treated in California convinced him that radical changes were needed in a system that placed private property above the needs of common people. In seeking to explain the significance of Woody's music, historian Charles J. Shindo argues, "Far from the simple country boy he claimed to be, Guthrie, as an Okie activist, created an image of himself and dust bowl migration that sought to center the migrant in the debate over American capitalism."[1] This radical questioning of capitalism was furthered by Woody's experience in Los Angeles, as is noted by Darryl Holter in the introduction to his book on Woody in the City of Angels. Holter writes, "The Los Angeles years solidified and shaped Woody's subsequent work. Perhaps more importantly, his songs, popular image, and politics formed a legacy that evolved through years of terminal illness and expanded exponentially after his death."[2] While in Los Angeles, Woody became involved with labor organizers and communists, but as Nora Guthrie suggests, Woody was not an innocent duped by the left. He was motivated by his radical faith in the people and "commonism." He believed that the people working together would triumph over the forces of greed who sought to divide them.[3]

The Oklahoma in which Woody reached maturity was not today's bastion of conservatism. Instead, Woody's Oklahoma was the home of a vibrant Socialist Party that included strong elements of Christian socialism in its popular ideology. The Socialist Party of Eugene Debs in the Southwest did not champion a materialistic atheism. Rather, the socialist movement in states such as Oklahoma embraced a millennial tradition in which the meek would inherit the earth. The Socialist Party, accordingly, often did well in areas where Pentecostal groups such as the Church of Christ enjoyed popular support. In *Grass Roots Socialism,* historian Jack Green observes, "In the early 1900s the new holiness sects of the Southwest clearly represented the primitive Christianity of the oppressed. The holiness movement was a 'radical opponent' of materialism and modernism in the established churches, and in that sense was a product of the same kind of class consciousness that led poor people to socialism."[4] Thus, Woody grew up in a region where no fundamental conflict was assumed between religious views and radical political ideology, although the philosophical differences between socialism and communism seemed somewhat blurred in Woody's thinking.

The threat posed by socialism to the established political order and parties in Oklahoma was neutralized during World War I, when patriotism was employed as a pretext by the government and vigilante groups to suppress radicalism. Woody's father, Charley Guthrie, was part of this process as a small-town real estate entrepreneur whose ambitions exceeded his talents. He sought political office by employing the tactics of race and red-baiting, asserting that the Socialists in Oklahoma wanted to resolve the race issue through encouraging intermarriage. In the oil boom of the early 1920s, Charley lost out to the big business interests rolling into the state, and the family became destitute. In addition, the family home was destroyed by fire, and in a separate incident Woody's sister, Clara, was killed when her dress caught fire. Many locals blamed Woody's mother Nora for Clara's death, and she began to behave in an eccentric fashion — wandering the streets in various states of undress. In June 1927, Nora allegedly poured kerosene on Charley and struck a match. Nora was diagnosed with Huntington's disease and was institutionalized. Charley was badly burned but survived, moving to Pampa, Texas, in order to live with relatives. As for Woody, he attempted to live on his own and fared poorly in school before joining his father and siblings in Texas.[5]

Arriving in Pampa just as the depression was striking the country in 1929, Woody helped his father manage a boarding house. Woody married Mary Jennings, who was sixteen years of age, in October 1933. He did not let the responsibilities of marriage force him into the confinement of a regular job — not that there was all that much steady work available in Pampa in 1933. Two years later Woody's first child was born, and he attempted to support the family by painting signs, reading fortunes, and playing music. As the dust bowl engulfed the Texas Panhandle, Woody responded by writing songs such as "Dusty Old Dust," which would later become part of his *Dust Bowl Ballads* recording. Woody was also becoming increasingly restless, and in 1937, leaving his family in Pampa, he headed out to California to see what the great migration from the dust bowl really meant to the people. Although Mary was not enthusiastic about Woody leaving the family and shirking what many would consider his responsibilities, she recognized her husband's restless spirit. Explaining his actions, Woody asserted, "I had a crazy notion in me that I wanted to stay down and out for a good long spell, so's I could get to live with every different kind of a person I could, to learn about all kinds of jobs they do, and to live with them for a long enough time to find out it was time to move on."[6] Woody's belief that life in all its varieties was to be experienced and celebrated was also evident in a letter he penned in February 1937 following the birth of his niece, Mary Ann Guthrie. Woody's advice to the new arrival in the world was, "Concentrate long and deep upon life and living — death and dying — who, what, why we are as we are and where we are going. This is more valuable than schooling. Go. See. And do!"[7] Following this counsel, Woody decided the road would be his school. In early 1937, he set out for California, promising to later send for Mary and his two daughters when he found a job and place to live.

Hitchhiking and riding the freight trains, Woody experienced the prejudice and discrimination to which the dust bowl migrants were being subjected. He also received an education on the history of indigenous, American radicalism; he heard many former and current members of the Industrial Workers of the World (IWW) speak of the Wobblie minstrel Joe Hill, a Swedish-born immigrant and martyr who was executed in 1915 by a Utah firing squad for an alleged robbery and murder. His life would later be eulogized in Woody's music. Woody began to carry around a copy of the *IWW Little Red Songbook* which purported to fan the fires of discontent.[8] The road was providing Woody with an opportunity to learn about the inequities of American capitalism and radical efforts to alter the system.

After considerable rambling, well chronicled in *Bound for Glory*, Woody settled with relatives in Glendale, California. He was able to get a radio spot with his cousin Jack on station KFVD, operated by Frank Burke. Woody was more talented than Jack and soon established a successful show accompanied by Maxine Crissman, whom Woody insisted upon calling Lefty Lou. The program, featuring ballads, hymns, hillbilly tunes, and Woody's running commentaries on social conditions, was a hit and allowed Woody to bring Mary and the kids to California.

Woody's education on conditions in California was fostered by his radio show and the people's response to it. In order to get more material for his show Woody attended organizing efforts among the pickers, Communist Party events, and did some reporting for Frank Burke's progressive newspaper *The Light*. Calling himself the "hobo correspondent," Woody traveled around the state reporting upon the exploitation of the migrants who flocked to California to pick fruits and vegetables, only to find themselves unemployed or unable to earn enough money to support a family. Stranded outside Barstow in September 1938 with hundreds of unemployed men, Woody told readers of *The Light*, "These people are mostly the ones who tired of marching with the starvation armies of wandering workers and grown wary of the smell of rotting fruit crops. Bewildered and flat broke, they are trying to get back somewhere or other where the meals come oftener." In another report, Woody concluded, "Migration in California has no doubt slowed down, and it looks like the railroads and the city police officers have suddenly decided to detain all migratory workers along the roads that they can in order to have free labor for their pea and bean patches. The constant dread of the wandering worker is to be arrested by some city officer, charged with idleness or vagrancy and sent in almost chain gang style to the bean patch to work without pay."[9]

In addition to his writing for *The Light*, Woody became increasingly involved with the organizing efforts of California communists. In 1938, Woody celebrated the pardon of labor leader Tom Mooney, whose conviction for planting a bomb during a 1916 Preparedness Day Parade in San Francisco was disputed by many on the political left, by composing "Tom Mooney is Free." Ed Robbin, who was a correspondent for the communist *People's Daily World* and also provided commentary for KFVD, asked Woody to perform the song for a Communist Party function. When Robbin inquired as to whether the folk singer had any reservations about being associated with the party, Woody replied, "Left-wing, right-wing, chicken-wing — it's all the same thing to me. I sing my songs wherever I can sing 'em. So if you'll have me, I'll be glad to go." The crowd loved Woody's tune, especially the last line saying that now it was time to free the rest of California.[10]

Communist organizer Dorothy Healey described Woody as a regular performer at party fund-raising activities during the late 1930s in California. Woody also wrote a column for the *People's Daily World* that appeared on the editorial page under the heading "Woody Sez." The column, which eventually included 174 commentaries and ran from May 1939 until January 1940, featured Woody's cartoons and such down home philosophy as "I ain't a communist necessarily, but I have been in the red all my life."[11] The communist publication tended to be less doctrinaire than its New York City equivalent the *Daily Worker* and enjoyed a circulation in the tens of thousands during the 1930s. A close reading of the columns indicates that Woody was a great deal more complicated than the country bumpkin persona he sometimes assumed in his writing. Beneath the colloquialisms and the frequent misspellings is an intellectual whose writing articulated the suffering as well as the longing of the dust bowl refugees for a better life. Woody's pieces do not rely upon quotations from Marx and Lenin, but they certainly reflect a strong sense of class consciousness and disdain for what capitalism had accomplished for common working people.

In his first "Woody Sez" column, Woody introduced himself to readers in what he termed his "awgowbyografie." When describing his early years in Okemah and Pampa, Woody failed to mention the tragedies that plagued the Guthrie family. Instead, Woody emphasized the exploitive nature of American capitalism by asserting that bankers had forced farmers off their land in the Southwest. Unable to make ends meet in Pampa, he headed to California hoping to find his relatives, "but I didn't know for shore wich rr-bridge they was a livin' under, so you see I was a travelin' practically without a magnete. I mean a compast. I didn't know whre the heick I was a goin'." Of course, Woody did find these relatives, although not actually living under a bridge, and they helped him obtain his radio show. Woody indicated that he was happy to have an opportunity to write his columns because he had "a Hillbilly's Eye View of the whole Migration Labor movement from the South to the Pacific Coast. An' because I figgered it wood be helpful to my people, the dustbowl refugees, I was tickled to get the chanct."[12]

Woody chronicled and championed the common people with a strong sense of class consciousness, often employing populist rhetoric. On May 18, 1939, he observed that the wealthy were concerned that providing relief to the poor might lower the standard of living. Woody defined the standard of living as home, car, clothes, groceries, radio, an electric ice box, and a job with decent wages. These were things that the people did not have because the wealthy "got it from you an' me." He continued with this theme of exploitation, describing Wall Street as the place where "the workers git worked on an the reapers get reaped — as the farmers get plowed under." Woody concluded that Wall Street speculators were rattlesnakes who made "easy street impossible for the people."[13]

Normally, Woody tried to interject some humor into his denunciation of the grafters, but he had little time for levity when fellow migrants were attacked. Woody was angered by an article in the reactionary *Los Angeles Times* that asserted the migrants were nothing more than gold diggers seeking to take advantage of the taxpayers and property owners of California by collecting relief. An incensed Woody wrote: "Scenes of Life in a Trailer Camp city were painted to call your attention to the untold, inhuman suffering that these people are willing to go thru — just for some of that 'esay relief money.' How the Sheriff's Force cleaned out the jungle and drove the Shak dwellers out of the River Bottom and set fire to their cardboard Houses, and destroyed their patch-work shelter — was told about — not to make you feel in your heart a genuine sorrow for your brothers and sisters of our American Race that's got to live in such places, but to try to make you believe that these Underprivileged people designing in their hearts to Dig Some Easy Gold — of your taxpayers."[14] In this defense of his fellow migrants, Woody drops many of his colloquialisms and writes in a more straight-forward fashion. He maintained that all his people wanted was a chance to work and earn a living.

Woody's connection to the everyday lives of the common people was evident in columns that commented upon such basic concerns as housing, loan sharks, high utility costs, and health care. To Woody, decent housing was a basic human right to which all were entitled. He described houses as homes to "raise children in; but depression America corporations and banks were using houses to rob workin' folks by charging exorbitant rents." Woody continued this argument the following day by observing that policemen were employed to protect the property of the wealthy. He stated, "A policeman will just stand there an let a banker rob a farmer or a finance man rob a workin' man. But if a farmer robs the banker — you wood have a hole dern army of cops out a shooting at him."[15] These thoughts regarding the law as an instrument of class oppression used against the people would lead Woody to embrace social banditry and populist outlaws such as Pretty Boy Floyd.

In addition to bankers and landlords who were supported by a corrupt legal system, Woody had nothing but contempt for loan sharks and private utilities earning immense profits at the expense of the poor. In several columns, he discussed widows, Native Americans, and veterans whose gas or electrical services were cancelled. An angry Woody proclaimed, "Dear Gas Companies: Uneducated, unenlightened, and uninformed as I am, provides me with a magnificent opportunity and elegant excuse to tell you here and now that I oftentimes have nightmares in which there go crawling and creeping species of creatures similar to those which are symbolized by the practices you use."[16]

Woody's venom for furniture dealers was also apparent. They applied high rates of interest to the purchases by working-class people, who could not afford to pay cash up front for their goods. Casting the creditors into the same circle of hell as bankers and utility companies, Woody wrote, "Dear Credit People: I have come to the conclusion after long meditation, jealous forethought, and silent prayer, that you are a bunch of Low Down Thieves... and I am unable to think otherwise." Personalizing the issue as he often did in his columns, Woody complained that it was difficult for his twenty-one-year-old brother George to get married because creditors were attempting to "enslave, degrade, depress, deprive, and otherwise 'rob' our young folks that's a falling in Love, and a getting married."[17]

Woody also addressed basic issues of health care in a column reporting that his family was expecting a baby. The singer understood that doctors, like everyone else, had to make a living, but he simply could not comprehend how a physician could charge as much for his services one night delivering a baby as a working man earned in six months of labor. Woody contemplated, "Funny how one feller can hit a few licks of some sort of 'inspired work'— like a doctor or a lawyer, and take all the inspiration out of you for a year." Celebrating the dignity and worth of labor, Woody in his unique way appeared to call for a system of universal health care, insisting, "I believe in a government wholesale price on labor, delivered to your house cause they double the pressure, triple the increase, and quadruple the price at the hosspistol."[18]

In denouncing the creditors and advocating for health care, Woody appears to fit within the reform tradition of Roosevelt's New Deal. The paradoxical Guthrie, however, also espoused more revolutionary sentiments in his "Woody Sez" columns. On June 24, 1939, Woody sounded like Karl Marx proclaiming that the workers had nothing to lose but their chains. Stopping just short of calling for a revolution, Woody exclaimed, "Down with Wall street. Down with salary loan sharks — down with the rape made finance fiends — We are civilized to the brink of poverty, slavery, an slaughter. If this be treason — make the most of it." Continuing in this revolutionary vein several days later, Woody insisted, "Lots of the big money boys is a willin' to have you a workin' for their Freedom — an' in pursuit of their Happiness but that is like a puttin' the constitution down in Pig Latin. To expect help, groceries, freedom and fair chance from a selfish, greedy, whole-hog, profiteer — so like milkin' a dead cow, it won't work."[19] Despite such a pessimistic forecast for reforming the American system, Woody did not totally depart from Popular Front cooperation with antifascist liberals such as Franklin Roosevelt.

During the summer of 1939, before the signing of the Hitler-Stalin Non-aggression Pact in August, Woody supported the re-election of Roosevelt. He continued to denounce those exploiting the common people, but he appeared to tone down his rhetoric a bit, providing a less incendiary or revolutionary approach to the political and economic crisis of capitalism. Instead, Woody returned to extolling the virtues of the migrants and poor. On July 7, he discussed his comfort level when walking down "skid row" in Los Angeles, asserting that he trusted hobos more than the "playfolks that populate our banks and hotels." In another piece about the migrants, Woody maintained that they were honest and true because they were forced to live in a state of nature with few possessions and empty bellies. Woody proclaimed, "You Land

Shirks, and other Friskers, listen to me, the hungrier you make us, the wiser we get... cause all of the good books on religion advise you to fast and think... and the fastest you can think is when youre right hungry." Woody also praised how John Steinbeck portrayed the migrants in *The Grapes of Wrath*, writing, "John's book is out to show you just how exactly what th Arkies, an the Oakies, the Kansies, and the Texies, an all of the farmers an workers has to go through — so's somebody can make a profit off of em. John's book was a little to poetry — like to ever take a holt among the real, genuine 'dusties' — but it will hit right where folks don't know what other folks has to go through — except by books." At three dollars, the singer concluded that the migrants would scarcely be able to afford Steinbeck's novel, perhaps explaining Woody's apparent preference for John Ford's film version over the book.[20]

While Woody reaffirmed his faith in the people, he also continued to defend the Communist Party and its supporters. On July 17, 1939, he reported that former party member John Leech was testifying before the House Un-American Activities Committee (HUAC) and denouncing communism. Woody labeled Leech as a Judas figure, observing, "But that is the way it was when they nailed the carpenter to the cross — they took the words of the folks that didn't know anything about him, and then — a feller named Judas, that deserted his party — sold out his teacher an his own soule — for about 30 hunks of silver."[21] Woody also defended union leader Harry Bridges. The United States government wanted to deport the Australian-born labor boss of the longshoremen for his alleged Communist Party ties. Woody asserted that Bridges believed that the union movement was Americanism, and "Abe Lincoln said the same thing." The folk singer believed that Bridges was in trouble because of the red-baiting pursued by William Randolph Hearst and his media empire. According to Woody, "When a guy comes out a raisin' hell a bout the migertory workers, and hoboes, and poor folks, worken people, and scares hell out of em with cartoon and old storys in a newspaper — an rule em by fear — like the Hearst papers does — I ain't got no use for em."[22]

In this diatribe against Hearst, Woody, as was often the case, was more precise in denouncing the grafters than articulating how exactly change was to come about in the world. However, he maintained a simple vision in which a nation governed by the working people would usher in progress, while in a country "run by Money rule, you got rotten politicians, rotten banks, rotten crops, rotten clothing, rotten gangsters, and rotten ever thing."[23] The vision of a workers' state, which ostensibly existed in the Soviet Union, appeared to describe Woody's ideal government. Yet the often ambiguous Woody spent little time and energy waxing poetically about the worker's paradise in the Soviet Union. While often defending communism and adhering to essential aspects of the party line, the singer was an American who wanted to create a people's government in the United States that would harken back to the founding principles of the Declaration of Independence — that all men are created equal. Thus, after meeting a Japanese family that had migrated to the United States in search of freedom, an empathetic Woody observed, "That's how come the U. S. A. to get started — and that's what has kept her a goin.... Freedom. Folks is a lookin for Freedom. Here and herafter, the best thing they ask for is Freedom. A job of work, a fair chance an Honest Share of the stuff they produce ... they got that much a coming to em, and they are dadgum shore a goin to Get It. They'll cross oceans, fight wars, migerate like birds, go through hell's high waters, or anything else 1000 times — to get Freedom."[24]

This was Woody's paradise. An America where the common people could find fulfilling work and be free from exploitation. Woody placed little faith in organized religion. Instead, he believed in the millennial return of the working-class carpenter who would bring peace, equality, and justice to the world. The folk singer envisioned an earthly paradise in which, "Should the Master appear again on earth, that he would take a look at the sinners ... as He did before. Religion is to forget yourself and work for the good of others. Outside of that there is no religion ... no progress ... no hope for you, your neighbor, your coming grandchildren. Find out who is causing the Trouble here in this old World — remove the power from their hands — place it in the hands of those who aint' Greedy — and you can roll over and go to sleep."[25] More interested in ends than means, Woody continued to perceive communism as a possible path through which to usher in the commonwealth of equality called for by the Prince of Peace.

In 1939, however, it became even more difficult to be a communist in the United States; the Nazi-Soviet Non-aggression Pact was signed in August and on September 1, 1939, the Germans invaded Poland. The Popular Front policy of collective security against fascism was abandoned as Stalin, convinced after the Munich crisis of 1938 that the Western democracies would not stand up to Hitler, determined that the interests of the Soviet Union could be best served by forming a temporary alliance with the Nazi dictator. The shift in policy of the Communist Party in the United States made it apparent to many critics that American communists were simply following the dictates of the Soviet Union and exercised little independence. Yet Woody did not desert the party. Instead he shifted from supporting the antifascist Popular Front to denouncing capitalistic war for exploiting the working class. Although he generally continued to support the New Deal and Roosevelt for re-election in 1940, Woody downplayed the upcoming election in his columns for the fall of 1939. He would not repudiate his leftist sympathies and increasingly focused attention on questions of war and peace in his writing. A playful Woody commented upon a lost songbook, suggesting, "Well you will find some of them songs to be purty dern left handed. They was so left wing I had to write em with my left hand and sing em with my left tonsil, an string my gittar up backwards to git eny harmony out of em."[26]

Woody also wrote a column describing how he was sitting home, "buried about 6 foot deep in some dialecticle matternilisation, and it was a speakin a bout what was real, an what was just pure old imagining," when his children told him they wanted to play and eat, but said they wanted real, not imaginary oranges.[27] For Woody, the future was always about the children and creating a better world for them. He increasingly wrote about the impact of the war in Europe on children, and he endorsed the Soviet policy of viewing World War II as a capitalist conflict. He observed, "See where Hitler is a gonna jump on the wimmen & children, too, an everybody else says, if you jump on em, we'll jump on em too, which makes it look like theyre a goin to get jumped on." A few days later, Woody found the origins of the war to lie in the "private ownership of scarce resources." He lamented, "Some war. Seems like theyre a fightin to see who owns what.... Well if the country belonged to ever body init they coodent no fights break out." War, according to Woody, would remain a problem as long as civilization was based on the profit system. In support of peace, Woody urged workers, who were strapped financially, to donate a day's pay to maintain the *People's Daily World* as one of the few voices against war and fascism.[28]

Despite Woody's appeal for a more peaceful world, war was a reality in Europe and Asia. Never acknowledging that his analysis also supported Soviet self-interest, Woody concluded that the war was a failure, squandering precious resources needed by the people. He denounced the European war in the most vehement terms, urging Americans to resist policies of conscription or to aid the British, which would draw the country into a war benefitting corrupt politicians and capitalist profiteers. Woody exclaimed: "War is a game played by maniacs, who kill each other. It is murder, studied and prepared by insane minds, and followed by a bunch of thieves. You can't believe in life, and wear the uniform of death. There are certain men who never think of any other thing besides slaughter. They are blood soaked butchers and they are believed to be heroes. Three fifths of the people decide to murder the other two fifths, who must take up killing in order to stay alive. Locate the man who profits by war — strip him of his profits and war will end."[29]

In late 1939, the "Woody Sez" columns concentrated on issues of war and peace, but Woody continued to rail against the exploitation of the working class by big business and profiteers, while calling for a more collectivist future. He envisioned the United States as one big union which everyone could join, concluding, "Now, if you an em an everybody all belonged to the same big union — an then th union was to guarantee you a job all of th time — why heck — we cood all be richer than we are by a dang sight."[30] In another column, however, Woody indicated that he was growing restless in California. He speculated that he was the "dirtiest of the Dustbowlers," and he might be the next

The People's Daily World *and Indigenous Radicalism* 55

to migrate.³¹ On January 7, 1940, Woody wrote his final "Woody Sez" column for the *People's Daily World*. As usual, Woody did not bid farewell to all his readers, friends, or family. Woody's adherence to the Communist Party line following the Nazi-Soviet Pact resulted in a parting of ways between the radical folk singer and progressive radio station owner Frank Burke. With nothing to hold him in California and restless once again, Woody returned to his family in Texas before he headed off toward the new promise land of New York City.

Woody's adherence to the Communist Party line in the 1930s led to accusations that the folk singer was a party member who slavishly followed the dictates of Joseph Stalin. Nora Guthrie tends to dismiss the party membership claims, insisting that her father was practical rather than ideological. Besides not having the patience for the paperwork necessary to maintain a party membership, Nora argues that communism was too narrow for Woody and his constantly evolving political thought made it impossible to follow a doctrinal party line. She adheres more to Woody's concept of "commonism" by concluding that Woody believed the answer to the world's problems could be found in the common people coming together and sharing their ideas and resources.³² This idea is more akin to the philosophy of one big soul preached by Jim Casy in Steinbeck's *The Grapes of Wrath*.

Biographer Ed Cray accepts Nora's view that her father lacked the discipline and ideological commitment to be a party member. On the other hand, Ronald Cohen, in his examination of Woody and the Communist Party, finds no contradiction in Woody's admiration for the Communist Party and his celebration of the American people. Like many in the 1930s, he was attracted to the party's basic domestic goals of greater democracy, "while resisting any slavish obedience to Party doctrines or dictates." He was more a follower of Eugene Debs and Abraham Lincoln than Lenin or Stalin, but he perceived communism as offering a vision of equality, democracy, and peace. Cohen concludes that Woody was "a Red, but, of his own stripe — no contradiction in a political climate where anything was possible, as Woody demonstrated."³³ As for Woody, he remained elusive on the subject, quipping, "I ain't a communist necessarily, but I have been in the red all my life."[34] Woody later suggested that he might have joined the party sometime in 1937, but usually he dismissed the witch hunts of reactionaries looking for communists. In 1939, he wrote in one of his notebooks, "Well Ever Body is a callin' ever body else a communist. They called Roosevelt that. They called Upton Sinclair that. They called Hughey Long that. They called EPIC that. They called Ham & eggs that. And now they've got the government Inspectors out a huntin' the Communists and Red Activities, and Revolts — such is life! Accordion to all the neighbors, all of the other neighbors are communists."[35]

Woody's concern about government surveillance was certainly warranted as the FBI files on the musician totaled several hundred pages and continued even after disease limited his activities. After examining these files, Aaron J. Leonard concluded that the FBI had difficulty in establishing Woody's party membership, but "settled on the view that, card-carrying or not, Guthrie was to be treated as a communist."[36] Thus, the Stalinist label that critics placed on Woody never disappeared in some quarters; even as many in his home state prepared to celebrate Woody's centennial in 2012, the *Oklahoma Constitution* denounced his politics. In an editorial, the conservative publication asserted, "It is clear that Woody Guthrie was a philosophical communist, one who wrote for a communist newspaper. One could even say Guthrie was the most extreme sort of communist — a Stalinist."[37]

A close reading of the "Woody Sez" columns from the *People's Daily World*, however, does not support such a simplistic depiction. Instead these columns provide ample evidence that the California years of the late 1930s were a crucial period in which Woody investigated the living conditions of the dust bowl refugees and formulated a radical hybrid political ideology that incorporated elements of Christian socialism, social banditry, populism, Jeffersonianism, collectivism, and, yes, even communism into his philosophy of "commonism." Woody never recanted his communist past and beliefs, but as David Shumway suggested in an insightful essay on Woody's legacy, "If we are to understand Woody Guthrie's place in our cultural history, we can only do so by acknowledging his indigenous radicalism."[38] The "Woody Sez" columns for the *People's Daily World* illuminate the complexity of Woody's radicalism. Woody's vision of a better world for all of God's children attempted to fuse elements of traditional, American radicalism with Marxism. At times Woody's adherence to the Communist Party line makes him appear as something of a "Hillbilly Apparatchik," who slavishly follows the dictates of the party. But in his celebration of the common people and the promise of American life he was very much a traditional, left-wing, American populist, as exemplified by his belief in "commonism."

My search for Woody Guthrie in California provided essential insights into understanding how Woody formulated a radical analysis of American capitalism, which did not seem to work for many common people such as the Guthrie and Briley families. But the development of Woody's political consciousness was hardly complete, and New York City beckoned with new opportunities and a door opening to a world far beyond the experiences of Okemah and Pampa. After some difficult early days in New York, Woody thrived in the rich cultural environment of the city. As the product of a poor family who could not afford vacations, it is easy to identify with both the fear and excitement Woody found in New York City. At age twenty-one, I had never flown in an airplane or traveled beyond Texas and Oklahoma. An academic career and various fellowships finally opened the opportunity to grow and travel. Fulbright study opportunities have taken me to Japan, Amsterdam, the Middle East, and Eastern Europe. And for some strange reason I have always felt at home in New York City — a location I visit at every opportunity. It seems to have all the intellectual stimulation and entertainment that I was missing in Childress: Major League Baseball, theater, museums, bookstores, lectures, concerts, film festivals, and conversations. It would be easy to get caught up with the cultural elitism of New York City, but the hard-working people of New York actually have quite a bit in common with their counterparts in Oklahoma, Texas, and California. In New York City, Woody found artists, working-class people, political and union activists, and a new love with whom he shared his dreams for a better world.

Chapter Three

Woody in New York City: "Woody Sez" and the *Daily Worker*

Woody Guthrie arrived virtually penniless in New York City during the winter of 1940. Although his first residency in the city lasted only about a year, it was a formative period in his life; after a brief sojourn in the West he would return and make New York his home. As Nora Guthrie observed in an interview, Woody's initial experience in New York City was crucial for his intellectual growth and development. The rich cultural environment of the city opened his mind to new ideas, but he never lost his confidence in listening to his inner self and the common people of the dust bowl where he was born and raised.[1]

After arriving in the city, Woody composed "This Land Is Your Land," although he would not record the song for several years. He was touted for his songs and performances, which captured the voice of common Americans in a similar fashion as did Steinbeck's writing. Woody recorded his album *Dust Bowl Ballads* to critical acclaim, and his authenticity was embraced by musicologist Alan Lomax. Woody's popularity led to several lucrative radio contracts, and he even brought

Mary and the children to live with him. The commercial opportunities, however, conflicted with Woody's political agenda as outlined in his columns for the communist *Daily Worker*. This resurrection of his "Woody Sez" pieces will form an essential source for this chapter. In his writing for the *Daily Worker*, Woody sometimes assumes the role of the country rube in the big city, but overall they constitute an increasingly more sophisticated radical critique of the American political scene. Eventually, however, Woody's radio sponsors became uncomfortable with the folk singer's politics. In frustration, Woody gave up his *Daily Worker* column. Fearing that he was losing his independence, however, he finally rejected the political compromise of a commercial radio career and took Mary and the kids back with him to California.

Woody was initially invited to New York City by his friend, actor Will Geer (perhaps best-known today for his role as Grandpa in the popular 1990s television series *The Waltons*) who was appearing on Broadway in the cast of *Tobacco Road*. The city appeared to offer opportunities for Woody to perform, and if he could obtain some musical jobs, he might earn enough to send for Mary and the family that had expanded to three children. Woody sold his rather dilapidated Chevrolet and obtained enough money to buy a bus ticket that would get him as far east as Pittsburgh. When he arrived in Pittsburgh, it was snowing, and Woody attempted to hitchhike in the frigid weather. Luckily, he got a ride from a forest ranger who took him to Philadelphia and purchased the forlorn musician a bus ride to New York City. He moved in with Will and Herta Geer and their six-month-old daughter. Borrowing Herta's guitar, Woody raised some funds by singing in bars along the Bowery. After saving enough money for a week's lodging, Woody moved into a room at Hanover House near the New York Public Library. It is there in February 1940 that Woody composed his most famous song, originally called "God Blessed America."[2]

In writing what would become better known as "This Land Is Your Land," Woody was responding to Irving Berlin's "God Bless America" as performed by Kate Smith, and which was dominating American radio and jukeboxes in early 1940. Based upon his life experience, Woody found that the way Berlin embraced American exceptionalism hardly considered what the folk singer observed on the dusty plains of Oklahoma and Texas, the fruit orchards of California, and the Hoovervilles of desperate families seeking work. To Woody, Berlin's song had become, according to Robert Santelli, "a sonic elixir, a numbing narcotic that placed the nation's destiny in a God that hadn't yet figured out what to do with the nation and had given people the idea that little, if anything, was wrong with their country." Woody believed that a good song told the truth, and he found the Berlin tune to be false. Woody took on the responsibility to document in song the plight of the American people, and then to express the hope of a better tomorrow. Santelli, in his history of Woody's anthem to America, concluded that, similar to Berlin, Woody loved America, but he did not exhibit blind faith or patriotism. Instead, "Guthrie didn't whitewash the country's imperfections. Rather what he did was tell it like it is, as indicated by what he wrote at the end of the page, 'All you can write is what you see.'"[3]

While Woody was pleased with the song, he did not immediately share the piece. He first recorded the song in 1944 for Moe Asch, who finally released the song in 1951 as part of a Woody Guthrie children's collection. Instead, Woody was more focused on making a name for himself in New York City. On February 25, 1940, he appeared at the Mecca Temple in Manhattan, performing at a benefit for Spanish Civil War refugees. Woody's big break, however, came when Geer arranged for him to perform at a gala benefit for Steinbeck's Committee for Agricultural Workers. Although unknown to the audience, Woody demonstrated confidence, charisma, and authenticity. Clad in a blue work shirt and rather dusty cap, he shared some observations about being part of the "Rape of Graft" show before launching into "Do Re Mi." He told the audience, "You know, Oklahoma is a very rich state. You want oil in Oklahoma, just go down a hole and get it. If you want coal, why we've got coal in Oklahoma. Jus' go down a hole and get it. You want lead, we've got lead mines. Go down a hole and get you some lead. If you want food, clothes, groceries, just go in a hole ... and stay there."[4] Woody's performance was enthusiastically received by the

New York City audience. He met figures from the city's music scene who would later be influential in his career, including Pete Seeger, Aunt Molly Jackson, Lead Belly, and composer Earl Robinson. Steinbeck embraced Woody's authenticity, proclaiming, "He sings the songs of a people, and I suspect that he is, in a way, that people. Harsh voiced and nasal, his guitar hands like a tire iron on a rusty rim, there is nothing sweet about Woody, and there is nothing sweet about the songs he sings. But there is something more important for those who will listen. This is the will of the people to oppose and fight against oppression. I think we call this the American spirit."[5]

Woody's songs also excited Alan Lomax, Assistant Director of the Archives of Folk Song at the Library of Congress, who proclaimed the folk singer "Shakespeare in overalls" and invited Woody to the nation's capital to make his first recordings. To Lomax, Woody's performance in March 1940 at the Forrest Theater was a turning point in American folk music. It was the moment when, as Lomax biographer John Szwed suggested, "the folk revival in America was born." Although excited about Woody's potential, Lomax recognized that the singer was really "a highbrow disguised as a primitive ... the double disguise of the true revolutionary."[6]

Three months later, Woody showed up at Lomax's home, and the musicologist spent several days recording Woody's music and stories. Lomax was instrumental in forging Woody's early career. He encouraged Woody to work with Seeger on a project that would become called *Hard Hitting Songs for Hard-Hit People* — Woody's title for a collection of American social and political protest songs.[7] In addition, Lomax arranged for Woody to record his *Dust Bowl Ballads* for RCA Records and employed his contacts in the radio industry to obtain spots on such programs as *Pursuit of Happiness, Back Where I Come From, Adventures in Music,* and *We the People,* where Woody could be discovered by a larger audience. He even obtained an endorsement contract from the Model Tobacco Company, and Woody served as the host for the company's radio show, *Pipe Smoking Time.* This commercial success allowed Woody to bring his family to New York City.

These business associations, however, did not halt Woody's political activities. He continued to perform at many Communist Party functions, and he was able to resume his "Woody Sez" column with the *Daily Worker*. A close examination of these columns reveals that despite the publicity he garnered on the radio, Woody remained committed to his radical vision of "commonism." On April 2, 1940, the *Daily Worker* introduced its new columnist by remarking, "Woody that's his name. He's a native of Oklahoma who's come East for a time. He can tell you about the Dust Bowl, the original characters of *The Grapes of Wrath* and of the latest letter he got from John Steinbeck. He strums a guitar, sings people's songs and writes columns for the *Daily Worker*." Mike Quinn of the *Daily Worker* enthusiastically proclaimed, "Sing it, Woody, sing it. Karl Marx wrote it, and Lincoln said it, and Lenin did it. Sing it, Woody, and we'll all laugh together." The folksy image of this introduction to readers was maintained in some of Woody's first columns as he assumed something of a "country bumpkin in the big city" persona.[8]

For example, he commented on the difficulties he encountered in navigating the New York City bus and subway systems. Woody wrote, "I believe there is more of New York underground than on top. New York is funny. The streets are half a block long and three blocks wide. And the town is half a town wide and three towns high. I have remarked elsewhere that everybody has got to go in the hole every morning to get to work. You might say the workin folks had to go underground to get anywhere." Woody concluded the piece by complaining how expensive it was to travel around the city, noting, "Boy it really takes the nickels to live here. You can't get to first base unless you make 84746 fone calls and ride 85756 buses every day. You got to spend sixty cents in nickels to see about a dollar job. Then you got to spend the rest of the dollar to get to the right place at the right time."[9]

While Woody maintained his country-boy take on the big city, he was increasingly political in his columns. Woody was critical of war profiteers, capitalism, bankers, the Roosevelt administration, and Jim Crow, while continuing to focus on the daily concerns of working people and his Okie migrants. Overall, these are similar themes to those Woody developed in his pieces for the *People's Daily World*, but with greater concern for racial issues. The radicalism that was fostered in California was alive and well in New York City. And Woody's writing could also display considerable venom, as was evident in a column discussing British imperialism in which Woody demonstrated his break with Popular Front collective security. Describing the British Empire as representing the biggest gang of thieves in the world, Woody commented, "Half of the movies I been to in the last 2 years showed the British a sending soldiers and guards and cops and deputies and policemen out into the wild country of the mountains and deserts of India and Africa and Asia. They pay you $1 a day to act as a robber for them, and give you a badge and a soldier suit and a helmet and a gun and they explain murder on such a basis as makes it seem all right."[10] In the post-World War II world, Woody would level similar critiques of American imperialism.

The anti-imperialist theme was evident in another piece in which Woody denounced capitalism for promoting war and empire. Coining a new term coperialist — which did not catch on — Woody asserted, "It's the tribe between the capitalists and the Imperialists — a class right in there that ain't never made plain in the books — and they're the boys like senators and congressmen and governors and such, that ramrod the capital business of the Imperialist Moguls."[11] As war raged in Europe, Woody followed the party line that the fighting was a capitalist struggle, and he was opposed to any effort on behalf of the Roosevelt administration to have the United States support the British against the Nazi onslaught. Although Roosevelt was increasingly convinced that the United States should side with the British, he recognized the strong antiwar sentiments of many Americans, as exemplified in Woody's columns. Thus, as he sought election to a third term in 1940, Roosevelt publicly maintained a policy of neutrality that he would later abandon after winning re-election and introducing the Lend-lease legislation to aid the British and other victims of Nazi aggression.[12]

From Woody's perspective war only benefited the capitalist class, and so he also focused upon domestic issues threatening American democracy. In an April 21, 1940 column, he denounced the crime of lynching. He observed that in his home town of Okemah a black woman and her son were hanged from a river bridge, and postcards of the event were sold locally. He did not, however, acknowledge that his father might have been involved with this Okemah lynching. Instead, Woody describes an artist friend's painting of a lynching that stymied his sometimes humorous approach to issues of exploitation. Analyzing the piece of art, Woody wrote, "This painting is so real I feel like I was at a lynching and it somehow or another just takes all of the fun and good humor and good sport out of you to sit here and realize that people could go so haywire as to hang a human body by a pole and shoot it full of Winchester rifle holes just for pastime."[13] In addition to his concern for racial injustice in the United States, Woody was worried about how the war crisis was curtailing immigration, such as that of Jews fleeing Nazi persecution. Addressing the nativism in America advocated by fascist groups, Woody observed, "Folks what's born in Foreign Countries can't help it. They went to a lot of work and trouble a gettin here — most of us is here by accident anyway — but the fellers that jump on you and make trouble for you just because of the place you was born . . . well, all I got to say is that 2,000 years ago we had 'em, and we got plenty of 'em right now, and 2,000 years from now they'll be out arresting you and a having your trial, a trying to prove you was born up on the moon."[14]

While it broadened his focus, Woody's time in New York City did not mean that he had forgotten about his fellow dust bowl migrants. In referring to Farm Security Administration photographs of destitute migrant families, Woody was quick to remind his New York readers that the Okies were not about to give up in their struggles against the profit system. Woody concluded, "When they do take a notion to get going and get together, and organized and fight for what's right, they'll surprise the whole world, and in all probability strike at the right place stronger and faster than any of us can imagine at the present time."[15]

He also commented upon reports that John Ford's film adaptation of *The Grapes of Wrath* was drawing small crowds in rural Oklahoma. Woody pointed out, "Well, the old world don't like to smell its own B.O. and besides us 'Oakies' aint got the two bits to go on, and the 'bloakies' that robbed us dam sure don't want a vision of it a lookin' em right square in the face."[16] Woody also returned to dust bowl themes in another piece, arguing that lots of things terrify a rich man, "but you cannot scare a man who has lost his land to the dust and landlords."[17]

Woody was becoming a little homesick for his people and desired to see his family, so he convinced Pete Seeger to accompany him on a journey that would take the two men into the South and to Woody's Southwestern roots. Woody planned to maintain his *Daily Worker* column with commentaries from the road trip. On May 22, 1940 he wrote a passionate farewell to New York, insisting, "There is one only one New York, and if you don't see it, you are doing yourself and your country an injustice, it's got the best of the least for the most, and the most of the least for the least, and the biggest bunch of people on earth that work like dogs for a living, and the biggest bunch that live a lifetime and never hit a lick of work."[18]

Woody's columns from the road were initially more on the lighter side, and he seemed to delight once again in rambling and conversing with the people along the way. In some of his early road columns, he expressed disbelief that a family of four lived in a twenty-room mansion while so many people were without shelter, and Woody complained that a dentist had no business charging him five dollars to extract a tooth. In addition, he confessed that he had stopped shaving while traveling so that he could give his face a break just as his stomach was taking a rest as meals were often hard to find.[19] But when it came to the Ku Klux Klan, Woody was hardly so jovial. In his column of May 31, Woody denounced the Klan, proclaiming, "The KKK gangs are a coming out on a bronc, shute No. 3, rider No. 7, but I'll lay a 2 to 1 he gets throwed. Anybody that's yellow enough to have to put a sack over his head to do his daily work, well, he just caint win, 'cause he caint see good enough. . . . Anybody gets so far off track as to go around with a sack over his head is just to lose out, well just because he don't believe in what he's a doing." In conclusion, Woody expressed his contempt for Klan members who had beaten an interracial couple.[20]

After numerous car breakdowns and adventures, Woody and Seeger made it to Oklahoma in early June. They initially stayed in Oklahoma City with Communist Party organizers, Bob and Ina Wood, who recruited the musicians to entertain for striking workers, a meeting of the Southern Tenant Farmers Union, and an encampment of the unemployed along the Canadian River.[21] In response to Ina Wood's complaint that Woody had not produced a union song for women, the folk singer stayed up all night and, with Seeger's help, wrote "Union Maid." Will Kaufman describes this song as "one of the great anthems of the wartime and postwar labor movement." In his manuscript version of the song, contained in the Woody Guthrie Archives, Woody credits the inspiration for the song to African-American activist Annie Mae Meriwether who was sexually brutalized and almost murdered for daring to join the interracial Sharecroppers Union in Alabama. In his notes to the song, Woody wrote, "Mrs. Meriweather (*sic*) was the Union Sharecropper lady that Vaughn Riles and Ralph McQuire stripped naked and beat up; then hung her for dead up to a rafter in the little shack."[22]

Conditions in Oklahoma were the subject of several *Daily Worker* columns as Woody reported on the difficult economic circumstances confronting working-class people in his home state. As Woody described, Community Camp in Oklahoma City — which he claimed was "the world's biggest Hooverville" — reflected the dire straits in which the profit system had placed many of his fellow citizens. Woody wrote, "The camp is mostly under a grove of trees, little old patched up shanties ain't got no paint, dug down a foot or so to solid footing for a dirt floor, hammered out buckets and cane are valuable building material, and the cold damp runs you out into the sunshine quick as old sun shows his head." Defending his people against an accusation by a more affluent woman that the poor would not know what to do with better accommodations, Woody asserted, "Baloney. Give them a tile kitchen, and it would be spotless. Rich folks don't ever do no homework. It's the homeless folks that clean up behind you."[23] While he generally critiqued the deplorable living conditions for the poor in Oklahoma, Woody expressed some optimism regarding the organizing potential of the poor, as exhibited by the Workers Alliance, that had developed a food stamp plan to aid starving people in Oklahoma City and Tulsa. He called for the program to be implemented throughout the state. Woody concluded that the city and country people needed to unite as, "90% of the Human beings in the world is inwardly on the Same Side, but they are just being kept apart by those who want them apart."[24]

His road trip did not prevent Woody from continuing to denounce efforts to draw America into the war in Europe. He chronicled that he and Pete were given a ride by two young men who were considering enlisting in the military. They could not understand why Woody was not eager to defend his country. After pointing out that he had no argument with European boys who were trying to feed their families just as he was, Woody hoped that his young traveling companions would resist the drumbeats of war. He concluded, "Well, they ain't got no hourse, no land, no home, no job, no money, no groceries, nothing but a bunch of debts, and they just feel like that aint worth dying for." Woody also reported on a conversation that he had with a preacher living in the homeless camp. The preacher was concerned about the threat of war and asserted that the European conflict was the devil's work. Woody then asked him who was working with the devil, and the preacher replied, "It's th' RICH FOLKS. They start all of these wars — and then yell for us poor folks to come do their dying for them. All I got is community Camp, A $7 house on a dry sandy river bed, alongside a garbage dump — I wouldn't fight for That."[25]

Following their stay in Oklahoma, Woody and Seeger journeyed to Pampa so that Woody could have some time with Mary and the children. Seeger who came from a privileged family was rather shocked by the poor conditions, like those of the homeless camps, in which Woody's family lived. After only a few days in Pampa, Woody was restless and ready to return to New York City, while Seeger continued his journey to the West Coast. The Woody-Seeger pairing was always a rather strange one. Woody thought Seeger rather odd in that he did not drink or chase women. As for Seeger, he noted the differences between the two men, concluding, "I was an intellectual from New England, and he was a self-made intellectual from a small town in Oklahoma. He was determined not to let himself be changed.... I was eager to change." Seeger, who was six years younger than Woody, also credited his elder with teaching him a great deal about life. Seeger stated, "His ability to identify with the ordinary man and woman, speak their own language without using the fancy words, and never be afraid. I learned from him how just plain orneriness has a kind of wonderful honesty to it that is unbeatable."[26]

For the trip back to New York City, Woody gathered up Bob Wood and several of his comrades who were heading to the Communist Party national convention, to be held in Madison Square Garden. Woody described his return to the city in a humorous column for the *Daily Worker*, remarking, "A lot of folks in our caravan was a coming to New York for their first time. After we got out of the Holler Tunnel, I says, Well, Boys, what do you think of her? One old boy in the back said, I bet I sunburn the roof of my mouth — but it'll be worth it — he looked out the window as we drove down the street and he said, God a mighty, dadburn my hide, is ALL of them people here for the convention? — Another ol boy said, Well, yeah, but they just don't KNOW it yet."[27] Woody attended this convention, which nominated Earl Browder for President. He gave his Pontiac to Wood and the other Oklahoma Communist Party members for their drive home before throwing himself into pursuing his musical career in the big city.

As Woody began to enjoy some success with his music and radio appearances, he continued to write his column for the *Daily Worker* — denouncing warmongers and the profit system. Reflecting the breakdown of the Popular Front, Woody was increasingly critical of Roosevelt and the New Deal, arguing that the President and Democratic Party were preparing the nation for war. Woody condemned a resolution by the Oklahoma Democratic Party to enter the war in support of the British. Woody asserted, "The rich folks way of running a country has fizzled again, and before they'd come out and admit it, they'd kill you and me just as willingly as a sticker in a slaughter house ... by hissing us onto each other. They'd even spend our money to furnish the guns." Woody warned his readers to beware of the Roosevelt administration, observing, "Don't be in favor of any body just because you used to be. That's like trying to — well, sometimes, it's like trying to fly a wrecked plane. For instance, Roosevelt." In another piece, Woody questioned the New Deal, referring to Roosevelt's programs as the "nude deal" that had done little to alleviate the poverty of American workers and farmers. Woody wrote, "We called for a new deal once. We got a Nude Deal. Now the way lords are playing poker for blood, and they're glaring at each other over a pile of six guns . . . and if it so happens that you are in debt, broke, down and out, over worked, under fed, or in the red — maybe you ought to holler for a new deal your self."[28]

Woody believed the system was broken, and he denounced Congress for creating HUAC to persecute anyone who might call for fundamental changes to the capitalist system. Comparing the New Deal to a dilapidated automobile, Woody argued that Congressional committees such as HUAC were formed "to keep you from spotting anything that's wrong, and to frail the daylights out of you for not putting on a big smile, and just setting there in the middle of the road, not moving a dadburn inch in either direction — with a big silly grin on your face, nodding gently and sweetly to all of the folks and waiting for the dam thing to take you somewhere to dinner. It just ain't done."[29] Woody's reaction to the problems confronting Americans and a world of refugees was the Marxist refrain that the common people of the world must unite to overthrow the capitalist system. Speaking to the dust bowl migrants and refugees from the European conflict, Woody proclaimed, "Someday I look for them to all migrate in the right direction and just camp down here on good old Wall St., and just sort of raise our voices, and fists, and maybe our families there."[30]

In the late summer of 1940 as Congress debated whether to impose conscription on the nation, Woody was increasingly adamant in his opposition to war. Woody warned that conscription would lead to "the packing plant of War, where men are made into hamburger meat, young boys into steaks, engineers into chops, and the college kids are flying disconnected, disassociated, unrelated, disenfranchised, dispossessed, worthless, useless, moneyless, homeless, hunks of human anatomy." Instead of planning for war, Woody suggested that the government put young men to work building safe roads, schools, hospitals, factories, and housing. Woody also insisted that big business in Europe needed to realize that the Yanks would not be coming to bail them out as America had done during the First World War. Reflecting strains of isolationism that were popular among both the American left and right, Woody argued that the working people of the United States had plenty to do on the home front. He wrote, "We ain't more 'n scratched the surface over here, so if the Yanks do any going and coming, it ought to be to go down to work, and come down and get paid, and go up on a vacation and come up and get paid, and go on a trip and come and get paid, and go put in a crop and come up and get paid, and go build some houses and come up and get paid, and go down and get a snort, and come up and see me sometime."[31]

Although the fog of war could draw considerable anger and class resentment on Woody's part, overall his columns in late summer and fall of 1940 were more innocuous, with discussions of the weather and music often occupying his attention. For example, Woody called upon the people to enjoy more old-fashioned get-togethers with music, dancing, and laughter. Woody urged the workers to "have their dancing, wining, dining and romancing, their jokes, their fun, and belly laughs, within their own meetings and parties, because it's like this, it would make us a lot more independent of the profit system, and if profit was made, it would be for your own system." Still, the old Woody "commonism" would crop up in his *Daily Worker* pieces. He perceived little difference between Roosevelt's New Deal and his Republican opponent, businessman Wendell Wilkie. Woody argued, "I wouldn't be surprised to learn that the same man wrote up both platforms. I sometimes wonder who writes up their speeches. When you select one of the bunches, they'll appoint the bunch on their cabinets, and the same old boot heels will scar the White House desks. Same bunch of heels." Expressing his discontent with a system that left many Americans without breakfast, a bitter Woody reiterated one of his favorite sayings with a rather revolutionary twist when he asserted, "Detroit has got men of wheels. Pittsburgh men of steel. Birmingham men of iron. New York men of gold. Reno men of silver. Los Angeles men of the ocean, and Oklahoma's got men of the dust. All of these men has got women and kids. Take it easy. But take it."[32]

Despite such calls for action, Woody in his final columns for the *Daily Worker* seemed to express some concern that he was losing touch with the common people amid his blossoming radio career in New York City. He complained that publicity was the bread and butter of New York entertainment, concluding, "Well, they don't grow no stuff to eat here. I guess they got to keep busy at something. So they all get out and manage each others Publicity. Half of New York is Publicity Managers and the other half has done been managed out of everything they got." In addition to his discomfort with the publicity game, Woody could not believe that he had to purchase an appointment book to keep up with his engagements. Speaking of his next performance, Woody lamented, "They say lots of literary celebs will be there. I'll be there to look everybody over — unless I got lost in traffic."[33]

Woody's growing discontent with the New York City scene was apparently due in great part to the growing pressure of radio sponsors for Woody to tone down his radical politics. He had also brought his family to the city, and Mary welcomed the more comfortable life style that Woody's radio career was bringing to the Guthrie family. Accordingly, Woody published his last column for the *Daily Worker*, a rather innocuous piece on folk music, on November 14, 1940. In response to allegations that he was a communist, Woody wrote his patron Alan Lomax in September 1940, asserting, "They called me a communist and a wild man and everything you could think of but I don't care what they call me. I ain't a member of an earthly organization, my trouble is I really ought to go down in the morning and just join everything." Feeling growing pressure, Woody feared that he had compromised his beliefs in the pursuit of money. Describing Woody's radio work in New York City, his biographer Joe Klein commented,

"There was no room for slyness or spontaneity, not to mention politics or 'polli-TISH-uns.' Woody had been hired more for his on-the-air delivery than for his cleverness, or even his songs. It was his casual, natural country feel that was salable. But playing the rube wasn't much fun unless there was an element of surprise — the quick, caustic, understated, unexpected comeback that cut four or five different ways was the only thing that made the act morally defensible. Without the needle, he was just another singing hick who trafficked in a swarmy, vulgar sort of self-depreciation for the city folks, singing only the blandest songs and telling the limpest stories...."[34]

Woody became increasingly angry with the moral compromises he had made, and he began to push back against the demands of the radio shows. For example, he walked off the set of *Back Where I Come From* when director Nick Ray wanted to drop singer Lead Belly (whom Lomax had discovered in a Louisiana prison) from a program because listeners would not be able to understand his thick Southern accent. Woody developed a close friendship with Lead Belly — which will be pursued in greater depth in the chapter on Woody and race — and he refused to take further instruction from Ray. (Ray went on to become a distinguished director of films such as *Rebel Without a Cause* [1955].) Woody was also unhappy with his corporate-controlled job hosting *Pipe Smoking Time*. On New Year's Eve 1940, Will Geer arranged for Woody to perform at the home of actress Katharine Cornell, but the folk singer was offended by the fancy party and its upper-class participants. He begged Geer to get him out of the party. Two nights later he returned home from his last *Pipe Smoking Time* show and abruptly informed Mary to pack up the children as they were leaving New York and heading back to California. Although Mary and the children were not exactly pleased with this decision, they placed their possessions in the new Pontiac that Woody had purchased on credit and were soon on the road. Describing Woody's decision to depart New York, Will Kaufman wrote that after the travesty of folk singing on his radio program and "apparently sickened by his self-betrayal and his political weakness, Guthrie uprooted himself and his long-suffering family and fled from the one and only New York, whose capitalist temptations had finally overpowered the revolutionary potential he had initially celebrated."[35]

In *Bound for Glory*, Woody paints a far more romanticized version of his disillusionment with and departure from New York City. The autobiography, however, conveniently leaves out Mary and the children and his wife's perspective that Woody's political involvement destroyed their relationship. In his book, Woody walks away from an audition at the Rainbow Room in Rockefeller Center and finds solace among the common folk of the city. After the temptations of the big city, Woody was back with the people, embracing "commonism." Woody proclaimed:

> I walked along, the day just leaving out over the tops of the tall buildings, and sifting through the old scarred chimneys sticking up. Thank the good Lord, everybody, everything ain't all slicked up, and starched and imitation. Thank God, everybody ain't afraid. Afraid in the skyscrapers, and afraid in the red tape offices, and afraid in the tick of the little machine that never explodes, stock market tickers, that scare how many to death, ticking off deaths, marriages and divorces, friends and enemies, tickers connected and plugged in like juke boxes, playing the false and corny lies that are rung in the wild canyons of Wall Street, songs swept by the families that lose, songs jingled on the silver spurs of the men that win. Here on the slummy edges, people are crammed down on the curbs, the sidewalks, and the fireplugs, and cars and trucks and kids and rubber balls are bouncing through the streets, I was thinking, 'This is what I call bein' borned an' a-living'; I don't know what I call that big high building back younder that I left.'[36]

In reality, Woody was hardly confident as he left New York City in early January 1941. As he contemplated a cross country journey accompanied by his wife and three children and with few economic prospects awaiting him in California, Woody expressed a degree of anxiety often missing in his public persona, writing, "Well, I guess the main reason *Pipe Smoking Time* Fired me was on account of I done just what they told me to do and it was no good. It didn't make me feel none too good because it sounded like too much war — so what I done wasn't good — so I'm broke again. I feel natural but just ain't satisfied."[37] Woody eventually found temporary employment with the Bonneville Power Administration, where he produced some of his best music. But his marriage to Mary did not survive the retreat from New York City and the trek west. Woody would eventually return to New York, throw himself into the union movement, and struggle against fascism, while also meeting the love of his life.

In the search for Woody Guthrie, his 1940 experience in New York City is crucial. It is the time when he composed what would become his most famous song, "This Land Is Your Land." In addition, his columns from the *Daily Worker* demonstrate his commitment to the radical perspective that was shaped by the dust bowl and his experience in California. Woody, nevertheless, was tempted by commercial success and family responsibilities to compromise his political ideas. In the final analysis, Woody was unable to reconcile his belief in "commonism" with the glitter of New York City — no matter how attractive it might seem. But it would cost him his first marriage. He was able to find his political voice again in the Pacific Northwest but providing for his family was another matter.

Searching for Woody Guthrie has allowed me to reconsider some of my own values and decisions. Coming from a similar background, it is easy for me to understand the temptation of New York City's rich cultural and intellectual environment. Yet in embracing this vibrant world, it is often difficult to avoid a sense of betraying one's family and roots. Albuquerque, New Mexico is not New York City. Yet it did allow me to escape Childress, but probably not all its baggage. My father often cautioned me about getting "too big for my britches" with advanced college degrees, and I often get the impression that former high school classmates may view me as an elitist. In addition, on a much smaller stage than Woody, I have struggled with some of the same kind of compromises as Woody did. I was fortunate to find a teaching position that I loved and that provided some security for my family. Nonetheless, as an individual who has publicly acknowledged his leftist politics in writings and activities, I have been criticized for pursuing a career in the more elitist environs of an independent private school rather than public education. In response, I would say that there is some validity to this critique. On the other hand, I believe that I have made some valuable contributions during my tenure at Sandia Prep, and I have no apologies to make. Although not all the students at Sandia Prep come from wealthy families, child psychologist Robert Coles in volume five of his *Children of Crisis*, titled *Privileged Ones*, argues that there is important labor to be done with the education of more affluent young people.[38] But Woody was unable to make such compromises. We have the wonderful music he produced as he continued his search for pure old "commonism," at great personal cost.

Chapter Four

Woody and the Bonneville Power Administration: Twenty-six Songs in Thirty Days

His one-month position with the Bonneville Power Administration (BPA) presents something of a detour in the search for Woody Guthrie, before the folk singer returned to New York City to grapple with issues of war and peace while pursuing love. Nonetheless, Woody's experience in the Pacific Northwest offers some key insights into his life and values. Woody had rejected the compromises necessary for a traditional commercial radio career, yet this decision placed his family in desperate financial straits. Woody needed a job and accepted a position with a New Deal agency, even though he was often a critic of what he comically called Roosevelt's "Nude Deal." Yet the development of public power to benefit the lives of the common people was a concept that Woody could support. To earn the daily tender, as we have all learned in our lives, there are some compromises that have to be made — it is simply a question of which compromises one is willing to make without sacrificing core principles.

Although the quality of the songs he produced in the Pacific Northwest were somewhat uneven, "Pastures of Plenty," "Roll On, Columbia, Roll On!," "Grand Coulee Dam," and "Biggest Thing That Man Has Ever Done" certainly represent some of his best work. In his study of the Columbia River songs, Greg Vandy argues, "They present a powerful thesis that the American worker, given the opportunity, has the power to turn deserts into orchards, and rivers into a force strong enough to defeat Nazi Germany. They are a deeply patriotic salvo from a man whose patriotism would wrongly be questioned. They are a refutation to anyone who suggests that the government doesn't have any business helping the common man. The songs are also an optimistic answer to the despairing questions that arose from the Dust Bowl. In fact, what we have come to realize is that Woody Guthrie's Columbia River songs are a direct answer to his Dust Bowl ballads."[1]

Woody also recognized the significance of his work for the BPA. In a letter to his friends Elizabeth and Harold Ambellan, Woody described the Pacific Northwest as "one of the prettiest places you ever looked at." Analyzing the government building of dams in the region, Woody wrote, "Uncle Sam is putting big power dams all along the river to produce electricity for public ownership and distribution through the People's Utility Districts in every town and countryside and the main job is to force the private owned concerns to sell out to the government by selling power at lower rates and by making deals with the National Defense Industries such as the big aluminum, chrome, and manganese plants, the up and coming lighter metal for Uncle Sam's Flying Fortesses."[2] It is interesting to note here that in addition to proclaiming the potential of public power to enrich the lives of working people, Woody was suggesting that public power could enhance the nation's military preparedness. While Woody in his columns for the *Daily Worker* and performances with the Almanac Singers voiced vehement opposition to American participation in the gathering global war, this letter, written a few weeks before Hitler's invasion of the Soviet Union, represents Woody's changing perspective on the conflict as dam construction could also contribute to the people's struggle against fascism.

Such grandiose ideas, however, were not on Woody's radar screen as the Guthrie family traveled across the country in January 1941. They had made a brief visit to Washington D.C. to mend fences with Alan Lomax after Woody departed from his New York City radio shows. Woody hoped that he might be able to resurrect a career with KFVD or other radio stations in the Los Angeles area, but Woody had burned most of his bridges and contacts with his abrupt departure from California the previous year. In his study of the dust bowl migrants, historian Charles J. Shindo notes that Woody was becoming somewhat out of touch with the migrants. Many migrants were obtaining jobs with the burgeoning California aircraft and defense industries, while culturally they were becoming more drawn to country and western music rather than the folk protest ballads preferred by Woody. Shindo argues, "Far from the simple country boy he claimed to be, Guthrie, as an Okie activist, created an image of himself and the dust bowl migrants that sought to center the migrant in the debate over American capitalism. In the end, however, Guthrie failed to understand the unity of politics, economics, and traditional values in Okie culture, and in seeking to change the migrants' status in the political economy, Guthrie distanced himself from the migrants' self-expressed concerns."[3]

Nevertheless, many migrants and their families struggled to find food and shelter, and the Guthrie family grappled with basic survival. Woody finally found a place to live when his old friend Ed Robbin from the *People's Daily World* informed Woody that the house next door to him was vacant. Woody simply moved Mary and the children into the humble house. When finally confronted by the landlord, Woody used his charm to secure permission to stay in the abode with a small rental payment. Robbin also noticed that Mary was growing increasingly frustrated with the family's financial problems and Woody's often irresponsible behavior. She told Robbin, "It's as though he hated the idea of making a lot of money. Never could hold onto a dollar when he had it. Spent it or gave it away. Or drank a good deal of it with the people he met in bars or friends and musicians."[4]

In letters to the Almanac Singers in New York City, Woody provided a more positive take on his situation. He had little to say about the family, but Woody was looking to secure a publisher for his *Hard Hitting Songs* manuscript and also mentioned that he was going to head downtown "and see if I got any unemployment insurance a coming to me, and how to go about a getting it."[5] He expressed no regrets about withdrawing from his New York City radio shows, criticizing compromises made for commercial purposes and praising the Almanacs for maintaining their allegiance to the truth and music of the people. In writing about money, which was in short supply for Woody and Mary, he insisted, "It looks like the more money you make the worse it cramps your writing. Same way with singing or anything else. But the way you old boys are set up there in your old loft I imagine there ain't no way in the world you could let money cramp you. The more dough you go to making the more you got to run around with the white collars. I hope you don't ever let their ideas soak in on you.... We ain't on the money side and dont fight with money, but we use the Truth and its like a spring of cold water."[6]

The letter to the Almanac Singers also makes it clear that Woody was missing the excitement of New York City; he complains that the California sunshine was giving him spring fever and making him somewhat lethargic. Politics were simply more intense in New York City than California, and Woody proclaimed, "New York is about the revoltingest place in the country. You can always go out and take a look at the rest of the country, but fights, gun fights, strikes, police and legion raids, and everything, and then when you go back to New York, you'll see it just a little bit plainer, or the same thing in just a little cleaner looking glass; you'll see the working folks marching up and down the streets, having meetings, talking, preaching, and always going the rest of the country just one better."[7]

Meanwhile, the Guthrie family struggled in their Los Angeles shanty residence. One day the toilet overflowed, and a frustrated

Woody packed the family into the car. They fled Los Angeles, ending up in the small town of Columbia, California in the Sierra foothills where Woody tried to earn some money by singing in local bars. In early May 1941, the family received a forwarded letter suggesting that the BPA was interested in Woody serving as the narrator for a documentary on the building of the Grand Coulee Dam on the Columbia River. He was asked to submit some paperwork, but an impatient Woody decided that he did not have time for the forms. He once again packed up Mary and the kids and headed toward Portland, Oregon.

Although Woody was visited in Los Angeles by director Gunther Von Fritsch about appearing in the documentary film to promote the work of the BPA, the agency claims no final decision had been made to hire Woody when he walked unannounced into the Portland office of the agency on May 12, 1941. Woody was originally recommended for the position by Alan Lomax, who maintained his faith and interest in Woody despite his disappointment that Woody had turned his back on the radio shows Lomax helped the folk singer procure.[8] Nevertheless, Stephen Kahn, who was in charge of public relations for the BPA, had some misgivings regarding Woody's politics. He, accordingly, decided to sign Woody to a one-month contract rather than the initially proposed one-year deal as the shorter agreement would not require approval from his superiors in Washington D.C. Kahn also sought the endorsement of his supervisor, Paul J. Raver, known for his conservative political orientation. Woody strolled into Raver's office, sang a few songs, and emerged with a one-month contract for $266.00 to write songs for a projected BPA promotional film. Although the sum was not large, Woody and Mary were delighted with the money, which provided them temporary food and shelter in Portland. And in need of work, Woody seemed to have no problem complying with the loyalty oath required by the Department of the Interior under the Hatch Act of August 2, 1939. Woody signed and answered no to the question: "Do you have membership in any political party or organization which advocates the overthrow of our Constitutional form of government in the United States."[9] Considering Woody's political activities, it is unclear whether he was being somewhat disingenuous here or simply failed to see the Communist Party as a threat to Constitutional principles. But most importantly Woody had work, and the family had food.

The project to which Woody signed on was an enterprise that would bring regional planning and rural electrification to the Pacific Northwest, just as the Tennessee Valley Authority (TVA) enhanced the quality of life for many people in Appalachia. The BPA would harness the power of the Columbia River by constructing the Bonneville and Grand Coulee Dams. Then, the agency worked with local farmers to create People's Utility Districts (PUDs) "to contest the power of private utilities, large landowners, banks, and insurance companies." In addition to providing public power, the BPA proposed an ambitious irrigation project that "envisioned an orderly relocation of farmers from across the country who would work small plots of land on the Columbia Basin."[10]

To promote the BPA agenda, Kahn and Von Fritsch produced the documentary *Hydro* (1939), which was influenced by New Deal filmmaker Pare Lorentz who addressed the dust bowl in *The Plow that Broke the Plains* (1936) and documented the achievements of the TVA in *The River* (1937).[11] *Hydro* was a short film of approximately thirty minutes with limited national release. It relied primarily upon technical and financial arguments to encourage the formation of PUDs. However, the BPA remained under attack from public utility companies, and many voters remained suspicious of this extended government activity. BPA information officer Kahn was convinced that another film was needed to better capture the spirit of the project. He concluded, "You have to have something that will introduce entertainment value and will go away lifting people's spirits and singing their songs. You know, someone said, 'I don't care who writes your laws if I can sing your songs.'"[12] Von Fritsch was brought back to direct the new film entitled *The Columbia: America's Greatest Power Stream*.

Woody was initially proposed as both a narrator and singer for the film project, but Kahn was somewhat uncomfortable with Woody's politics as well as his nasal twang. Kahn decided it would be best if Woody concentrated upon songs that captured the spirit of the BPA goals. Meanwhile, Woody found housing for his family, but his new Pontiac, which was rather battered after making the trip to California and up to Oregon, was repossessed by the finance company when Woody failed to keep up with the payments. Woody needed a way to get a feeling for the region before he composed his songs, but the agency was not about to lend the folk singer — who had a well-deserved reputation for being rather rough on automobiles — a government car. Instead, the BPA assigned public information officer employee Elmer Buehler to serve as Woody's chauffeur. Mark Pedelty, in his study of the "Columbia River Songs," insists that Buehler's role was essential to Woody's success in capturing the beauty of the Pacific Northwest. Pedelty writes, "Buehler provided quick and easy entry into the world of the Pacific Northwest. Guthrie was hired to portray that world in song, without any prior experience, an extremely daunting task. Guthrie wrote directly about what he was shown in that whirlwind tour across Oregon and Washington. If the better songs read as travelogues it is because they reflect Guthrie's actual experience. A magnificent countryside and massive construction projects were paraded before Guthrie in quick succession. Guthrie allowed Buehler to shepherd him from site to site without controlling the itinerary himself. The guitarist was able to jot notes and write music in the back seat, entertained by a parade of mountains, cliffs, and cascades."[13] As for Buehler, he was impressed with how Woody interacted with common people along the road, but they did not converse a great deal as Woody spent most of his time sitting in the backseat scribbling notes and trying out songs with his guitar — a sustained work ethic that Woody did not always exhibit. Buehler, however, did insist that he usually had to drive with the windows down due to Woody's body odor, a result of his rather notorious aversion to bathing.[14]

 Woody's discipline contributed to one of his most productive periods as he compiled twenty-six songs in his thirty days with the BPA; however, only three of these songs actually made it into the film, whose release was delayed by the Second World War. *The Columbia: America's Greatest Power Stream* finally premiered in 1949, and it was not the type of feature film originally envisioned by Kahn. Instead, it was only twenty-one minutes in length and recycled a considerable amount of footage from *Hydro*. Of Woody's twenty-six songs, only "Roll On, Columbia, Roll On!," "Pastures of Plenty," and "Biggest Thing that Man Has Ever Done" are employed in the film and will constitute the focus of analysis in the remainder of this chapter. It was not until the late 1980s, however, that a recording of all the Columbia River songs was released by Folkway Records.[15]

Many environmentalists and contemporary activists wonder today how Woody could have lent his voice to the BPA, which damaged the natural environment and deprived many Indigenous people of their traditional fishing rights. Scientific research indicates that the BPA dams impede salmon migration, impound harmful chemicals, and impact fish health and reproduction. Among the species that have become extinct is the Snake River Coho, which was last observed in 1984. Scientists estimate that the current salmon population of the Columbia River system represents less than three percent of the original numbers. There is a strong consensus among biologists that if four dams on the Snake River, a tributary of the Columbia, are not dismantled, additional species in the region will be endangered. Industrial and recreational fishing interests, in cooperation with the tourism industry, have lobbied to remove the Snake River dams. This has angered farmers and conservatives in the Pacific Northwest who perceive them as urban elite environmentalists conspiring with the federal government to deny local access rights. Thus, the forces that were once arrayed against the BPA dam-building agenda are now fighting to maintain the dams.[16]

The question that troubles many contemporary reformers is how did that icon of the American left, Woody Guthrie, come to be associated with a program of giant technology threatening the environment and Indigenous people on behalf of vested economic interests? Mark Pedelty answers this question by suggesting that Woody's opinions and politics were somewhat circumscribed by the fact that he held a government position that, by necessity, forced him to produce a degree of propaganda in support of his patron, the BPA. This propaganda, however, was in support of government programs with which Woody essentially agreed. It reflected the faith of the old left in technology and heroic factory workers, which often characterized socialist realism in the 1930s. Pedelty concludes, "Guthrie was not above producing propaganda, but he did so with a conscience, choosing when to place his craft at the behest of institutional interests. The music he made in these contexts may be less artful than the great majority of his work, but it was also more immediately and directly effective. For a musician like Guthrie, art is judged not just by emotional impact, aesthetics, or critical insight, but must also have a meaningful political impact."[17]

Thus, Pedelty argues that Woody includes elements of irony in the Columbia River songs that undercut the propaganda. For example, in "Roll On, Columbia, Roll On!" Woody celebrates the beauty and power of the untamed river, yet he is advocating for a project that will curtail this raw natural beauty and power. A few verses later he relates damming the Columbia to the triumph of manifest destiny in the Pacific Northwest by mentioning Indian removal and the hanging of Indians who resisted white progress.[18] There is certainly some evidence for irony here as Woody was hardly an advocate for American expansionism and exceptionalism at the expense of Native Americans. He was quite cognizant of the Native American experience in Oklahoma, where tribal holdings were often exploited by oil companies and banks. In addition, Buehler, his BPA driver, asserted that Woody loved meeting Native American fishermen, concluding, "He was very much interested in the Indians that were up there. He looked upon them as the common people too."[19] Woody, however, was hardly clueless as to the impact of the dam construction on the salmon population in the region. He wrote Millard Lampell of the Almanacs, expressing his reservations about the environmental impact of the project by asserting, "Some factories are dumping refuse & chemical garbage onto the nation's greatest salmon power stream, the Columbia River. Millions of fish are destroyed and the Indians are plenty sore."[20]

Pedelty also detected strong elements of irony in "The Biggest Thing that Man Has Ever Done," in which Woody compared construction of the Grand Coulee Dam with the Biblical tower of Babel. According to Pedelty, "It does not take a lot of imagination to get the point" that Woody was attempting to make regarding the limits of technology. In support of his argument, Pedelty notes that in later versions of the song, Woody expressed reservations regarding the atomic bomb and energy.[21] On the other hand, "Pastures of Plenty" tends to present an unambiguous portrait of Woody's people and the possibilities of the BPA project to enrich their lives. Woody describes the suffering of the dust bowl migrants who were responsible for harvesting the crops of rich landowners in Arizona, California, and Oregon. But all these people want is their own land, and Woody concludes that the Grand Coulee Dam will make this dream a reality for the struggling migrants.[22] Thus, "Pastures of Plenty" convinced professor Richard Nate that Woody believed it was possible that the New Deal "could make the dream of a 'promised land' in the West finally come true."[23] Accordingly, the dams constructed by the BPA were part of what historian Richard Lowitt termed the New Deal vision of a planned promised land.[24] Guthrie scholar Will Kaufman places Woody's enthusiasm for the BPA within the context of the artist's acceptance of modernity. Kaufman writes, "Guthrie became evangelical about electricity and industrial production, determined henceforth to associate folk music with modernity rather than with the antique ruralism with which it was so often associated."[25]

Placing a little less faith in the New Deal and modernism, Arlo Guthrie, nevertheless, argued that his father believed in the possibilities of government planning as outlined by the TVA and BPA. Arlo explained, "He saw himself for the first time as being on the inside of a worthwhile, monumental, world-changing, nature-challenging, huge-beyond-belief thing. It was bigger than him, and frankly there weren't many things he considered bigger than him. Most people are the center of their own universe, and it's rare that you get a chance to participate in something that you know is bigger than you and your country. He saw this as a big deal. He felt there was a real purpose here, an urgency. He believed what was happening here was not only good, but needed."[26] In his book on the Columbia River songs, Greg Vandy is in agreement with Arlo. He acknowledges, however, that Woody was aware of potential threats the BPA projects posed to the environment.

Despite these warnings, Woody supported the dam construction as a means through which to improve conditions for the common people. The BPA could be perceived as the manifestation of "commonism," for seen through the lens of war and depression hardships, the benefits to the people were hard to pass up. The dam project was his idea of a realized democratic socialism. It was what "man could do to remake America and help people."[27]

The many ambiguities inherent in a massive project such as the BPA were also addressed by filmmaker Elia Kazan in *Wild River* (1960). Kazan's film features an idealistic TVA bureaucrat, Chuck Glover (Montgomery Clift), whose job it is to remove elderly matriarch Ella Garth (Jo Van Fleet) from her ancestral home to make way for the TVA dam that will control flooding and bring electrification to the region. But this progress will come at the cost of Ella Garth's way of life. In the final analysis, she is evicted from her property and dies shortly thereafter. Kazan's sympathies were originally with the TVA and Glover, but as he developed the film project he was increasingly drawn to the defiance of Garth, expressing the ambivalence that characterized much of Kazan's cinema.[28]

A composition such as "Pastures of Plenty" does not appear to reflect this ambivalence, but in letters written after his BPA job was finished, Woody seemed less certain that the plight of his Okie migrants was about to change due to New Deal policies. Woody wrote to the Almanac Singers (whom he insisted upon calling "My Beloved Talcum Powder Singers or Seed Catalog Singers") that after his work with the BPA concluded in early June 1941, he spent time visiting the many shantytowns in the Portland area and found living conditions terrible. Rather than encouraging dam construction to relieve their plight, Woody was urging the Okies to embrace their culture and get themselves free from a popular culture that featured only the lifestyles of the rich and famous. Woody explained that he told the Okies:

> You folks are the best in the West. Why don't you take time out and write up some songs about who you are, where you came from, where all you been, what you was a lookin for, what happened to

you on the way, the work you done and the work you do and the work and the things that you want to do. Your songs so far are not your songs, but songs that somebody else has put in your head, and for that matter, not your own life, not your own work, troubles, desires, or romances: why had you ought to sing like you're rich when you aint rich, or satisfied when you aint satisfied, or just like you hear on these nickel machines and over the radio? Every one of them would lean and look towards me and keep so still and such a solemn look on their faces, there in those little old greasy dirty hovels that it would bring the rising sun to tears.

Therefore, Woody concluded that it was the duty of folk singers such as the Almanacs to "see to it that the seeds are sown which will grow into free speech, free singing, and the free pursuit of happiness that is the first and simplist birthright of a free people. For with their songs choked and their pamphlets condemned, their freedom will be throttled down to less than a walk, and freedom of going and coming, of meeting and discussing, of course, freedom will just be a rich man's word to print in big papers and holler over his radio."[29]

With the Nazi invasion of the Soviet Union, Woody welcomed the Almanac Singers into the struggle against fascism, but he cautioned that war songs should include tributes to the working people who will bring about the final victory of public ownership. Woody was also ready to rejoin his colleagues, asserting that Mary and the children would stay on in Portland with some friends temporarily before heading back to Texas where they would live with relatives. According to Woody, "She says for me to go on with you Almanacs, and that she thinks it's about the best thing that ever happened to me; a thing I always did hold out for, it's organizing me, dam it, organizing me."[30] In reality, Mary was a little less enthusiastic than Woody's letter to the Almanacs might indicate, and the couple's temporary separation following Woody's job with the BPA proved to be permanent.

Woody returned to New York City and joined with the Almanac Singers to encourage labor organization and denounce the fascist threat. While he continued to embrace the dust bowl migrants, he would not live among them again. Woody loved the Okies, but like Thomas Wolfe he had changed and found it difficult to go home again. He preferred the intellectual and artistic stimulation of New York City. The search for Woody Guthrie does not return to Oklahoma and Texas, but Woody always carried with him the dust bowl heritage of his early years. In a similar fashion, after college and graduate school, I never again quite felt comfortable in my home town of Childress; however, I remain appreciative of my parents and the many residents who work hard and attempt to treat everyone with respect. While not exactly New York City, Albuquerque was rather cosmopolitan in comparison with the Texas Panhandle, and I was able to explore new possibilities. As for Woody, the BPA and Pacific Northwest was something of a diversion before he returned to the political fray in New York. However, he did break permanently with Mary after his burst of activity in Portland, and he headed toward New York City where he would fight the good fight against fascism and discover the love of his life.

Chapter Five

Woody and World War II: The Struggle against Fascism

The Second World War was a terrible time of global death and destruction, and the Holocaust demonstrated the ultimate depravity of humankind. For Woody Guthrie, however, the world conflict offered an opportunity for the common people in the United States and around the world to rise up and seize control over their lives and global resources, while defeating the fascist forces of greed, private property, and racism. Thus to Woody, the war, however painful, was worth the sacrifice as it would usher in the socialist millennium. During this time, Woody was also creating a new personal world with Marjorie Greenblatt Mazia and a child on the way, whom Woody insisted upon calling Railroad Pete. This new world's dawn was crushed by the Cold War, McCarthyism, the death of Cathy Ann Guthrie (Railroad Pete), and Woody's diagnosis of Huntington's disease. Before looking at the collapse of Woody's dreams, the search for Woody Guthrie must first examine the world he believed that his love for Marjorie and Railroad

Pete could create alongside the destruction of fascism. In understanding Woody and ourselves it is essential to look at the dreams, remembering Robert Kennedy's quote, "There are those who look at things the way they are, and ask why... I dream of things that never were and ask why not?"[1] Woody Guthrie was trying to create that better world when he returned to New York City and the Almanac Singers in the summer of 1941.

When Woody arrived in New York, the Almanacs were preparing for a tour that would take them to the West Coast in support of the labor movement and a changing perspective on the war in Europe — that of urging collective security and action against the fascist threat. Membership in the Almanac Singers was fluid. Core members Woody, Pete Seeger, Lee Hays, and Millard Lampell were often supplemented by Pete Hawes, Baldwin "Butch" Hawes, Bess Lomax Hawes, Sis Cunningham, Arthur Stern, Cisco Houston, and Josh White. According to Lee Hays, who was from Arkansas, the name Almanac Singers was chosen because farmers only kept two books in their homes: "the *Bible* to guide and prepare them for life in the next world, and the Almanac to tell them about conditions in this one."[2]

Despite having just returned from the West Coast, Woody signed on to the new tour with considerable enthusiasm, linking the issues of antifascism and union organization. In early 1941, almost 2,500,000 American workers were on strike, many of them responding to organizing drives by CIO unions, such as the United Automobile Workers, United Steelworkers, and United Electrical Workers, in a surge of industrial unionism that cultural historian Michael Denning describes as "a kind of social reconstruction."[3] As a social movement, the CIO sought to address issues of Jim Crow in the workplace and provide workers with a greater voice in management decisions. This more militant approach, especially in contrast with the American Federation of Labor (AFL), however, was tempered as the nation drifted toward war in the summer of 1941. With Hitler's invasion of the Soviet Union, the CIO began to shift its policies toward support of Roosevelt and even conscription, and after Pearl Harbor the labor organization opposed strikes that might undermine the war effort — although numerous wildcat strikes indicate considerable dissent with this decision. As for the Almanacs, they dropped antiwar songs such as Woody's "Why Do They Stand There in the Rain," but performed labor songs from their album *Talking Union* (1941).

As the Almanacs traveled across the country, Woody passionately linked the struggle against fascism abroad with supporting the union movement at home. He described the enthusiasm of seamen in Cleveland from the National Maritime Union (NMU) — a labor organization with which Woody would later be involved when he joined the Merchant Marine — for the union solidarity endorsed by the Kentucky coal region union anthem, "Which Side Are You On?" Woody wrote, "Made you feel so good to see all of these guys, just hard working sailors, there in their hall walking, talking, smoke a flying and big long tables full of piles of papers, pencils, and red hot arguments, sizzling debates, and questions and answers banging away from the tables and the platform, shooting the living hell out of Mister Hitler and anybody else of his particular way of thinking, the goons, ginks, company finks, spies, rats, stools, hired thugs, was called out, put on the spot, and exposed, and mailed back home."[4]

Woody also cautioned the Almanac Singers that workers could easily spot a phony, and singers who aspire to sing and write songs of the common people need to shun Hollywood, Broadway, Tin Pan Alley, and other such "baloney." True artists do not look down upon the common folk but are part of the people. Thus, the Almanac Singers must insert themselves into the union struggle and "fight, fight, fight." Woody maintained, "The Almanac Singers don't just sing Union Songs or tell just Union stories, or pull only Union Jokes. The one thing that's give them a free ticket into the biggest meetings of the Union is because we have seen the fight within the fight, and the fight for higher pay and the fight to always get ahead and get higher and progress, and our songs and ballads are a history and record of the battles the Union has won, and the job and the work that the Union has done, and everyone from coast to coast, Union Men, Women, and Kids are prouder of that one thing than anything else, the battle they fought barehanded, and won."[5]

Woody also linked the union movement and the struggle against Hitler, in which the Soviet Union was doing the brunt of the fighting. But Woody also insisted that Hitler and Nazi Germany were representative of domestic fascism that workers must fight through their democratic unions. Woody concluded, "The Unions in this country are deadliest enemy of Hitlerism and all kinds of fascism, and are out to bring a quick end to any kind of an ism that even smells like Hitlerism, and the quickest way the Union can bring about this end, the better it'll suit the Union. Hitler ain't just a feller a running around loose over there in Nazi Germany, he's the mad, crazy, greedy people in this world, and this world is pretty well populated with his kind, folks that somehow believe in living fat and lazy off of the hard work of you and me, and our folks. Hitler hates Unions. He hates the Soviet Union, because The USSR is a solid Union Town, and Hitler caint never crack it, let alone take it."[6]

Woody expressed few qualms about having his music associated with the communists and Soviet Union. Commenting on one CIO rally, the folk singer asserted, "The Soviet consul member was there, Nicki Somebody, and he listened to our songs and wanted to know where he could get all the records we ever made. He's gonna send a big batch of them over to the Soviet Union because, he said, this is the first time in America he's heard music that sounds like Soviet Worker's Music and Singing. If they take a sudden notion to produce these records over there, naturally you know what that might lead to — hell, we might sell a whole flock of them. Its damn good to hear that the Almanacs and Union folks over here in the USA guessed so close to the Real Truth in selecting and choosing to back this kind of music."[7]

Before an Almanac concert in Milwaukee, Woody reaffirmed that the CIO and Stalin's Red Army were fighting the same enemy. Like Hitler in Europe, big business in America was "hijacking a dollar, a farm, a town, county, state or a whole country." But the Red Army, in solidarity with the CIO, was fighting these forces of greed, and Woody enthusiastically concluded, "The Red Army boys sing about their Union Battles and Rich Landlord Battles, and Poor Farmer Fights, Sharecropper Skirmishes, and will stab and cut and fight back at the

Nazis as long as there's a pocket knife or club or flint rock handy." Woody concluded that sitting on the banks of Lake Michigan and contemplating the struggles of the people "just naturally makes me think of the 6 million CIO folks over here that's putting up the same fight, standing on the side of Britain and the Red Army and battling for the same thing — a world where everybody's got a good job at honest pay, and nobody can lock a chain around your neck or keep you from voting. The world can be had."[8]

Woody with his authentic Okie background was the moral conscience of the Almanac Singers, whose other members hailed from more middle-class roots. He was the real proletariat, and the other members of the group deferred to him. But Woody could be somewhat arrogant, and antagonism was evident in the group — especially between Woody and Millard Lampell. Describing Woody's relationship with the other Almanacs, biographer Joe Klein notes, "He was the group's inspiration, the moral leader, the old master . . . and he never let anyone forget it. He was forever intimidating the others with his political and musical rectitude — and his Oklahoma credentials — they were all dilettantes compared to him. . . . Woody, the dust bowl refugee, was the group's repository of proletarian wisdom, the ultimate arbiter of taste. He was impossibly arrogant, affecting a general air of impatience with the other Almanacs' hopelessly urban, middle-class sensibilities, rarely raising his voice but maintaining his authority with grunts, shouts, and paralytic stares."[9] The Almanacs, however, confronted more serious problems than personal relationships and attitudes.

As Woody and the Almanac Singers threw themselves into the antifascist struggle and CIO labor organization, they were increasingly attacked and criticized for supporting the Communist Party. In early 1942, the Almanacs were at the crest of their popularity with a projected record contract with Decca and an acclaimed February 14, 1942, appearance on the radio program *This Is War*. Three days later, the *New York World Telegram* reported that the program's organizers were shocked to learn that the Almanacs were associated with the Communist Party, and the show's producers promised that the

Almanacs would not be featured on future *This Is War* broadcasts. The *New York Post* followed with a similar denunciation of the Almanacs. Although they did not officially disband until 1943, the Almanac Singers were finished — an early casualty of the Red Scare that came to dominate the post-World War II period. While the Almanacs identified with many of the progressive causes pursued by the Communist Party, including opposition to Jim Crow, Robbie Lieberman, in his history of folk music and communism, argues that the Almanacs were not party members, nor did they enjoy financial support from the party organization. But they were done in by their association with the movement politics of the Popular Front. Lieberman writes, "Their connection to the Communist Movement inspired the Almanacs' work in many ways. It is therefore hardly surprising that the basic political tenets of that movement — such as the importance of the defense of the Soviet Union and the belief in the working class as the primary agent of change — affected the content of their songs. The Almanacs were skilled song writers, and these songs were more than slogans. But their lyrics did not contradict the party line. Their independence was illustrated not by their political outlook so much as by their cultural theory — their commitment to the use of folk and topical songs as weapons."[10]

In defense of the Almanacs' shifting political positions, Bess Lomax insisted that the Almanacs were victims of the rapidly changing international political scene in the late 1930s and early 1940s. Lomax remarked, "Every day, it seemed, another once-stable European political reality would fall to the rapidly expanding Nazi armies, and the agonies of the death camps were beginning to reach our ears. The Almanacs, as self-defined commentators, were inevitably affected by the intense rivalry between the 'warmongers' and the 'isolationists'.... We hoped the next headline would not challenge our entire roster of poetic ideas."[11] Lee Hays also resented the idea that the Almanacs were mindless doctrinaire followers of the party line. He explained that if Winston Churchill changed his position on defending the Soviet Union, then surely the Almanac Singers could shift their music to support a war on both domestic and international fascism. "All of a sudden," explained Hays, "it became one war, instead of two, and here was some chance of beating fascism on its own ground, which everybody was for. But it sure knocked hell out of our repertoire."[12]

While the Almanacs wrestled with the communist issue, Woody was focused upon more personal concerns as he had fallen in love with a young dancer from the progressive Martha Graham Dance Company, Marjorie Greenblatt Mazia. In late January 1942, Marjorie accompanied her friend Sophie Maslow to the Almanac apartment on a mission to obtain Woody's cooperation for an experimental dance revue called *Folksy*. Both Woody and Marjorie would later insist that they fell in love at first sight that afternoon. Marjorie came from a different world than Woody. Her parents were Russian Jewish immigrants with a more cosmopolitan perspective than Woody's dust bowl roots. Marjorie's mother was a creative woman who wrote poetry, and her father was a businessman with intellectual interests. As for Marjorie, her passions were art and dance. When she was eighteen, Marjorie married a Philadelphia accountant Joe Mazia, but she spent a considerable amount of time commuting to dance rehearsals and performances in New York City. Marjorie and Woody began to see more of one another, and the singer moved into the New York apartment of the dancer, who helped Woody focus on writing his autobiography. By June 1942, Marjorie was pregnant, and Woody was delighted, insisting upon calling the unborn child Railroad Pete. The next month, Marjorie disappointed Woody by returning to live with her husband in Philadelphia where she could have the best possible care for the baby that was due in February 1943. The plan was for Marjorie and Railroad Pete to join Woody in New York by April. The long-distance affair proved difficult, and Marjorie considered ending her relationship with Woody. He survived the separation by penning long letters to Marjorie and compiling a journal dedicated to Railroad Pete in which Woody waxed poetically about a better world that was coming into being with the defeat of fascism and birth of Railroad Pete.[13]

Guthrie biographer Joe Klein describes Woody's drawings of Railroad Pete as depicting "a tough little cuss who walked around with his hands jammed into his pockets and sock cap over his eyes, the world's best union organizer and fascist fighter, who could knock Nazi planes from the sky simply by spitting at them and wipe out entire panzer divisions the same way."[14] In a similar vein, Will Kaufman argues that in the Second World War, Woody blended the personal and the political, envisioning a better world in which he would find personal happiness with Marjorie and Railroad Pete in a global environment where fascism, greed, and racism were defeated and the Okies and union people could find peace, prosperity, and happiness. Kaufman writes that Woody fashioned "a conception of the war that would, above all else, embrace the major aims of the American communist movement: antifascism, anti-capitalism, anti-imperialism, and international labor solidarity.... His strategy was to devise a narrative that could equate the Soviet struggle with that of the American workers.... Guthrie's narrative of the war was also bound up in his courtship with Marjorie Mazia — a signal example of the manner in which Guthrie's devotion to the workers' struggle could drive even his most intimate relationships."[15]

Woody's persistence would eventually win out, and Marjorie did leave her husband in April 1943 after the birth of Cathy Guthrie on February 6th of that same year. Railroad Pete proved to be a girl, but Woody never seemed to be disappointed and embraced Cathy with the beloved nickname "Stackabones." An examination of Woody's letters to Marjorie and journal entries dedicated to Railroad Pete provide ample evidence for Kaufman's argument that Woody equated his political beliefs in the defeat of global fascism with his vision of a better tomorrow with Marjorie and his new family. Woody developed a rather simplistic dialectic to describe the global struggle, combining the personal with the political. Woody asserted, "All I ever done was to simply show here and there that the people in the fight all around the world are lined up on two sides. Love. Greed. There are no middle grounds — no halfway limbs."[16]

However, the anxiety he often expressed over his relationship with Marjorie and the outcome of the war indicate that Woody recognized this better world would not be achieved without a struggle. Thus, Woody wrote to Marjorie and Pete on November 17, 1942, expressing his love, growing frustration with the Almanacs, and hatred for fascism. And it is interesting to note that Woody often referred to Marjorie as Mama, and she reciprocated by calling him Baby—terms of affection that in some ways symbolized their relationship as Marjorie was often a mothering or nurturing figure who had to organize and focus the more undisciplined and childlike Woody.

Attempting to define love, Woody wrote, "You love somebody you can think with, and work with; and when you find somebody with any or all of these things, or any blend and mixture of them, you love them. That is, you think of them often, and want to be with them every minute." Woody goes on to explain that he never felt like this about anyone before Marjorie. He also clearly admired Marjorie as a fellow artist and believed that he could share and express ideas that Mary Guthrie would never be able to understand. Nevertheless, Woody, as an artist, complained to Marjorie about an elitism that was creeping into the music of the Almanac Singers. Rather than drawing their inspiration from the common people and their music, too much consideration was being given to intellectuals and politicians in the Almanacs' choice of music. Woody lamented, "Lord knows, I never sing nor play one single word or note that is not for the help of the working classes to know more, feel better, use up, and to own and control this world they have built, but still, could you take the best Marxist in the country and trot them out on the stage over two or three rough rehearsals and yell, Dance!"[17] Thus, the artist and proletarian in Woody were certainly willing to challenge the dictates of the party as he placed greater faith in the natural instincts of the people rather than Marxist intellectuals.

Woody insisted that purity in art was necessary to defeat fascism as artists, whether dancers or folk singers, would have "to tell what fascism is, what it is doing to the world, what it is out to get, and what we are going to have to do to stop it." He then proceeded to lecture Marjorie on the dangers of fascism which he likened to slavery, proclaiming, "Raped, murdered, living in whoredom and working like animals. This is a whole atmosphere, that floats over our towns and farms and cities and whoever breathes of it, somehow or another, turns the wrong direction, does the wrong thing, says the wrong word, or somehow or another, frustrates our organizing together. The whole fight is that Hitler says we can't have a human union, and we say that we can. There's no separate, personal, and individual hope or lifelong dream or even the most outwardly successful appearance of such a thing, until fascism is fought and killed. I'm just an ordinary little guitar picker but these things are getting to be mighty plain to me."[18] Thus, the personal happiness of Woody, Marjorie, and Railroad Pete were bound to the defeat of fascism.

Woody returned to similar themes in his letter of December 9, 1942 to Mama and Railroad Pete. Responding to a letter from Marjorie in which she expressed fear that their complicated relationship would never work out, Woody insisted that to sometimes be discouraged was human, but they must never lose sight of the goal for which they were fighting: "Our only dream is to be together for as many years as the good lord sees fit to give us." Again linking the personal and political, Woody explained that the only thing that could prevent their happiness was the human greed embodied in fascism. And like the soldiers on the battlefield, it was their duty to fight fascism in their daily lives. Woody argued, "The war is going to last until fascist human greed is erased from the human mind and fascist suffering wiped from out of the heart, and there's not much of a thing known as personal salvation for you or me or anybody else until this war is fought and won." But dedication to the struggle did not cancel out hopes, dreams, and plans for the future. Woody concluded, "I know our plans and our hopes, and I roll them over in my mind all of the time, because I know that I fight and hate and preach and do everything that I can against fascism because it says I, you and me, can't dream a dream, hope a hope good enough to get together and fight for it. Hitler knows that once you get a glimpse of your higher hopes, you turn at once into a vicious anti-fascist soldier. . . ."[19]

In late 1942, Woody was lamenting his separation from Marjorie and displayed greater introspection and included less political reflection on the evils of fascism in his letters. Woody talked of leaving New York and moving to Philadelphia so that he might be closer to Marjorie as she prepared to give birth. The letter takes a practical turn as Woody insists that he needs to be near his love in order to be better organized and focused in his work. Rather than denouncing the profit system, Woody assures Marjorie that he could be a traditional breadwinner for the family. Woody proclaimed, "My daily job, as I see it, is to make money, get money, find money, discover, invest, earn and procure money, and then to save money, and hold onto it, can it, bank it, bury it, or otherwise just swing onto the long green. Honey, money is part of our dream, and it will git for us the things, the little things in life that make the big things; I've been a little careless with my money, but with very little coaching from you, I know I could learn to save it."[20]

Continuing in this reflective mood, Woody commented on his marriage to Mary and thanked Marjorie for urging him to maintain contact with his three children from this marriage — a promise that Woody proved rather weak in implementing. Woody asserted that he and Mary had married too young and simply drifted apart as they grew and developed. He just "had to leave and do her the justice of letting her discover a new life with a person more companionable." As for Woody, he received an excellent political education while taking to the road, but "I got too self-reliant, too sure of my ability to get out along the streets and pick up a dollar, too selfish and unreasonable in my ways, and the worst is that I missed all of the fun and belly laughs of family life, circles of friends, and the intimate little talks and gossiping with neighbors which lightens and brightens everybody's life so much."[21] Woody concludes the letter by telling Marjorie and Pete how much he loves them, seemingly enough to abandon the road and perhaps take his place in the post-World War II comfort of the suburbs.

In early 1943, Woody was still despondent about being separated from Marjorie, but he seemed less inclined to adopt a more traditional lifestyle. He confessed to being lonesome but observed that they should put their problems in perspective, considering the sacrifices so many around the globe were making in the fight against greed and fascism. Woody wrote, "Let's remember the people everywhere that are seeing a hundred times as much sorrow and suffering, yes, even rape and robbery and death, seeing all of the bloody sights that the world's worst maniac can brew up in the deadwood cellars of his mind;

let's compare what war is doing and what we're going through with what the friends in Europe, China, and the men on the seas, and in the trenches and in the tanks and planes are suffering. Yes. I'm just writing this down here because I know you already look at things in this way. I guess I'm writing it down for my own self, too."[22]

The appeal of a more traditional domestic relationship is rejected in this letter as Woody returns to the antifascist struggle. The country bumpkin persona Woody sometimes assumed in public was cast aside as he shared his observations after reading Russian writer Maxim Gorky's *Mother*. Revealing his intellectual credentials, Woody credits Gorky with providing inspiration for those taking up the fight against fascism, concluding, "Gorky has written this book to cause you to pick up and wake up and find your place in the war and in the world, and to give you loving people who done exactly this when most of the world was against them. He takes this little bunch of revolutionary world-changers, and he makes their hearts and minds come alive to you, and he shows you that no human being can rest easy until he has found his place in the clear-out fight of greed and love." Woody closed his letter with the optimistic observation that the war was ushering in a better world, writing, "This war is now advertised as the march of the Common Man to freedom, and the people everywhere are glad to get in and work, fight, live, die, forget their own self entirely, and to win the better world."[23]

Woody echoed similar themes, minus the doubts he sometimes expressed about their relationship in letters to Marjorie, through his journal conversations with Railroad Pete. Woody explained to Pete that his mother was a woman of hope, exclaiming, "She has more hope per square inch than anybody else. Hopes about this, and hopes about that, hopes about you, about me, about all of the relatives, hope about lots of people, all people, I ought to say. She's what's called a planner. I guess she make more plans in a day than fascism could tear down in a century." Despite his own difficulties growing up and the contemporary context of a global war, Woody's advice to Pete is upbeat for the singer had found purpose in his music, Marjorie, Pete, and the struggle against fascism. Woody cautioned his unborn child, "Remember, Pete, this world is good at worst, just one old rough and tumble trip of fun. Don't let the old defeated folks make you see life as hopeless, not too sad and blue, because in all this oozing filth there is the young, the brave, the growing, and the new.... Love life. Love people. And love being here."[24]

This embracing of life, however, did not prevent Woody from launching into a sermon warning Pete about the danger fascism posed to the freedom and happiness that was his birthright. Woody defined fascism for Pete as the "greed for profit and the greed for the power to hurt and make slaves out of the people." Essentially, fascists were bullies who could be defeated by common people of all colors, religions, and creeds uniting and fighting together. Thus, Woody argued that the Second World War was a positive moment in history because the bullies and the racists were on the retreat. Woody confided to Pete, "I'm not a Jew and I'm not a Negro, but when people are held down, hung, and killed because of the color of your skin, that is where the fight must be fought and won, no matter what it takes to do it. Until Race Hate is wiped out once and for all, life on this earth will be a narrow hell hole, a cowardly and greedy and a hell of a place to live." Expecting Pete to join the fight against fascism and racism, Woody also encouraged Railroad Pete to get the most out of life by embracing the dignity of work, concluding, "Glorify the greasy gloves and the overalls and your house will be crowded and your mind alive and your ideas so many you cant count them — because work is new and old every day. And will be, too, on tomorrow."[25]

With the arrival of Cathy Ann Guthrie to replace the mythical Railroad Pete, Woody seemed to enter the dawning of a new world. His autobiography had been well received, and he had Marjorie to help him organize his life and music. While Woody was an enthusiastic supporter of the war effort, Marjorie was afraid that he would chafe under the discipline of military life. To avoid Woody being drafted, she reluctantly agreed to the plan of Cisco Houston that he and Woody would join the Merchant Marine. They were accompanied by Jim Longhi, a young law student whom Cisco met at a Communist Party summer retreat. Woody immediately began to teach Longhi some guitar chords so the three comrades could form a trio and entertain their shipmates.[26] In June 1943, the trio set sail on the *William B. Travis* — named after the defeated commander of the Alamo; as an inexperienced seaman Guthrie was assigned to kitchen duty. The supplies and troops carried by the Merchant Marine were vital to the Allied cause, and these missions were not without considerable danger — more than six thousand seamen from the Merchant Marine had lost their lives in service by mid-1943. Off the coast of Sicily, the *William B. Travis* was hit by a torpedo and eventually sank. Woody was uninjured and returned to New York in October 1943, at which time the family moved into an apartment on Mermaid Avenue in Coney Island. Woody, however, was still subject to conscription, so he and his friends signed on for another voyage on the *William Floyd* which again took them to the Mediterranean Sea and made them the target of fascist torpedoes. In March 1944, they were back in the United States, and Woody was recording for Moe Asch. By the middle of May, the friends were sailing on the *Sea Porpoise*, where they insisted upon entertaining an integrated audience of soldiers below deck during an attack. While lending support to the invasion of Normandy, the *Sea Porpoise* was torpedoed. As they went below deck to fetch their guitars off the sinking ship, Woody, Houston, and Longhi helped shipmates escape. This proved to be Woody's last voyage. Allegations of his membership in the Communist Party caused him to lose his seaman's papers shortly thereafter. Without a deferment, Woody was drafted into the Army in March 1945.

Woody's experience with the Merchant Marine offered him an opportunity to participate directly in the fight against fascism, and he exhibited considerable bravery under fire. In letters and journal entries he wrote while on these dangerous voyages, Woody continued to develop his political ideas, displaying considerable support for the Soviet Union and communism in the struggle against fascism. But the organized doctrinal discipline of the party was another matter. Nonetheless, Woody's broader "commonism" seemed to have some room for communism. In a letter to Pete Seeger, Woody apologized for missing the singer's wedding and rather nonchalantly informed his friend of the sinking of the *William B. Travis* with the loss of one seaman. Woody concluded, "We had quite a trip and seen a lot of sights, learned a lot more about how terrible and vicious a thing Fascism-Nazism really is. The people of those countries are on their way up the ladder of human freedom, and since all of the conceivable kinds and styles of slavery have already been worn out on them, they certainly cain't go back to any of those forms, but only on and on to a world that is owned and operated for everybody."[27]

In a shipboard letter to Marjorie in 1944, Woody was considerably more political and evidently missing Marjorie's companionship. Woody reported that there was a great deal of talk shipboard about the war and its aftermath. Welcoming the advances of the Red Army, Woody wrote, "Town after town, dozens of them, hundreds of them, are freed by the Red Army every hour, day and week. We wonder what effect this is having on the countries the Reds are not entering, that is what form of government will be set up to replace the Nazi? The question is already well set in Russia of course where they have their communist or soviet form. I am of the opinion that surely there will be very similar workers governments set up as fast as each country is set free by the allies." Thus, Woody seems to accurately anticipate the postwar world in Eastern Europe, but he certainly did not forecast the emergence of the Cold War. He assumed that the postwar governments in Western Europe and the United States would reflect the triumph of antifascist workers. These governments would not oppose Soviet-style regimes in Eastern Europe and would also usher in the end of colonialism with the dissolution of the British Empire. Separated from Marjorie, and always a bit more sexually aggressive than his lover, Woody also believed Soviet equality better promoted healthy sexual relations between men and women than did the societies of the United States or Western Europe. Celebrating sexuality Woody proclaimed, "It seems like man-woman and the whole business of sex, even venereal disease, are all pretty well cleared up in Russia. I think most of them have already found their right sweethearts and family and since there's no crooked laws and lawyers to abuse them for sex, rob them for romancing, make slaves of them for being male and female, sex, to them, is something that takes place as easy and as natural as the sun moving across the sky."[28]

Woody also shared his experiences ashore with the *Daily Worker*. In great detail he described the destruction that the Allied bombing wreaked upon the people of Palermo, but Woody concluded that the destruction was necessary in order to rid the world of fascism. Woody wrote, "The people of Sicily and the people of Italy understand that fascism cannot be dynamited from a nation with ice cream cones. No, it takes the bomb. It takes the three inch, the five inch, the twelve and sixteen inch shell. The shell explodes and does not know the difference between the hideout of your enemy or the parlor of your friend." He also lamented that the destruction was worse because fascism had not been nipped in the bud earlier in places such as Spain. He argued, "We waited until the fascist germ wiggled its way into every street, alley, neighborhood. The cancer of slavery actually found its way into every home. Now, it is good to see that the people of Italy and of Sicily understand the terrible blasting that is necessary to dislodge and to destroy the fascist disease. The people know."[29] Woody, however, failed to acknowledge the many columns he wrote for the *Daily Worker* during 1940 in which he vehemently maintained that the war in Europe was not a conflict in which the United States should become involved.

Woody closed the letter on a more positive note, observing that out of the death and devastation a better world for the common people would arise. The folk singer concluded, "Everybody knows that the next step is out of the slavage, and into the new daylight of a workers world. Because the workers just simply will not bother to rebuild a world in which they cannot be free."[30] In another letter to the *Daily Worker*, Woody was enthusiastic about how people's music might unify working families and encourage solidarity in the construction of a workers' paradise. Recounting how he, along with Cisco Houston and Jimmy Longhi, entertained the troops on a Liberty ship, Woody discussed the power of union songs — many of which the soldiers had never had the opportunity to sing. Confronting death and danger on the high seas, these soldiers needed to sing out good and loud about their hopes and dreams. Woody proclaimed, "Men of all colors, all tongues, all States, out here on this big ship, finding their own selves, and finding their own words, their own minds, their own feelings, thoughts, plans and their own Union." After this taste of union song and power, Woody argued that the troops would not be content to return to a United States in which popular music was dominated by Tin Pan Alley and wealthy record companies that wanted to distract the common people from coming together and creating one big union. Woody believed that in the postwar union world, the people would be listening to "Union songs about the Union Man fighting for his Union World. And Big Money can just take its old sissy funny crop, and dump all of it over into the ocean, like we done with the British Tea!"[31]

Woody's initial reaction to the use of the atomic bomb against Imperial Japan mirrored his arguments to the *Daily Worker* that the death and destruction of the war was necessary for a better tomorrow. This optimism, however, was overshadowed by personal problems and the breakdown of Woody's faith in the wartime antifascist alliance. Woody's experience in basic training and teletype school as the war wound down lacked the excitement and sense of purpose that his service with the Merchant Marine provided. Further, release from military service and finally marrying Marjorie did not necessarily bring happiness, as Woody had to deal with the emergence of the Cold War and McCarthyism as well as personal problems. The hope contained in the war letters to Railroad Pete dissipated rather quickly. In the search for Woody Guthrie, the war years are crucial for understanding the type of sacrifices Woody believed would be necessary for working-class people to realize the dream of "commonism" free from fascism, racism, greed, and the profit system. In many ways it reminds me of the 1960s counterculture when I believed that I was part of a movement to create a fresh beautiful world free from materialism and conformity, which had fostered war along with racial, economic, and gender inequality and discrimination. In hindsight, it is easy to see many of the excesses that undermined the counterculture, along with the oppression of the establishment. Nonetheless, I miss the dream of the 1960s that made me believe that I was part of a larger community and movement to transform the world. I recognize my youthful naiveté and that change is usually more glacial in its pace — transforming the culture one day, task, and person at a time. For someone as idealistic as Woody, it was probably inevitable that the postwar world would not fulfill the expectations he outlined in his letters to Marjorie and Railroad Pete. Compromise was also difficult for Woody, and while we all face challenges in our lives, I never had to confront the types of tragedy Woody confronted in losing his daughter Cathy or in finding himself increasingly trapped within his body as Huntington's disease stopped him from fully expressing his thoughts and ideas.

Chapter Six

Woody and Postwar Disillusionment: The Korean War

The search for Woody Guthrie enters a dark phase as we examine the post-World War II years and his eventual institutionalization at Greystone Park Psychiatric Hospital in New Jersey. His dreams of a new world born out of the antifascist struggle were destroyed by the Cold War and McCarthyism, which sought to prevent change by dismissing all reformers as agents of Soviet Communism. Woody's changing political perspective during this period is perhaps best reflected by the series of songs he wrote questioning the war in Korea. The Korean War songs also indicate that disease was making it more difficult for Woody to be as articulate in song as he had been during the depression and World War II. However, the cycle still clearly demonstrates his dissatisfaction with the Cold War and post-World War II American democracy. Woody refused to desert the Communist Party in its hour of need, but he was spared the harsher denunciations of McCarthyism as he struggled with personal demons: Cathy perished in a fire, his relationship with Marjorie deteriorated, and he was drinking heavily. He took to the road before his official diagnosis of Huntington's disease. Before he finally lost control of his body, Woody continued to write and sing about a better world. Despite his many trials and tribulations, Woody never lost sight of his precious "commonism." This is the inspiration that Woody Guthrie still provides for many of us as we go about our daily lives and try in our small ways to implement that better world Woody envisioned.

Woody was inducted into the Army on May 7, 1945, and assigned to Sheppard Field, Texas for basic training. Marjorie was concerned that Woody would chafe under military discipline, but he initially seemed to embrace military service as part of the struggle against fascism. In a letter to Marjorie, he asserted that he was proud to be part of the war effort and that the military discipline was good for him. Proclaiming that he found a purpose in the Army, Woody wrote, "Here, there are several million men demanding that I do something for them every minute of my day, and whether my job be dumping butt cans or writing on the post typewriter, marching, eating, sweeping with broom or a mop, saluting, I can see that all of this is the very kind of an appreciation of my society that I have never been quite able to catch onto and realize." In a rather unusual note for the individualistic singer, Woody concluded, "It is here that I will learn some of the rules and regulations that I can put into practice for living no matter where I go or what I do."[1]

After thirty-one days of basic training, Woody was assigned to teletype school at Scott Field, outside East St. Louis, Illinois. After Japan surrendered, Woody saw less purpose in his military career, and his letters are full of complaints about military life. To his friends Harold and Elizabeth Ambellan, Woody expressed regret that he was unable to "throw my two grenades before the Japs quit and laid down their guns."[2] The employment of the atomic bomb against the Japanese also failed initially to cause Woody any concern, although he would later express reservations with America's atomic diplomacy. Woody informed Marjorie that his fellow soldiers were enthusiastic about Japan's surrender, and his arguments for using the bomb against

Japan echoed the justifications put forth by President Harry Truman for ordering the destruction of Hiroshima and Nagasaki. Woody asserted, "I am in favor of the use of the atomic bomb. After fair warning to civilians, the bomb knocks out the Jap fascist Army Air Force, War Factory, the Navy, and cuts the war down by many bloody months, useless blood of both sides. The Atomic Bomb and short war will kill fewer men on all sides than TNT and a long war."[3]

Woody also associated the Japanese unconditional surrender with the entry of the Russians into the war against Japan. However, he did not anticipate the later argument by revisionist historians that the atomic bomb was employed quickly to prevent the Soviet forces from gaining territory in postwar Asia. Woody, nevertheless, assumed that the war would result in a communist government coming to power in China. He argued that the people would not accept Chiang Kai-shek as their leader because he was corrupt and because during the war he was more concerned with fighting his communist allies rather than the fascist Japanese. Woody concluded, "It is going to be lots of fun watching the people of China pass up Chiang Kai Chek."[4]

But as the war ended, Woody saw less need for his continued military service, and he believed that as an artist he was needed in the struggle to create a better postwar world. In a rather lengthy letter to Marjorie, he complained about a Betty Grable film, *The Dolly Sisters*, which encouraged common people to pursue the American dream of materialism by conforming and encouraging women, as in the case of Grable's character, to find a wealthy husband. According to Woody, the real history of people's struggles against the profit system was ignored by a popular culture that sought to ignore "commonism" and replace it with "escapism." Woody asserted, "This is why you attend such movies as *The Dolly Sisters*, because it makes you feel that for the day at least the world is fine and glorious, there are no hungry mouths, no rich, no dying, no slaves, no garbage on your street, no low wages, no high prices, no black markets." He believed that liberals were at fault for their reluctance to promote conflict that might interfere with profits, but this was the struggle that "the progressives and revolutionaries" always depicted. Woody argued that the enemy of the people is the artist who "would try to distrust, to hate the other on account of the state in which we were born, or the color of our hair and skin. He takes his orders from some higher brains who consciously keep us in an endless quarrel and he uses our culture as a noise and a babble not to tell us the true fact and make us know more but to fill our eyes and ears with the thoughts that the world under his rule is a good rowdy hard place to be, and that you ought not to bother your cute little head with troubled worries."[5] Concluding on a more optimistic note, Woody credited Marjorie with being the type of artist who embraced the struggles of common people to better their lives.

Woody's relationship with Marjorie was somewhat troubled as Woody longed to leave the military and re-enlist in the fight against domestic fascism. His letters described considerable sexual longing, expressing some disappointment that Marjorie was not as interested in sexual activities as Woody, who described himself as a great lover. For example, in one letter he explained how important masturbation was to him due to a strong sex drive. Woody also expressed interest in oral sex, but he concluded, "I could see that in spite of your good trying, the business of sex for sex's sake wasn't very strongly in you. To me it was the center of everything. I wanted it to be intellectual and beautiful, even scientific, but there still is a wildness that I would like to feel, a self-forgetfulness, a more daring and thrilling, surprising something."[6] These sexual observations were apparently resolved when on furlough, Woody married Marjorie on November 13, 1945. Their honeymoon was spent at the Guthrie apartment on Mermaid Avenue, and Woody was finally discharged from military service on December 21, 1945. Until his discharge, Woody continued to write erotic letters to his wife. Other women received similar correspondence, including an admirer by the name of Annette Berger who informed Marjorie of her letters from Woody. This preoccupation with sexuality was an increasing focus in Woody's life and seems to offer evidence of the obsession that often characterizes Huntington's disease.[7]

Woody, however, perceived the postwar world as offering more than just greater sexual freedom. He threw himself into such activities as Pete Seeger's People's Songs project, labor organization, fighting

Jim Crow, and political dissent against the Truman administration. Following his discharge from the Army, Seeger envisioned the formation of a loose-knit organization that would disseminate folk music to unions and other progressive movements for change in the postwar world. This idea resulted in the formation of People's Songs. The first issue of the *People's Songs Bulletin* on February 6, 1946, captured the goals Seeger had in mind. The *Bulletin* proclaimed, "The people are on the march and must have songs to sing. Now, in 1946, the truth must reassert itself in many singing voices. There are thousands of unions, people's organizations, singers, and choruses who would gladly use more songs. There are many songwriters, amateur and professional, who are writing these songs. It is clear that there must be an organization to make and send songs of labor and the American people through the land."[8] The group's founders included other members of the Almanac Singers, as well as Woody — an inspiration to many folk singers — who agreed to serve on the board of People's Songs.

Woody wrote a rather long and humorous piece on his introduction to the organization, describing his arrival for a meeting in Seeger's Greenwich Village apartment basement. Woody was met by Pete's wife Toshi who was dealing with an ancient piece of sewer pipe. He informed her, "I am a firm believer in this idea of a People's Songs organization, because we can carry more filth out of this town in one year than that old sewer pipe took away in a Century and Three Quarters." According to Woody, Seeger described the purpose of People's Songs as, "To organize all of us that write these songs for the labor movement, to put all of our collection of songs into one big cabinet, and to send any union local any kind of song, any kind of a historical material about anything they might need, and to shoot it out poco pronto, in today and out tonight."[9]

But Woody was glad that the meeting was short of speakers and long on singing, as a spontaneous hootenanny broke out among the gathered musicians. An enthusiastic Woody proclaimed, "I'd heard boatloads of soldiers, sailors, towns full of bombed peoples, villages full of peasants and guerillas, heard all of these sing in the sounding hole of my guitar, but this little room shook as much as any boat, village, or town that I heard the people sing in. I would include all boxcars, saloons, churches, jails, nails, houses, of wood, iron, steel, marble, hard rock or granite." In conclusion, Woody asserted that People's Songs would help to "win our new world just around this next bend." And he could not resist referring to his beloved Cathy or Stackabones, remarking, "My daughter Cathy dances only to a song when it is a People's Song," and this held true for all the children in her nursery school.[10]

The postwar environment witnessed a considerable rise in strike activity as many unions, after adhering to a no strike pledge that they would not interfere with war production, sought to assure their position in the economy as wartime wage and price controls were terminated. In January 1946, the electrical workers joined the meat cutters, steelworkers, and auto workers in the postwar wave of strikes and labor unrest. Woody, Pete Seeger, and Lee Hays flew to Pittsburgh to perform for workers who were on strike against Westinghouse. In his account of the Pittsburgh rally, Woody marveled at the beauty of air travel before getting down to the politics of the labor meeting. Woody in awe gushed, "The lights from towns and farms were a sight I had never seen before. I've walked up mountains and pulled over humps in cars and trucks, but never just lifted over a whole range of them like a big bird." In Pittsburgh, over twenty thousand people marched through the streets of the city. The former Almanacs performed before an appreciative crowd, and copies of music from People's Songs were tossed from high rise buildings to the people below so they could sing along. Woody believed that the rally was evidence that "commonism" was dawning for American workers, and he asserted, "There was so much of that electric surge of life in the air that it would make a new person out of you if you would let it take hold of you. Every speaker was a fighter and a lawyer and a teacher and a preacher. Every charge against the company we made plain. There was jokes, yells, and hate in the voices. I could hear the voices of people fighting a fight. Ten Thousand in one big union camp."[11]

Buried in this optimistic spirit was an observation foreshadowing the growth of McCarthyism that would soon place labor on the defensive. Woody noted, "We sang 'Solidarity Forever' and the papers said the rally started off with a communist song. Oh. Well. Any songs that fight for the cause of the workhand is a communist song to the rich folks."[12] Although in this comment Woody was somewhat dismissive of the threat posed by the anticommunist movement, the Cold War and the Red Scare proved to be powerful forces that would essentially destroy People's Songs and curtail the growth of organized labor. William Chafe, in his history of the post-World War II United States, argues that reform efforts, racial minorities, women, and workers seeking to expand the benefits of the New Deal were labeled as communists in the politics of fear that swept through the United States during the early years of the Cold War. Chafe writes, "Organized labor reeled from a series of legislative and political defeats, with internal divisions sapping almost all of the energies displayed in the immediate aftermath of the war. Surrounding all these developments was a pervasive aura of anticommunism — a new Red Scare — so powerful that many social causes identified with liberal principles could be tarred by opponents with the fatal brush of being called subversive. While for many Americans the postwar years brought unparalleled prosperity and good fortune, for those most concerned with dramatic progress on issues of equality, these same years brought a shrinking vision and a sharply reduced sense of possibility."[13] The CIO began to expel communist leaders who had played a significant role in the early struggles of industrial unionism, while the power of organized labor was curtailed by such legislation as the Taft-Hartley Act. In contract negotiations, organized labor refrained from pursuing a more progressive social agenda and seeking a role in management decisions, focusing instead on the issues of wages, hours, and benefits.[14]

Meanwhile, People's Songs was also under the surveillance of the FBI and HUAC, along with their anticommunist allies in the media. In his study of People's Songs, Robbie Lieberman argues that in addition to harassment from the political right, the folk music movement lost its support from organized labor who retreated before the anticommunist juggernaut. Lieberman also insists that while many of the artists associated with People's Songs came to maturity during the Popular

Front and were sympathetic to the goals of the Communist Party, especially during the party's depression heyday, these musicians did not blindly follow the hard line the party increasingly assumed in the postwar world (although Woody Guthrie proved to be somewhat of an exception to this observation). People's Songs went bankrupt after placing many of its resources in the failed 1948 Progressive Party Presidential campaign of Henry Wallace. Lieberman concludes that People's Songs lack of success in connecting with its intended working-class audience "had more to do with broad historical and political changes over which they had no control. The cold war and anticommunism, change in the labor movement, and the Communist movement's return to orthodoxy all played a significant role in limiting People's Songs' audience."[15]

As the nation moved away from the promise of a new dawn for working people after their sacrifices in the fight against fascism, Woody's politics seemed to veer even more toward the left. He was not afraid to defend the Communist Party. He asked record producer Moe Asch if the party line was changing after Woody learned that the American party leader Earl Browder, whose policies favored accommodation with the Roosevelt administration during the war, was out of favor. In 1944, Woody had praised Browder's book on the Teheran Conference and was inspired to write a song championing wartime cooperation. While serving in the Merchant Marine, he wrote the *Daily Worker*, "Enclosing a song called the 'Ballad of Teheran,' I'd like to dedicate it to Earl Browder, to his wife, Raisa, and to Joe Stalin, Winston Churchill, and to Franklin D. Roosevelt. And to every drop of Union blood in all the Union Veins around the world tonight."[16] Yet Woody had no problem when the party responded to the emerging Cold War by dumping Browder in favor of the more hard line William Foster. Woody believed that it was important for the party to resist the efforts of capitalists to rob the people of the gains for which they fought the Second World War.

Woody told Moe Asch that anyone battling for the common people would be labeled a communist by such groups as HUAC and by reactionary big business. He was prepared to suffer the slings and arrows of the anticommunist movement, asserting, "If your works gets to be labelled as communist or even radically leaning in the general direction of bolshevism, then, of course, you are black balled, black listed, chalked up as a revolutionary bomb thrower, and you invite the whole weight of the capitalist machine to be thrown against you." Woody continued, "I have decided, long ago, that my songs and ballads would not get the hugs and kisses of the capitalistic 'experts,' simply because I believe that the real folk history of this country finds its center and its hub in the fight of the union members against the hired gun thugs of the big owners. It is for this reason I have never really, sincerely, expected nor daily prayed, nor hoped for a single solitary minute for a penny's worth of help from the hand of our landlord and ruler."[17]

Woody also wanted to make it clear that communist labels were not exactly a case of mistaken political identity. Whether Woody was a card-carrying member of the Communist Party remains problematic, but his sympathies were certainly clear. He refused to criticize the party and its leadership, while insisting that socialism offered the only hope for a better tomorrow. Woody wrote, "The job to be done is to get this thing called socialism nailed and hammered up just as quick as we can. I believe this just as much as I believe my own name and lots more. We've got to pay whatever it costs to get socialism in here just as early as we can. That is the big job. This is the only job worth working on. Socialism is the only job worth wasting any time or strength on. It's the only job that'll give you and me and all of us a good job we can be really proud of. Socialism won't skip a single one of us. It'll not make hoboes nor bums nor dirty backdoor tramps out of any of us." He concluded, "The biggest thing that ever happened to me in my whole life was back in 1936 the day I joined hands with the Communist Party. I'll stick to my words, don't you worry your head one minute about that."[18]

While Woody railed against the Red Scare and maintained his support for organized labor, he also continued to compose his music, although he was dissatisfied with a series of songs he did for Moe Asch on the executions of Sacco and Vanzetti in the 1920s. Nonetheless, he took considerable pride in the children's music he was producing for

Cathy, and his faith in a better world was increasingly focused upon his little Stackabones. Woody's world, however, was shattered when Cathy perished in yet another Guthrie family fire just days after her fourth birthday. Woody relates that on February 9, 1947, he was singing for and supporting striking Phelps Dodge workers in Elizabethtown, New Jersey. Marjorie and Cathy were in the family's Mermaid Avenue apartment when Marjorie, who was four months pregnant with Arlo, left for five minutes to go across the street and purchase some fruit. During the brief time that Marjorie was gone, a fire started in the apartment, apparently caused by an electrical short in a cord from the wall plug for the family radio. The fire seriously burned Cathy, who was rushed to the hospital. Woody returned home that evening around midnight and found a note urging him to come to the hospital immediately. When he arrived at the hospital, as Woody described, Cathy was trying to keep everyone in good spirits, but the burns were too severe. Cathy died on February 10. Woody initially tried to celebrate Cathy's brief life by living up to what he termed her "progressive spirit." Woody proclaimed that he and Marjorie planned to "go right on and to have our next several babies in the same progressive and social minded ways we raised Cathy on. Cathy was a citizen here, ran our careers, ran our works, gave us our best thoughts, visions, ideas, plans." Trying to finish his account of the accident on an optimistic note, Woody concluded, "So let's not feel low and lonely like we might like to feel, but let's feel high and almighty like Cathy would ask us to feel. Let's take faith in her four happy years, and let's keep on singing and dancing at our Hootenannies and at our nursery schools and in our studies, the way Cathy would like for us to do. And let's keep on marching and fighting, too."[19]

A few weeks later in a letter to Pete and Toshi Seeger, Woody was still celebrating Cathy's life. He asserted, "Her four years were wild and full. She was a full reasoned citizen around here, a taxpayer, a human, and a voter. She decorated and ran this house here. Her decorations are still here to let us look at them every day and night and get brighter. She did not leave us as a robbery or a loss, but as a complete gain. She put the neighborhood several generations ahead of itself, woke up many friends, and set many folks to loving one another that used to be hard enemies." In describing Cathy's final hours, Woody explained, "She never said one word of hurt, one complaining word, nor one hint nor crack that she was in pain, not one sour look, never did she lose her smile in all of her wrapping and paddings." Demonstrating the tremendous impact Cathy had on his life, Woody concluded, "She had the real spirit of a People's Dancer and of a People's Singer and if I ever display any signs of either spirit it will be because of what Cathy taught me with great patience and pain during her trip through here."[20]

Woody, however, had placed so many of his hopes and dreams in Stackabones that it was virtually impossible to maintain the progressive optimism with which he initially approached her tragic death. He hit the road shortly after Cathy's accident, spending time in Pampa, Portland, and Los Angeles before returning to Mermaid Avenue for the birth of Arlo on July 10, 1947. Connecting the personal with the political, Woody lashed out at the capitalist system, blaming greed for Cathy's death. He asserted that Phelps Dodge was guilty of holding back technological advances that would have allowed for a better and cheaper grade of copper wiring. This innovation might have been able to prevent the fire that killed Cathy. Woody insisted that capitalists were responsible for attacking union pickets at the New Jersey Phelps Dodge strike, while producing "cheap fraudulent grades of steel, copper, rubber, products of every sort and of every kind that take the lives of our loved ones right in our own house and home. I actually think that this whole age of wrecks, blasts, fires, explosions, crackups and crashes, is caused half by a hateful carelessness of a worker that hates Taftism and hates McCarthyism, and hates low grade dangerous and deadly kinds of cheap tricky greed and profit products of the mine and mill."[21]

Seething with anger, Woody struggled to find a sense of direction. He pursued numerous writing projects; including two novels that were not published until after his death. He enjoyed spending time with Marjorie and his growing family of Arlo, Joady, and Nora. But Woody was quite restless, quarreling with Marjorie, drinking heavily, visiting skid row, and seeking female companionship. He was even convicted in November 1949 for writing pornographic letters to Mary Ruth Crissman, the younger sister of his former singing partner Lefty Lou. Woody agreed to seek counseling to avoid incarceration. Woody's absences from the family home on Mermaid Avenue became more frequent after being diagnosed with Huntington's disease. He reacted to this medical news by fleeing Marjorie, the children, and New York City. Woody sought refuge with friends outside of Los Angeles, where he fell in love with Anneke Van Kirk Marshall, age twenty. Anneke was soon pregnant, and Woody was granted a divorce so that he could make Anneke his third wife. For a short time, Woody appeared to be in remission, but by September 1954 his behavior was again quite erratic. Anneke and Woody returned to New York City where he checked into the hospital. Anneke could no longer take the strain of the relationship, and she filed for divorce. Marjorie, who meanwhile had remarried, took over the task of looking after Woody.[22]

During this personal crisis, Woody maintained his radical analysis of American capitalism, racism, and imperialism. He was a vocal critic of the Korean War (in which 54,000 Americans perished along with perhaps one to two million Koreans) at a time when there was little tolerance for dissent. President Harry Truman responded to the incursion of North Korean troops across the thirty-eighth parallel into South Korea on September 25, 1950, by dispatching American forces to the defense of South Korea and requesting that the Security Council of the United Nations brand the North Korean regime an aggressor and authorize action to repel the invaders. The President described the Korean situation in the most dire circumstances, asserting, "The attack upon Korea makes it plain beyond all doubt that Communism has passed beyond the use of subversion to conquer independent nations and will now use armed invasion and war."[23]

Despite such grave rhetoric, the war proved to be a tough sell with the American people. Over 60 percent of Americans, according to the Gallup Poll, favored withdrawal from Korea in January 1951. Nevertheless, loyalty oaths, Congressional investigations, blacklists, and vigilante actions sought to limit dissent. On August 2, 1950, in New York City, for example, several thousand opponents of Truman's

Korean intervention rallied despite the failure of city authorities to grant them a parade permit. The dissidents, identified by the *New York Times* as "mostly leftists," were assaulted by mounted police who charged into their ranks, severely beating several protesters. The mood of intolerance was also evident in a New Jersey General Motors plant when four workers attempted to distribute antiwar leaflets. The activists were beaten by their fellow workers and forced to evacuate the premises. In an example of corporate and labor cooperation, General Motors and the United Auto Workers agreed that the four protesting workers should be terminated and expelled from the union. Commenting upon the suppression of Korean War dissent, historian Robin Brooks argues, "Unlike other conflicts, the Korean War began during a period of greater peacetime repression than the country had ever known; as a result the government itself, with committees of the House and Senate playing a role equal to or greater than that of the administration branch, played an enormous role in quashing dissent, leaving very little room for the efforts of the would-be vigilantes."[24]

This intolerance for protest and freedom of speech was evident throughout American culture. HUAC investigations into allegations of communist subversion in the Hollywood film industry culminated in the blacklist and imprisonment of the Hollywood Ten for contempt of Congress. In response, the film studios abandoned controversial social problem films in favor of Biblical epics and escapist fare. The music industry also suffered from the blacklist. Pete Seeger was enjoying considerable commercial success as a member of the Weavers, who recorded such hits as "Goodnight, Irene" and "Kisses Sweeter than Wine." Although Seeger had left the Communist Party, his former association with the organization came back to haunt him in February 1952, when FBI informant Harvey Matusow testified before HUAC. Matusow denounced the Weavers for their alleged communist connections. The singing group quickly became a victim of the blacklist as concert dates were cancelled, and by December 1952, the Weavers disbanded. Seeger biographer Allan M. Winkler concludes, "The Weavers were at the height of their popularity, making more money and hammering out more songs than ever. Suddenly, like the clap of thunder on a sunny day, their bubble burst. They were the ones being hammered. A Red Scare more disturbing than the one that followed World War I left them reeling under charges of being communist subversives."[25]

Although Woody was more vehement than Seeger in denouncing the post-World War II Red Scare and the liberal abandonment of progressive causes, he failed to attain the commercial success of Seeger and the Weavers. Thus, he did not generate the sort of attention that led to denunciations before Congressional committees and blacklisting efforts by corporate sponsors. Plagued by personal and health problems, Woody, although still under government surveillance, enjoyed a degree of obscurity in the early 1950s that provided him the freedom to continue his condemnation of capitalism, Jim Crow, and American foreign policy during the Korean War. He had little use for President Truman, and in 1948, Woody campaigned actively for the Progressive Party candidacy of Henry Wallace. Frustrated with Truman's upset electoral victory, Woody penned an open letter to the President, proclaiming, "If you ever so much as lay a small claim to be a human with a brain, a soul, a heart, a mind, a feeling... take a look at these bills you are signing to make more high explosives to blow us all off of the map. Your face will look a whole lot blanker if the little atoms blow our world away and all of your pals and kinfolks along with the rest of us."[26]

Woody's view of the atomic bomb grew more critical after his initial burst of enthusiasm that the Hiroshima and Nagasaki bombs had ended World War II. Written just after Woody first learned about the new technology's use against Japan, "Freedom's Fire" was a patriotic song that celebrated the destruction of Japanese fascism and credited America with shining the light of freedom on Hiroshima. By 1947, Woody, however, was focusing upon the threat nuclear weapons posed for humanity with the song "Dance Around My Atomic Fire." Woody's belief that atomic technology was a threat rather than a boon for humanity and world peace was apparent in his song "One Thing the Atom Can't Do."[27] By the time of the Korean War, Woody equated atomic diplomacy with his critique of American imperialism and capitalism.

The degree to which Woody found common ground between his personal and political discontent was evident in a piece entitled "Why Is it?", written sometime in 1951. In this notebook entry the singer bemoans, "Capitalism is the gospel of hate and not love. It's offices practice the acts of hate and not acts of love. Then feel empty and miserable and full of greedy hate, but don't let them make you feel guilty nor full of hate. I pronounce my own self not guilty. I pronounce the capitalist system guilty."[28] Woody's increasing discontent with the American political system and the development of a national security state was evident in a series of songs he wrote condemning U.S. military intervention in Korea. Most of the songs were written in Torrango Canyon, California, at the same time that Woody was forging a relationship with Anneke Van Kirk Marshall in the winter of 1952. There is a degree of repetition as well as sexual imagery in the series of songs — which may be reflective of Woody's illness as well as his separation from Marjorie and the fact that he was beginning a sexual relationship with a woman twenty years his junior.

In his first Korean piece, written in 1951 and entitled "Thirty 8th Parallel," Woody urged American troops not to cross the thirty-eighth parallel into North Korea. Instead of invading North Korea, Woody urged American soldiers to drop their guns and shake the hands of their alleged enemies. With "Deep in the Mud," Woody portrayed the Korean War as a quagmire in which Americans would become bogged down in a conflict that was none of their business. This would be similar to metaphors later used to describe the Vietnam War, and "Deep in the Mud" echoes Vietnam-era protest songs such as Pete Seeger's "Waist Deep in the Big Muddy" (1966). Woody repeats similar themes with "Jeep in the Mud," but he writes from a Korean or Chinese perspective, asking the Americans why they came to Korea with their Wall Street jeeps. The narrator tells the Americans to take their jeeps back home before they become stuck in the mud of the Korean peninsula.[29]

More themes of stalemate are found in "Korean Quicksands," "Korea War Tank," "Korean Boggyhole Blues," "Korea I'm Alone,"

"Korea Send Me Home," "Korean Quickstep," "Korea Bye Bye," "Korean Blues," and "I Don't Want Korea." These songs, however, are not told from a Chinese or Korean point of view. Instead, these tunes are written from the perspective of American soldiers and employ the omnipresent voice and vision of Woody urging that the solders throw down their guns and return to the home front. Gallup Public Opinion Polls indicate that Woody's views were not out of step with many Americans who supported withdrawal from Korea. In "Korea Send Me Home," Woody takes on the persona of a soldier begging to be sent home because he never believed in the Korean War, concluding "please send me home-e-home!" The problem, however, was that American boys were being sent home in body bags as the fighting bogged down into a bloody stalemate along the thirty-eighth parallel. Woody described this frustrating fact in "Korean Quicksands," proclaiming that Americans were becoming neck deep in blood as they fought in the Korean rice fields. To avoid this quicksand of blood, Woody proposed in "Korea Bye Bye" that the United States apologize to the Korean people and bring the boys home. In the Korean cycle of songs, Woody also connected with a theme reflective of soldiers in all wars: a desire to be reunited with their sweethearts on the home front. In "I Don't Want Korea," Woody assumes the voice of a young soldier who has a girlfriend named Ruth back home with whom he desires to resume a relationship. The soldier announces that he has no use for the Korean War and refuses to be "a slave to the American government."[30]

Themes of repressed sexuality were also evident in "Korea Ain't My Home," "Korean Beauty," "Korean Baby Goodbye," "Korean Waltz," "Korean Boogey," "Korea I Love You," "Korean Girly," and "Korea and Me." In the group of songs, Woody seems to equate his own sexual longing at this troubled time in his life with the sexual frustration of soldiers serving on the front lines in Korea. Suggesting themes of making love and not war (which would become a familiar countercultural refrain during the Vietnam War era) Woody wrote in "Korean Beauty" that if the world could see his Korean queen, then "none of these young wild-haired soldier boys would never be able to pull down a trigger spring for the rest of their days." Here, Woody comments upon the relationships between American servicemen and Korean women that became an issue for the U.S. military establishment during the Korean War and the ensuing American military presence in Vietnam. A closer reading of the songs, however, seems to indicate that in fixating upon both Korea and the prospect of divorce from Marjorie, Woody was equating Korea with his second wife. In "Korean Girly," Woody asks his Korean "honeybun" to "please shoot me, please boot me back home!" While in "Korean Boogey," Woody apologizes to his Korean "cutey" for hurting her pride. Evidently experiencing a great deal of guilt over his treatment of Marjorie, Woody in "Korea I Love You" tells his "Sweet Korea" that "nobody loves you like I do!" And he concluded, "If you love me like I love you, Wall Street can't crack our love in two." But in the final analysis, the escape of the road and a younger lover were beckoning, and in "Korea and Me," Woody insisted that both he and Korea simply had to be free.[31]

Although sexuality was something of an obsession with Woody at this point in his life, the songwriter was still able to engage the Korean War with political satire. In "Mr. Sickyman Ree," Woody challenged the Truman administration's characterization of President Syngman Rhee's Republic of Korea (South Korea) as a model democracy. Woody also had little patience for General Douglas MacArthur, expressing his approval of the General's removal in "Korea Mackarter." Critical of MacArthur's advocating the employment of nuclear weapons in the Korean conflict, Woody proclaimed that it was time for "Korea Mackarter" to fly home "as he wants to kill every home I see in Korea!" Demonstrating even less respect for the General, Woody, in "Korea Korea," referred to MacArthur as "Mach Arsser" and urged American soldiers to desert and grab "a glass of beer." In "Han River Woman" and "Han River Mud," Woody acknowledged the civilian causalities that occurred when the main bridge across the Han River was demolished during the early days of the war.[32] Charles J. Hanley, Sang-Hun Choe, and Martha Mendoza write that engineers gave "no warning to the throng of civilians and retreating soldiers who were walking and riding, in bumper-to-bumper traffic, across the lengthy span. Hundreds were killed in the explosion, and many more fell to their deaths or drowned when surging crowds pushed them into the gaps created in the bridge."[33]

Although the Korean War cycle of songs was not indicative of Woody's best work, they nevertheless reflect a radical analysis often missing from discussion of the Korean War. In addition, the Korean War songs were certainly part of Woody's broader Cold War critique. For example, the folk singer lamented the executions of Julius and Ethel Rosenberg for ostensibly communicating the secret of the atomic bomb to the Soviets, concluding, "You, Rosenbergs did more than any other pair I know of to keep my United States from flying over and laying these atom bombs on the tables of every nation in the world."[34] Of course, Woody's movements and statements were monitored by the Federal Bureau of Investigation, but Woody's illness spared him from being called before HUAC as was his colleague Pete Seeger. Nonetheless, the antiwar and civil rights visions of Woody would be resurrected during the political and cultural turmoil of the 1960s.

Woody's reservations regarding the Korean War and foreign policy of President Truman have also found support among historians. In *The Unfinished Journey*, William Chafe argues that the roots of the Vietnam War may be found within the Korean conflict. Chafe asserts that the Korean War encouraged the United States to pursue a policy of military containment, established a precedent for waging war "by executive authority alone," reinforced "the tendency in American foreign policy to support dictatorship in the name of freedom," and "highlighted the potential brutalization of American soldiers unable to distinguish friend from foe."[35] Supporting the arguments made by Chafe, Arnold A. Offner, in his study of Truman's Cold War policies, concludes, "Throughout his Presidency, Truman remained a parochial nationalist who lacked the leadership to move the U. S. away from conflict and toward détente. Instead, he promoted an ideology and politics of Cold War confrontation that became the modus operandi of successive administrations and the U. S. for the next two generations."[36] During a difficult time in his life, Woody continued to envision a world beyond Jim Crow, McCarthyism, and the Cold War where children, such as Railroad Pete or Stackabones, could live free from the scourge of war, poverty, and racism.

Woody's disillusionment in post-World War II America offers some important life lessons in seeking to obtain some balance between one's vision of a better world and an often-harsher political reality. Personal problems and challenges in the postwar period often led to a more strident political stance on Woody's part. He refused to denounce the Communist Party while maintaining his faith in "commonism." According to Nora Guthrie, the key to understanding her father is that even in moments of political and personal despair, he never lost his faith in the power of love. The heart and the common people, not the politicians, know the difference between right and wrong, and love will eventually triumph.[37] In many ways this was my faith during the 1960s as a member of the counterculture. As a more mature person I recognize that the eventual victory of Woody's vision is more evolutionary than revolutionary, but we must continue the struggle. Thus, Woody's critique of postwar America and the Cold War offered an example for a younger generation in the 1960s questioning the anticommunist crusade that culminated in the tragedy of the Vietnam War.

After this more detailed biographical overview of Woody's life, the next phase in our search for Woody Guthrie and his legacy will lead us into the examination of specific issues that are crucial to understanding the man along with his music and values. We will examine Woody's faith in Jesus as an agent of social change, his identification with outlaws as primitive rebels against capitalism, his proclamation that the union movement was his personal religion, his calls for racial justice after growing up in a racially intolerant environment, and finally his contradictory views on women that included both elements of respect and sexual exploitation. In these issues, we see Woody exhibiting his faith in "commonism" and in the power of love, as alluded to by Nora Guthrie.

Chapter Seven

Woody and Jesus: The Working-Class Carpenter and Christian Socialism

Growing up in the Texas Panhandle, I was exposed to the powerful influence of evangelical Christianity that also dominated the religious upbringing of Woody Guthrie. For my family this religious background fostered a conservative orientation, while Woody drew upon the Pentecostal tradition to fashion a version of Jesus as a working-class carpenter who fought for a more equitable division of God's resources. Growing up, I attended an Assembly of God church with a congregation of white working-class people — the men often wearing ties along with their best overalls. As a boy, I witnessed faith healing, speaking in tongues, and the employment of poisonous snakes in religious ceremonies. My parents were believers who kept the faith; they felt assured that obedience to God and living a good life would gain them in heaven all the comforts they were denied during their earthly existence. As I grew older, I was a great disappointment to my parents for rejecting their view of fundamentalist Christianity. I do not really expect to be reunited with them in a heavenly paradise.

While I try to respect the religious views of those who disagree with me, it is my perception, from a somewhat Marxist orientation, that vested economic interests often employ the promise of a heavenly paradise to assure that workers will not rebel against their conditions. This is the argument that the IWW minstrel Joe Hill made in his famous song, "The Preacher and the Slave."[1] Woody agreed with Hill that religion is often employed to manipulate the people, but he nevertheless maintained a belief in Jesus as a social reformer. I sometimes lament the loss of this connection to my roots, but I simply cannot seem to find Woody's faith.

In recent years, Christian evangelicals have increasingly embraced the Republican Party and its conservative principles, and not even the sexual escapades of Donald Trump can shake this faith. In *One Nation Under God*, historian Kevin M. Kruse argues that since the depression, corporate interests and the Republican Party have maintained that the United States is a Christian nation whose founding religious principles are under assault from New Deal and Democratic big government programs bent on undermining American individualism.[2] For example, in the 2004 Presidential election, the emphasis of the Democratic Party upon such issues as job creation in the economically-depressed state of Ohio was apparently trumped by the emotional issues of same-sex marriage and abortion, which evangelicals perceived as more threatening to their way of life than an economy in decline.

This reading of the 2004 election resulted in a series of jeremiads from the political left bemoaning the influence of Christians upon American politics. In an opinion piece for the *New York Times*, liberal economist Paul Krugman termed President George W. Bush a radical who "wants to break down barriers between church and state." In his influential book *What's the Matter with Kansas?*, Thomas Frank speculated as to why the working class in Kansas, a state with a progressive tradition, would allow themselves to be manipulated by evangelists and the Republican Party into voting against their own economic interests. Kevin Phillips, a former adviser to President Richard Nixon (whose writings are now often embraced by those on the political left), lamented the formation of an *American Theocracy* in which evangelists, hoping for the Biblical "end of time" battle of Armageddon, promote military conflict and crusades in the Middle East.[3]

In 2016, Republican nominee Donald Trump took a somewhat different approach, emphasizing economic issues and placing the blame for the decline of the American working class on bad trade deals and immigration, while promising to build a wall that would halt illegal immigration from Mexico. Trump maintained evangelical support by asserting that issues such as abortion and same-sex marriage should be left to the states, while promising to appoint conservative judges opposed to expanding the liberal social agenda. To protect Americans from terrorism, Trump also proposed bans on Muslim immigration to the United States — a move that proved popular with many Christian evangelicals. But for those expecting Trump to turn around the economy for the working class, the appointment to his cabinet of bankers and anti-labor, wealthy chief executives of major corporations as well as large tax cuts for the wealthy do not bode well for the future.

Such dire predictions, however, fail to account for the more complex role played by Christianity in American politics and history. The legacy of progressive Christian activism in the political arena is rich with examples: the Great Awakening; evangelical abolitionism; Walter Rauschenbusch and the Social Gospel; Dorothy Day and the Catholic Worker Movement; Martin Luther King Jr. and the Civil Rights Movement; the crusade of individuals such as Daniel and Philip Berrigan and William Sloane Coffin against nuclear weapons and the Vietnam War; and Jim Wallis, editor of *Sojourner* magazine, who calls on Christians to follow the example of the Christian social justice legacy by combining the quests for spiritual meaning and progressive social change. In *The Soul of Politics*, Wallis argues, "We need a personal ethic of moral responsibility, a social vision based on bringing people together, a commitment to justice with the capacity also for sustainability, a restored sense of our covenant with the abandoned poor and the damaged earth, a reminder of shared values that call forth the very best in us, and a renewal of citizen politics to fashion a new political future."[4]

In his music, writings, political commentaries, and life story, Woody Guthrie epitomized the values of the progressive Christianity envisioned by Wallis. Woody's songs, combining themes of Jesus and working-class politics, helped common people address the economic inequalities of depression-era America. Perceiving no fundamental contradiction between Marx and Jesus, Woody believed communism was simply common sense and followed the Biblical obligation to share God's resources.

With his eclectic politics, Woody insisted that both communism and Christianity extolled the common ownership of the means of production — in other words, "commonism." Although he rarely quoted directly from scripture, or from Marx and Lenin for that matter, Woody was apparently influenced by such Biblical passages as *Acts* 2:44–45, in which early Christians are charged to "sell their property and possessions and divide them among all according to each one's needs." The angry God of the Old Testament was of little interest to Woody, who was drawn to the New Testament and the promise of Jesus as a messiah bringing social justice to a troubled world. Biblical passages such as *Matthew* 19:16–24 present Jesus as the champion of the poor. When a young man asks of Jesus what he must do to find heaven and attain eternal life, Jesus responds that one must forget about worldly goods, sell his possessions, and share the money with the poor. The young man, who was wealthy, departed in disappointment. Jesus then instructed his disciples, "It is easier for a camel to pass through the eye of a needle than for one who is rich to enter into the kingdom of God." Woody was also attracted to the activist Jesus who chased the "money changers" or bankers out of the temple in Jerusalem, asserting, "My house shall be a house of prayer, but you are making it a den of thieves" (*Matthew* 21:12–14).[5]

Woody was the product of a milieu in which Jesus was the champion of the poor and meek, who would inherit the earth as taught in the Sermon on the Mount. Woody was born during a time in rural

Oklahoma when the Socialist Party, under the leadership of Eugene Debs, used the region's populist tradition to foster a following in the Southwest. During the first two decades of the twentieth century, the class conflict in the state was exacerbated by growing farm tenancy and absentee landlordism. Socialists in Oklahoma embraced a millennial Christian belief that the poor would inherit the earth. In *Agrarian Socialism in America: Marx, Jefferson and Jesus in the Oklahoma Countryside, 1904-1920*, Jim Bissett asserts that there was no hypocrisy in Socialist leaders employing religion to attract support for the party platform. Political gatherings often resembled revival camp meetings and included prayers. Bissett writes, "Marxism and Christianity achieved a synergy in the Party, combining in a unique way to strengthen the movement. Thus, while the Marxist ideas that socialists brought to Christianity energized the democratic, communitarian strain in evangelical Protestantism, religion simultaneously deepened and made relevant the Marxist ideological core of the Socialist Party. The resulting message became all the more powerful."[6] Thus, Woody grew up in a region where no fundamental conflict was assumed between religious views and radical political ideology.

Oklahoma Socialists also embraced the cult of Jesus, which comprised an essential element of Woody's left-wing political thought. Socialists in Oklahoma expressed reverence for Jesus, emphasizing his working-class origins and eventual betrayal by the political elites and capitalists. This was the Jesus loved by Woody in his music and writing. In *American Jesus*, Stephen Prothero asserts that Woody and the Socialists of Oklahoma were hardly unique in their celebration of Jesus. Prothero observes that the paradox of Jesus in American culture is that he is embraced by "Christian America and multireligious America" as well as by secularists. Prothero, thus, concludes, "To see Americans of all stripes have cast the man from Nazareth in their own image is to examine, through the looking glass, the kaleidoscopic character of American culture."[7]

To Woody and many Oklahomans suffering through difficult times, Jesus was the champion of the dispossessed, who would not desert them even during their exile to California when the dust bowl destroyed their farms. Yet while growing up in the religious environment of rural Oklahoma, Woody's family did not attend church on a regular basis. This changed, however, following family tragedies that destroyed their home and left Woody's older sister Clara dead, his mother Nora institutionalized, and his father Charley severely burned. After joining his father in Pampa, Woody underwent a religious conversion experience. He began to play music with his uncle Jerry P. Guthrie and Reverend Eulys McKenzie of the Church of Christ. According to Woody's biographer Joe Klein, McKenzie "was a gentle man with a kind heart — even though he had a reputation for giving wild fire-and-brimstone sermons every Sunday — and he convinced Woody that it was important to make a spiritual commitment and be baptized by total immersion."[8] Although he soon stopped attending church on a regular basis, Woody maintained an active interest in Jesus and the Bible.

It is not surprising that Woody was initially attracted to an outsider Pentecostal denomination such as the Church of Christ. Fundamentalist Christians believe that those who are saved or born again will go to heaven. Christians who engage in such worship practices as speaking in tongues or faith healing insist that these gifts indicate a greater degree of spirituality. More mainstream denominations such as the Methodists frown upon such emotional outbursts. Accordingly, the Pentecostal churches were home to the poor tenant farmers who believed that God was withholding his gifts of healing and tongues from the wealthier, more established churches. Historian Jim Bissett concludes, "Thus, God himself understood what the rest of society seemed to have missed; in God's eyes, the impoverished farmers who worshipped in fundamentalist churches were superior to their political and economic enemies."[9] Like the disgruntled preacher Jim Casy in *The Grapes of Wrath*, Woody was searching for the one big soul.

His religious principles, however, did not hold Woody back from leaving his family in Texas and joining the exodus to California. As Woody observed the mistreatment of the dust bowl migrants, he did not lose his faith in Jesus. When describing his experience riding the rails with the unemployed and dispossessed for his autobiography *Bound for Glory*, Woody evoked the cult of Jesus. Sitting around a campfire in Redding, California, with a group of men seeking work, Woody observes an intelligent-looking young man who is approximately twenty years of age. He is speaking of the need for a social vision in the country. The young man asserts that the people need to get together and build things like dams, railroads, factories, and ships. He excitedly brings the image of Jesus into the discussion, proclaiming:

> That's what 'social' means, me and you and you working on something together and owning it together. What the hell's wrong with this, anybody — speak up! If Jesus Christ was sitting right here, right now, he'd say this very same damn thing. You just ask Jesus how the hell come a couple of thousand of us living out here in the jungle camp like a bunch of wild animals. You just ask Jesus how many millions of other folks are living the same way? Sharecroppers down South, big city people that work in factories and live like rats in the dirty slums. You know what Jesus'll say back to you? He'll tell you we all just mortally got to work together, build things together, fix up old things together, clean out old filth together, put up new buildings, schools and churches, banks and factories together, and own everything together. Sure, they'll call it a bad ism. Jesus don't care if you call it socialism or communism, or just me and you.[10]

This statement well articulates Woody's view of "commonism" and the type of primitive Christian socialism or communism extolled in the Biblical book of *Acts*. It is a utopian religious vision that Woody maintained even as he became involved with the Communist Party during his time in California from 1937 to 1940.

With his "Woody Sez" columns for the *People's Daily World*, Woody might have been following the Communist Party line in his denunciation of war, but opposing military conflict also fit well with the New Testament conception of Jesus Christ as the Prince of Peace. And depictions of Jesus were a staple of Woody's columns. Woody attacked bankers, landlords, furniture dealers, utilities, and doctors for charging the poor usurious interest rates and exorbitant fees. Woody evoked the Biblical image of the dispossessed as God's chosen people, asserting, "You Land Shirks, and other Friskers, listen to me, the hungrier you make us, the smarter we get . . . cause all of the good books on religion advise you to fast and think . . . and the fastest you think is when you're right hungry." And Jesus served as an excellent model for inspiring the people to combat the bankers and capitalists. Woody insisted, "Today we need to make a Whip of small organizations in small movements — an bind them and wind them into one great big 'Whip' — an drive not only the Money Changing Ideas and thoughts out of their own mind, or bodily Temple — but also so to drive the Money Changers out of the Temple of our Nation."[11] Woody believed that the people did not have to wait passively for the return of the messiah; instead, they could follow the example of Jesus and overthrow the exploiters — ushering in an earthly paradise of equality based upon the teachings of Jesus.

Woody envisioned an earthly paradise in which all people would enjoy equal access to the planet's resources. He dreamed of an America where the common people could find meaningful work and be free from exploitation. Woody placed little faith in organized religion, believing instead in the message of the working-class carpenter bringing peace, equality, and justice to the world. Embracing the Jesus who taught that "the last shall be first, and the first will be last" (*Matthew* 20:16), Woody wrote, "Should the Master appear again on earth, that he would take a look at the churches, a look at the sinners, and associate himself at once with the sinners . . . as he did before. Religion is to forget yourself and work for the good of others. Outside of that there is no religion . . . no progress . . . no hope for you, your neighbors, your coming grandchildren. Find out who is causing the Trouble here in this Old World — remove the power from their hands — place it in the hands of those who ain't Greedy — and you can roll over and go to sleep."[12] Woody was more interested in ends than means, and he seemed to have no problem with the Communist Party if it could help build the commonwealth of equality called for by the Prince of Peace.

While eventually settling in cosmopolitan New York City, Woody retained his faith in Jesus the redeemer, which was inoculated in his more rural upbringing. In the winter of 1940 after arriving in New York City, Woody wrote "Jesus Christ Was a Man," or as it is sometimes called "They Laid Jesus Christ in His Grave." He gazed out the window of his rooming house and observed that the poor of New York City were cold and hungry, while the wealthy were "drinking good whiskey and celebrating and wasting handfuls of money at gambling and women." The folk singer concluded that if Jesus Christ were to preach his message regarding the redistribution of wealth on the streets of New York City, "They'd lock him back in jail as sure as you're reading this." In "Jesus Christ Was a Man," the working-class origins of the man from Galilee are celebrated. Jesus is a brave carpenter who preaches that the rich should give their possessions to the poor. Woody told Alan Lomax that Jesus was an outlaw like Pretty Boy Floyd and Jesse James — an outlaw who "stole from the rich and gave to the poor." In this composition, Woody was clearly influenced by minstrel Billy Gashade's "Jesse James" ballad, which Woody rewrote as a social protest song in 1939. Jesse James is laid in his grave by his supposed friend "that dirty little coward" Robert Ford, while Jesus, the carpenter who championed the poor, was betrayed by "a dirty little coward called Judas Iscariot." The Jesus presented by Woody in "Jesus Christ Was a Man" is also a revolutionary, who will return to earth with a sword in his hand to achieve justice for the common people.[13]

Despite its destructive force, the Second World War persuaded Woody to present a less apocalyptic vision of his religious ideas. Woody perceived World War II as a collective effort against fascism; an efffort that had the potential to fashion an era of democracy and prosperity for the common people of the world. Thus, he downplayed Jesus as a revolutionary or socialist outlaw in "Jesus Christ for President," which was later recorded by Billy Bragg and Wilco. Just as the Communist Party returned to the Popular Front strategy of cooperating with bourgeois democratic regimes such as Franklin Roosevelt's New Deal, "Jesus Christ for President" presented Jesus in a less revolutionary guise, willing to work within the electoral system to create a more equitable and just society. The capitalists and money changers still need to be driven from the temple, but in the song the process does not require a violent revolution. With the carpenter as President, the crooked politicians will be dispatched from office, while jobs and pensions are guaranteed for young and old. But whether socialist outlaw or democratic politician, Jesus would provide the peace and prosperity foretold in the New Testament of which Woody was so fond.[14]

In "This Morning I Am Born Again," written in January 1945, Woody reiterated the example of Jesus transforming the world into an earthly paradise, except the masses could implement the carpenter's vision themselves through the union movement. It would not be necessary to have Christ as King or President. Sounding more like Joe Hill in dismissing the Christian sense of personal redemption in being born again, Woody asserts that he no longer dreams of pearly gates and streets of gold. Instead, Jesus's vision of one big human family could be found in the temple of the union hall. The people had within themselves the power to reinvent the postwar world in the image of Jesus's teachings.[15]

But the emergence of the Cold War, anticommunism and McCarthyism, and conservative reaction against the gains made by the union movement during the New Deal prevented the realization of the utopia envisioned in "Jesus Christ for President" and "This Morning I Am Born Again." Despite personal tragedy and the chilling political climate of the postwar period, Woody maintained his faith in both Jesus and the Communist Party. In a letter to his relatives in California, Woody insisted that the communist belief in the common ownership of the means of production was the answer to the world's economic problems. And even as his health deteriorated, Woody refused to alter his views on the promise of communism. In one of his last letters, he stated that he could not vote for President Eisenhower in the 1956 Presidential election. Woody proclaimed, "Eisenhower can't be my big chiefy bosseyman till he makes all my United States alla my races all equal. . . . I vote for only communist candidates.

Anyhow they'll be the ones to ever even partways try to give birth to my racey equality."[16]

Nor did Woody believe that Jesus had forsaken him. During his extended hospitalization, Woody referred to Jesus as his doctor. Although there is no indication that Woody's faith in the communist vision of Jesus faltered, in his final years, suffering from a crippling disease, the singer increasingly evoked Jesus as a personal savior. Realizing his desperate straits, Woody wrote his father "maybe Jesus can think up a cure of some kind." But Charley Guthrie died before his son. Woody wrote to his sister Mary Jo Edgmon, urging her to not be too sorrowful as their father was earning his heavenly reward. Although Woody had often quarreled with Charley over politics and never seemed able to please his father, the son did not mention his father's hatred of socialism or his racial prejudice. Instead, Woody celebrated Charley Guthrie as a good Christian, who "passed on into his great, good, ever loving heavenly hi holy Saintly reward as through the promises of my Savior, my dear sweet Jesus, my Christ."[17] On October 3, 1967, Woody finally succumbed to the disease ravaging his body. He was a loyal disciple of Jesus who attempted through his association with the Communist Party to implement the master's teachings regarding social justice and "commonism."

There is an assumption in the popular culture today that religion and Jesus are the exclusive property of the political right. Examining the music and politics of Woody Guthrie suggests there is a rich legacy in American history which those on the political Christian left might draw upon in the struggle for social justice. The story of Jesus in America goes well beyond issues of abortion and same-sex marriage. In his reading of the Bible, Woody perceived no fundamental conflict between the principles of communism and the teachings of Jesus Christ that the selfish grafters should be driven from the temple of America and that God's resources be shared among all people. Jesus, the Bible, and Christianity are contested legacies within American history and not the exclusive property of any one political ideology, as some contemporary evangelicals appear to assume. Although some progressive Christians may be uncomfortable with fully implementing the radical ideas espoused by Woody, his perceptions of Jesus and "commonism" offer an example of social justice upon which Christians and even non-Christians may continue to draw. As Jim Wallis asserts, "The truth is that most of the important movements for social change in America have been fueled by religion — progressive religion. The stark moral challenges of our times have once again begun to awaken this prophetic tradition. As the religious Right loses influence, nothing could be better for the health of both church and society than a return of the moral center that anchors our nation in a common humanity."[18] Woody's response to Wallis would likely be an amen!

Examining Woody and Jesus has brought back many memories of my family. They shared Woody's faith in Jesus, but instead of being empowered to challenge the prerogatives of entrenched political economic elites, they remained stoic and long suffering while waiting for their heavenly reward. In addition, they clung to Old Testament Biblical passages that the Assembly of God ministers interpreted in a way that justified segregation and miscegenation laws and denounced gays and lesbians. As a young boy, I witnessed emotional religious services with people speaking in tongues and faith healing. But it is too simple to poke fun at these working-class people whose faith, even if often misplaced, provided many with a survival manual during difficult times. And I still do not know what to make of the phenomenon of speaking in tongues, where these rather inarticulate, plain people poured forth an unknown language followed by an articulate interpretation. I cannot envision them as sophisticated or devious enough to engage in fakery. As a young man, I witnessed numerous examples of faith healing through prayer, but I often wondered if these "miracles" were more manifestations of the power of positive thinking if one believed strongly enough in prayer and God's healing power. On a personal note, when I was in junior high school, my maternal grandmother took me to one of the tent revival meetings of evangelist Oral Roberts, who eventually accumulated enough wealth to establish his own university. Throughout my early years, I had suffered seriously from asthma and remember believing that I would die from being unable to breathe. After Roberts prayed for me while placing a vise grip on my forehead, I never again suffered from asthma. Perhaps I had simply matured and "outgrown" the disease, but that is not what my religious grandmother thought. And when I became a non-believer, the healing was not retroactively revoked.

The bottom line is that I never found the conservative Jesus of my parents as appealing as the radical, progressive Jesus espoused by Woody. I did not simply want to survive this world, but rather to change it. Thus, during my religious youth I disappointed my parents by identifying with Woody's perception of Jesus — a revolutionary outlaw who would overthrow the system of capitalist exploitation that enslaved the working class. For Woody, outlaws such as Frank and Jesse James, Billy the Kid, Belle Star, the Dalton Gang, and Pretty Boy Floyd were champions of the poor against the banks and big business, implementing the revolutionary social change emphasized by Jesus in his teachings. Woody, however, would eventually reject this romantic vision of violence as rather simplistic and dangerous.

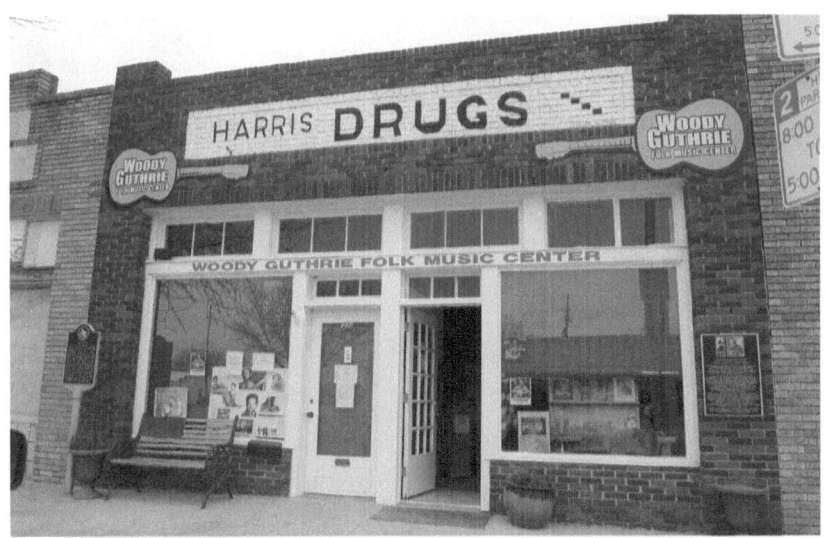

Harris Drug Store in Pampa, TX, where Woody Guthrie once worked. It's now home to the Woody Guthrie Folk Music Center.

The author at Harris Drug Store counter where Woody once served ice cream and sodas.

Message board from the Woody Guthrie Folk Music Center in Pampa, TX.

The author at park bench outside Harris Drugs in Pampa, TX.

The author with his wife, Kathleen, at Woody Guthrie Folk Music Center.

Poster from Bound for Glory, 1976. Courtesy of Photofest.

Woody Guthrie, 1942. Courtesy of the Woody Guthrie Archives.

"Welcome to Okemah."

The Okemah, OK, water tower.

Woody Guthrie statue, Okemah, OK.

An Arlo Guthrie concert at the restored Crystal Theatre in Okemah, OK, for Woodyfest Centennial.

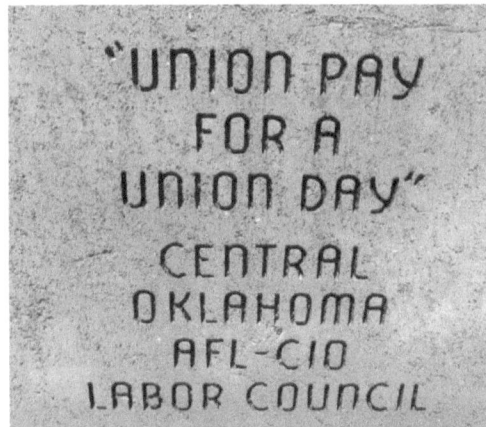

Commemorative brick in Okemah, OK, from the AFL-CIO honoring Woody Guthrie and the union idea.

The author and his eldest daughter, Pam, at Woodyfest's Centennial in 2012.

Bandstand at Woodyfest 2012 in Okemah, OK.

Chapter Eight

Primitive Rebels: Woody and the Outlaw Tradition

In his classic work *Primitive Rebels*, Marxist scholar E. J. Hobsbawm describes social banditry as "little more than endemic peasant protest against oppression and poverty, a cry for vengeance on the rich and the oppressors, a vague dream of some curb upon them, a righting of individual wrongs. Its ambitions are modest, a traditional world in which men are justly dealt with, not a new and perfect world."[1] During the late 1920s and early 1930s as the nation and world suffered through the crisis of capitalism known as the Great Depression, social banditry was practiced and celebrated among the destitute of American society in the rural Midwest and Southwest of the United States. Figures such as Bonnie and Clyde, Baby Face Nelson, John Dillinger, and Pretty Boy Floyd were often perceived by the people as Robin Hood types, fighting against the banking system that had driven many farmers from their homes.[2]

These primitive rebels or outlaws were celebrated in the music of Woody Guthrie, who drew upon the history and traditions of his native Oklahoma to pen ballads of tribute to such outlaws as the Dalton Gang, Billy the Kid, Belle Starr, Jesse James, and Pretty Boy Floyd, as well as the fictional Tom Joad. These songs played upon folk traditions in which outlaws were perceived to be defending the people against injustices perpetuated by legal institutions on behalf of the business community. Angered by the terrible conditions in which many common people lived during the depression, Woody proclaimed, "Writing is no profession for a man these days. With all these poor folks wandering around the country as homeless as little doggies, what I should do is strap on a couple of six-shooters and blow open the doors of the banks and feed people and give them houses. The only reason I don't do that is because I ain't got the guts."[3]

Woody, however, was a far more sophisticated political thinker than is usually acknowledged. He recognized the limitations of social banditry for building the type of egalitarian society Woody spoke of in his songs and writings. Resorting to individual violence was perhaps personally satisfying, but such actions contributed little to the construction of a lasting commonwealth for the people. Thus, true revolutionaries needed to abandon the romance of the gun and the idea of regeneration through violence. The creation of a better world and Woody's dream of "commonism" required the discipline and organization of the labor movement or Communist Party. The symbol of Tom Joad seems to reflect the idea of how an individual might be embodied in the masses: as Tom explains to his mother, he will be there when the cops are beating up a guy or people are fighting to be free. Losing sight of oneself in the struggle for "commonism," or Steinbeck's one big soul, may be found in Woody's autobiography, as are the themes of Christian socialism, antifascism, and the union movement that are also contained in Woody's songs. Nevertheless, the outlaw always remained a somewhat attractive figure for Woody. The evolution of Woody's thoughts on social banditry is described by scholar Mark Allan Jackson in his book *Prophet Singer*. Jackson writes, "In effect,

Guthrie may have started out singing outlaw songs because they appealed to the 'rugged individualist' tradition from which he came. But by the early 1940s, he had moved beyond this perspective and had created several outlaw ballads having both men and women struggling to right the wrongs occurring around them and exhibiting the author's own growing social consciousness."[4]

While Woody developed a sense of class consciousness in his work and thought, he, nevertheless, recognized the struggle of individualistic primitive rebels in the United States and often celebrated them in his music. Hobsbawm describes primitive rebels as belonging to the culture of pre-capitalist or peasant societies and thus outside of the American experience. Yet Woody's outlaws often represent subsistence farmers whose agrarian way of life is under assault by government and business interests who want to take their land and pursue more large scale commercial and capitalist ventures. Woody's outlaws, thus, are part of American and world historical resistance to the exploitation of laboring people.

In terms of my search for Woody Guthrie, the themes of outlaw violence fit well into the major changes both myself and American society were undergoing during the 1960s. As a boy growing up in Texas, television Westerns were a staple of my existence. The issues were simple. There were the good guys and the bad guys, symbolized by white and black cowboy hats. I was on the side of truth, justice, and the American way — as portrayed by my hero Gene Autry. Maturation in the late 1960s brought the realization that life was not quite so simple. Drawn to the Civil Rights Movement and protests against the Vietnam War, it occurred to me that many of my heroes championed the violent expansion of a white America at the expense of minority groups such as the Native Americans. While advocating peace and opposing the war in Vietnam, many on the political left, nevertheless, were attracted to the concept of regeneration through violence which historian Richard Slotkin argues dominates much of the nation's history. Slotkin writes, "The first colonists saw in America an opportunity to regenerate their fortunes, their spirits, and the power of their church and nation, but the means to that regeneration became the means of violence, and the myth of regeneration through violence became the structuring metaphor of the American experience."[5]

The Weatherman faction of SDS was enticed by the notion that violence, or bringing the war home, could in some fashion pave the way for a revolution that would destroy American capitalism and imperialism. Frustrated that peaceful protest was not influencing the government to alter its policies in Vietnam, some youth embraced violence and the outlaw tradition as the answer. As a member of SDS, I was attracted to the visions of revolution, but eventually embraced the notion that change is more evolutionary and comes through daily actions and by influencing one person at a time. Thus, teaching rather than revolution became my way of working toward a better world. Again, Woody's guidance was invaluable. His thoughts on the outlaw tradition helped provide some understanding and historical context for my own battles against the establishment.

In terms of Woody's music, perhaps his best-known outlaw ballad is "Pretty Boy Floyd," which has been performed by numerous artists, including Bob Dylan, Arlo Guthrie, The Byrds, Joan Baez, and Wall of Voodoo. Woody presents Floyd as an Oklahoma farmer who got into trouble with the law for defending his wife's honor and became a bank robber seeking to help his fellow farmers who were losing their land to the banks in depression America. Most contemporary historians provide a less flattering portrayal of Floyd. Born Charles Arthur Floyd in Georgia on February 3, 1904, Floyd moved to Oklahoma in 1911 where the family struggled to earn a living. Even before the depression struck America, Floyd was in trouble with the law and was sentenced to prison in 1925 for his role in a payroll robbery. After being released from prison, Floyd was allegedly involved with a number of bank robberies. Witnesses described him as a "pretty boy" — providing the nickname that the outlaw purportedly detested. In June 1933, Floyd was accused of being involved with the so-called Kansas City Massacre in which two FBI agents were shot and killed. Floyd, however, maintained that he was not present at the shoot-out in Kansas

City. Acclaimed by FBI Director J. Edgar Hoover as Public Enemy No. 1, Floyd was shot and killed by FBI agents led by Melvin Purvis on October 22, 1934, in East Liverpool, Ohio. Floyd's body was placed on public display in Sallisaw, Oklahoma, and his funeral was attended by approximately 30,000 people, many of whom perceived Floyd as a Robin Hood figure fighting for the poor against the banks. It is this perception of Floyd that Woody embraces in his song composed in March 1939 — five years after the death of Pretty Boy Floyd.[6]

In Woody's ballad, Floyd's life of crime began in Shawnee, Oklahoma, when a fight ensued between Floyd and a deputy sheriff who cursed the farmer in the presence of his wife. The lawman was armed with a gun, and Floyd killed him with a log chain in self-defense. Becoming a fugitive from the law, Floyd was often blamed for crimes that he could not have committed. While conceding that Floyd eventually resorted to robbing banks, Woody portrayed the outlaw as a Robin Hood figure seeking to aid the distraught farmers of Oklahoma. In Woody's ballad, Floyd used the money taken from the banks to help farmers pay their mortgages and save their farms. Woody's Floyd provided a car load of groceries for the families on relief on Christmas Day; farmers told the story of a mysterious stranger who asked for a meal and then left a thousand-dollar bill for the farmer and his family. Describing Pretty Boy Floyd as a man of the people who fought against the predatory banks and sought to more justly distribute the wealth, Woody closed his song with one of his most famous lines that still resonates within contemporary America:

> Yes as through this world I ramble,
>   I see lots of funny men,
> Some will rob you with a 6 gun,
>   And some with a fountain pen.
> But as through your life you'll travel,
>   Wherever you may roam,
> You won't never see an Outlaw drive
>   a family from their home.[7]

Woody does not necessarily assert that his version of Floyd's life was historically accurate, rather his song was based upon the stories told to him by Oklahoma farmers who knew Floyd well. According to Woody, "Something went haywire and Pretty Boy took to outlawing. Still he had more friends than any governor Oklahoma ever had. He went to packing shooting irons, blowing his way into the banks where the people's money was. Grabbed big sacks of it up and took it out and strewed it and scattered it everywhere, and give it to the poor folks all up and down the country. He had the right idea but he had the wrong system."[8] In this commentary, Woody acknowledges the limitations of the individualistic primitive rebels whose solitary acts of rebellion and retribution failed to provide the type of collectivist action required to overturn the profit system.

Nevertheless, Woody remained fascinated by outlaws, many of whom, like Pretty Boy Floyd, had their origins in his home state of Oklahoma and the surrounding areas of Kansas and Missouri. For example, in his song "The Dalton Boys," Woody sings of bank robbers Bob and Emmett Dalton. The Dalton brothers were originally lawmen, but after allegedly not being compensated for their services, they turned to a life of crime by robbing banks and seeking refuge in the Indian Territory of Oklahoma. On October 5, 1892, Bob was killed, and Emmett was severely wounded when the gang attempted to rob a bank in Coffeyville, Kansas. Woody's conclusions regarding the Dalton Boys are a little more ambiguous than his eulogy of Floyd; he wonders whether the boys have gone to glory or "pur-ga-tory."[9] Woody was also ambivalent when writing about the infamous female outlaw, Belle Starr. Born in Carthage, Missouri, Starr established a reputation as an outlaw in the Oklahoma Territory following the Civil War. She served a prison sentence for stealing horses and was mysteriously murdered on February 3, 1889. In his song, Woody focuses upon Starr's alleged eight lovers, including outlaws Cole, Jim, and Bob Younger; Cherokee Blue Duck; husband Jim Reed; Frank and Jesse James; and the notorious Civil War Confederate guerrilla leader William Quantrill. The folk singer neglects to consider what drove Starr to a life of crime and concludes his song by wondering whether Belle Star walks the streets of heaven or resides "somewhere below."[10]

Geographically, Woody moved out of Oklahoma's folklore to write of the legendary Billy the Kid. Historian and Billy the Kid biographer Robert M. Utley argues that the outlaw's fame should be placed within historical context. At the time of his death in 1881, Billy represented a changing America that was "undergoing momentous transformation from an agricultural realm to an industrial nation." Utley concludes that Billy the Kid's image as an outlaw/hero was solidified in the depression and during World War II when "the notoriety of the young hero strengthened during these dark years and never dimmed." Woody plugged into this cultural moment with his version of Billy the Kid, who was a singing and fun-loving young man popular with the Mexican women. Yet he was also the product of an environment where a gun was the only law, and Woody claims that Billy had killed twenty-one men before he was gunned down by lawman Pat Garrett, "who once was his friend." Guthrie scholar Mark Allan Jackson observes that Woody's song was based upon a 1927 tune penned by Andrew Jenkins, but in Woody's version of the outlaw's story, Billy is not a "young lad" who "went to the bad," but rather a "young outlaw who threatened the wrong man."[11]

Woody did not dwell upon what drove the Dalton Boys, Belle Starr, or Billy the Kid to a life of crime, as he did with the contemporary outlaw Pretty Boy Floyd; however, he insisted that perhaps America's most famous outlaw of the nineteenth century, Jesse James, was drawn to a life outside of the law by the actions of big business, in cahoots with the legal system, committed against his family. In his introduction to *Hard Hitting Songs*, Woody argued that outlaws were the product of a greedy profit system, writing, "These outlaws may be using the wrong system when they rob banks and hijack the rich traveler, and shoot their way out of a gamblin' game, and shoot down a man in a jewelry store, or blow down the pawn shop owner, but I think I know what's on these old boys' minds. Something like this: 'Two little children a layin' in the bed, both of them so hungry that they can't lift up their head....'"[12]

Thus, Woody perceived Jesse and Frank James as men forced into a rebellion against the authorities because the railroad companies wanted the family farm and the Pinkerton detectives firebombed the James home — killing a younger brother and maiming the mother of the infamous James brothers. Woody asserted, "It was the Railroad buyers that sent the bullies down to push folks off their farms in the county that the railroad was coming through, but some folks just naturally don't push so easy. Jesse James and Frank was them kind of men. You just didn't drive them around like cattle. Yeah, and we still sing about Frank and Jesse. There wasn't a sissy bone in their body. They never drew a scared breath. They drew some fast ones, but they weren't scared." In "Jesse James and His Boys," Woody described Jesse as a brave Robin Hood figure who "took from the Rich and delivered to the Poor." He would "never harm a child nor frighten a Mother and her Babe," and when running from the law, Jesse "found a Welcome in every cottage door."[13] In fact, Woody explained to Alan Lomax that Jesse was so popular in Oklahoma "that there's about ten or fifteen guys in ever town that claims to be him and they got the bullet holes to show it." According to Woody, there was an old drunk in Okemah who claimed to be Jesse, and when jailers stripped him for a bath, it was discovered that "he had the identical bullet holes that the Jesse dang James was supposed to have but, uh, there was a lot of other guys around there too and they all had so many bullet holes in 'em that they couldn't decide on a pattern so Jesse is done gone but he is still with us."[14]

Within the popular culture of the Great Depression, bankers were often presented as villains and bank robbers as sympathetic outlaws, similar to Woody's depiction of Jesse James as a folk hero. In 1939, director Henry King released *Jesse James* starring Tyrone Power, Henry Fonda, and Nancy Kelly. The film portrayed the railroad tycoons and Pinkerton detectives as ruthless villains in their quest for land and use of violent tactics, forcing the James brothers to live outside the law. Woody, who loved the movies, wrote a rousing review of the film for his "Woody Sez" column in the *People's Daily World*. Woody praised Frank and Jesse James as victims of the railroad owners, who hired hoodlums to drive the farmers off their land. Even though the railroad men bombed their home, the James brothers continued to fight the corrupt railroad interests. Woody insisted, "No wonder folks likes to hear songs about the outlaws — they're wrong alright, but not as dirty and sneakin' as some of our so-called 'higher ups.' "[15]

In his depiction of the James brothers, Woody seems to have anticipated the primitive rebel thesis presented by Hobsbawm. Jesse represents agrarians battling against centralizing and modernizing forces seeking to destroy the independent way of life embraced by the farmers or peasants. Many contemporary historians, however, question Hobsbawm's arguments, and more recent scholarship on Jesse James challenges the portrayal of the outlaw as a rebel against predatory business interests. Pulitzer Prize-winning historian and biographer T. J. Stiles asserts that Jesse was a "bushwhacker" or Confederate guerrilla who was still attempting to promote the Confederate or KKK agenda in Reconstruction Missouri following the Civil War. Stiles writes, "Jesse James was not an inarticulate avenger for the poor; his popularity was driven by politics — politics based on wartime allegiance — and was rooted among former Confederates. Even his attacks on unpopular economic targets, the banks and railroads, turn out on closer inspection to have had political resonances. He was, in fact, a major force in the attempt to create a Confederate identity for Missouri, a cultural and political offensive waged by the defeated rebels to undo the triumph of the Radical Republicans in the Civil War."[16]

Woody might be shocked to learn that he was eulogizing an advocate of Jim Crow, but he recognized the limits of individual outlaws engaging in violent rebellion. The necessity of more collectivist action was evident in Woody's celebration of the union movement and of Jesus as a champion of socialism. In 1940, for example, Woody composed "Jesus Christ Was a Man," or as it is sometimes called "They Laid Jesus Christ in His Grave," comparing Jesse James and Jesus. Both men were advocates for the poor but were betrayed and killed. James was shot in the back by Bob Ford as the legendary outlaw attempted to adjust a picture frame in his home, while Jesus was sold

Woody and the Outlaw Tradition

out for thirty pieces of silver by "a dirty little coward called Judas Iscariot." Jesus was killed because he preached that "the poor would win the world," but, unlike Jesse James, the carpenter from Nazareth would have the final word. He would return to earth with a vengeance and, "It would be better for you rich if you'd never been born!"[17] In this violent imagery, Jesus was clearly placed within the tradition of the socialist outlaw.

Social banditry, however, did not agree with Communist Party orthodoxy, which emphasized collective action rather than individual adventurism. The party line and Woody's faith in "commonism" were more apparent in "This Morning I Am Born Again," written in January 1945. In this composition, an earthly paradise for the common people is achieved not through violence but rather through the union movement. In the song's conclusion, Woody writes that he envisions a new tomorrow where the human race will become "just one big family" within the "union place."[18] The transition from social banditry to a more collectivist solution is perhaps best illustrated in Woody's epic "Tom Joad." The outlaw Tom Joad becomes a model for how the individual rebel may transpose his interests into those of the collective, or Jim Casy's "one big soul," to create a better tomorrow and a better world.

If we are to take Woody at his word, the song "Tom Joad" was based on John Ford's film rather than Steinbeck's novel, and the structure of the composition is, indeed, closer to that of the cinematic version. Thus, Woody concludes "Tom Joad" with Tom departing the family but telling his mother that through the death of Preacher Casy, he was finally able to envision the world as one big soul. Tom Joad declares that his mother and family will see him wherever people are hungry and fighting for their rights.

In his introduction to the song for *Hard Hitting Songs*, Woody compares Tom Joad with the men he knew growing up in Oklahoma, writing, "The story of Tom Joad is one that a lot of boys went through. From the Oklahoma penitentiary — to his home in the dust bowl, and then they had to get away to California — had to pick up their old car and pull out — and his mother and his dad, and his sisters and brothers found out about the thugs and the firebugs and the guards and the deputies that guard the fields and the rich man says 'are mine' — 'You keep off.'" Woody argues that his song was not written for the company guards, police, and vigilantes who persecute the people, but perhaps, like Tom Joad's struggle, it might have an impact as "a guard or a deputy can always come over on the real people's side."[19]

Steinbeck drew upon a rich American protest tradition for his novel, and the fictional Tom Joad has served as an inspiration for activists and artists. However, scholar Zoe Trodd insists, "Within the protest tradition, the ghost of Tom Joad has breathed the most fire through Woody Guthrie," who "saw in *The Grapes of Wrath* a blueprint for the protest future."[20] In a similar vein, historians Bryant Simon and William Deverell credit Woody with turning Tom Joad "into a dogged union organizer with an uncompromising Popular Front agenda. Perfectly mirroring Guthrie's own down-home, left-wing politics, his Tom Joad addresses the battle between the rich and the poor, and the need for working people to stick together if they ever want to end their hardships." Simon and Deverell conclude, "Telling a 'true' story of the people was not enough for him. It was the starting point in a call to action. In other words, where the movie ends, Guthrie's Tom Joad begins."[21]

Woody's vision of Tom Joad as an actor in the American protest tradition who bears witness to the inequities of American life is kept alive in Bruce Springsteen's "The Ghost of Tom Joad;" a rousing interpretation of this ballad by Rage Against the Machine interrogates the myth of the American dream. Springsteen released *The Ghost of Tom Joad* album in 1995 when it was apparent that the Ronald Reagan conservative revolution and Bill Clinton's globalization left many American workers in places such as Youngstown, Ohio, demoralized and out of work. In a review of Springsteen's album, Paul D. Fischer credits the rock star with drawing upon Woody to bring back Tom Joad. Fischer concludes, "Under Tom Joad's unwavering gaze, questions of what can and must be done to address injustices and inequalities inevitably arise. Springsteen makes middle-class listeners self-conscious of their relative advantages, and by his own responses to parallel circumstances provides a model for conduct in everyday life."[22]

Nevertheless, there is always the danger that more contemporary artistic visions of the depression era may produce a sense of nostalgia for a simpler time — as is evident in Hal Ashby's film *Bound for Glory*. But even in the wake of a rising wave of conservative politics, historians Simon and Deverell perceive hope in the Tom Joad of Steinbeck, Ford, Guthrie, and Springsteen. They argue, "This Tom Joad is still dangerous, or at least frightening, to those counties and schools and school boards that still flirt with banning *The Grapes of Wrath* from classrooms. Banning the novel is a simpleminded indefensible action, but in the bans, which still take place, we see the ghost of Tom Joad. There's power there, there's the sixty-year-old Tom Joad still breathing fire."[23] Thus, in the search for Woody Guthrie, "Tom Joad" signifies an important bridge between Woody's infatuation with outlaws violently challenging the established order and a belief in a more inclusive union movement that, similar to religious belief, had the power to fundamentally transform America and the world. Like the mythical Tom Joad, Woody devoted much of his adult life to the union struggle.

Chapter Nine

"I'm Sticking to the Union": Woody and Labor

As is evident in his musical compositions, correspondence, and voluminous journals, Woody Guthrie believed in the transformative power of the union idea. Although Woody walked many picket lines and entertained thousands of striking workers, his direct participation in union politics was rather limited — with the exception of his World War II Merchant Marine experience. While enlisted he joined the National Maritime Union (NMU), which challenged the International Seaman's Union organized by the American Federation of Labor. In regard to the union movement, Woody was more of an idealist than an organization man.

His religious and political values often overlapped: Woody perceived Jesus as a radical who would usher in a millennium of equality among the working people of the world, with the carpenter and the masses able to achieve this better world through the union movement. Yet the post-World War II America, of which Woody expected so much, proved to be inhospitable to organized labor, even though it had witnessed considerable growth during the Great Depression and World War II. Cold War and McCarthyism tactics employed postwar fears and insecurities to associate the labor movement with communism. Organized labor responded to the postwar reaction by purging union leaders with leftist political associations. In addition, labor leaders retreated into the bread and butter unionism of pensions, benefits, and wages while abandoning the transformation of American capitalism to provide workers with a greater voice in business management. Republicans in Congress also began to curtail the power of unions through such legislation as the Taft-Hartley Act (1947), which limited strike activity and required union officials to sign anticommunist oaths. Unionized workers, who had surged to almost half of the workforce, began to decline — reaching the feeble figure of approximately ten percent within the contemporary labor force. Today, organized labor in the United States lacks the transformative and countervailing power that Woody envisioned.[1]

Thus, my search for Woody Guthrie takes place in an America that, to a great extent, has abandoned the union dream of Woody, Tom Joad, and Jesus the working-class carpenter. I grew up in a union family as my father was a member of the railroad brotherhoods. One of my earliest memories is accompanying my father to a picket line, where I remember tossing some pebbles at strikebreakers. My father seemed proud of me and explained why I never wanted to be a "scab." Nevertheless, his union membership did not prevent him from suffering numerous layoffs from the shops at the Fort Worth and Denver Railroad. During his periods of temporary unemployment from the railroad, my father struggled to find work and even went from door-to-door offering his labor for hire. Finally, while working on a railroad wrecking crew, he suffered a massive coronary. After he passed, my mother continued to draw some benefits from his railroad retirement pension, which were helpful during her final years.

Before matriculating to the university, I assumed that it would be possible to find a working-class job in Childress and perhaps join a union. However, an early marriage and my enthusiasm for history education altered these plans. Years later, after completing the comprehensive exams for my dissertation, I accepted a teaching position with an independent school that did not recognize teaching unions and tenure, as did the public schools. In fact, I taught for almost forty years on a year-to-year contract. I even became part of management, serving almost a quarter century as the assistant head of school. In this administrative capacity, I was in charge of school discipline for students, and I also supervised faculty. I like to believe that my working-class background and educational struggles in high school made me more sensitive to the concerns of students and teachers. In hindsight, my perception is that while many students appreciated my sense of compassion during their disciplinary hearings, many teaching colleagues viewed me as an administrator who was a threat to their jobs — and they had no union protection against management. Nevertheless, I remain sympathetic to teachers' unions and oppose the mantra of many conservatives that the unions are responsible for the problems in American public education. These opinions are inconsistent with my educational career and open me to accusations of hypocrisy. In my defense, I am basically proud of my work as an educator, but I certainly acknowledge the gap between my politics and job description, exposing compromises with which I am not sure that Woody Guthrie would have agreed.

These compromises were also made during a terrible time for organized labor in the United States. During the 1970s, as I moved out of graduate school and into the workforce, a wave of wildcat strikes occurred throughout the country. Labor activists were challenging traditional union leadership, which during the post-World War II era negotiated contracts providing for greater wages and benefits while conceding management control of the workplace. This lack of autonomy left many workers disillusioned and alienated, struggling to regain some sense of control over their lives on the shop floor. Despite the promise at the beginning of the decade, most of these reform efforts failed. By the end of the 1970s, the working class of America was in disarray. Conditions only got worse in the 1980s. Organized labor suffered a major defeat in 1981 when President Ronald Reagan fired the striking airplane controllers and destroyed their union, the Professional Airplane Traffic Controllers Organization — a setback from which labor is still attempting to recover. Many workers suffered from the economic impact of "stagflation" and lost their jobs to automation and to outsourcing in cheaper international labor markets. Disillusioned workers blamed affirmative action programs, illegal immigration, and minorities for the deteriorating economic status and politically deserted the New Deal coalition to vote for Richard Nixon and Ronald Reagan — a movement that continues today with white working-class support for xenophobic businessman Donald Trump. Summarizing the impact of the 1970s upon the working class, historian Jefferson Cowie argues, "How a republic of anxiety overtook a republic of security may be the seventies' greatest, and most tragic, legacy. The social and political spaces for the collective concerns of working people — the majority of citizenry — dissolved from American civic life when the nation moved from manufacturing to finance, from troubled hope to jaded ennui, from the compromises and constraints of industrial pluralism to the jungles of the marketplace. The seventies marked the end of a political order, the end of a movement, and the end of an era. Most of all, it was the end of a historically elusive ideal: the conscious, diverse, and unified working class acting as a powerful agent in political, social, and economic life."[2]

The search for Woody Guthrie is important for in his work and life we can observe the union idea of equality and unity so missing from contemporary divisive political rhetoric. Guthrie scholar Mark Jackson concludes that the key to Woody's thought was his vision of a better world, personified in the almost religious dedication to the idea of equality contained in the idealized conception of union. Jackson writes, "In his songs, Guthrie denounced fascism, race hate, and greed — and celebrated the promise of the unity of men and women in various forms. He wanted all Americans to join together to demand justice for themselves, so they could have shelter and food, dignity, and joy — all gained through the people's 'union feeling.' "[3] It made no sense to Woody that a few rich folks owned the farms, banks, and factories, while most people worked hard and received little. Such a system was illogical to Woody, and his dust bowl experience convinced him that the American dream was a cruel hoax. "Commonism" and the union idea in which the people shared and worked together made more sense to Woody than American capitalism.

Growing up in Oklahoma and Texas, Woody had little exposure to the union movement. The Socialist Party enjoyed considerable support in the Southwest during the late nineteenth and early twentieth centuries. But the Socialist movement in the region was virtually destroyed during World War I, amid allegations that Socialists failed to support the war effort and were seeking to promote a Bolshevik Revolution within the United States. Woody became more aware of the possibilities for progress by the common people that the union movement offered as he rode the rails and learned more about the history of groups such as the IWW. In addition, Woody had direct experience in California organizing farmworkers in the fruit orchards and vegetable fields. But as Woody made clear in his introduction to a songbook edited by Moe Asch, the early union years in California were difficult. Woody observed, "Labor in general, at that time, was in the nickel and the penny stages, very few strong and well run unions but lots of tear gas and guns being used by hired thugs and all kinds of vigilantes. The movement could not pay me enough money to keep up my eats, gas, oil, travel expenses, except Five Dollars here and Three there, Two and a Quarter yonder, at places where I sung."[4]

These challenges convinced Woody to seek better prospects in New York City, but the lessons learned in California's fields made Woody a union man. Woody's commitment to labor was quite evident in his introduction to *Hard Hitting Songs for Hard-Hit People*. Seeking to assert the fundamental Americanism of the union idea, Woody insisted that it was the concept of "one big union" for which Abraham Lincoln had surrendered his life. Woody concluded that Lincoln's union dream had been stolen, proclaiming, "The Banking men has got their Big Union, and the Land Lords has got their Big Union, and the Merchants has got their Kiwanis and Lion Club, and the Finance Men has got their Big Union, and the Associated Farmers has got their Big Union, but down south and out west, on the cotton farms, and working in the orchards and fruit crops it is a jail house offense for a few common everyday workers to form them a Union, and get together for higher wages and honest pay and fair treatment." Woody goes on to explain that the songbook chronicles how big business, with its hirelings in law enforcement, has persecuted and prosecuted efforts by working people to organize. Woody concluded, "They call you a red or a radical or something, and throw you and your family off of the farm and let you starve to death.... These songs will echo that song of starvation till the world looks level — till the world is level — and there ain't no rich men, and there ain't no poor men, and every man on earth is at work and his family is living as human beings instead of like a nest of rats."[5]

For Woody, the idea of one big union aligned well with his religious faith in Jesus and Christian socialism. Nora Guthrie asserted that the key to understanding her father was his love for the common people. Thus, in writing about the one big union in *Hard Hitting Songs*, Woody exclaimed, "Most Folks believe in Union. They believe in One Big Union. Preachers preach it, screechers screech it. Talkers talk it. Singers sing it. One Big Union has got to come. You believe in it. I know you do. You believe in it because the bible says You'll all be One in the Father. That is as High as Religion goes. Then on over there somewhere it says, God is Love. So you see that the Reason you got Religion is so's everybody can all be One in Love."[6]

Accordingly, Woody threw himself into the union struggle: he composed songs such as "Union Maid," joined the Almanac Singers in support of CIO organizing efforts in 1941, signed up for the Merchant Marine during the Second World War (he viewed the global conflict as a struggle between the union idea and fascism), and, after the war, embraced the union movement as the means to confront Jim Crow and McCarthyism. The union idea and its capacity for love also saved Woody from descending into revolutionary violence as he witnessed the way his dust bowl migrants were treated in California. More religious apocalyptic visions were evident in a song called "Final Call," which Woody originally composed in February 1939. In "Final Call," Woody spoke of an army of workers that would march through the "plentiful valley" and destroy the rich man in order to create "a world of plenty here for one and all."[7]

Images of revolutionary violence were also on Woody's mind in a journal entry dated March 1941 and written in Los Angeles after Woody had retreated from the compromises associated with his brief New York radio career. Woody asserted that he was not necessarily in favor of revolutionary violence, but he was growing increasingly frustrated and angry with the economic inequality that plagued his family and most American workers. He proclaimed that it was time for the common people to stand up and demand their fair share of the earth's resources from the wealthy hoarders. Writing to his fellow workers, Woody insisted, "You plant and raise everything they got. You make everything they got. There's a whole army of you, and just a little bunch of them. You need more things. They got more than they need. I hope to God that you don't have to hurt nobody in getting your fair and honest share." Woody then proceeded to make an analogy with pulling an abscessed tooth; he observed that if a rotten tooth is causing you trouble, then you need to "fix it, yank it out and throw it away and forget about it." The same was true in the political world, and the people should not be afraid to employ their strength to create a better world.[8]

Woody credited the union movement with offering him a viable alternative, through collective action, to revolutionary or outlaw violence. In a commentary on the song "When You're Down and Out," Woody wrote that like many dust bowl refugees in California, he was "herded around like a Hereford steer at cutting time." He believed the migrants could deal with the drought conditions, but not the bankers who "would not listen to reason." Woody explains that he became so angry that he wanted to do something to help his people, but, "I didn't know whether to sing to 'em or shoot at 'em and I thought about a couple of pearl handed 44's, and about the money in the banks, and about the hungry people." Relieved that he did not succumb to robbing and shooting, Woody concluded, "I found a better way to beat the rich men and the bankers at their own game, and that's the Union, the C.I.O., or any of its unions." The union boys were the only ones on the side of the farmers and migrants "through thick and thin."[9]

Over two million American workers were on strike in the summer of 1941, and Woody was enthusiastic when the CIO invited the

Almanac Singers to entertain and encourage the striking laborers. He told his communist friend from California, Ed Robbin, "Being along with the Almanac Singers is some sort of treat to me, as it is packing my head full of this stuff called Organization. Something that I still need a heap more of."[10] Woody was impressed with the discipline displayed by CIO organizers as they sought to move beyond the skilled crafts approach of the American Federation of Labor (AFL) into a mass movement of industrial unionism. The radical achievements of the CIO are chronicled by historian Robert H. Zieger, who asserts, "Beginning in November 1935 and for a decade thereafter, industrial workers organized powerful unions. Aided by a friendly federal government, workers staged innovative sit-down strikes and wrested contracts from some of the most bitter-end corporations. They created permanent industrial unions that boldly intruded into political and governmental arenas. They challenged managers and supervisors at work sites and on shop floors throughout the country. They staged mass demonstrations. Through their leaders, they pressed a social democratic public agenda. They often welcomed communists and other radicals as their leaders and spokesmen." Zieger concludes, "The CIO projected manly strength. Its picket line confrontations, its military like logistical innovations, its centralized organizing campaigns, and its enormous public demonstrations made it seem like an irresistible juggernaut."[11]

Woody was attracted to this militancy and projection of strength. Following the United States' entry into the Second World War, Woody perceived the CIO as the way to combat Jim Crow at home and fascism abroad by empowering the working people of America. While Woody and others on the political left would later be disappointed with the CIO and organized labor for purging alleged communist members and a mixed record on race relations, there were no such reservations during the antifascist struggle of World War II. In August 1942, Woody lauded the CIO radio show *Labor for Victory*, proclaiming, "The leaders of the CIO are showing that they are wide awake to the threat of fascism, by their union planning that has shown itself to be the best in all fields, the waterfront plan of Harry Bridges, the Murray plan [steel], the Oil Workers plan, the seamen in the NMU, and it is this same kind of clear forecast that takes advantage of the radio, films, records, etc., in bringing the culture of unionism to the working people."[12]

Woody expanded these ideas in a long piece entitled "Union Show Troup," extolling the contributions of the Almanac Singers to the union struggle and urging other artists to join the fight. Woody felt artists must be "militant" in support of the people and abandon the "fakery" of Hollywood. The Almanacs were willing to become actively involved in strikes; thus, "our songs and ballads are a history and a record of the battles the Union has won, and the job and the work that the Union has done, and everywhere from coast to coast, Union Men and Women and Kids are prouder of that one thing than anything else, they battled and fought barehanded, and won."[13]

According to Woody, artists could not remain neutral, and it was incumbent upon them to decide which side they were on. Pointing out that the first thing Hitler did after gaining power was to abolish independent unions, Woody proclaimed there were only two sides: "the union side and the Hitler side." Woody related Hitler to domestic fascism within the United States and defended the Soviet Union who was doing the brunt of the fighting against Nazi Germany. He argued, "Hitler aint just a feller a running around loose over there in Nazi Germany, he's the mad, crazy, greedy people in this world, and this world is pretty well populated with his kind, folks that somehow believe in living fat and lazy off of the hard work of you and me, and our folks. Hitler hates Unions. He hates the Soviet Union, because The USSR is a solid Union Town, and Hitler caint never crack it, let alone take it." Thus, artists needed to become "good soldiers for the working people" and "good union members."[14]

In "Union Show Troup," Woody also cautioned his readers about becoming infatuated with the outlaw tradition to which the folk singer was also attracted. The problem with the outlaw, Woody warned, is that he was usually alone and bound to be defeated by law enforcement. Woody explained that outlaws employed the wrong means to redress their grievances, observing, "The outlaw tries to whip the world down to his size and then he finds out that the world is a whole lot bigger than him... so by yourself, even with a couple of Tommy guns, you're beat before the cards are dealt." Despite songs such as "Pretty Boy Floyd," Woody insisted that neither he nor the folk tradition glorified outlaws. Instead of surrendering to the misguided individualism of social banditry, Woody concluded it was better to "join the union and bring your complaints to the shop steward, or from the floor of the union meeting. This keeps your job, and you don't have to turn out to be bad men to get some changes made."[15]

In a piece entitled "War Songs & Work Songs," Woody described the United States as one big union and employed the image of the nation as a train bound for glory. Woody wrote, "Our country here is called the Union. Union of our whole big forty eight states over which in various boxcars I've rolled and been rolled. The word 'union' means 'all hooked together' like a big rolling train. The people in the fast locomotive and the cars behind it are our forty eight states full of our work and our goods and our stuff we make." Woody, however, cautioned that this train to freedom could be derailed by Americans who used racial prejudice to divide the union of the American people. Those sowing such racial discord would be supporting Adolf Hitler.[16]

Similar themes of the war against fascism as a union struggle were evident in Woody's letters describing his Merchant Marine experience. Returning to the United States on a Liberty ship after being torpedoed off the coast of Italy, Woody praised the seamen, exclaiming, "The crew was as fine, as hard working, and as calm, brave a bunch of men as I will ever see in this world. They were tops. Men and boys of all kinds and all colors. Working together in friendship and unity. Our only ills and troubles came from the captain and the chief steward. We drew up petitions to remove both of them from duty in charge of the lives of workers."[17] Thus, rather than resorting to the violent outbursts of outlaws, the grievance procedures of the union could provide relief from bosses who exploited their workers. In another letter, he explained how seamen and transported soldiers proclaimed Woody, Cisco Houston, and Jimmy Longhi as the "Union Boys" and begged to be entertained with union songs as many were being introduced for the first time to the union idea. As a good union man, Woody also credited his union, the National Maritime Union, with fostering this fellowship among the troops. Woody reported, "While men are aboard ships, and while they are ashore, the NMU gives them the same working spirit. The NMU gives lots of us our first toehold, and teaches us how to speak out, to stand up and how to use your mind, how to be a man. How to do all kinds of political union work. How to step lively. How to sing. How to sing in your soul."[18]

Woody's support for the union movement, as well as the more accommodating World War II politics of the Communist Party — in which communism was characterized as Americanism — convinced the folk singer to support the candidacy of Franklin D. Roosevelt for a fourth term in 1944. By advocating legislation such as the Wagner Act, Roosevelt's New Deal created the National Labor Relations Board and fostered collective bargaining. Woody warned workers about being complacent regarding Roosevelt because it played into the hands of the Republican Party and its Presidential candidate, Thomas Dewey. Warning that the 1944 electoral contest was about the differences between slave and free labor, Woody proclaimed that "the union side is the Roosevelt side." Woody asserted that Hitler and the Republicans sought to trick the people by dividing them, but the union was coming "because you're on your way down there to register your name down. The new world is coming because you're not letting your son down, your dad, your sweetheart that's out there in all of that blood and smoke and burning oil." Declaring that he was proud to be on the blacklists compiled by Republicans such as Dewey and FBI Director J. Edgar Hoover, Woody concluded, "I live union. I eat union. I think union. I see union. I walk it and I talk it. I sing it and I preach it. I squash my feet and my fingers in it and breathe it from our sun. I see this world as a union world or a slave world with nothing in between."[19] Roosevelt was elected to a fourth term, but was in poor health. He died from a cerebral hemorrhage on April 12, 1945. Party regulars at the 1944 Democratic National Convention had forced Roosevelt to dump his progressive Vice-President Henry Wallace in favor of Missouri Senator Harry Truman. After assuming the Presidency, Truman embraced the Cold War, struggled to protect the gains made by labor during the 1930s, and instituted Loyalty Review Boards in response to the anticommunist Red Scare. It was not the leadership Woody envisioned when he called for the re-election of Roosevelt.

As the war's end approached, Woody, however, maintained his faith in the union idea. To his listeners on New York City radio station WNEW, Woody announced that he was a union man and proclaimed, "The folks all around the world have been fighting now for a hundred centuries to all be union and to all be free and I sing the songs that tell you about that." Urging his radio audience to send letters of support, the singer concluded, "I speak for the union people that see a union world and that fight for a one big union all around the world."[20] In "This Morning I Am Born Again," Woody insisted that Jesus's teachings of equality could be realized within the temple of the union hall.[21]

Woody's hopes for a union world were dashed by the emergence of the Cold War and McCarthyism. Despite this reactionary environment, Woody, nevertheless, rededicated himself to the union struggle. In a letter to Duncan Emrich, Chief of the Archives for American Folk Songs, Woody said that he wanted to place additional songs in his collection at the archives, but he felt that the atmosphere in Washington, D.C., had changed. Woody explained that the last time he was in the nation's capital with a group of labor leaders, he had to surrender his guitar case; guards had objected to his stickers that stated, "This machine kills fascists" and "Support the General Motors Strikers." The folk singer quipped, "Do you suppose they felt like I was controlling the thoughts of the American citizens a little too much?"[22]

On a more serious note, Woody participated in the postwar CIO organizing drive among textile workers in the South. He also went to Winston-Salem, North Carolina in support of a strike by the Food, Tobacco, and Allied Workers (FTA) where he composed the song "Against the Law" (later recorded by Billy Bragg and Wilco for the *Mermaid Avenue* albums). However, he was disappointed that his performances for the striking workers were segregated by the FTA.[23] And the CIO Dixie campaign proved to be a failure. CIO historian Robert H. Zieger cites a number of factors that account for this lack of success, pointing to "the drive's lack of red-blooded militancy, its isolation of the left, its overwhelming concentration on textiles, its lack of political content, and its failure to exploit black workers' enthusiasm."[24]

In terms of Woody's commitment to the postwar union struggle, it is worth remembering that the day his beloved Cathy perished in a fire, the musician and activist was away from home in New Jersey supporting striking Phelps-Dodge electrical workers. Woody later penned a ballad about union organizer Mario Russo who was killed in clashes between the police and strikers. Sending the song to People's Songs, Wood asserted, "I wrote up this ballad after I'd sung down there at the rally of the Phelps Dodge workers in Elizabethtown on February 9th, the day they met to celebrate their strike was won after 8 months and 3 days. This was the same Sunday night when I came home with my guitar to find that a copper wire had shorted out in our front room causing a fire that took the life of our little four year old daughter, Cathy Ann."[25]

Despite this personal tragedy and growing disillusionment with the timidity of the postwar labor movement, Woody committed to the 1948 Progressive Presidential candidacy of Henry A. Wallace. Woody made numerous campaign appearances around the country on behalf of Wallace, describing the former vice president as a union man who, unlike Truman, would seek peace with the Soviet Union. In the song "Wallace Day," Woody composed a union hymn in which the common people supporting Wallace would "build heaven on this earth all full of union men."[26] The promising potential of the Wallace candidacy, however, was discredited by accusations that the candidate was the tool of the Communist Party, and Wallace failed to carry any state. In an electoral surprise, President Truman defeated Republican challenger Tom Dewey and segregationist Dixiecrat candidate Strom Thurmond.[27]

A distraught Woody expressed his displeasure with the election results and the postwar political climate in a letter to Marjorie's mother, Aliza Greenblatt. Woody seemed to lose his usual faith in "commonism" as he lamented that voters had ignored candidates "with love, with brotherhood, and with faith and union in their hearts" in favor of "our present maniacs in office, men and women that worship at the altar of greed, and dwell in a sweat of neurotic fear and hate." Always thinking of the children, Woody complained that under the current system they would never be able to receive "rewards equal to their works and their talents." Instead, an angry and pessimistic Woody concluded, "Under our present bunch of laws and lawmakers, well, all of the big piles of public money seem to go over to the crooks, the thieves, the gamblers, the gangsters, and the racketeers, the fellers who believe in robbery, rape, crime and disgrace."[28]

The union idea upon which Woody had invested so much of his faith, time, and energy during the Second World War was under attack in postwar America at the same time that Woody also suffered from personal tragedy and deteriorating health. Despite his anger and disillusionment, Woody maintained his belief in "commonism" and the concept of one big union. This included the dream of racial equality, to which Woody increasingly devoted his energies. Woody's efforts to promote racial harmony were apparent with his music, which lauded blues artists such as Huddie Ledbetter better known as Lead Belly, and political commitment to battling lynching and racial hate groups such as the KKK, whom Woody equated with domestic fascism. Although Woody's health situation prevented his active participation in the Civil Right Movement, his music and example inspired a younger generation of folk singers and activists, both black and white, to launch a crusade against racism and segregation that continues to resonate with contemporary efforts to create a more just and egalitarian America.

Chapter Ten

Woody and Race: Taking on Jim Crow

In the search for Woody Guthrie, the folk singer's evolution on questions of race certainly resonates with me. The rural environment of Oklahoma and the Texas Panhandle in which Woody grew up during the 1920s and 1930s did not promote racial harmony and understanding. Woody's racial prejudices were a product of his upbringing, and progressives were quick to call out Woody on these discriminatory attitudes. To his credit, Woody was able to overcome these stereotypes and racist attitudes to broaden his definition of "commonism" and the union idea to be racially diverse.

In terms of my own life and that of many other white Southerners there has been a similar path of self-discovery. But just because America elected a black president in 2008 does not mean that the nation has moved beyond its major problems with both overt and institutional racism. The Black Lives Matter movement well documents the tense relationship between the black community and law enforcement; the racial economic divide also persists, and the prison-industrial complex system constitutes a modern form of slavery. While demographic trends are making America a more racially diverse nation, the Presidential campaign of 2016 provided ample evidence of a white backlash against diversity. This movement away from inclusion was encapsulated in President Trump's failure to denounce Nazi marchers in the streets of Charlottesville, Virginia. Woody's legacy of overcoming his background of prejudice and becoming an activist in the struggle against racism remains an inspiring example for us all.

My parents never preached the Klan message of hate and violence, but they certainly embraced the conventional racist assumptions of their white community and sought to pass these along to their children. The community of Childress, in which I grew up, had segregated schools and neighborhoods; the black section of town was called "niggertown" and the streets were unpaved. The word "nigger" was commonly used in our home, and the Bible was often touted as providing support for segregation. Perhaps because I read so much, which always made me feel somewhat of an outsider in Childress, I was often uncomfortable with this language and racism. For example: I remember as a child going to buy some fireworks. There were also several black families purchasing items at the same fireworks stand. I wanted a device that moved rapidly on the ground before exploding and was popularly known as a "nigger chaser." Somewhat self-conscious of the nearby black families, I asked for the firework by using its brand name, "Texas Twister." The salesman had no idea what I was talking about, loudly proclaiming, "Do you mean nigger chasers. What the hell is wrong with you?"

And I often did feel that there was something wrong with me because I questioned the basic values of my parents, church, friends, and community. I even got to know some of the black kids through my employment at the local cemetery as part of Lyndon Johnson's Neighborhood Youth Corps, which provided work opportunities for impoverished youth. We dug graves together, but whites were always supposed to operate the machinery, such as the lawn mowers. I, however, have no common or mechanical sense and could never figure out how to start the lawn mowers. So when the boss was gone, a young black man, Robert Alexander, helped me get the mower running. And since I was more comfortable with a non-motorized tool, such as a hoe, he would mow while I chopped weeds. When we saw the boss returning, however, we quickly changed back to our racial job descriptions.

I would like to say that this experience made me an advocate for racial toleration and understanding when our community finally got around to implementing the *Brown v. Board* decision during my junior year in high school. But although friendly with a number of black students, I usually lacked the courage to openly espouse my doubts about the racist environment in which I was raised. Thus, I found myself engaging in self-censorship and often uncomfortably laughing at the racist banter of many peers. And it is quite embarrassing to acknowledge that the word "nigger" was part of my vocabulary. To put it quite simply, I often conformed to the racist assumptions of my family and friends. I was rescued from this conformity at West Texas State University, hardly a bastion of radicalism, where my professors offered me an opportunity to reinvent myself and establish a degree of comfort in openly questioning many of the conventional wisdoms upon which I was raised. Beginning with my years at the university, where friends and teachers called me out for racist assumptions and language, I have dedicated my studies, social activism, teaching, writing, and family life to the promotion of a more racially diverse society. Perhaps the thing I am most proud of is my children, who have grown up embracing friends of color and who recognize the continuing power of racism in our society, which must be addressed in our lives and actions. Understanding Woody's struggles with overcoming racial prejudice has helped me come to grips with my own racist past.

Examining one's family history in regard to subjects such as race is uncomfortable, but it is probably somewhat easier for me to discuss this topic as my parents are deceased. When Woody composed his autobiography *Bound for Glory*, his relationships with his father and many other family members were somewhat strained. Thus, Woody presents his Okemah upbringing in a somewhat nostalgic fashion. He seems to honestly confront the mental health issues of his mother, but he fails to realistically describe the racial environment of Oklahoma in the early twentieth century. Instead of presenting himself as a young man whose racial views evolved over time, the Woody of Okemah is a full-blown antifascist who is opposed to racial intolerance. He describes Okemah as "an Oklahoma farming town since the early days, and it has about an equal number of Indians, Negroes, and Whites doing their trading there."[1] There is no mention of the race riots or lynching of black people that often characterized the Oklahoma of Woody's youth.

In describing his life after moving to Pampa in 1926, Woody depicts the Texas Panhandle community as a former oil boom town whose farm land is being ravaged by the dust bowl. Before he eventually departs for California, Woody makes it clear that he has no patience for the religious and racial intolerance sweeping through Europe. When asked about how he perceives the rise of fascism, Woody replies, "Hitler an' Mussolini is out to make chaingang slaves outta you, outta me, and outta ever' body else! An' kill ever'body that gets in their road! Try to make us hate each other on accounta what Goddam color our skin is! Bible says to love ya neighbor! Don't say any certain color!"[2] When Woody takes to the road, he has no problem riding the rails alongside unemployed black people. A young, black traveling companion named Wheeler complains to Woody about racial prejudice, calling it a "skin problem." Lamenting the power of racism over the people, Wheeler explains, "Like you can help what color you are. Goddamit all. Why don't they spend that same amount of time and trouble doing something good, like painting their Goddam barns, or build some new roads?"[3] Woody concurred with Wheeler's analysis, replying that the rich were trying to divide the people and that the solution to the crisis of the depression was a unified people working together across racial lines.

Thus, the Woody Guthrie of his autobiography emerges from the native soil of Oklahoma and Texas as a champion of racial equality. Reality, however, was far more complex. Segregation was evident in all aspects of life, ranging from voting to housing to education, when Woody was growing up. Mark Allan Jackson, in his analysis of Woody's music, reports that a young Woody and some of his friends even adorned blackface and provided the residents of Okemah an impromptu minstrel show.[4] Oklahoma was also a dangerous place for its black residents. Klan membership in the state grew during the 1920s, accompanied by an increase in lynching. Forty-one lynchings were reported in the first three decades after statehood.[5] On May 31, 1921, perhaps the nation's worst race riot in history occurred in Tulsa, Oklahoma. In his book on the riot, James S. Hirsch notes that thirty-eight people were confirmed killed, including ten white people, but the actual number killed in the fighting may have exceeded 300 — and almost all the victims were black residents of the city. Hirsch goes on to comment that while an allegation of a black elevator operator touching a white woman was the ostensible reason for the explosion of racial hate, the primary motivating factor was white resentment over the emerging prosperity of a black business community and middle class in Tulsa. Thus, the riot caused the destruction of the black Greenwood business district. Hirsch writes, "1,256 homes were burned in a thirty-six-square block area of Greenwood, including churches, stores, hotels, businesses, two newspapers, a school, a hospital, and a library — in short, all the institutions that perpetuated black life in Tulsa. The burned property was valued between $1.5 and $1.8 million — more than $14 million in 2000 dollars. Many homes were looted before being torched, but no white rioter was ever convicted for his or her crime."[6] It was a blow from which the black community in Tulsa never completely recovered. Although Woody never commented on the Tulsa race riot and was only nine at the time, it is difficult to imagine that he was not aware of the violence in Tulsa, which was only about fifty miles from Okemah.

Racial violence also struck closer to home for Woody with a lynching in Okemah on the evening of May 24, 1911, a little over a year before Woody was born. The racial violence was the outgrowth of a confrontation between a white police officer and the black Nelson family. The officer was killed, and the authorities arrested Laura Nelson and her teenage son Lawrence. About a week after their arrest, a mob led by the local Klan broke into the jail, capturing the mother and her son. Laura Nelson's baby was supposedly abandoned in the confusion and rescued by a black family. Laura was reportedly gang raped before she and Lawrence were taken to a bridge approximately six miles west of town, where they were lynched. As was common with many public lynchings, photographs were taken of the victims hanging from a trestle and later sold as postcards to commemorate the occasion — making lynching a ritualized act of political murder. Woody's father Charley was a member of the local Klan and apparently participated in the lynching. Charley's brother Claude proudly told Woody's biographer Joe Klein that Charley was involved with the hanging of the "niggers." While laughing, Claude Guthrie informed Klein that he knew that "rascal" Charley was "in on it."[7]

Although he never acknowledged his father's Klan membership or participation in the lynching, Woody was aware that Laura and Lawrence Nelson were murdered in his home town. Later, he composed the song "Don't Kill My Baby and My Son," dealing with the lynching. The song, which was never recorded, has some historical inaccuracies, but it well conveys the pain of Laura Nelson who feared for the lives of her son and baby. Although the lynching occurred before Woody was born, in the song he is a young boy wandering the streets of Okemah, when he hears the wails of a black woman in the jailhouse. In his notes on the composition, Woody wrote that the mother's cries were "lonesomer than all of the animals in the wild places that I've run into." Wood asserted, "The Negro lady had a right new baby, and a son that was doomed to be hung by her dead body with the rise of the morning wind, and my dad told me the whole story." In conclusion, Woody noted, "Several years has gone by and I wrote this song down, because that lady's wail went further, went higher, and went deeper than any sermon or radio broadcast I ever heard."[8] It is interesting to observe that the song tends to exonerate Charley, who is credited with informing his son of "many a sad tale about the old black jailhouse." Woody returned to the topic of Charley's racial attitudes in his novel *Seeds of Man* (written in the late 1940s, but not published until after Woody's death), but the racial ideology of his father would remain somewhat ambiguous and ambivalent.

Despite Woody's efforts to downplay the racist environment in which he reached maturation, it is difficult to disagree with the conclusion reached by Mark Allan Jackson, "Considering the mass of prejudices toward African Americans in his nation, state, town, and family, it would be surprising if Guthrie grew up unbiased."[9] In addition, some of his early California journals offer evidence of this prejudice. Many of these notebooks included racist caricatures of African headhunters and natives. In one, a white missionary is talking to an African who tells him, "The chief says for you to go back and teach your people how to live in houses."[10] These caricatures and racial stereotypes do not reflect the hate and violence of a Klansman, but they do indicate the prejudicial attitudes to which Woody was exposed while growing up in rural Oklahoma and Texas.

These racist assumptions were also present in Woody's KFVD radio broadcasts. He seemed to have no problem employing the word "nigger" in his songs and commentaries. On October 20, 1937, Woody introduced and sang Uncle Dave Mason's racist, "Run, Nigger, Run." In response to this overt racism, Woody received a letter from a young black listener, Terrence Howell, who wrote, "You were going along quite well in your program this evening until you announced your 'Nigger Blues.' I am a Negro, a young Negro in college, and I certainly resented your remark. No person or persons of any intelligence uses that word over the radio today."[11] Woody was embarrassed when Howell challenged his racial attitudes, and he responded by reading the letter during his next broadcast. He apologized profusely and promised to never use that word again. And Woody proved to be a man of his word as he took up the cause of racial equality and became a fierce opponent of hate groups such as the Klan.

Woody's opposition to Jim Crow ties in well with his attraction to the Communist Party as he became active in organizing efforts among California farmworkers. With the crisis of capitalism as exposed by the Great Depression, the 1930s were what political scientist Harvey Klehr calls "the heyday of American communism." Klehr writes, "The 1930s marked the height of Communist influence in America. This was an era in which the Party emerged from the fringes of national life and managed to play a supporting role in some of the greatest dramas of the day — the fight for unemployment insurance, industrial unionism, collective security against fascism, and others."[12] Among these other issues was the struggle for racial equality. While Klehr observes that black membership in the party remained relatively low, the Communist Party did attract considerable attention and support for its opposition to the Klan and racial segregation, and for advocating such causes as anti-lynching legislation, the organization of a Sharecroppers Union in Alabama, the legal defense of the "Scottsboro Boys" (who were accused of raping two white women riding the rails in Alabama), the extension of unemployment benefits to black workers, and even the racial integration of Major League Baseball. Woody shared these sentiments and stood alongside the Communist Party, as was often reflected in his "Woody Sez" columns for the *People's Daily World* and *Daily Worker*.

Certainly an element of Woody's enthusiastic support for the organizing efforts of the CIO was the union's opposition to racism and to the skilled craft unionism of the AFL, which limited black membership. In his notes for the satiric "Hallelujah, I'm a Ku Klux," Woody wrote, "They say the Ku Lux are against the CIO. That's enough to make me join the CIO tomorrow. When you got to hide your face to do it, boy, you're going against your own self, and when you try to go around horse-whipping people or smearing hot tar and loose feathers on 'em — that's just as mean and low as you can fall. No CIO Union has ever treated folks this way." In earning the opposition of the Klan, the CIO demonstrated its commitment to democracy and racial equality. As for the Klan, Woody denounced the secretive organization as serving the interests of the wealthy. Woody concluded, "The Ku Klux, or the Klip Joints or whatever you call 'em are to my notion the wrongest tribe of folks I ever seen. There's the Outlaws that took money from the rich and gave it to the poor, but the Ku Klux, some strange way, always side in with the Rich Guys. If they beat up a Rich Man it's because a Richer one told them to."[13] In these comments, Woody attempted to build a bridge between the poor white and black workers against the capitalist class.

During the Second World War, Woody continued to perceive the fight for racial equality as a key component of his one big union idea.

Fighting the Klan and Jim Crow was part of the struggle against fascism. To Woody, Hitler and the Klan were simply sides of the same coin, representing the forces of greed, which sought to exploit workers and employ racial and ethnic prejudice to divide the people. Woody believed that World War II would destroy both domestic and international fascism, ushering in the new dawn of "commonism." In his essay entitled "War Songs and Work Songs," Woody blasted the racial divisions promoted by Nazi ideology, arguing, "A song tells you we're all the same color under our skin, and in a blood bank, the color is all the same. Hitler would like me and you to fight each other all over the place just because we're a little different color, or shape or size, or something; but songs had ought to tell me how to like you and work with you and be your friend, and fight side by side with you." Concluding his piece with the metaphor of the American people on a train bound for freedom, Woody warned that racial division might derail the locomotive, writing, "What if somebody in one of the cars was to say, 'I'll unhook this car because a red man, or a green man, or a black man or a polka-dotted man made all of this carload, an' I don't like them colors of folks — so I'll unhook this car — ' you'd be doing just perzactly what Adolph would like for you to do — hurting the work of your own American people . . . and doing the Nazi army a big, big favor, because Hitler says he's got people bought and paid for to spread just such crazy notions around and keep our train from being 'Union,' 'United.' And from making it to Freedom."[14]

Woody insisted that it was the responsibility of artists to keep the freedom train on track. Soldiers needed to better understand the cause for which they were sacrificing their lives. The artist must help the soldier comprehend "who and the enemy, fascism really is, how deadly and murderous Nazism is, and all about the end of race hate, Jim Crow, and such likes, KKKism, and lynching. . . ."[15] In another piece on the war, written while he was at sea, Woody asserted that antifascists around the world were fighting for freedom, and he defined this term as including economic security as well as personal expression. The way to achieve this freedom was the union idea of the common people working together. The forces of greed would try to divide the people by appealing to racism, but Woody preached that the workers of all colors must remain united. He closed on an angry note by addressing those who succumbed to fascism, "You are called the Axis by some. You are called the Nazis, the Fascists, the Sons of Heaven, the Super Men! Baloney! Horse Manure! You are the Ku Klux! You are the Vigilantes! You are those who think that you own us and our labor! You are those who have let your own blind greed cut you apart from the spirit of our union. You are turning into a heap of dung at a very high rate of speed."[16]

Woody carried the fight against the domestic fascism of the Klan into the postwar period when progressive champions of racial unity were accused of supporting communism. However, Woody's evolution from his racist upbringing to an activist in the cause for black liberation cannot simply be viewed through the lens of politics. Music and Woody's love of the blues, along with his appreciation for black artists such as Lead Belly, were essential elements in broadening Woody's racial vision. As Woody wrote in one of his journals, "We got a week called Negro History Week but it would take more than just one week to sing all the good Negro songs that I picked up along my road."[17] Woody appeared to identify quite closely with the saga of Lead Belly, with whom he formed a meaningful friendship.

Lead Belly was born Huddie William Ledbetter on January 20, 1889, in segregated Louisiana. Earning his living primarily as a musician, Lead Belly ran into problems with the law. In 1918, he was imprisoned in Texas following an altercation over a woman that resulted in the death of a male relative. Seven years later, he was pardoned by Texas Governor Morris Neff who enjoyed the prisoner's music. However, this freedom was short lived. In 1930, the bluesman was sentenced to Louisiana's infamous Angola Prison Farm after stabbing a white man during a fight. It was while he was incarcerated at Angola that Lead Belly's music was recorded by folklorists John and Alan Lomax. Impressed with these recordings, the Lomax family appealed to Louisiana Governor Oscar K. Allen to parole Lead Belly, and the convict was released from prison in 1934. Following prison, Lead Belly worked for the Lomax family before finally settling in New York City.

It was through Alan Lomax that Woody met Lead Belly who was a regular on the radio program *Back Where I Come From*.[18]

Woody became good friends with Lead Belly and his wife, often spending the night at the Ledbetter apartment. According to Alan Lomax's biographer John Szwed, Woody perceived Lead Belly as "the real thing, who had been tossed into southern prisons as brutal as concentration camps and survived them physically and spiritually, who had come out of them whole and laughing and joyous and confident." As for Woody, Lead Belly believed he offered proof that poor Southern whites could accept blacks. Szwed concludes, "Both singers came from oil boomtowns in the Southwest and knew many of the same songs, the stories of the cowboys, the epics of the railroad workers, oil riggers, and hobos, the plights of lonely women and men, the ballads of the broken-hearted."[19] The comradery between Woody and Lead Belly epitomized the interracial harmony of "commonism" and the one big union.

Describing his friend, Woody wrote that Lead Belly understood that all people get the blues — "High price blues. No money blues. No clothing blues. No home blues. No man blues. The no war blues. The no nothing blues. Leadbelly is an artist that sees all of these things." Woody goes on to assert that he was first exposed to the blues when, living on his own at age thirteen, he traveled into eastern Texas and Louisiana. He concludes that listening to the blues of the black people in this region provided him with an essential education in life and music. The folk singer proclaimed, "I learned all I could from Negro shoe shine boys, cotton workers, farmers, and the whole spirit of these people. I did not read in papers nor in books, but in their talking and singing and their home made music. This music speaks an awful plain language." Thus, Woody believed that black music was the sound of the people and deserved an honored place in the union struggle against fascism. Lead Belly and blind black harmonica player Sonny Terry felt the "same as any of us about southern conditions that came from Jim Crow, Poll Tax, rotten houses, rotten land."[20]

After Woody was drafted into the Army, he wrote Marjorie, voicing his opposition to segregation and embracing the role played by black citizens and soldiers in the struggle against fascism — both foreign and domestic. Although the training facilities at Sheppard Field in Texas were segregated, Woody expressed admiration for his black comrades, writing, "These Negroes are full of spirit such as the Jews under Hitler fascism in Europe. It shows up here. If the prize for military neatness, spirit and marching is given in the right hands, these hands will be Black Hands. The songs they sing have set every back bone of our 90,000 servicemen and women here at Sheppard Field on fire. And I know that this is just a little pin speck in the big map." Woody also insisted that if asked to entertain the black troops, as he had been at Fort Dix, he would not perform in a segregated hall "where Race Hate is the boss." The singer concluded, "I have not offered to sing in their Jim Crow Halls and I would shovel manure and call it a manly art before I would change my Race policy one single inch."[21] And Woody practiced what he preached. While in the Merchant Marine, Woody, Cisco Houston, and Jimmy Longhi were entertaining troops in the hold of a ship under torpedo attack. When Woody heard the voices of black soldiers coming from a nearby toilet, he insisted that the black men join the other troops. When the black soldiers pointed out that segregation prevented this mingling, Woody decided that he would just have to sing in the black toilet — upsetting the white troops. To head off a potential riot during the stressful torpedo assault, an officer decided that a temporary exception to racial segregation would have to be made, and the black soldiers joined their white colleagues for the impromptu performance of the Merchant Marine Three.[22]

After his discharge, Woody incorporated the struggle against Jim Crow, racism, and the Klan into his post-World War II union organizing efforts. For example: when he went to Winston-Salem, North Carolina, in support of a strike by the Food, Tobacco, and Allied Workers, Woody added a verse advocating racial unity to the traditional union song "You Gotta Go Down and Join the Union." The fight for racial equality in the South was always a difficult one, and Woody was surprised to learn that he was performing the song at a segregated venue.[23] In this case, however, Woody bent his opposition to segregated facilities in support of union organizing. Woody also denounced the segregationist housing policies of New York City real estate developer Fred Trump — the father of American President Donald Trump. In October 1950, Woody signed the lease for an apartment in the public housing project that became known as Beach Haven. Rather naïve, Woody was shocked to learn that the real estate developer took advantage of the "restricted covenants" approved by the Federal Housing Authority to create a racially segregated housing project. An angry Woody responded by denouncing his landlord's racist policies, asserting, "I suppose old man Trump knew just how much racial hate he stirred up in the bloodspot of human hearts when he drawed that color line here at the Eighteen hundred family project by the name of Beach Haven. I suppose old man Trump knows how many drops of sad tears and crazy fears it caused my family in and out of Beach Haven to feel and fall heir to."[24]

Woody also penned numerous songs based upon newspaper accounts of postwar discrimination against black citizens and veterans. In a letter to Moe Asch, Woody lamented about "these lynchings, hangings, tarrings, featherings, and blindings that have been taking place around our good nation." He enclosed a song called "The Blinding of Isaac Woodard," which told the story of a black veteran who, after fighting in the Pacific, returned to his home in South Carolina. Holding an honorable discharge and still dressed in his Army uniform, Woodard attempted to use a "whites only" bathroom at a South Carolina bus station. He was taken off the bus by the local police and taken to the jail where he was severely beaten and as a result lost his eyesight. Telling the story from Woodard's perspective, Woody has his narrator conclude that he does not understand, "How you could treat a human like they have treated me." He fought against fascists in the war, "but I can see the fight's not over, now that I'm blind."[25]

In addition to the Woodard ballad, Woody wrote to Asch about recording "The Killing of the Ferguson Brothers." This song focuses upon the killing of two black veterans by a white policeman in Freeport, New York, after they protested being refused service at a bus station cafeteria. An all-white jury failed to indict the police officer. In "Buoy Bells from Trenton," Woody denounced the conviction of the

"Trenton Six," a group of black men convicted in 1948 of murdering a white man in New Jersey despite coerced confessions that were not supported by other evidence gathered in the case. Woody also penned "The Ballad of Rosa Lee Ingram," telling the story of a black sharecropper and mother in Georgia. Rosa Lee Ingram, along with two of her sons, was convicted by an all-white jury of murdering a white man who was attempting to rape her.[26]

Woody's songs, however, were not simply about black victimhood. "The Ballad of Harriet Tubman," written by Woody in 1944 and revised in 1953, celebrates the heroism of the former slave who escaped to the North and then risked her life nineteen times by returning to the South to help enslaved people escape bondage. Assuming the voice of Tubman as narrator, Woody's song promotes black agency, activism, and resistance. With the advent of the Civil War, Tubman called upon President Lincoln to arm blacks, so they could assume their just place in the struggle for freedom. Guthrie scholar Mark Allan Jackson credits Woody with recognizing the revolutionary and radical nature of Tubman's contribution to American history.[27]

Woody was also willing to assume personal risks in his fight against racial bigotry, as was evident in his response to the so-called Peekskill riots. On August 27, 1949, black entertainer and activist Paul Robeson was scheduled to provide a concert at Peekskill, New York — a Jewish summer resort area. Robeson had performed in the area on previous occasions with no problems, but the Cold War anticommunist hysteria had changed the environment. Robeson was accused of proclaiming, while addressing the World Peace Congress in Paris, that black citizens would not defend the United States against Soviet aggression due to America's history of racism. The concert was postponed when local mobs attacked audience members and threatened Robeson with lynching, while the Klan allegedly burned a cross on a nearby hillside. Robeson's appearance was rescheduled for September 4, and with security provided by numerous unions, the concert was free from violence. There were serious problems, however, following the performance as cars exiting the site were attacked by mobs organized through local Veterans of Foreign Wars and American

Legion chapters; approximately 140 people were injured. Woody had attended the show with Lee Hays, Pete Seeger, and Seeger's wife and child. Their car was attacked, and Woody placed his shirt over the windshield to protect the party from shattering glass — although Hays observed that Woody had no sense of timing as he had used a red shirt. Woody attempted to capture his reaction to the riots in a series of *Peekskill Songs*. The most powerful of these may be "My Thirty Thousand," which celebrates the eventual triumph of racial equality over the forces of hate. It was later recorded by Billy Bragg and Wilco.[28]

Peekskill was not Woody's last major foray into the battle against racism. In 1953, after he left Marjorie and his family, Woody took up residence with his new lover Anneke Van Kirk Marshall in the Florida Beluthahatchee estate of Woody's friend Stetson Kennedy. There, Woody continued his contributions to a series of anti-racist songs, which Guthrie scholar Jorge Arevalo Mateus calls the *Beluthahatchee Blues*. Mateus argues that while this cycle of songs are not strictly "blues" in form or structure, "They represent Guthrie's ability to focus on topics that may be construed as 'Southern' in sensibility and culture at a time in his biography which has generally been overlooked or regarded, incorrectly, as a period of diminished and fading creative capacities." On the contrary, Mateus finds the *Beluthahatchee* cycle to reflect a "fecund mixture of resolve, turbulence, and serenity."[29]

Woody first met Stetson Kennedy at Alan Lomax's New York City apartment in the mid-1940s, and the two men often appeared together supporting progressive causes and opposing the Klan. Coming from a relatively affluent Florida family, Kennedy left the University of Florida in 1937, finding employment with the New Deal's WPA as a folklorist and teaming with African-American novelist Zora Neale Hurston to produce the *WPA Guide to Florida: The Southernmost State* (1939). Unable to join the war effort due to a back condition, Kennedy accepted a position as Southeastern editorial director of the CIO's political action committee in Atlanta. In this capacity, he published monographs exposing limitations imposed upon voting and democracy in the South through the poll tax, white primary, and literacy tests. Following the war, Kennedy risked his life by infiltrating the Klan and the Columbians, an Atlanta-based neo-Nazi organization. These undercover activities and subsequent testimony led to criminal convictions for the leaders of the Columbians. Kennedy's efforts to infiltrate the Klan and Columbians were later recounted in a memoir, *The Klan Unmasked* — although some critics argue that Kennedy tended to overemphasize his role in unmasking the Klan. In 1952, Kennedy ran for Governor of Florida, and Woody composed a campaign song "Stetson Kennedy," which was later recorded by Billy Bragg and Wilco. With the Klan and right-wing extremists threatening his life, Kennedy left the United States for Europe in 1953 and spent almost a decade living abroad in exile. His Beluthahatchee estate remained a refuge for artists during this time.[30]

In 1945, Woody wrote to Kennedy, expressing admiration for his work and vowing to visit Florida — a state that Woody had missed in his travels. Woody credited Kennedy with exposing the inroads fascism was making in the South by fostering racial division and blaming blacks for the poor economic conditions of the region. Woody wrote, "The erosions of racial hate, poll tax, sharecropping, and cheap labor that grow so well where homes and schools are so bare, all of these the home style fascists will try to use as the perfect setting in which to get their start. If these conditions of poverty did not exist the fascists would create them in order to pretend to cure them, but the Christian American Fascists, like the Fascists in Italy, Germany, or anywhere else, cannot really point to even one neighborhood in which they cured poverty, because it is the ignorance caused by poverty that keeps fascism alive, and this is why they fight trade unions so hard, because the trade unions have been the only cure for poverty on the face of the earth and there is no other answer to the Southern problem of filth, disease, backwardness, and rotten politics." Railing against what he termed Christian American Fascists, Woody concluded the letter by remarking, "It is only in ignorance that their breed of laws can pass, and any office holder who passes a Christian American Fascist law to keep his folks in their swamps of misery is as much a Fascist as ever walked the sidewalk."[31]

By 1951, Woody and Marjorie were discussing a divorce, and the troubled folk singer followed up on his promise to visit Florida and sought refuge at Kennedy's estate. Kennedy's compound, however, was under siege by the Klan. According to biographer Ed Cray, Woody agreed to help Kennedy defend his home and was soon taking target practice with his patron's rifle. The Klan eventually did make an appearance in a convoy of pickup trucks, but Woody and other defenders were prepared for them. According to Cray, "Amid the gunfire and a hail of falling twigs and leaves, the panicked Klansmen circled the driveway in front of Kennedy's home and sped off, never to return."[32] After a few weeks, Woody went back to New York City before finally leaving Marjorie and the children to take up residence in California. In 1953, Woody, accompanied by Anneke Van Kirk Marshall, again sought refuge at the Beluthahatchee estate. Describing his Florida experience, Woody wrote to Moe Asch, asserting, "We kept right on making us up our fighting Jimmy Crow balladsongs while we were off down in them raceyhate Florida jungles and she made up several songs & stories & articles & pieces & storysongs & ballads just a good as some of my very best ones."[33]

Woody failed to forge a singing and performing duo with Anneke, but the songs composed during his journeys to Florida certainly provide ample evidence of his contempt for Jim Crow and the Klan as manifestations of American fascism. In "Genocide" (1952), Woody accuses the Klan and the forces of hate of promoting genocide against blacks. In his notes to the song, Woody proposes a more evolutionary than revolutionary solution, suggesting that the answer to racism may be best found in the voting booth rather than in resorting to violence. Woody wrote, "Your Ku Klux Klan calling for a few more millions of my white skin'd people(s) to come with full force and full violence and kill the body and soul of my darker skin'd people(s) just as fast as they walk up to a pollybooth or to my voting box to tell my whole world around what your are thinking and hoping when you drop your finger down on that voting machine."[34] Yet in other songs from this cycle, such as "Pistol Packer" (1953), "Hold On" (1953), and "Beluthahatchee

Blues" (1953), Woody appears more prepared for a violent revolution against American racism. In the Florida swamp, Woody, nevertheless, seemed to find some idyllic refuge in nature with such songs as "Peace Town" (1953), "Chopping Axe Blues" (1953), and "Seeds of Man" (1953).[35] But perhaps his mood about race is best reflected in a tribute he addresses to Harriet Tubman. Woody tells Tubman that he "hopes he can do everything to live up to what she, John Brown, Abraham Lincoln did about slavery. More than a good 99 percent of everybody I know feel just about the same way that I feel about going right on and working and fighting till we kill that old snake of slavery that you and your breed and your reed and your creed and your kind crippled as bad as you've crippled it." Woody closed his tribute to Tubman with the salutation of "your friend."[36] Jorge Arevalo Mateus summarizes the *Beluthahatchee* cycle as placing Woody on the side of "democracy vs. hate and genocide" in a final conflict that was "not race war, but counterracist war."[37]

While Woody, like many Americans, tended to perceive racial issues in terms of black and white relations, he was certainly aware of America's multicultural and multiracial nature and origins. It is interesting to note that, despite growing up in Oklahoma where there was a large Native American population, American Indians are not often the topic of Woody's songs. He seems to have a more assimilationist approach toward Indian nations such as the Cherokee, who were forcibly moved to Oklahoma by President Andrew Jackson in the infamous Trail of Tears. Woody seems to have perceived the Cherokee farmers as similar to the white "Okies" with whom he grew up. In "Will Rogers Highway," Woody paints a picture of farm tenancy that placed Oklahomans on the road to California. Speaking of the love that the people of Oklahoma had for Rogers, Woody wrote, "Will Rogers was born in Oolagah in the nation of the Cherokee — and a hundred thousand followed him from old Oklahoma to Los Angelese."[38] The Will Rogers Highway or Route 66, named after a man of Native American ancestry, was rough on the migrants, but tenancy and the dust bowl made them refugees on a contemporary trail of tears.

In songs such as "The Chinese and the Japs" and "The Germans and the Japs," Woody made clear his contempt for Japanese fascism. He writes that fascism in Japan would be destroyed by "Allied Cannonballs," and when the Yanks made it to Tokyo it would be "Oakie Dokio."[39] Racism was a key element in the Pacific War. As historian John Dower notes in *War Without Mercy*, American racism was directed toward the Japanese people, while Hitler and Nazism, which had misled the German people, were seen as the enemy on the European front.[40] Many Americans were also frustrated with the Roosevelt administration's concentration on Europe as they wanted revenge against the Japanese for the attacks on Pearl Harbor and the Philippines. Woody was initially somewhat ambivalent about the atomic bombing of Hiroshima and Nagasaki, and he consistently concentrated his rhetoric and music on the ideological threat posed by Hitler. On the other hand, Woody's apparent misgivings regarding the incarceration of Japanese Americans within internment camps is evident in *Bound for Glory* when Woody and his partner Cisco Houston defend a Japanese-owned restaurant against a New York City mob. To hold back a group of sailors intent on injuring a Japanese family, Woody burst into song. At the same time, Cisco made a speech pointing out that fascists were spreading rumors of Japanese sabotage to keep the people of America racially divided. Houston proclaimed, "Listen folks. These little Japanese farmers that you see up and down the country here, and these Japanese people that run the little old cafes and gin joints, they can't help it because they happen to be Japanese. Nine-tenths of them hate their Rising Sun robbers just as much as I do, or you do."[41]

His experiences in California also acquainted Woody with the work of Mexican laborers in the fruit orchards and vegetable fields. In addition, Woody read, and recommended to his friends, Carey McWilliams's classic study *Factories in the Field*. Thus, it is not surprising that one of Woody's best songs was based upon the discrimination confronting Mexican farmworkers in the United States. In "Deportees" (1948), Woody was incensed over newspaper accounts of a California plane crash in Los Gatos Canyon during which thirty-two people perished. The plane was carrying deportees from the Braceros guest worker program back to Mexico. A newspaper account in the *New York Times* listed the names of the flight crew and a security guard, but the Mexican laborers were simply referred to as deportees — inspiring Woody's song of protest that still resonates well in contemporary America. Woody's biographer Joe Klein described "Deportees" as "the last great song he would write, a memorial to the nameless migrants 'all scattered like dry leaves' in Los Gatos Canyon."[42]

Woody's journey from the racist environment of Oklahoma and the Texas Panhandle in the 1920s and 1930s to playing music alongside his friend Lead Belly, to fighting the domestic terrorism and racism of the Klan, and to composing songs such as the *Beluthahatchee* cycle and "Deportees" constitutes the radical transformation of a man and an artist. Dealing with a similar background, it is certainly a story that resonates with me. I have not made the contributions that Woody made to the struggle for racial equality, but I like to think that in my teaching and the raising of my children, I have been able to make some difference. Despite the pushback against a diverse America which the 2016 elections seemed to represent, I have great hope for the future when I look at of the attitudes of my children and their friends. They accept and respect without question the LGBTQ community along with racial and cultural diversity. The following powerful quote from Woody's biographer Will Kaufman well describes Woody's transformation and is one to which I, and others brought up within a racist environment, should relate. Kaufman writes that in places such as Peekskill and the swamps of Florida, Woody "had knowingly put himself in harm's way to stand up to terror in the name of racial solidarity and antifascism. He had by then traveled a long road from the casual, thoughtless racism of his youth, having been painfully educated into a capacity for greater wisdom and racial empathy. In the process, his journey — a virtual *bildungsroman* in itself — had proved something uplifting. Racists are not born, but made; and they can be unmade."[43] Woody's relationship with women, however, did not provide such a straightforward trajectory.

Chapter Eleven

Woody and the Women's Question: Advocate for Equality and Sexual Libertine

In the search for Woody Guthrie, the folk singer's attitudes toward women provide essential clues to understanding the man. Woody's relationships with women were often complex as well as contradictory. In the abstract, Woody respected women and credited them for the essential role they played in the union struggle against capitalist exploitation. However, when applying the feminist principle that the personal is the political, Woody often fell short of his esteemed ideas in his interactions with women. Woody could be quite sentimental and charming, as his early love letters to Marjorie well attest. He also loved the innocence of children, as noted by his letters to Railroad Pete and his later admiration for Stackabones. His children's albums embrace childhood and family; he was a house husband for three children on Mermaid Avenue, while Marjorie served as the primary breadwinner for the family. Yet Woody struggled with family responsibilities, which he perceived as limiting his freedom of movement and expression. He twice deserted wives and children for the road and other female companionship.

In the late 1940s and early 1950s, before he was institutionalized, Woody became seemingly obsessed with sexuality. His letters to Marjorie and other women were increasingly erotic and pornographic, with Woody even spending some time in jail for sending this material through the mails. A number of these passages from correspondence found in the Guthrie Archives well be quoted, not to shock readers but rather to provide evidence of Woody's erotic fascinations. And he would sometimes combine his political observations with sexual commentary in his writings, such as in "Union Love Juice," which will be examined later in this chapter. Of course, this sexual obsession may be traced to the control that Huntington's disease was beginning to exercise over Woody's thoughts and behavior by the late 1940s and early 1950s. But there also seemed to be elements of the sexual libertine in Woody's thought; he compared himself to romantic artists such as Walt Whitman and Aleksandr Pushkin and complained about the efforts of society to censor and regulate his behavior and writing. After his brief third marriage to the young Anneke Van Kirk Marshall, Woody's rambling days were over. He became increasingly dependent upon the remarried Marjorie as his Huntington's disease took over his mind and body. An admirer of women for their courage and beauty, Woody's transformation from traditional to progressive values on race was less evident in his opinions on women.

While Woody's trajectory in regard to race often resembles my own journey, it is more difficult to identify with his ideas on gender and sexuality. Nevertheless, I was brought up in a home that adhered to the gender stereotypes of post-World War II America. My mother was a stay at home mom who raised the children, while my father served as the breadwinner. Thus, when he was laid off from his job, and my mother entered the workforce, he was depressed and his manhood was threatened. I probably gave these gender roles little thought until my freshman year in college, when my girlfriend Cecelia (who was a senior in high school) became pregnant. In traditional fashion, we married. However, our embarrassed parents insisted that we elope, and there was no formal marriage ceremony. Cecilia worked and was the primary caregiver for our child, Pam, while I pursued my education. Cecilia also eventually obtained her college degree, but we essentially followed rather traditional gender roles. Married at such a young age in the late 1960s, we tended to miss the sexual revolution of the era. While I often enunciated radical political ideas, our family certainly lived a more traditional lifestyle. Pam rebelled against this lifestyle by developing a more "hippie" approach to life: she emphasized living in harmony with nature and rejected the idea of being tied down to an occupation or career. Cecelia and I moved in different directions, and, after twenty years of marriage, we divorced. She found a nice partner who shared many of her values. She later died from kidney disease.

As for me, I remarried a health educator, Kathleen, and we have three children. Initially, Kathleen stayed home with the children, but, since our ages are significantly different, she returned full time to work when I retired from teaching. While Kathleen is more conservative politically than I, she has challenged many of my lackadaisical attitudes toward household responsibilities. She correctly pointed out that when it came to issues of feminism, I often talked a good game but was rather reluctant to make the personal political. This old dog is not too elderly to learn new tricks, and I believe that I am doing a better job of reconciling my progressive principles with my daily activities. In Woody's case, his political allegiance to the one big union that assured racial and gender equality was not always evident in his personal relationships with women and his family. This discrepancy led to a great deal of pain in Woody's life, offering important lessons about the challenges of implementing our ideas in daily life.

The centrality of women to Woody's political philosophy was evident in a comment he made in the early 1940s, observing, "I guess that I have lived such a life that most of my thoughts are about politics — and most of my politics is about women. If you think men run the world, always remember the women run the men."[1] This perspective was defined in Woody's 1942 song "She Came Along to Me," recorded by Billy Bragg and Wilco in the first volume of their *Mermaid Avenue* recordings. The song refers to the powers of a woman, in this case Marjorie, and by implication all women, to transform a man such as Woody. If he could truly know Marjorie, then he would know all the women, whose brains and organizational skills have all too often been ignored by society. Woody observes that in reality "the women are equal and may well be ahead of the men." Woody and Marjorie came from different backgrounds, but opposites often attract, and Woody gave Marjorie credit for making him a better man and the world a more progressive place. He concludes, "But never, never, never, never could it have been done if the women hadn't entered into the deal like she came along to me."[2]

"She Came Along to Me" ties in well with the active role Woody assigned to women in the union movement. In *Hard Hitting Songs*, for example, Woody acknowledges the important role played by women such as Aunt Molly Jackson in the struggle for union recognition. Jackson is credited with composing songs such as "I Am a Union Woman," "Kentucky Miner's Wife Hungry, Ragged Blues," "I Love Coal Miners, I Do," and "Kentucky Miners' Dreadful Fate." Born probably in 1880, Jackson was raised in humble circumstances. Her father was a Kentucky coal miner, and her mother died from tuberculosis when Jackson was six years of age. Jackson was married twice to coal miners — the first of whom died in a mining accident. Her father and brother were blinded in yet another mining explosion. Jackson served as a nurse and midwife in Harlan County, Kentucky, where she was often arrested for unionizing activities. During the Harlan County Coal War, she was "discovered" by the Dreiser Committee, which was investigating conditions in coal country. Jackson made fund-raising appearances for the miners in places such as New York City where she met and performed with Woody. She eventually moved to New York City, where she died in 1960.[3] Woody admired Jackson's courage and music, calling her the "best ballad singer in the whole country." Introducing her music for *Hard Hitting Songs*, Woody wrote, "Some folks just ain't quite got the nerve to say what they think is right. But some day they'll wish they had. You ain't a scared of nobody, Molly.

I know it. I've been around you enough to know that. And you can't stay around Molly for even a few minutes, but what she'll speak out something that is so good, so true, and so honest, that it'll stick in your head as long as you live."[4]

Woody had similar words of praise for Jackson's half-sister Sara Ogan. Her song credits include "I Am a Girl of Constant Sorrow," "I Hate the Capitalist System," and "Come on Friends and Let's Go Down." Observing that Ogan's contempt for capitalism was based upon personal experience in Kentucky coal country, Woody explained that her father, husband, and one of her babies had died from breathing coal dust. Thus, Ogan's authentic songs were "deadlier and stronger than rifle bullets, and have cut, a wider swath than a machine gun could. She sings about the Union ... the One Big Union that has got to come ... when the farmers and the working folks all over everywhere get together, shake hands, and stand side by side, and back to back, a fighting hell out of the big rich guys that say they own all the land, all of the hills, all of the crops, and all of the coal and iron and gold that's down under the ground."[5]

Jackson and Ogan provide good historical examples for Woody's classic "Union Maid," which the songwriter later maintained was based upon the life of African-American activist Annie Mae Meriwether. Meriwether had been sexually brutalized and nearly lynched for supporting the interracial Sharecroppers Union in Alabama. A revised version of the song in the Guthrie Archives makes the connection with Meriwether clear, but the more popular and better-known version of "Union Maid" features a young woman who refuses to be intimidated by the violent threats of company thugs and vigilantes. Her example inspires the union men to stay strong and stick to the union.[6] Woody's perception of women exhibiting physical courage was also apparent in his World War II song "Miss Pavlachenko." This song is a tribute to the Soviet female sniper Luidmilla Pavlachenko, who was alleged to have killed more than 300 Nazi soldiers. In an annotation to the song, Woody wrote, "I have a feeling, that if any brand or breed or style of fascist ever invades our United States, from inside, top side, bottom side, east side, west side, north or south side, there will be lots of good fighting women find all kinds of ways to wipe them out."[7] Thus, Woody viewed women in the abstract as equals who would stand alongside men in the struggle against fascism and forge the union world of "commonism."

In his personal relationships, however, this degree of equality was more problematic. For example, he abandoned Mary and three children in his pursuit to understand the larger family of man and the one big union. This decision was not taken lightly; Woody did eventually bring his first family to live with him in California, New York City, and Oregon before finally settling upon a divorce from Mary. While Mary blamed the failed marriage upon Woody's allegiance to political commitments over those of family responsibility, Woody sought to place a more positive spin on the unraveling of the relationship. In February 1940, after arriving in New York City for the first time, Woody commented on his separation from Mary. He described his wife as "a good easy going girl" who knew how to handle him. When threatened by the dust bowl and lack of work in Pampa, Woody asserted that he and Mary agreed that it would be best for the family if Woody went on the road to look for work. Woody wrote, "It's a pretty tough thing to have to be apart from your family for so long at a time but sometimes you cant hardly do nothing else. We didn't have any serious trouble or arguments. She never did give up. She said whatever I done she filt like it would be for the good of the kids and the whole family."[8] Woody concluded that he and Mary underestimated how difficult their financial situation would become, but he appreciated the fact that Mary always put her kids first. Following rather traditional gender roles, Woody did not assume that caring for the children was his primary responsibility, but he also struggled with expectations that the male should be the primary breadwinner for the family.

After rejecting the political compromises of a commercial radio career and after the brief family sojourn in Oregon, Woody returned to New York City without Mary and the children. He fell in love with Marjorie and began to pursue a divorce from his first wife. Marjorie encouraged Woody to maintain a relationship with his first family, and Woody continued to speak of Mary in positive terms, while downplaying their differences. In a letter to Marjorie, Woody explained that he and Mary had married too young and simply drifted apart over time. Thus, he had to leave so that Mary would have the opportunity to find a more appropriate companion. While admitting that he sometimes missed the warmth of a family, Woody asserted that hitting the road was essential in order to find a way to make himself useful. He confessed that in his wanderings he "got a smattering of political understanding, that is, enough to see the general hopes of most of the people, and to make my work play some kind of part in their hopes."[9] Here, Woody suggests that his larger political obligations trumped his family responsibilities, but in many of his early letters to Marjorie there is a tenderness and charm that seems to indicate that Woody was capable of making the personal political.

In a letter dated November 17, 1942, Woody recalled his first meeting with Marjorie after he walked her home from the Almanac loft apartment. A romantic Woody noted, "I remember very clear just what kind of a night it was, and I can see a picture of your face, your hair, and your breath turning to steam in the air in the fog of that chilly night. I didn't know you then, not well, but you seemed so friendly, so sincere and serious, somehow or other, that I will always remember just exactly how you looked." Marjorie was what he had been searching for in his ramblings, and Woody was in love. To Woody, after he found Marjorie, "Life was getting bigger and plainer, and shaping itself into something almost so good and healthy that I didn't dare to hope for too much of it. To me, that's what this old word 'love' has always meant. I've looked a lot of places for it, but I never found this. I knew I would know it if I ever run into it, know it almost at first sight, and know that that was what I was looking for." Never at a loss for words, Woody was rendered almost speechless by his first night with Marjorie, concluding, "But this was the night that I saved up all of my nerve and strength and thought up all of my best speeches and novels and articles, and lectures and treatises and essays and notes and comments and just about then I finally mustered up the nerve to say, 'You're sweet.'"[10]

Woody, however, was insecure about his relationship with Marjorie. He explained in their correspondence how fascism constituted a threat to their love, which was also complicated by the fact that Marjorie was pregnant with Woody's child, while still married to another man. In another letter, Woody proclaimed that in his ramblings, he realized that he was missing love and the intimacy of family. Now that he had found true love with his soul mate, he embraced his responsibilities and talked about finding work and securing a solid financial foundation for his family.[11]

Vowing to establish a more traditional lifestyle with the woman he loved, Woody penned long journal entries to their unborn child, whom Woody insisted upon calling Railroad Pete. In these writings, Woody praised the beauty and talent of Marjorie, and he explained how the Second World War would allow Pete to grow up in a world free from fascism. Woody also envisioned a brave new world with equality between men and women. Woody believed that Railroad Pete would have no problem in the future if he proved to be a girl, telling Pete, "Girl or boy, you will be loved an equal amount. A girl can do just as much in any field as a boy, to beat fascism — although I'm hoping this is one monster that your eyes wont have to see."[12] And Woody was certainly true to his words, celebrating the birth of Cathy Ann Guthrie and championing her innate appreciation for "commonism."

While at sea with the Merchant Marine during the war, Woody also expressed his anticipation of a strong union world free from fascism, but he cautioned that this community of equality would have to begin in the homes of union people. In a notebook entry, Woody asserted, "I have seen all kinds of workers in their union halls and in their homes. And they exercise their minds and mouths on Union subjects more (at home). Your mind starts out around your house with the little specific things and it flies on out to the big and the general. You'll have to pardon me when I say 'big.' There are no 'bigger' thoughts than the Union of your family with the world."[13] Thus, Woody projected a postwar world in which he, Marjorie, and Cathy would form a union family based upon mutual respect and gender equality, uniting the personal and the political.

After returning from the Merchant Marine and enlisting in the Army, Woody's dreams of a harmonious and traditional family were often missing from his correspondence. His letters at this time increasingly focused upon themes of sexuality and expressed sexual frustration. His sexual frustrations were not quelled by his marriage to Marjorie on November 13, 1945. After the marriage and shortly before his discharge from the military, Woody wrote that he was feeling desperate and lonely — and he was becoming preoccupied with sexual thoughts, bragging about how frequently he could masturbate. Concentrating upon his sexual desires, Woody informed Marjorie, "I find that it is my desire to see myself and all others sexually happy that keeps my gates open to all of the histories and sciences."[14] Tension between Woody and Marjorie was apparently exacerbated by her reluctance to perform activities such as oral sex or to engage as frequently in sex as Woody preferred. During his final months in the military, he began to write love letters to other women, such as Annette Berger, although there is no evidence that he followed up these letters with actual relationships.[15]

Although he performed at various union venues and continued to write songs, Woody was unable to find full time work following his release from the Army. He became primarily a house husband, while Marjorie worked as a dance instructor. Woody enjoyed playing with Cathy and making music with her, but he seemed to have too much time on his hands. His thoughts increasingly turned toward sex. Woody also began to act upon these sexual thoughts by writing pornographic letters and instituting sexual affairs. These obsessions were only exacerbated following Cathy's tragic accident and death. Unable to cope with Cathy's death, Woody deserted Marjorie and their new child, Arlo. He hoped to find solace on the road, but Woody was miserable and conflicted. On May 9, 1947, Woody wrote Marjorie, complaining that her letters were always more "about business affairs than about hot passions. You lose sight of the little fact that we found even Stacky somewhere in the lands of our passions. I've tried everything I know to get you to slide out of the business land and ooze on over to the lovers land." Woody concluded the letter with the hope that the couple would be able to renew their sexual relationship, writing, "Dont be afeared so much that my love juices are dropping down into pages of letters to any other girl, nor into words spoke into my other lady's ears. This hasn't took place and its not going to happen. So just keep your girdle and yer pants on, Turtle, and save every little drop of your boxing and wrestling, debating, arguing, blowing, biting, kissing, screaming, fucking, laying and hip swinging for me."[16]

Just a few days later, however, Woody was feeling less sexually frisky. A despondent Woody wrote his wife, "Your old man is in bad shape. You don't know and I cant tell you how bad these last few days have tasted to me. I don't know what has hit me. I've never felt this low before. And when I did it didn't last this long. Homesick. Lonesome. Miserable and every other thing that is lousy and no good."[17] Finding the road lonely and desolate, Woody returned home and attempted to forge a life with Marjorie. In an August 1947 journal entry, Woody acknowledged the pull of the road — especially after Cathy's death, who in so many ways symbolized his idealistic hopes for the postwar world — but he pledged that he would do his best to foster a marriage based upon gender equality. Woody asserted, "If I can just take a new hold on all of my old pieces and grab my hands down here in Marjorie's hopes and around her plans. Our plan to work a good long program of dances of hers an songs and folk ballads of mine. To tour. To travel. To have nine kids and all of them ours."[18]

Despite such lofty goals, Woody could not seem to control his sexual thoughts and behavior. In another notebook entry from that same month, Woody was again critical of Marjorie's lovemaking, proclaiming in sexist language, "I don't really believe in whores, whore houses, nor in whoredom. But I'd like to be married to some pretty woman that had enough sense to know how to give me all of the fancy works that a whore does."[19] Woody was also composing essays that combined his passion for unionism with his obsession for sex. In a piece entitled "Union Love Juice," Woody suggests that love, as exemplified by the union of all people and the freedom of sexual expression, would destroy greed and racial hatred. Woody concluded the erotic piece by proclaiming, "I am the suck and the deathless touch of all tongues. I feel the outer and the inner shapes of your moving teeth. I drink down your jaws sexified, rolly, passionate honey and tell all of you racial haters that you can't even wiggle as a germ in my union love juice."[20]

The desire for sexual freedom seemed to trump Woody's plans for a more traditional marriage and home. He openly pursued other women, including friends of Marjorie. This was evident in Woody's reaction to performances of *Finian's Rainbow* (1947). Woody was flattered that the Broadway production, co-written by Popular Front composer E. Y. Harburg (whose music credits include the film score for *The Wizard of Oz* [1939]), created a character named Woody Mahoney. The character is described as a merchant seaman who has just returned from fighting fascism in the South Pacific. In the satirical musical fable that is critical of Southern racism and politics, Mahoney is a fighter for the rights of the common people.[21] Nevertheless, Woody was critical of the production's conclusion in which Mahoney gives up his fight for social justice to settle down with the female lead — something Woody insists that he would never do. In a piece on the play, Woody exclaimed, "No girl, outside of the union, no matter how hot, how steamy, how active, how shaped up, how goodly stacked, could even so much as cause me to lose fifteen minutes in getting up my road to my next union local." After bragging that he had walked away from many women who tried to distract him from his union religion, Woody concluded, "I'm Woody the union man. Woody, the union worker, and my guitar is my factory machine, my machine that kills Fascists."[22]

Nevertheless, Woody was not quite ready to let go of sexual themes in his reaction to *Finian's Rainbow*. Addressing Pearl Lang, who danced with Marjorie in the Martha Graham group and played the female lead in the production, Woody compliments her singing, dancing, and body. Calling her his little sister, Woody introduces a strong note of sexual tension by asserting, "Never did much want you for my sister, well, just because there is not so many things at my age I can do with you if you're my sister."[23] The infatuation with Pearl Lang was minor compared to the allegations of pornography lodged against Woody in 1949.

The charges stemmed from sexually explicit letters Woody sent to Mary Ruth Crissman; the younger sister of his former KFVD singing partner, "Lefty Lou." Contained in some of the letters were newspaper clippings describing grisly murders. The letters and clippings were graphic enough for the Los Angeles police department to consider Woody temporarily a suspect in the notorious Black Dahlia murder. Woody, however, was convicted of using the mail system to transport pornographic material. He was able to avoid serious jail time by agreeing to enter treatment at the Quaker Emergency Services Readjustment Center in midtown Manhattan. The rehabilitation center focused upon cases of sexual deviance — which, within the context of the sexually repressive 1950s, usually meant men who were suspected of homosexuality.[24] Woody denounced the charges against him as politically motivated slander created by reactionaries who sought to silence his voice amid the postwar Red Scare. He also seemed to perceive himself as a sexual libertine whose freedom to be sexually expressive was being curtailed by the political establishment, as well as by Marjorie, who sought to force him into a traditional marriage and family.

To Woody, the personal was political, and sexual liberalism was a form of political free expression. In November 1947, Woody was writing a notebook focusing upon conflict. He asserted, "Every thing you see in this book is a conflict. Every word is a conflict. In conflict with this system of low pay. And in conflict with this world here of high runaway prices. In conflict with you because you and me fooled around and let the big duds rob us blind and drive us around full of conflict."[25] Woody also examined the personal side of political and national conflicts. He complained that frustrations with high prices led to parents spanking their children when they should be knocking "away at the head of this criminal robbing we live under." He was critical of a culture and political system that sought to censor open expression of sexuality, which was a natural right and a natural thing to do. Woody proclaimed, "Who tries to teach me to feel ashamed of me in my body here is my worst criminal. Whoever hates my body is a coward. Whoever is afraid of my naked flesh can't even see my naked thoughts. And you've got to see all my naked thoughts before you can feel any of your freer feeling to the kinds of good works that you pick to do. There are not a few around me, but many lunatic cowards who've been taught that I'm insane."[26] In this entry, Woody seems to anticipate the later diagnosis that disease might have played a role in his sexual politics. However, he rejected this interpretation. He believed that the effort to limit his sexual expression was part and parcel of the repressive post-World War II environment orchestrated by fascist big business interests, with whom even Marjorie sometimes seemed to be in cahoots.

In a series of notebook entries for October 1949, when he faced an obscenity conviction for his erotic letters to Mary Ruth Crissman, Woody equated his prosecution with the Red Scare and governmental efforts to silence political dissent. He was being pursued through the corrupt legal system because he advocated "one sure cure for most of our ills. Get rid of this blind capitalist system quick." As for the judge hearing his case, Woody had nothing but contempt, proclaiming, "My judge cain't even say the word, sex, without thinking the word, maniac. I'd ought to be up on that judging bench looking down at him." An unapologetic Woody also heaped scorn on the probation officer assigned to him by the court. He complained, "That word obscene means of the low and common people. I think my words talk more for the common people than my probation officer does. He cant force my people to talk the King's old rotten English." Woody concluded that his songs would "do more good for public morals than that stuck up proud head of a probation officer."[27]

While Woody was able to avoid prison time from the obscenity charge, his marriage to Marjorie was rapidly deteriorating. He perceived his wife as part of the political conspiracy to limit his freedom of expression, often symbolized by the desire to pursue other sexual partners and the freedom of the open road. For example, in an October 1947 journal entry addressed to his infant son, Arlo, Woody asserted, "Don't let marriage slow you down." Marjorie was beautiful and a wonderful mother, but he and his wife viewed "the world from such different clifftops that I doubt lots of time if we see eye to eye and puss to puss." Woody concluded his advice by insisting, "No human here among us has got any right to walk up to another human being and tell you what to do, and when and how to do it."[28] By December 1952, Woody was writing that he could not love his wife anymore and that it was necessary for him to keep moving.[29]

While in California, Woody met Anneke Van Kirk Marshall, the twenty-year-old wife of an aspiring writer David Marshall. She was an art student who came from an academic family. According to Woody's biographer Joe Klein, Anneke was mature for her age. She was "headstrong, rebellious, (but not very 'political'), and something of a bohemian, given to wearing long peasant skirts and going about with no shoes."[30] Infatuated with Woody, Anneke agreed to accompany the older man to Stetson Kennedy's Florida retreat, Beluthahatchee. Initially, the sexual liaison with the younger woman seemed to energize Woody. He wrote Moe Asch that while in Florida the couple "kept right on making us up our fighting Jimmy Crow balladsongs while we were off down in their raceyhate Florida jungles and she made up several songs & stories & articles & pieces & storysongs & ballads just as good as some of my very best ones." A few months later, Woody wrote Asch that he and Anneke were coming back to New York City and that they were hoping to produce a new album of progressive songs. Woody concluded, "I've been turning out better & louder & ruffer & vulgarar & obscener & sexier songs at my same old ratespeed of one or more gooduns a day & my guitar sounds different some but better all around to my ears."[31] This resurgence, however, proved short lived. Woody's health deteriorated, and Anneke was unable to care for both her ailing husband and a new baby. The marriage culminated in divorce. Woody was hospitalized; the remarried Marjorie oversaw Woody's health care and finances.

Many of Woody's best songs, such as "Union Maid," spoke of equality between the sexes and acknowledged the power of women. Yet in his three marriages Woody had difficulty translating these abstract ideas into practice. He enjoyed his children and loved his wives. He often spoke about a union household based upon equality, but the lure of the open road proved to be too tempting. To Woody, his rambling seemed to represent individual freedom as well as a commitment to the larger family or union of "commonism." Perhaps this idea is best laid out in Woody's autobiography *Bound for Glory*. While Woody goes into considerable detail about his parents and growing up in Okemah and Pampa, Mary and his first family are left out of the story. Instead, Woody is single but drawn to a young woman, Ruth, at one of the migrant camps. She would like Woody to stay with her, but Ruth also understands that with his music Woody has a gift to help the people. Ruth recognizes that Woody must continue with his rambling and singing, but she holds out hope that one day he may return to her. In response, Woody asserts, "An' I swore a long time ago I'd stick to my guitar an' my singin'. But most radio stations they won't let you sing th' real songs. They want you to sing pure ol' bull manure an' nothin' else. So I cain't never get ahold of money an' stuff it'd take to keep you an' me in a house an' home...."[32] Thus, Woody was unable to reconcile his longing for a traditional home with the freedom of the open road.

The gap between the personal and political in Woody's treatment of women was also apparent in his attitudes toward sexuality. While he expressed romantic devotion and love for Marjorie, Woody's rambling nature was also apparent in his sexual liaisons with other women. He often expressed an unwillingness to let this sexual freedom be controlled by marriage vows of monogamy. Nevertheless, his increasing focus upon eroticism and the sexual nature of his letters to Marjorie and other women during the late 1940s and early 1950s probably resulted from his Huntington's disease, which causes obsession. Psychologist Arthur Falek argues that rejection by society is common for individuals diagnosed with the disease as it "has been associated with loss of inhibition and, in particular, inappropriate sexual advances."[33] Such advances were certainly apparent in the sexually explicit letters to Mary Ruth Crissman and Marjorie's friend Pearl Lang.

Woody's assertions of sexual freedom, however, sometimes struck a more political note; he seemed to perceive himself as a sexual libertine, challenging the narrow social and cultural conventions of a repressive capitalist society. For example, Woody sometimes compared his poetry with that of Walt Whitman, Carl Sandberg, and the Russian Aleksandr Pushkin. Woody criticized these esteemed intellectuals for not writing in a style to which the common working people of the world could relate. Woody argued, "Whitman makes glorious the works, labors, hopes, dreams, and feelings of my people, but he does not do this in the sorts of words my people think, talk, and dance and sing." According to Woody, the same was true for Sandberg and Pushkin, who "praise, describe, pay their thanks and their tribute to my people, but not in words my kind of people think. So I've got to keep on plugging on."[34]

Woody concluded that his willingness to deal openly with issues of sexuality allowed him to advance beyond the work of his fellow American writers Whitman and Sandberg. In another journal entry addressed to the authors, Woody exclaimed, "You can't live one tenth as passionate as me. You have been penned up. I have grown free. Both of you afraid of the female, the woman. Both of you scared of the breast and the belly. Both of you paying good words to my workers, both of you scared of the woman I come from. Both of you lonesome. Both of you lost."[35] This passage may also be interpreted as expressing some reservations regarding Whitman's sexual orientation, but Woody was prepared to push boundaries where sex and politics intersected.

For example, Woody challenged the nation's miscegenation laws, which were not overturned until the 1967 Supreme Court *Loving* decision. In "My Big Mixed Race," Woody celebrated interracial relationships; he wrote, "If there was only one way of knowing just how many bellies rub together in my 48 states tonite, to turn out my big mixed race that'll win out over guns with love and hugs and winks and jokes alone...." Employing sexual imagery, Woody concluded, "This joking and this dancy rubbing which will outnumber atom bombs, deputy guns, all kinds of burning crosses, my miracle of being able to breed and seed and bear six more of my hot blood to stand in the place you tried to kill with all your guns...."[36] But there were some limitations to Woody's willingness to push social boundaries.

Displaying more conventional postwar attitudes, Woody expressed reservations when he and Marjorie accompanied a young unmarried woman to what he termed a "baby killer place." Woody urged the woman to not have the abortion and instead place the child for adoption with a loving family. The woman countered that she "was being more political revolutionary and broadminded, and modern minded" to not bring a baby into the repressive post-World War II environment. Woody continued to argue with the pregnant woman, insisting that her child might grow up to "put the last finishing touches on the very system of profit worshiping that all of us hate and want to see dead."[37] He lamented that in the final analysis the woman elected to kill her baby. In this exchange, Woody demonstrated little support for the progressive idea that true sexual freedom would provide women with control over their bodies and reproductive decisions.

Woody also expressed discomfort with same sex male relationships. After being institutionalized, he complained to Marjorie about "homosexuals" in his hospital ward. He wrote, "Two more homosexuals did go to bed together right here in a bed right next to my own a few nights ago but my attendant here chased them outta there beds when I pointed out the pair of unnatural lovers to him. Our ward has really got forty men here that are well known homosexuals."[38] In this letter, Woody reflects dominant popular and medical prejudices of the time against same sex relationships. The capitalist society of 1950s America viewed homosexuality as a threat to the family, and the American Psychiatric Association classified homosexuality as a mental disorder until 1973. Many scholars of Cold War culture note the extent to which anticommunist crusaders coupled concerns with assertive women, masculinity in crisis, homosexuality, and national security. K. A. Cuordileone argues, "It is hard to escape the conclusion that underlying the excesses and inanities of the anticommunist imagination — of which the image of the subversive-as-homosexual was the most lurid — was an anxiety about troubling trends at home as well as abroad, not least among them sexual disorder." And David Johnson, in his study of Cold War persecution of gays and lesbians in the federal government, goes so far as to suggest, "In 1950, many politicians, journalists, and citizens thought that homosexuals proved more of a threat to national security than Communists."[39]

Thus on the question of sexual orientation, Woody found himself on the side of the national security state in opposition to personal freedom. Here, the progressive champion of "commonism" was on the side of domestic fascism. Yet Woody had demonstrated the ability to transform his views when he changed his opinions on race. Disease denied him the opportunity to evolve his thoughts and actions on treatment of women and what has become an activist LGBTQ community. On the other hand, Woody certainly recognized that he was queer and an outsider who challenged the conservatism, conformity, and consumerism of postwar American capitalism. In a 1947 journal entry, Woody expressed his impatience with those who labeled him a sex maniac. Woody proclaimed, "But if I took the other road these same several yellers would scream that I'm a queer. I fully aim at this time, dear lay man and lay woman, to walk up and to run bare back down both of these trails and to get my soul known again as the two both, the sexual maniac, the saint, the sinner, the drinker, the thinker, the queer. The works."[40] Woody, accordingly, was willing to embrace the perception of himself as a deviant or queer — somewhat similar to the way gay activists in the 1990s began to employ the term queer as a positive description, which emphasized their desire to highlight their differences with a sense of pride. In the 1960s and 1970s, the alienation described by Woody in his journal entry was transformed into identity politics by the LGBTQ community, celebrating their differences from mainstream society. One would like to believe that given the opportunity to continue his journey as a progressive thinker, Woody might have become a supporter of the LGBTQ community and might have reconciled the gap between theory and practice on issues of women's equality and self-determination.

 I maintain this faith in Woody because in so many ways his journey parallels my own political evolution. I grew up in a racist, sexist, and homophobic environment, and despite setbacks to progressives in the 2016 elections, I remain convinced that America today is a far more egalitarian nation than the one into which I was born. Today, I'm married with a family and transgender son. I have worked hard to make the personal political in my relations with family and friends, as well as with my attitudes on race, gender, and the LGBTQ community. It is a journey of tolerance and understanding on which I continue to travel and an odyssey of self-discovery that was aborted for Woody by disease. Nora Guthrie believes that the most essential concept for understanding her father is his tremendous capacity for love captured in the following passage: "Command love to operate in you and through you to heal, to help, to lift, to bless, to cleanse and to spread the good work and the good news that the day of human hate and fear and dark lostness is all over and all gone and a day of new bright command at your hand."[41] Thus, Woody's life as a voyage of unfolding love is an example that continues to inspire despite the detours and disappointments one encounters in life.

Chapter Twelve

Woody's Songs: *Dust Bowl Ballads*, 1940

The trajectory of Woody's life and thoughts are essential in the search for Woody Guthrie, but one cannot ignore the songs and music through which Woody expressed his love for humanity. Thus, the next path for exploration is three chapter-length examinations of Woody's recordings which shed considerable light upon his political development and hopes for the future. This investigation of Woody's music will begin with his most classic and quintessential album, *Dust Bowl Ballads*. Alan Lomax encouraged RCA producer Robert Wetherald to record this album in 1940. It includes Woody's description of the dust storms sweeping through the Great Plains and the human toll paid by migrants seeking a new life in California. The second album is *Struggle*, recorded for progressive music producer Moe Asch just as the Second World War was ending. *Struggle*, which includes compositions such as "1913 Massacre" and "Ludlow Massacre," evokes a note of historical continuity for the progressive fight. And Woody envisioned that the union movement, in which he placed so much faith, would launch a new struggle against the profit system, racial discrimination, and domestic fascism in the postwar period. This postwar struggle, however, proved disappointing for Woody and other progressives because of the advent of the Cold War and McCarthyism.

This sense of disillusionment is examined in a postwar project commissioned by Asch. It focuses upon the convictions and executions of Italian anarchists Sacco and Vanzetti for an alleged murder and robbery committed during the post-World War I anti-immigrant environment and the first Red Scare. Woody was dissatisfied with his Sacco and Vanzetti album, which Asch did not actually release until the more receptive political atmosphere of the 1960s. Woody's disappointment with the Sacco and Vanzetti songs mirrors the personal and political crisis of Woody's life in the post-World War II period. A closer examination of Woody's *Ballads of Sacco & Vanzetti*, however, reveals a musical heritage that addresses essential issues of immigration and xenophobia that continue to resonate in American history and politics — making the legacy of this album particularly significant in a way that is often overlooked.

While Woody's songs covered a myriad of topics concerning the experiences of America's common folk, *Dust Bowl Ballads* is his most personal recording; in this album he describes the depression-era experience of his family and other dust bowl migrants from Oklahoma and the Texas Panhandle. Essentially, Woody was depicting the human tragedy of a man-made disaster — a lesson that politicians who deny the evidence of global warming seem destined to repeat. The human suffering that Woody sought to capture in his music is exemplified by the Shaw family from Boise City, Oklahoma, which is related in filmmaker Ken Burns's documentary *The Dust Bowl* (2012). Unable to protect her one-year-old daughter Ruth Nell from the dust engulfing the family home, Hazel Shaw took her baby via train to Enid, Oklahoma, where the storms were somewhat less severe. But the dust in the baby's lungs caused Ruth Nell to die. That same day, Hazel's "Grandma Lou" also passed away. The grieving family planned a dual funeral service for April 14, 1935 — a day that would become known as Black Sunday when the region was struck by perhaps the worst dust storm of the era. Woody described this day in "Dust Storm Disaster." More family members were almost lost in the storm that halted the funeral procession. After burying his daughter, Charles Shaw, unable to see through the thick dust, had to crawl five blocks across Boise City on his belly to see if his five-year-old niece Carol had made it back to her home. Carol was safe, but the funeral was disrupted, and the family had lost their baby despite Hazel's best efforts to keep the dust out of the family home.[1]

In response to the onset of the Great Depression and to the falling grain prices, farmers in the Great Plains responded by increasing production — just as they had when prices rose during the First World War. However, this proved to be an environmental disaster: plowing vast acreages in the region destroyed the grass that could otherwise have prevented erosion. While some might place blame upon the individual farmers who increased the amount of acreage in production, historian Donald Worster, in his classic study of the dust bowl, concludes that the farmers of the northern Great Plains reflected the dominant capitalist culture. Seeking to explain the origins of the dust bowl, Worster writes, "Some environmental catastrophes are nature's work, others are the slow accumulating effects of ignorance or poverty. The Dust Bowl, in contrast, was the inevitable outcome of a culture that deliberately, self-consciously, set itself the task of dominating and exploiting the land for all it was worth." Worster concludes that the dust bowl "came about because the expansionary energy of the United States had finally encountered a volatile, marginal land, destroying the delicate ecological balance that had evolved there. We speak of farmers and plows on the plains and the damage they did, but the language is inadequate. What brought them to the region was a social system, a set of values, an economic order. There is no word that so fully sums up these elements as 'capitalism.'"[2] This critique of capitalism as an economic system fostering greed and negatively impacting common farmers certainly fits well into Woody's radical analysis of the profit system.

Cultural historian Charles Shindo argues that during the 1930s and early 1940s, the crisis of American capitalism in the Great Plains, as outlined by Worster, was best reflected in the cultural commentary of photographer Dorothea Lange, novelist John Steinbeck, filmmaker John Ford, and folk singer Woody Guthrie in his *Dust Bowl Ballads*. In his analysis of Woody's contributions to understanding the cultural impact of the dust bowl, Shindo asserts, "From Guthrie's dual role as Okie chronicler and political activist, we get a vivid picture of the dust storms, the dislocation, disruption, and despair of migration, the conditions of migrant life, and a sense of the migrants' traditions and values, along with an interpretation of the cause of the migrants' problems and suggested solutions." In taking a more radical approach than his contemporaries, Guthrie, according to Shindo, "rejected the passive resistance to corporate capitalism offered by Ford and was more radical than Lange or Steinbeck in calling for reform. Guthrie advocated a combination of Ford's familial values, Steinbeck's organic worker, and Lange's worthy victims. Guthrie, in essence, combined elements of each position into this role of folk singer/activist and therefore was able to speak to the migrants on their own terms while also speaking on behalf of the migrants to a larger audience."[3]

After being radicalized by his experience as a dust bowl refugee in California, Woody appealed to New York City intellectuals as an authentic voice of the Okies dispossessed by the banks and depression.[4] Alan Lomax was impressed with Woody's March 3, 1940, appearance at *The Grapes of Wrath Evening*, and the musicologist signed Woody for his *American School of the Air* radio program. He also convinced Woody to visit him in Washington D.C., where the folk singer agreed to record about forty songs and talk about his life. According to Lomax's biographer John Szwed, "It was not purity of tradition that he wanted from Woody, but to get him before the public as quickly as possible. Still there was a vérité feel to the sessions, the songs interspersed with stories of Guthrie's early life, his family, travels, and occupations, with some of his memories evoking strong emotions in him. . . ."[5]

The opportunity to get Woody's music before the public arose when R. P. Wetherald, a recording supervisor for RCA Victor, approached Lomax about recording an album of Southwestern music. Lomax recommended Woody as a vocal artist who would make the characters from *The Grapes of Wrath* come alive for listeners. RCA responded with a $300 contract for what would become *Dust Bowl Ballads* — a concept album of thirteen songs. The album actually ended up being recorded on fourteen tracks because of the length of "Tom Joad," in which Woody condensed the novel and film into a seventeen verse and seven-minute song. The album included such essential Guthrie compositions as "The Great Dust Storm," "Talking Dust Bowl Blues," "Pretty Boy Floyd," "Dusty Old Dust," "Do Re Mi," and "Vigilante Man." The songs were recorded on April 26 and May 3, 1940, and the album was released in July of that year. RCA Victor did little to promote *Dust Bowl Ballads*, and sales lagged with perhaps a thousand copies sold nationally. Reviews were also somewhat mixed; an elite classical music critic suggested that Woody's celebration of the common people might provide useful material for more serious composers. A more positive note was struck by Howard Taubman in the *New York Times*, who concluded that Woody's songs were not a "summer sedative. They make you think; they may even make you uncomfortable. . . . The album shows that the phonograph is broadening its perspective, and that life as some of our unfortunates know it can be mirrored on the glistening disks."[6] Woody, however, was not really discouraged by the reviews and limited sales as people were beginning to listen to his music. He was busy with singing appearances in New York City, and *Dust Bowl Ballads* placed $300 in his pocket. Politically, as Woody told the *Daily Worker*, the songs were progressive and "straight from the hearts and minds of the Okies." Woody said that he was proud "to have been born a shade pink, and didn't have to read too many books to become a proletariat, and you can guess that when you hear the records. . . . What I'm glad to see is working folks' songs getting so popular. I'm sure Victor never did a more radical album."[7]

Of course, *Dust Bowl Ballads* has only grown in stature since its original release. The album was re-released in 2000 by Buddha Records, and this release includes Woody's original liner notes. Woody's notes on the Buddha label are preceded by the comments of music critic Dave Marsh, who concluded that "sixty years after they were released, Woody Guthrie's *Dust Bowl Ballads* still deserve their place among the greatest American stories and songs." According to Marsh, the album realized Woody's ambition to attain the literary heights established by Whitman, Sandberg, and Pushkin in "becoming the voice of his people and in a way that remains intelligible many years later." Marsh also argued that in chronicling the dust bowl experience, Woody was able to move beyond the art of John Ford and Steinbeck by telling the story from the inside. Marsh proclaimed, "So the people in his songs are every day men and women, sweethearts sparking in the dark by saying goodbye instead of envisioning their futures, farmers who have seen a great wind plant their tractors under six feet of dust, crowds panicked as clouds turn day into night."[8] In a review of the Buddha release, critic Anthony Decurtis asserted, "Perhaps the lone salvation of human tragedy is that occasionally it finds its poets, the one person who lends enduring meaning to suffering and rescues dignity from disaster. The Dust Bowl crisis of the Thirties found its poet in Woody Guthrie. . . ." In his 2000 review, Decurtis reminded readers that Woody's music remains relevant, writing, "The lessons his songs teach are essential in a time that has its own problems with homelessness, displaced workers, bank failures, and farm crises."[9] And in the wake of the unrest and division following the 2016 national elections and the Trump Presidency, Woody's progressive ideas and vision of the common people of all races united in opposition to corporate greed and racial hate are needed more than ever.

Woody's understanding of the *Dust Bowl Ballads* is well articulated in the album's liner notes, in his introduction to the "Okie" section of *Hard Hitting Songs*, and in the recordings of his interviews with Alan Lomax. In his original 1940 liner notes, Woody makes a radical condemnation of American society, and it is surprising that a corporation such as RCA Victor was willing to include this message on a mainstream recording. Woody asserted that the songs of *Dust Bowl Ballads* did not belong to him. Instead, they were of the people. Woody explained, "They are Oakie songs. Dust Bowl songs. Migratious songs, about my folks and my relatives, about a jillion of 'em, that got hit by drouth, the dust, the wind, the banker, and the landlord, and the police, all at the same time . . . and it was these things all added up that caused us to pack our wife and kids into our little rattletrap jalopies, and light out down the Highway — in every direction, mostly west to California." Woody insisted that the dust bowl refugees simply desired freedom which he defined as "3 square meals a day and a good job at honest pay."[10]

Describing the Texas Panhandle where he lived when the dust storms began, Woody depicted high plains "flat as a floor, bald as an eight ball, with nothin' in the world to stop that North Wind but a barb wire fence about a hundred miles north, and all of them barbs is turned the same way ... where the oil flows, the wheat grows, the dust blows, and the farmer owes." He acknowledged that dust storms were nothing new to a place such as Pampa, but the 1930s were different because "your land turns into a sand dune, and your barn is half covered up, and you see tractors covered under, and farm machinery, and chicken houses dusted under, why, you scratch your head, and you pull your hair, and you walk the floor, and you think, and think, and think, but just can't see your way out."[11]

For many residents of the Texas Panhandle and Oklahoma, including Woody, the only solution appeared to be the promise of agricultural labor in California. In his history of the dust bowl, Donald Worster documents that twenty-three of thirty-two Texas Panhandle counties lost population during the 1930s as migrants left the land in search of jobs in places such as California. Worster observes, "There once had been a farmhouse on every quarter section in the region and now there were often as many houses abandoned as occupied. The people did not stop to shut the door — they just walked out, leaving behind them the wreckage of their labors: an ugly little shack with broken windows covered by cardboard, a sagging ridgepole, a barren, dusty yard, the windmill creaking in the wind. Ten thousand abandoned houses on the high plains, 9 million acres of farmland turned back to nature."[12]

In *Dust Bowl Ballads*, Woody chronicled the dust storms as well as the great migration to California, where the dust bowl refugees often encountered hostility, violence, and low pay in the fields and orchards. Woody's album notes, however, do not conclude on a pessimistic tone as he praises the work of the government camps established by the New Deal in California for the migrants. These camps, administered by the Resettlement Administration, also offered a glimmer of hope for the Joads in Steinbeck's *The Grapes of Wrath*. Nevertheless, the camps only provided temporary relief, and Woody believed that a more permanent solution would lie in restructuring of the capitalist system in a way that would allow the Okies to return home. Woody concludes his liner notes by observing, "I like to wore that highway 66 out myself, and when you turn around for a year or two and look at all of the folks that's down and out, bushed, disgusted, (but can still be trusted), you wish somehow or other, that they could get back to their old stompin' grounds, and pitch in and build this part of the country back up again ... but you know they can't do it unless some things are changed."[13]

Woody expresses similar views in his introduction to the "Okie Section" of *Hard Hitting Songs for Hard-Hit People*, which includes most of the *Dust Bowl Ballads* compositions. However, Woody insists that the failure of the capitalist system broadened the definition of the term Okie to include all dispossessed Americans. Woody wrote, "Almost everybody is a Okie now days. That means you ain't got no home, or don't know how long you're gonna have the one you are in. Sort of means, too, that you're out of a job. Or owe more than you can rake and scrape. Okies has come to include all of the folks that the rich folks has et up. I could sleep myself mighty comfortable with just that one name on my tombstone."[14] In his commentary on "Dust Bowl Refugee," Woody also expanded his definition of the migrants, observing that he and his family had moved to a little house on the back of a lot behind a Chinese family. Speaking of the Chinese neighbors, Woody noted, "They had come to this country to get away from war torn China. We was a trying to get away from the dust and bankers."[15]

In "The Great Dust Storm," Woody described the massive dust storm of April 14, 1935, which convinced many farmers to abandon their land, load up their jalopies, and rattle down the highway. He explained, "This is a true song. It is about the worst dust storm in anybody's history book. I was in what is give up to be the big middle of it. Right in there north of Amarillo, Texas. I'll never forget how my wife and kinfolks looked. That was before it hit. After it got dark, you couldn't see how nobody looked. You could just reach over and get them by the hand and stand there and wonder how it would all come out. It turned wheat lands into deserts. I've seen hills change direction down there." But as Woody made clear in "Dust Can't Kill Me," the Okies would persevere despite the forces of greed and nature arrayed against them. Woody proclaimed, 'Tractors a running your house down reminds me of war tanks. But tractors, dust, tanks, pistols, clubs, gas, or what, cain't blow me down, cain't kill me — that's what us Okies think."[16]

In "Vigilante Man," Woody documents that the migrants had more to deal with than dust as they encountered armed thugs, who perceived the refugees as threats to their jobs and communities — fears that still seem to motivate many contemporary Americans. According to Woody, the song has its origins in an event that occurred while riding the rails near Tracy, California. He and several others were rounded up by vigilantes and herded into a cow pasture during a driving rain storm. Woody and some of his companions decided to sneak back into town, where they were apprehended a second time. Woody relates, "This time I pulled off a joke on the cops and it made them mad. They took me off alone and made me get out in front of the car in the headlights, and walked me down the road about 2 miles. They left me out in the rain by a big bridge. I crawled down under the bridge and got in a big wool bed roll with a Canadian lumber jack. I ain't advertising the Canadian army, but them lumber jacks is about as warm a feller as you can sleep with.'[17]

Woody was also quite proud of "I Ain't Going to Be Treated This Way," which described migrants who were "going down that road feeling bad." The song depicted the spirit of Okie resistance, and Woody was pleased that the number was included in John Ford's *Grapes of Wrath*, which Woody described as having "more thinkin' in it than 99% of the celluloid that we're tangled up in the moving pictures today." Woody explained, "If you're over down in Oklahoma, or along the 66 Highway to California, and want to get to knowing somebody, some of the working folks, why just sort of saunter up along side of 'em, or past their gate, and hum this song — or whistle it. They'll come a running out and take you into the house to try to help them scrape up something to eat."[18]

In Woody's recorded interviews with Alan Lomax, the inspiration and experience for the songs contained in *Dust Bowl Ballads* are developed in greater detail. Woody told Lomax that when the great dust storm of April 14, 1935, struck, he was living in Pampa. Reminiscing, Woody stated that he and some of his friends were simply standing around, "and so we watched the dust storm come up like the Red Sea closin' in on the Israel children and any way, we stood there and watched the son of a gun come up and I am a tellin' you that it got so black when that thing hit we all run into the house and all of the neighbors had all congregated in different houses round over the neighborhood and around our town and we sat there in a little old room and it got so dark that you couldn't see your hand before your face. You couldn't see anybody in the room."[19] Woody went on to relate that one could turn on a light bulb in the room, but the dust was so thick that it offered no more illumination than a lit cigarette. And as the folks huddled in a darkened room battered by the dust and wind, Woody observed that people began to wonder if this was the end of the world.

Explaining that his people were more stoical than emotional, Woody noted that they concluded, "This is the end of the world. People ain't been living right. The human race ain't been treatin' each other right and robbin' each other in different ways, with fountain pens, guns, and havin' wars and killin' each other and shootin' round. So the feller that made this world, he's worked up this dust storm and there has never been nothin' like it in the whole history of the world. . . ." Thus, Woody wrote "So Long, It's Been Good to Know You," describing how the people responded to the dust storms by gathering in the churches with preachers bemoaning the state of the world.[20] In this passage, Woody touched upon the strain of fundamentalist or evangelical Protestantism that was so prominent in Texas and Oklahoma. Fundamentalist denominations believed that the dust storms heralded the apocalypse foretold in the Biblical book of *Revelation*. In addition, fundamentalist Christians associated the dust bowl with the plagues that God unleashed in *Exodus* upon the Egyptians who had refused to heed his commands. Thus, historian Neil Larry Shumsky concludes, "An observer in the Dust Bowl who recognized the common elements in the story of *Exodus* and their prophecy in *Revelation* could readily perceive the happenings in the Dust Bowl as the fulfillment of *Revelation's* prophecy." Shumsky credits Woody with comprehending that the dust bowl to the people of the Southwest was "an evocative and powerful reference to the *Exodus* and *Revelation* that correspond closely with this understanding of dust, of scripture, of God's nature, of history, of current events and of the future."[21]

Woody's profound connection to the people suffering the impact of the dust bowl was also evident in songs such as "Dust Bowl Pneumonia Blues," in which he described the consequences of constantly breathing the blowing dust. He told Lomax that the houses in Pampa were not built to keep out the dust that was accumulating every day, stating, "So every mornin' when you'd wake up, why you'd see where the dust had drifted in through cracks in your house, and it just made ... ripples and drifts all over the floor of your house and wherever the drafts of air went from one crack through all the rooms of your house. Why when you woke up in the morning, there would just be a big drift of dust in your house and in your hair, and your eyes and your whole face that stuck out from under the cover would be just covered up with dust and all of the combs and brushes and things on your dresser would be covered with dust. And breathin' that dust, naturally, there was lots of people that took down with a sickness that was called the dust pneumonia."[22] Woody's song talks about a condition that makes it impossible to breathe and causes death, such as that of baby Ruth Nell Shaw, but in denouncing bankers he made it clear that the agony was more than a natural disaster. In his study of the dust bowl, Donald Worster points out that the inorganic content of the dust was primarily fine silicon particles, along with bits of feldspar, volcanic ash, and calcite, which constituted a major health hazard resulting in silicosis of the lungs. For example, in the forty-five western counties of Kansas, where the dust storms were most intense, the death rate from acute respiratory infections was 99 people per 100,000, compared with a state-wide average of 70. Worster writes, "Many dust victims would arrive at a hospital almost dead, after driving long distances in a storm. They spat up clods of dust, washed the mud out of their mouths, swabbed their nostrils with Vaseline, and rinsed their bloodshot eyes with boric acid and water. Old people and babies were the most vulnerable to the dusters, as were those with chronic asthma, bronchitis, or tuberculosis, some of whom had moved to the plains so that they might breathe the high, dry air."[23]

How to respond to these economic and health threats was a dilemma for the residents of the dust bowl. Woody explained to Lomax that the exodus to the west was not an easy decision, observing, "They didn't know what to do. They sat around and talked there, for weeks and weeks. Hated to give up what they'd worked there for fifty years and been born and raised on. . . ." But they could not pay their debts which included a mortgage, farm machinery, fuel, and groceries. So when the farmers lost their land to the banks, they "just got up and they bundled up their little belongings, they threw in one or two little things, they thought they'd need. They couldn't take it all because they didn't have room. . . ." Despite their impoverished conditions, the dust bowl migrants held to the promise of widely circulated handbills that they would "have a wonderful chance to succeed in California." Woody concluded that he intended to tell his story in "Talking Dust Bowl," but he discovered that "it fits about several hundred thousand."[24]

Woody then pointed out to Lomax how the Okie migrants were betrayed by the false promise of good paying jobs and opportunity in California. Rather than being welcomed, the migrants were interrogated by the California authorities and "at the state line, they made several attempts to, uh, turn us back and to arrest us or to make us go back to where we came from. But we knew, we remembered the old tractor settin' back there covered up with dust, the cows standin' on top of the barn and lookin' out across that dead sea of dust and we said, no, mister, I'd rather be in jail here than sittin' down there on that farm." As Woody notes in his song "Do Re Mi," the basic problem for the Okies was that they did not have any money, and many were declared vagrants and were forced by the state to work for the growers without compensation. Thus, the fundamental issue was money, and Woody stated, "They don't ask you where ya got it, how ya got it, who you got it off or nothin' else, just so you got the do-re-mi, boy. That's the main thing. You can gamble for it, lie for it, steal for it, bum for it, beg for it, do anything else in the world for it, you can even chase people out of their house and home for it — do-re-mi."[25]

As Woody rambled on Highway 66 and through California, he was angered by the terrible conditions in which the migrants were living. He proclaimed, "They lived outside, like coyotes, around in the trees and timber and under the bridges and along all the railroad tracks and in their little shack house that they built out of cardboard and tote sacks and old corrugated iron that they got out of the dumps, why it just struck me to write this song called 'I Ain't Got No Home in the World Anymore.'"[26] In this composition, Woody was reacting to the hymn "This World Is Not My Home," which was popularized by the Carter Family and which essentially told the common people to concentrate upon their heavenly reward and not to worry about their everyday problems. According to Woody's biographer Joe Klein, Woody came to perceive the hymn as "encouraging the migrants to wait, and be meek, and be rewarded in the next life. It was telling them to accept the hovels and the hunger and the disease. It was telling them not to strike, and not to fight back. He was outraged by the idea that such an innocent-sounding song could be so ludicrous."[27] Instead, Woody's version was an angry testimonial to the way the Okies were treated by the bankers, police, and vigilantes, as documented by Rick Wartzman in his study of the efforts to suppress Steinbeck's *The Grapes of Wrath*. Wartzman observes that many people in California believed they were being invaded by a ragged army of the unemployed. The migrant community in Kern County, California, was branded as being full of "drunks, chislers, exploiters and social leeches." Illegal barricades limited the movement of Okie families, and the California Citizens Association, supported by the *Los Angeles Times* and American Legion, sponsored an "anti-Okie" petition to rid the state of migrants. Woody was determined to resist such oppression.[28]

In "Blowing Down the Road," or "Going Down the Road Feeling Bad" as it is often known, Woody made it clear that the migrants "ain't a-gonna be treated this way" anymore. While recognizing the limitations of armed rebellion and social banditry, Woody was, nevertheless, sympathetic to figures such as Oklahoma bank robber Pretty Boy Floyd. He told Lomax, "Pretty Boy got his and he is laying in his grave right today, but I want to venture to say without stretching the truth, that Pretty Boy Floyd is sung about on more lips and more mouths than and thought better of, in more hearts. He's all-around more popular than any governor that Oklahoma has ever had."[29] As Woody contemplated the conditions he described in *Dust Bowl Ballads*, he understood that it was time for fundamental change in American society. As historian Nancy Isenberg argues in *White Trash: The 400-Year Old Untold History of Class in America*, the American dream and social mobility have failed many of the nation's citizens.[30] The dust bowl experience made this fact clear to Woody, and he became a radical advocate for transforming American capitalism with a "commonism" that was multi-racial and included elements of communism, Christian socialism, populism, and Jeffersonian agrarianism. Of course, as historian Jeff Morgan suggests, Woody's contributions extended beyond *Dust Bowl Ballads* as his music and activism increasingly focused upon such issues as labor organization and fighting Jim Crow and fascism. Jerome Rodnitzsky proclaimed that by the 1970s, as Woody's range of vision expanded, "Black militant, woman liberationist, SDS member, labor organizer, student power advocate, Chicano farmer, or hard hat — all would sense Woody was one of theirs."[31] Nevertheless, *Dust Bowl Ballads* remains the best known of Woody's recordings and chronicles the events that radicalized Woody and fostered his belief in "commonism."

Even while living in New York City, Woody maintained a strong allegiance to his agricultural roots. In his introduction to the section on farming in *Hard Hitting Songs for Hard-Hit People*, Woody, for example, bemoaned the hard luck suffered by the American farmer who remains essential to national prosperity. Woody asserted, "The farmer is the man who feeds them all. He's a willing to give you a part, I'd say the biggest part of his crops in return for other stuff he needs, like a car, a fancy ice box, a linen dress, some overalls and work shoes, and a good radio and plenty of eats and drinks — but the hard luck was that you took his crops and you forgot to bring the other stuff down to him. It ain't hard to raise a crop. Ain't hard to miss one on account of dry weather. But when you give your crops and you don't get a dam thing back, well, boy, that's Hard Luck on The Farm."[32] In discussing "Seven Cent Cotton and Forty Cent Meat," Woody was a little more specific, reporting that farmers were earning low prices because the wealthy were organized and refused to pay farmers a just amount for their crops. Woody wrote, "They got them a Union, and they are a Union of Gamblers, Crooks, Racketeers, and Robbers. And songs like 'Seven Cent Cotton' will help to scare them crooked millionaires off your roost."[33] For Woody, the farmers also needed to form a union, similar to that of their labor brethren in the urban industrial centers of the nation, in order to combat the power of wealthy monopolists. As Woody increasingly focused upon industrial unionism in his music and political activity, he never forgot about his Okie roots chronicled in *Dust Bowl Ballads*.

In a February 1941 letter, Woody wrote his fellow Almanac Lee Hays regarding the importance of making soil conservation an essential element of a national policy about which all Americans needed to be educated. Blaming the current farm crisis on speculators and overexpansion brought on by World War I, Woody asserted that "saving our national topsoil had ought to be one of the first things on the list for national defense." He went on to complain, "Other classes of people haven't got even one little spark of real unity or sympathy for farmers or rural people, make fun of them, and treat them mean — and they could be taught right away that everybody stands on the shoulders of the man who stands flatfooted on the land and says, By God, I'm just a dam old farmer, but they just ain't no place I can stand, the land is the only place you can go for something to eat. I know, I been a farming right in here for nigh onto forty years."[34]

In his letter, Woody outlined several ideas to improve the lot of America's farmers. He called for the construction of "dikes, dams, terraces, deeper water wells, canals, ditches, and all kinds of irrigation." Politically, Woody envisioned a union of workers and farmers in a Farmer-Labor Party. He wanted Hays and Will Geer to take an active role in educating Americans regarding the importance of soil conservation for the nation's future. Hays and Geer would constitute a vanguard of agrarians as Woody proclaimed, "It's high time that the true facts and statistics on wasteage and plunder of the People's Soil be a solid rock of a new movement, theatrical, cultural, artful, and in every other way." Woody concluded his letter with a Biblical citation that Hays, the son of an Arkansas minister, would certainly find meaningful, "For Jesus said, 'The Poor shall inherit the Earth' — and we don't want it to be all wore out and eroded down as slick as an eight ball when you get it."[35]

Following up on his idea of cultural workers promoting agriculture, Woody penned a letter to Eugene Saxton of Harper & Brothers offering to draft a series of pieces, called "Soldiers in the Dust," that would describe agrarian conditions and aid farmers in supporting the war effort. Woody believed that a governmental plan was needed so that farmers could get "to the place where they can do the Allied Armies the most good and the Hitler Axis the most damage." Summarizing the plight of the Okies as the nation went on full war footing, Woody insisted, "More and more Federal Migratory Camps are needed so that a camp will be a home and social gathering and planning place instead of a hopeless and tangled trap, which, like the whole dust bowl was laid off onto the weather, but on closer looks, turned out to be nothing but humans in hack, breaking loose and running away from a pawn shop, looking for some hard work too and crawling from coast to coast a dozen times, if need be, to help Uncle Samuel win this war."[36]

As the war unfolded, Woody was increasingly focused on the idea of union, fighting fascism abroad and in America, and forging a new family. Yet Woody never forgot his people, and the album *Dust Bowl Ballads* remains one of the great cultural testaments to the crisis of American capitalism in the 1930s and to the everyday courage of common people to maintain their families and dignity in the face of economic, political, and social discrimination. In fact, every time I listen to *Dust Bowl Ballads*, I shed a few tears thinking about the great scar that the dust bowl left upon my family — especially my father.

As a young boy growing up in the early 1950s, I was able to witness some of the last major dust storms. I sat around the kitchen table in my maternal grandmother's home and watched the dust come through the windows and cracks in the walls, making breathing extremely difficult. And these storms were relatively mild compared to those of the mid-1930s, which Woody described in his songs. Nevertheless, the psychological aspects of the dust bowl and the depression appeared even worse than the storms themselves; my parents never seemed to put the Great Depression behind them. Going to work as a young boy robbed my father of the opportunity to attain an education or learn a trade. Both he and my mother spent much of their adult lives fearing another depression. Frugality was the family trademark. Instead of a private phone line, we were part of what was called a "party line" with multiple users who could listen in on one another's calls. My younger brother and I were often embarrassed by wearing the same school clothes day after day, and regular bathing was deemed an extravagance we could not afford. Saving electricity was also considered essential, and during the hot summer nights my father did not allow the use of the swamp cooler or any fans. Visits to the doctor were avoided unless it seemed to be a matter of life or death, and dentist appointments were simply off limits. I remain embarrassed at the poor state of my teeth, and my smiles remain rather tight-lipped. On Halloween, I went out to trick or treat with a twenty-nine cent Lone Ranger mask and a pillowcase to collect candy. As my father explained to me, "Them costumes is for rich folks." The family ideology could perhaps be summed up in my father's conviction that one could never have too much insurance. We, however, had shelter and food, although I sometimes left the table hungry. These family habits persisted after the death of my father, even though my mother had some money from savings, pensions, and Social Security. In fact, I am convinced that her descent into dementia came after she fell and broke her hip while trying to reach the bathroom in a darkened house. Nightlights were simply too expensive. But when I hear Woody's *Dust Bowl Ballads*, I remember their courage and love against tremendous adversity. I suppose in some ways I remain scarred by their dust bowl experience. It is an important legacy, and in Woody's *Struggle* album I found a historical message of resistance to exploitation that I wanted to carry into the 1960s and beyond with my own children.

Chapter Thirteen

Woody's Songs: *Struggle*, 1946

In 1976, record producer Moses Asch, director of Folkways Records, re-released the album *Struggle* by legendary folk singer Woody Guthrie. Woody had died nine years earlier after spending his last years institutionalized while suffering from Huntington's disease. The record was originally released by Asch in 1946 as *Struggle: Documentary #1*, but the proposed series of political albums envisioned by Asch and Woody failed to materialize owing to the post-World War II Red Scare and the composer's failing health and family issues. Asch asserted that the songs "Pretty Boy Floyd," "Buffalo Skinners," "Union Burying Ground," "Lost John," "Ludlow Massacre," and "1913 Massacre" were released on "Woody's insistence that there should be a series of records depicting the struggle of working people in bringing to light their fight for a place in the America that they experienced." Asch filled in the 1976 re-release with six other songs that demonstrated Woody's commitment to working-class consciousness and his opposition to Jim Crow, including "Struggle Blues," "A Dollar Down, A Dollar a Week," "Get Along Little Doggies," "Waiting at the Gate," "The Dying Miner," and the anti-lynching "Hang Knot." The record producer concluded that the nation's bicentennial was an appropriate time to resurrect Woody's political radicalism and to "give the struggling people a chance to know that one of their own did not let them down and his songs go on and on and on."[1]

While *Dust Bowl Ballads* is the best known of Woody's recordings, Woody used *Struggle* (released in 1946) to give notice that the historical battle of the working class to obtain their rights from the exploitive capitalist class did not end with the World War II struggle to defeat international fascism. With this album Woody announced that the fight to fulfill his vision of "commonism" would continue in the post-World War II American environment; and this fight would end Jim Crow by constructing an interracial union that included all workers. While Woody did not live to see the fulfillment of his dreams — at least some of which were attained in the Civil Rights Movement — he saw value in a rather existentialist philosophy that embraced the concept of struggle. For many of us who fought for social justice and against the Vietnam War, the mid-1970s seemed to usher in an era of personal indulgence, embodied in the disco scene and the abandonment of the fight to fundamentally reform American society. The celebration of the nation's bicentennial brought about a resurgence of patriotism and discouraged the critical discourse of the 1960s. During this nostalgic mood for a mythical America in which the dream of social mobility was within the grasp of all citizens, Hal Ashby's film *Bound for Glory* was released. It essentially de-radicalized Woody and suggested that the composer of "This Land Is Your Land," and America as a whole, had placed the economic travails of the depression behind them and were "bound for glory."

Asch's decision to release an expanded edition of *Struggle* in 1976 challenged this effort to downplay Woody's radical politics and reminded listeners of Woody's critique of capitalism and greed. As Wayne Hampton suggests in *Guerrilla Minstrels*, Woody was, despite many personal and political setbacks in the postwar period, driven by a sense of optimism and faith in the people alongside the concept of one big union to be achieved through a working-class struggle. Hampton describes Woody as "a thoroughgoing-mind guerrilla. He saw his music as a political tool, a weapon in the class struggle. His purpose as a singer and songwriter was to sing out in protest against the injustices of the world and to rally the people behind revolutionary change."[2]

Listening to *Struggle* in 1976 encouraged me to keep up the fight for progressive social change through the late 1970s and the Reagan years, which fostered the growing economic class divide in America. Like many other progressives, I find myself discouraged and despondent since the ascendancy of Donald Trump to the Presidency. This leads me to ponder the question, "What would Woody do?" The answer is obvious: it is imperative that we continue the struggle for social justice. It will not be easy. Greedy corporations are prepared to exploit the environment and the American workers, and their money — which translates to political influence—makes them very powerful. It will, indeed, be a struggle to fight their control over our society and government. But progressives must work to foster a stronger union movement and to recognize an interracial working class. The constant media focus upon the "white" working class plays into racial stereotypes that black and brown Americans, along with immigrants, do not work and are not part of the labor force. Woody fought for his one big union during the most trying of times, both politically and personally. The post-World War II period saw the emergence of a powerful national security state as the United States established military bases around the globe. Jim Crow remained firmly in power throughout the American South. Efforts at reform were reviled by the anticommunist movement and labeled as subversive. Dissent was curtailed through the efforts of HUAC and the FBI. The power of organized labor was curtailed by legislation such as the Taft-Hartley Act. Within this repressive political climate, Woody continued the struggle, while suffering through personal loss and the deterioration of his physical condition. Contemporary progressives need to follow Woody's example and maintain the struggle or resistance. And we must remember that with every two steps forward there tends to be at least one step backward.

    Woody's effort to engage in the postwar political battle through his music was quite evident in his correspondence with record producer Moe Asch. Although a man of the political left, Asch's background had little in common with Woody's. Moses Asch was born December 2, 1905, in Warsaw, Poland. His father was Yiddish language novelist and dramatist Sholem Asch. The family, fleeing anti-Semitism in Europe, migrated to New York City in 1915. After initially pursuing an interest in Yiddish music, Moses established Asch Recordings in 1940. After financial difficulties, Asch Recordings was reorganized in 1948 as Folkways Records. In addition to recording American folk and blues artists such as Lead Belly, Pete Seeger, and Cisco Houston, Asch published African, Asian, Latin American, and Eastern European folk music. Asch is recognized today for the essential role he played in the preservation of American folk music. Summarizing Asch's career, Alan Lomax remarked, "As an engineer and a very canny businessman, he used the record business to keep his rather isolationist countrymen sensitive to the wide range of the world. He's been extremely important in keeping America humane and urbane."[3]

After being inducted into the Army, Woody wrote Asch and his assistant Marian Distler about conditions at Sheppard Field in Texas. He was concerned that many of his comrades did not understand the struggle against fascism, complaining, "I run into about 50,000 good men here every day that sure as shit don't know." Woody was disappointed that most white soldiers did not care about the segregated conditions at the base. He wrote, "Jim Crow is here and it is bad. White and black get together once in a while out on a lecture in the field. Shows are Jim Crow. Prize Fights segregated. Barracks and chow are Jim Crowed to hell and gone. But both sides are waking up. This is like Prohibition. We are learning at least what we don't want." Woody went on to relate that he was impressed by the singing of black troops while marching in formation. He promised to write these songs down when possible, concluding, "Some are inclined to be vulgar and the others don't exist. I don't mean vulgar. I mean sensual."[4] If Woody, who was quite comfortable discussing sexuality, found the marching songs to be sensual, then the sexual content must have been rather graphic.

Woody's concern about segregation in the armed forces reflected his growing frustration with racism and Jim Crow in American society. These values were exhibited in an introduction to the song "Don't Lie to Me," which Woody included in a pamphlet entitled *Ten Songs by Woody Guthrie*. After crediting black labor with constructing the nation's railroads, Woody proclaimed, "Built the railroad and killed by the railroad. Never did ride the nice coaches nor drive the big engine on account of race hate called Jim Crow. But we're a fighting this war to kill fascism and Jim Crow is exactly the same thing as fascism, no difference I can see. And this song will be sung by me and by you a thousand years after fascism is killed, this song we'll sing first thing in the morning in our New Union World."[5] Here, Woody certainly seizes upon the historical importance of rail transportation to the history of the United States. Additionally, the 1896 Supreme Court decision *Plessy v. Ferguson* that upheld the segregationist principle of "separate but equal" was based upon streetcar transportation in Louisiana.

While only one of the original songs on the *Struggle* album focused directly on issues of race, Woody clearly believed that the fight against Jim Crow should take its place as one of the historic battles needed for all Americans to attain a decent life for their families. There was room for all races within the one big union tent. And Woody was particularly excited about the prospects for the *Struggle* album, telling Marian Distler, "I am building a GI House with my loan after the Japs is beat and Asch records are going to keep the walls painted and the weeds cut and the grass mowed and the floors swept."[6]

This idyllic view of postwar family life, however, did not stop Woody from sharing his enthusiasm with other women. While always professing his love for Marjorie, Woody continued an active correspondence with female admirers during his military confinement. One of his female correspondents was Charlotte Strauss. Amid discussions of music, love, and loneliness, Woody informed Strauss of how proud he was of the *Struggle* recording produced by Asch. Woody asserted that the songs on the album were "based mainly on actual scenes out of our struggles to build our trade unions and to be able to fight better to rid our landscapes of slums, filth, disease, idleness, broken bodies and rotten homes, also black markets, low wages, high prices." In exchange for all of her "good letters," Woody had Asch send Strauss a copy of *Struggle*. Encouraging Strauss to pursue her interest in song writing, Woody insisted that the young woman needed to get in touch with her own "empty places and feelings." As an example, he mentioned the song "You Got to Walk That Lonesome Valley," which Woody claimed to have performed in "a hundred saloons, whore houses, jails, union halls, and picket lines." Woody proudly concluded that he had changed the words of the song to "You got to go down and join the union."[7]

Woody perceived *Struggle* as the first of many albums that would focus on the postwar battle against domestic fascism. Before being released from the military, he suggested to Asch a series of songs based upon stories he heard from his fellow soldiers or read about in the newspapers. In his letter to Asch, Woody was excited about five war ballads. However, they reflect a somewhat morbid tone, and it is difficult to imagine them contributing to postwar morale and the union movement. "Ballad of the Big Ben" told the story of the *USS Franklin,* an aircraft carrier subjected to an attack by Japanese kamikaze planes. "What Kind of Bomb" focused upon the flight of the *Enola Gay* to drop the atomic bomb on Hiroshima. The sexually active musician was also concerned about venereal disease during the war, and in "VD Gunner" an infected serviceman attempts to kill the woman who passed the disease along to him. "Three Sisters" related the story of three young female resistance fighters in Europe. Two of the sisters killed themselves when the Germans took over their home, while the third was stripped naked. However, she employed her feminine wiles and was able to kill nineteen Nazi officers before resistance fighters rescued her. Woody believed that "Ballad of the Red Socks" showed the most promise with its story about two soldiers who were fighting the Japanese in the Pacific. One of the soldiers assumed that his buddy was dead and left him surrounded by the bodies of Japanese combatants, but his friend was later saved when his bright red socks revealed that he was an American soldier. The two friends were reunited at a hospital in San Francisco, where the soldier with red socks "meets his buddy that left him for dead and he cant talk on account of a busted wind pipe. They have a big laugh about the Red Socks."[8] Needless to say, Asch saw little commercial appeal in these "uplifting" ballads, and they failed to see the light of day.

Woody, however, proposed other projects that seemed to offer greater promise and would better fit with the union fight outlined in *Struggle*. After reading Carey McWilliams's book *Ill Fares the Land: Migrants and Migratory Labor in California,* Woody believed that cultural workers needed to tell the story of the Mexican laborers who tilled the fields in California. Woody exclaimed, "The other races all have their troubles, but I would judge that the Mexicans catch the roughest end of it all. They are allowed to come in, make their trip north, and then are herded back out as aliens and undesirables every year as the birds fly; only the birds are lots more welcome and fed better."[9] He also congratulated Asch for issuing the album *Honor the Poets,* featuring the work of such French intellectuals as Louis Aragon and Albert Camus. Woody admired the militancy of the French artists and concluded, "*Honor the Poets* is a right nice title, and its high time we honored the fighting poets in our own country. The revolution didn't hit us as yet. I wish it was here and our poets were singing the facts and the truth and the spirit."[10]

Woody was convinced that with albums such as *Struggle* he was in harmony with the French poets seeking to revolutionize their homeland. He informed Asch, "I have always taken the side I thought would help the workers in the lowest places to know their real fighting history, and to be proud to take their place, each in his own part of the fight from the cradle to the grave. I have never sung nor made songs just to entertain the upper classes, but to curse their clowning, reckless racketeers, and to warn the nervous ones that live and die by greed."[11] While staking his claim as an artist chronicling the struggles of the people to achieve "commonism," Woody was angry that colleagues such as Burl Ives and Josh White had deserted the people's music for the shallow commercialism of Tin Pan Alley and Hollywood. He condemned the capitalist system for fostering such betrayal and divisiveness, asserting, "It is all of this spying on each other that causes the newspapers to be full of killings, murders, rapes, robbings, divorces, shootings, stabbings, and every kind of disease, decay, rot, and degeneracy. This is the system which the owners would like to prolong, to keep alive, to prolong as long as they possibly can, because in the wild blindness of it all, they get all of us to fighting against one another, and rob us coming in the fields of production, and going, in the realms of distribution. This is the system I would like to see die out." After bemoaning that capitalism was responsible for the death of family members, Woody concluded, "It drove families of my relatives and friends by the hundreds of thousands to wander more homeless than dogs and to live less welcome than hogs, sheep, or cattle. This is the system I started out to expose by every conceivable way that I could think of with poems, stories, newspaper articles, even by humor, by fun, by nonsense, ridicule and by any other way that I could lay hold on."[12]

Woody followed up this proclamation by proposing to Asch a new series of songs to supplement the *Documentary Struggle* album, explaining, "The way these lynchings, hangings, tarrings, featherings, and blindings have been taking place around over our good nation, I have been working up an idea of an album of records, another issue of our *Documentary Struggle* album." But this time there would be a racial theme to the songs. Contemporary examples of violence and injustice directed toward black Americans would be addressed in "The Blinding of Isaac Woodward" and "Killing of the Ferguson Brothers." The crime of lynching in Woody's home town of Okemah was denounced in "Don't Kill My Baby and My Son," and Woody proudly wrote that Alan Lomax perceived the ballad to be one of the folk singer's best. The oppressive state institutions of the chain gang and poll tax were exposed in "Long and Lonesome Chain Around My Leg" and "Bloody Poll Tax Chain." The final song Woody proposed was "You Are the People's Army," in which he wrote, "You are the People's Army marching out of the hell of slavery, out of the storms of darkness, into the valley so bright; you are the People's Army marching through the fields of history, Over the mountain of sorrow, on to the city of light." In conclusion, Woody told the record producer, "I really believe that in this album you would have a document of the same tone as *Struggle* but brought up to date. The only real criticism I heard of the *Struggle* album was that it slipped too far back into history. Here is one that is happening right and left all up and down the country. I think that you could win the friendship of not only 13 million Negroes, but with that many other Nationalities and colors, poor White folks, and others." Woody said that he and his guitar were "hot and ready" to go on the project.[13]

Asch, however, was less enthusiastic about Woody's new topical songs. According to Asch's biographer Peter D. Goldsmith, the record producer believed that Woody's political song-writing had lost its spark. Thus, Woody "could still churn out long ballads about working-class struggles, but they tended to be rather literal and self-righteous."[14] Interest in a *Struggle* recording focusing on the black experience waned after Woody performed "The Blinding of Isaac Woodward" at an August 16, 1946, rally for Woodward at New York City's Lewisohn Stadium. Woody followed such performers as Milton Berle, Cab Calloway, Orson Welles, and Billie Holiday, and his performance paled in comparison with these stars. Woody had written the long ballad on various scraps of paper which kept blowing away in the windy stadium, and by the time Woody finished the song, he had lost much of his audience.[15]

Asch, nevertheless, had not completely given up on Woody. The record producer was making money off Woody's children's music, and he still had faith in Woody as a political composer. Asch suggested to Woody a cycle of songs on the executions of Italian anarchists Sacco and Vanzetti in the 1920s. Woody accepted the commission, but he abandoned the project in 1947; he was dissatisfied with the songs he had written. In a more accepting political environment and with the emergence of the folk revival, Asch finally released the Sacco and Vanzetti album in 1960. This cycle of songs will be discussed in considerable detail with the next chapter.

Woody, meanwhile, continued to propose numerous other projects to Asch such as an album on Abraham Lincoln, whom Woody described as "maybe the fullest grown man we ever did have for President. Its not no wonder that Abe could look right to the rocky bottom of any pair of eyes on the earth drunk or sober as their eyes might be, hurt, sick, crippled as their case might be."[16] Woody also reported to Asch and Marian Distler that there was considerable interest in the Pacific Northwest for an album collection of the Columbia River songs which he said were written for the Department of Interior while he "was on the exterior." Speaking of the BPA project, Woody proclaimed, "We've asked the weather question, the water question, the drouth question, the job and land and wage and price question, the roof and shelter question a thousand different ways and here is the whole answer, power owned by us that builds it.... If cheap public owned power is not our answer, well, I just don't guess there is an answer." Woody concluded that a collection of his Columbia River songs would encourage other such recordings, "I say the best possible use of any album of records may have is to make your fingers itch to write down your own song and your toes itch to dance it down."[17]

Asch failed to greenlight any of these projects, and the Columbia River songs were not released as an album until the 1980s. In fact, the only Woody political recording issued by Asch in the immediate postwar period was a new dust bowl album — *Ballads from the Dust Bowl* — that was released in 1946. Woody later referred to the album as his "*Grapes of Wrath* songs" that sound "like [songs] Tom Joad would love to hear."[18] In a more hospitable environment for political protest, Asch released an expanded version of *Struggle* that suggests Woody's music still had much to offer in its analysis of the historic struggle of the American working class.

The union idea is an essential element in Woody's thought. Three of the songs from the *Struggle* album deal with the coal mining industry — a logical point of focus because of the extreme danger miners faced underground, as well as the pivotal role coal miners played in early union efforts with the Western Federation of Miners (later incorporated into the IWW) and the United Mine Workers. In turn, unionization provoked violent opposition from the coal operators. Thomas G. Andrews, concentrating upon early twentieth-century labor wars in the coal fields of Colorado, argues that the legacy of the labor and management conflicts in the coal industry included "poverty, disease, discrimination, inequality, global climate change, war, and pollution" with the "environmental, social, political and economic aspects of these problems inextricably interconnected."[19]

As historian Archie Green well demonstrates, Woody builds upon a rich legacy of coal mining songs when he addresses the dangers faced by coal miners in "Union Burying Ground," "The Dying Miner," and "Waiting at the Gate" (the latter two songs chronicle the 1947 mining explosion in Centralia, Illinois). Coal mining has always been a dangerous proposition. From 1884 to 1912, approximately 43,000 miners died in accidents, while thousands more were injured. Increased unionization of miners during the New Deal era did little to alleviate accidents; between 1931 and 1945 over a thousand coal miners perished each year. And coal mining remained a dangerous occupation in post-World War II America. On March 25, 1947, the Number Five Coal Mine near Centralia, Illinois, exploded, killing 111 miners. In "The Dying Miner," or "Goodbye Centralia" as the song is sometimes called, Woody tells the story of a miner who survived the initial explosion, but who is succumbing to the afterdamp which saps the oxygen supply for the remaining miners. Drawing his inspiration from fourteen miners who survived long enough to write farewell notes, Woody's dying miner tells family and friends of his love and urges them to continue the struggle for better working and safety conditions in the mines. In "Waiting at the Gate" or "Miner's Kids and Wives," Woody relates the Centralia tragedy from the perspective of the families waiting at the mining gates to see if their brother, husband, son, or father would be rescued. In the immediate aftermath of the explosion at Number Five, eight wounded miners were recovered, while more than one hundred remained trapped below ground. In freezing weather, while the rescuers worked furiously to save the miners, families prayed and waited. But there were no more survivors, and the wait at the gate was in vain. And, indeed, Number Five was dangerous. Illinois Department of Mines and Minerals Director Robert Merrell was accused of ignoring repeated safety reports on the Centralia mine. A United States Senate sub-committee investigating these charges concluded, "There was negligence in the handling of safety conditions at Centralia."[20]

Woody's anger at mine safety was evident in his comment that "more and bigger and better cuss words" needed to be invented for him to adequately convey his disgust for companies that tried to "squeeze a extry dollar out of a working man's dead body." Woody, however, did not believe anthems to tragedies of working-class people in places such as Centralia contributed to a sense of helplessness or victimization. Instead, in "Union Burying Ground," Woody proclaims that with the death of every union miner in Centralia or the murder of a union organizer in the battle between labor and capital, the union movement would continue to grow. According to Woody, every new grave in the union burying ground brought a thousand new sisters and brothers to the movement.[21] There is a note of inevitability about the triumph of his union faith as expressed in "Union Burying Ground," but other selections from the *Struggle* album indicate that Woody's patience with the pace of union organizing was sometimes tested. And the folk singer continued to be attracted to outlaws and social banditry.

Woody's Oklahoma rural roots are evident by the inclusion of the traditional cowboy song "Get Along Little Doggies" in the *Struggle* tracks. This tune is hardly a romantic rendering of the cattle drive and the cowboy lifestyle. The cattle drive combined elements of drudgery and personal danger. Many of the drives originated in Texas and ended at the railheads in Kansas and Missouri or in the pastures of Wyoming, as in "Get Along Little Doggies." The cattle were also slow moving, caused dust to rise as they walked, and had a less than pleasant odor. The cowboys driving them often survived on biscuits and beans while sleeping on the ground, come rain or shine. Native Americans also objected to the violation of driving these herds through their traditional hunting grounds and would sometimes attack the drives. Cowboys were also the victims of rustlers, and stampedes could cost wranglers their lives and destroy herds. There was nothing romantic in the life of a cowboy, who was really an exploited laborer.[22] Exploitation of nature and labor is also a theme of "Buffalo Skinners." The buffalo of the Great Plains were slaughtered to make way for the construction of the transcontinental railroads. Byproducts of this process were the enforced settlement of the Plains Indians on reservations, as wards of the federal government, and the growth of a lucrative market in buffalo hides. Woody equates the exploitative origin of this market with the abuse of workers in other Western industries such as agriculture, coal, copper, and gold. In "Buffalo Skinners," a recruiter named Crego promises to pay the skinners good wages and provide transportation to the buffalo range. However, the expedition is beset by accidents and Indian attacks, and the food provided for the travelers is poor. When Crego fails to pay his workers, the buffalo skinners murder him. In commenting upon the "Buffalo Skinners," Woody writes, "This song just goes to show you what happened to one boss who forgot to pay up once too often. It shows you that the fellers that was doing the hard work knew all the time that the boss was gypping them, but they got sick and tired of his crooked work and left his bones to whiten in the sun that comes up every morning to some something like this, somewhere in the world."[23]

A similar theme of taking social justice into one's own hands is addressed in "A Dollar Down, A Dollar a Week." Woody denounced installment plans with high rates of interest for the purchase of consumer goods as exploiting the migrants pouring into California from Oklahoma. Writing in his "Woody Sez" column for the *People's Daily World* in 1939, Woody cast creditors into the same circle of hell as bankers. He referred to them as "Low Down Thieves" out to rob the people. In "A Dollar Down, A Dollar a Week," the protagonist purchases a car on credit, but every time he turns the wheel, it costs him. And when he takes his girl for a ride, he is pulled over by a speed cop and sentenced to sixty days in jail. When he gets out, his girl is with another man, whom he shoots and places in the graveyard.[24] In this song of personal revenge, the road to happiness is blocked by the business system, supported by the authorities. This line of thinking led Woody to flirt with the Robin Hood themes of social banditry contained in "Pretty Boy Floyd," which Woody originally recorded for the *Dust Bowl Ballads* album. Like many of the dust bowl migrants, he was attracted to Floyd and other Robin Hood figures, but Woody eventually rejected the individualistic approach of the outlaw. In other words, to bring about meaningful and lasting change, the collective action of the one big union was required — the type of collectivist vision Woody sang about in "This Land Is Your Land."

While there was plenty of racism in the Guthrie family history — including his father's apparent participation in an Okemah lynching of a black woman and her son — Woody's post-World War II collectivist, utopian vision imagined an America free from Jim Crow. Thus, *Struggle* contains the song "Hang Knot," denouncing lynching, even as Southerners in Congress continued to employ the filibuster to block federal anti-lynching legislation. *Struggle* also included "Lost John," a song about an escapee from a Georgia chain gang. Woody attributed this song to African-American musician "Blind" Sonny Terry. Woody described Terry as "the best of our blues men on the harmonica. He wandered around for several years over the south and his feelings are the same as any of us about southern conditions that come from Jim Crow, Poll Tax, rotten houses, rotten land. Sonny played around on street corners at daytime and in the barrel houses by night. He has lived closer to life than most of us. He knows how good and how bad people are and he puts all he knows into his mouth organ. You know the people of his south as you listen."[25] The influence of blues musicians, such as Lead Belly, is also apparent in the instrumental "Struggle Blues" by Woody and his Merchant Marine partner Cisco Houston. These three blues and racial protest songs provide a good introduction to a considerably larger outpouring of anti-Jim Crow themes in the early 1950s *Beluthahatchee Blues* compositions, written when the folk singer was staying at Stetson Kennedy's Florida compound.[26]

But perhaps the most important collectivist songs from the *Struggle* album are the historical narratives "Ludlow Massacre" and "1913 Massacre." Both songs evoke the historic struggle between labor and capital during the late-nineteenth- and early-twentieth-century industrialization of America. This was a crucial time in the American labor struggle, and Melvyn Dubofosky, in his history of the IWW, asserts that during this period "the triumph of the modern corporation and the corporate state did not seem final or inevitable."[27] Woody Guthrie, however, did not draw his inspiration from professional historians. Instead, in the early 1940s he was reading the autobiography of Communist Party organizer Ella Reeves Bloor, better known as Mother Bloor. In her memoir *We Are Many*, Bloor chronicles her labors on the political left with Eugene Debs and the Socialist Party, as well as her founding role in the Communist Labor Party during the early 1920s. Commenting upon Bloor in a 1941 *Daily Worker* column, Woody described the nearly eighty-year-old Bloor as one of the most energetic and youthful people he knew. Woody asserted, "She looks like she comes every day upon something she has been hunting for all of her life. That is because she knew what she was hunting for — and what she was planting — and now to wake up every morning and look all around her every day and see all of this good movement getting hundreds and thousands of times stronger, the day of her hopes and dreams must be today."[28] But in drawing inspiration for the *Struggle* album, Woody was more focused upon Bloor's first-hand account of events in Calumet, Michigan, in 1913 and Ludlow, Colorado, in 1914 — events which she described as "Massacre[s] of the Innocents."[29]

In the fall and winter of 1913, approximately 15,000 copper miners in Michigan's Upper Peninsula were on strike against the Calumet and Hecula Mining Company. The miners, who earned less than a dollar a day while working long hours under dangerous conditions, were primarily immigrants from Italy, Poland, Scandinavia, and the Austro-Hungarian Empire. As a Socialist Party organizer, Bloor was helping Annie Clemence, president of the ladies' auxiliary of the Western Federation of Miners, organize a Christmas Eve party for the children of striking miners at the Italian Hall. As a young girl was playing the piano, someone shouted "fire," and a frightened group of children attempted to run down the staircase. Clemence assured them there was no danger; however, panicked children seeking to flee the building became trapped on the staircase, and seventy-three were suffocated or trampled. According to Bloor, the doors at the bottom of the stairs, which opened on to the street, were held tight by deputies who wanted to discredit the union. Bloor testifies, "Afterwards, I saw the marks of the children's nails on the plaster, where they had desperately scratched to get free as they suffocated." This is the story which Woody tells in his haunting "1913 Massacre" with the refrain "see what your greed for money has done."[30]

In the aftermath of these deaths, the miners refused to accept burial funds from the company and marched the next day in a solemn funeral procession with seventy-three small caskets, amid an atmosphere that many feared would erupt into violence. Bloor goes on to document the efforts of the company to intimidate the miners during an inquiry into the Italian Union Hall fire, which failed to reach any definitive conclusions. Bloor relates that she lost contact with Anne Clemence, but the miners did achieve the eight-hour day, although the company was successful in thwarting union recognition. While the deaths of the children at the Italian Hall rarely make it into many contemporary history books, Woody's "1913 Massacre" ensures that the Calumet strike has not totally been forgotten.

In 2012, filmmakers Ken Ross and Louis V. Galdieri followed Woody's son, folk singer Arlo Guthrie to a Calumet, Michigan, concert, where he performed "1913 Massacre." The filmmakers found that the song resonated with many residents. Others sought to forget the events of 1913 in what was once the prosperous community of Calumet, before the copper mines were shut down. For no apparent reason, city leaders in 1984 decided to destroy the Italian Hall, which had remained structurally sound. Critics assumed that the destruction was an endeavor to erase a troublesome past. Many residents whose relatives perished in the tragic fire were uncomfortable with the demolition, and an arch was constructed in 1989 to commemorate the original site of Italian Hall. During a ceremony dedicating the arch citizens of Calumet held seventy-three roses to represent those who suffocated on the stairwell.[31]

In interviewing residents of Calumet, the filmmakers found relatives for whom the scars of Christmas Eve 1913 have never healed. These people consider the events of that evening a crime that was never properly brought to justice. On the other hand, the company continues to have supporters who refuse to acknowledge photographs showing the doors of Italian Hall opening outward rather than inward, suggesting that the doors had to be barred from the outside. These citizens of Calumet insist that the Christmas Eve deaths were simply a tragic accident and that Woody's song does a disservice to the copper company and town. Nora and Arlo Guthrie, however, informed the filmmakers that they are proud of their father's legacy of employing music to evoke lessons from the nation's past. Many of his songs continue to shed light upon the challenges and struggles of contemporary working-class people — a theme all too often missing from popular music today.[32]

In addition to "1913 Massacre," *Struggle* features "Ludlow Massacre," which is also described in Mother Bloor's autobiography. After her work organizing in the copper mines of Michigan, Bloor was sent by the Socialist Party to work with the coal miners on strike against the John D. Rockefeller-controlled Colorado Fuel and Iron Company. The families of the striking workers were living in tents at Ludlow, Colorado. Fearing for the lives of their children, Bloor describes how the miners' wives dug a cave inside the biggest tent, where they thought the children would be safe at night from a militia attack. On the evening of April 14, 1914, thirteen children and a pregnant woman were placed in the cave. According to Bloor, "That night the soldiers waited until all the miners were asleep. They stole around the colony and soaked the bottom of the tents with kerosene. Then they applied a match and there was a great burst of flame. The miners and their wives came running out of their tents, but there was a roaring wall of fire between them and the thirteen children and the pregnant woman in the cave. As they climbed out of the cave and before they could fight their way out of the blazing tent, the soldiers on the bridges started firing their Gattling guns. All their children who had been placed for safety in the cave were killed — not by the fire, but by the bullets of the soldiers."[33]

This is the story that Woody tells in the song "Ludlow Massacre." It has also been kept alive by the United Mine Workers with a monument to the slain at Ludlow, which is today a National Historical Landmark and is maintained by the National Park Service. Just off Interstate 25 near Pueblo, Colorado, the Ludlow Monument is worth a visit. Judging from the comments on the visitors' booklet it continues to provide an inspiration for those who question the capitalist exploitation of workers and children. I have visited the site on several occasions and reading the names and ages of the children who perished at Ludlow almost always brings me to tears. But the lesson of Ludlow should not be sadness, nostalgia, or victimization. Instead, Woody's song and the history of Ludlow are a story of resistance.

Historian Thomas G. Andrews laments that Ludlow is all too often presented as the victimization of miners who were, in reality, unafraid to take up arms in their defense. Andrews asserts, "By making victimization the main story line of a struggle in which strikers actually inflicted more deaths than they suffered, historians have treated men, women, and children who demonstrated tremendous capacity for action as having been almost entirely acted upon."[34] Thus, in his history of the Ludlow Massacre, Scott Martelle argues that the early-twentieth-century struggle in the Colorado coalfields was an example of class conflict come to the American West. Martelle writes that the striking miners "were fighting for their lives and livelihoods in a tableau established by the mine operators, and against an overwhelming system of corporate feudalism in which the U. S. Constitution was trumped by greed and prejudice. The militia's behavior was particularly troubling as it cast aside the Constitution — martial law was never formally declared — and embarked on a campaign of oppression that seems stolen from another country's history, not America's. . . . Against that backdrop, the striking miners can be viewed as freedom fighters in the time honored American tradition of rebellion against tyranny, and as men — and a few women — who helped crumble an egregious system of political corruption."[35]

In support of the miners' rebellious spirit and actions, Woody did not conclude his musical history of Ludlow on a note of victimization. Instead, Woody describes how the wives of miners in Trinidad sold potatoes in Walsenberg to acquire guns and ammunition, which the miners then employed against guardsmen.[36] These grieving laborers and their families were hardly helpless victims. It is the historical epics of *Struggle*, such as "1913 Massacre" and "Ludlow Massacre," along with the tribute to coal miners at Centralia, that record producer Moe Asch believed constituted Woody's best work.

Asch sought to follow the example set in *Struggle* by commissioning Woody to compose and record a collection of songs on the legacy of Italian anarchists Sacco and Vanzetti. Woody certainly took this assignment seriously, dedicating considerable research and a detailed collection of notebook entries to the martyred anarchists. While Woody considered the Sacco and Vanzetti songs his most important writing since the *Struggle* album, he encountered difficulties in completing the project; he was, at the same time, confronting problems in his personal life and perhaps showing early signs of Huntington's disease, which would institutionalize him in the mid-1950s. Although Woody was disappointed with his effort, he did record eleven songs, which Asch eventually released in 1960. The Sacco and Vanzetti recordings are often dismissed by music critics, but a close reading of these ballads, which will be the focus of the next chapter, reveals the considerable political and social insight often found in Woody's best work. Especially noteworthy is Woody's effort to establish a bond between the Italian immigrants to America and his dust bowl migrants — making the connection that all migrants of the world share a common history of struggle.

Chapter Fourteen

Woody's Songs: *Ballads of Sacco & Vanzetti,* 1946 and 1947

The saga of Italian immigrants Nicola Sacco and Bartolomeo Vanzetti was a major international event in the 1920s. For many people, their arrest, trial, and execution symbolized the xenophobic reaction of the American government to the new immigration from Southern and Eastern Europe following the First World War. The executions of Sacco and Vanzetti for alleged murders committed during a payroll robbery took place amid an atmosphere of political intolerance — the same atmosphere that witnessed the Palmer Raids and the first Red Scare, which silenced dissent and crushed a strong Socialist Party in states such as Oklahoma. Manipulated by the press and politicians, many Americans feared that the Bolshevik Revolution might be exported to the United States. The political milieu of the 1920s also fostered the growth of the Ku Klux Klan, which extended its reach and message of hate onto the national stage. The Klan also began to include Jews, Catholics, and immigrants from Southern and Eastern Europe as focal points for hate, in addition to black Americans — the Klan's traditional focus of its hatred. This climate of intolerance culminated in race riots throughout the nation — in which black people were murdered indiscriminately — and in the enactment of the Immigration Act of 1924, which imposed an immigration quota system that discriminated in favor of white Anglo Saxons from Western Europe. The executions of Sacco and Vanzetti, which occurred within this national mood of intolerance, are largely forgotten today. However, it is worth remembering the legacy of the two Italians in our current period of heightened racial and cultural insensitivity, just as Woody Guthrie resurrected their memory during another period of intolerance following the Second World War.

Many of Woody's biographers tend to dismiss the Sacco-Vanzetti recordings. Wayne Hampton simply states, "*The Ballads of Sacco & Vanzetti* are merely a few weak unenthusiastic, and unconvincing songs with which to remember the martyrs." Ed Cray and Joe Klein conclude that the Sacco and Vanzetti songs were ultimately a failure because they were too long and too polemical as Woody was growing increasingly frustrated with the political direction America was taking in the early Cold War years.[1] A closer examination of this cycle of songs, however, reveals that Woody's ballads fit well with the work of numerous artists who have labored to keep the story of Sacco and Vanzetti alive and relevant in American popular culture since the 1920s.

Just as Woody's work on *Struggle* inspired me in the 1960s and 1970s to fight against social injustice and to examine the historical roots of inequality in the United States, the Sacco and Vanzetti cycle of songs resonate today with me and with other progressives concerned about the 2016 elections. Donald Trump's successful Presidential bid gained its initial leverage from the businessman's xenophobic rhetoric against immigrants from Mexico and the Middle East. This vitriol has culminated in efforts to ban travelers from some predominantly Muslim nations and to get funding to build a wall along the U.S.-Mexican border. Trump and his supporters describe immigrants from these areas as a threat to both the physical and economic security of working-class Americans. Trump's demagogic language echoes many of the racist assumptions made during the 1920s that American traditions and institutions were under attack by immigrants from non-Anglo-Saxon counties. For example: after the First

World War, popular novelist and journalist Kenneth Roberts insisted that Southern and Eastern Europeans were taking American jobs and "were too frequently the source of unrest and dissatisfaction, as well as of sedition and of innumerable varieties of revolutionary and anarchistic doctrines." Concluding on a racist note that still seems to find some traction in contemporary America, Roberts wrote, "There are still many millions of good Americans who hold, in the innocence of their mistaken belief in the equality of mankind, that the person who believes in race purity is a snob: but before many years have gone by, he will be a benighted American who doesn't know that race purity is the prime essential for the well-being of his children and the continued existence of the things that made his country great."[2]

Woody was suspicious of prejudicial language and policies to "make America great again" whether they were directed at Italian immigrants, dust bowl migrants, union members, or people who were already the racial targets of Jim Crow and the KKK. Following the World War II crusade against fascism, Woody was disappointed with the reactionary politics of the postwar era, which, unfortunately, tended to mirror the "normalcy" of the 1920s. Nevertheless, he refused to surrender to the forces of reaction, even as he struggled with personal setbacks. Instead, Woody, with his cycle of songs on Sacco and Vanzetti, re-entered the political fray and attempted to establish a union among immigrants, white migrants, workers, and racial minorities. In other words, Woody's *Ballads of Sacco & Vanzetti* resonate today because the musician was seeking to build bridges. Quite the opposite of Donald Trump, who based his 2016 campaign and Presidential administration on building walls. Once again in my search for Woody Guthrie, the folk singer's life and music provided me with an example of how to live my own life. Rather than bemoaning the Trump Presidency, as a progressive it is my duty to remain active in the political struggle or resistance and to strive to make a difference every day. The story of Sacco and Vanzetti remains relevant and raises serious questions about the American justice system in our troubled times.

On April 15, 1920, the robbery of a shoe factory's payroll in South Braintree, Massachusetts, resulted in the murders of paymaster

Frederick A. Parmenter and security guard Alessandro Berardelli. The authorities charged Italian immigrants Nicola Sacco and Bartolomeo Vanzetti with the crime. Although the two men claimed their innocence, Sacco and Vanzetti were convicted and executed by the state of Massachusetts on August 23, 1927. Much of the testimony in the case focused upon the anarchist and antiwar beliefs of the two defendants. The prejudicial climate in which the trial was conducted is well illustrated by presiding Judge Webster Thayer's reported comment that he was going "to fry those anarchist bastards." The evidence against Sacco and Vanzetti was flimsy at best, and many observers of the trial believed the convictions were influenced by prejudice and discrimination against anarchists and the "new immigration" from Southern and Eastern Europe. These prejudices reflected the American political scene during the post-World War I era and the First Red Scare. Appeals from intellectuals in the United States and around the world, as well as global protests by workers, failed to halt the executions.[3]

On the fiftieth anniversary of their deaths, however, Massachusetts Governor Michael Dukakis, citing the prejudicial atmosphere in which the trial was conducted, signed legislation exonerating Sacco and Vanzetti. In proclaiming August 23, 1977, as Nicola Sacco and Bartolomeo Vanzetti Memorial Day, Dukakis stated, "Any stigma and disgrace should be forever removed from the names of Nicola Sacco and Bartolomeo Vanzetti, from the names of their families and descendants, and so, from the name of the Commonwealth of Massachusetts, and I hereby call upon all the people of Massachusetts to pause in their daily endeavors to reflect upon the tragic events, and draw from their historic lessons the resolve to prevent the forces of intolerance, fear, and hatred from ever again uniting to overcome the rationality, wisdom, and fairness to which our legal system aspires."[4]

The issues of equal justice before the law pointed out by Dukakis explain why the case of Sacco and Vanzetti continues to resonate in American culture. The saga of Sacco and Vanzetti is kept alive in the poetry of Edna St. Vincent Millay and William Carlos Williams, in Ben Shahn's painting *The Passion of Sacco and Vanzetti*, in Sherwood Anderson's play *Winterset*, and in the music of Joan Baez, Irish folk singer Christy Moore, Ska band Against All Authority, and classical composer Anton Coppola.[5] Nevertheless, the case remains on the fringes of popular culture. As LeRoy Ashby notes in his narrative history of American popular culture, the "ultimate arbiter of entertainment as a whole in the United States has been the revered profit motive."[6]

Accordingly, many creators of popular culture remain afraid to touch the legacy of Sacco and Vanzetti because of their association with anarchism. In his study into the anarchist backgrounds of Sacco and Vanzetti, Paul Avrich documents that the two men were followers of the Italian anarchist Luigi Galleani, who was suspected by the American government of involvement with the bombing of Attorney General A. Mitchell Palmer's home. Galleani was deported in June 1919, and Galleanist Andrea Salcedo died in May 1920 while he was in the custody of the Federal Bureau of Investigation. Although Avrich asserts that he finds it impossible to establish the innocence or guilt of Sacco and Vanzetti for the South Braintree murders, he concludes, "Both men, it must be emphasized, were social militants, advocates of relentless warfare against government and capital. Far from being the innocent dreamers so often depicted by their supporters, they belonged to a branch of the anarchist movement which preached insurrectionary violence and armed retaliation, including the use of dynamite and assassination."[7]

This is the historical context in which the trial of Sacco and Vanzetti was conducted, and this guilt by association continues to exert considerable influence. But not all scholars concur with the portrait painted by Avrich. Emphasizing the dignity of the defendants through their ordeal with the American legal system, the authors of the influential text *A People and a Nation* assert, "Sacco and Vanzetti's main offense seems to have been their political beliefs and Italian origins." Howard Zinn, author of the best-selling *A People's History of the United States*, also offers a more positive take on the politics of Sacco and Vanzetti in his introduction to the 1984 reprint edition of Upton Sinclair's *Boston: A Documentary Novel of the Sacco-Vanzetti Case* (1928). He insists, "They believed, as anarchists usually do, that the resources of the earth should be distributed fairly equally among all people; that decisions should be made collectively in small groups in touch with one another; that such a system of equality in wealth and political power would make crime, punishment, and prison unnecessary."[8] But in order to implement this vision, a class struggle would be necessary, culminating in a general strike by the working class and the overthrow of the capitalist system. Thus, Sacco and Vanzetti were a threat to the political establishment which had a motive to prosecute the Italian anarchists. In addition, Zinn concludes that the state was never able to provide a motive for Sacco and Vanzetti to engage in the Braintree robbery, as the stolen payroll was never recovered.

Even with the positive readings provided by Zinn and other scholars, many remain reluctant to embrace Sacco and Vanzetti as victims because the xenophobia and anti-radicalism of American culture retains a strong hold upon the popular imagination. Thus, keeping the story of Sacco and Vanzetti alive has fallen upon the more marginalized elements of popular culture on the political left, who recognize that the saga of the two Italian immigrants reminds us of the dangers inherent in limiting freedom of expression and curtailing civil liberties. Woody Guthrie's *Ballads of Sacco & Vanzetti* fits into this progressive political tradition. It is preceded by socialist Upton Sinclair's novel *Boston* (originally published in 1928, the year after the executions of Sacco and Vanzetti) and followed by Italian filmmaker Giuliano Montaldo's *Sacco and Vanzetti* (1971). Montaldo's film resonated with audiences in both the United States and Europe amid the global upheaval of the late 1960s and early 1970s. In the current political climate of fear and anxiety, perhaps it is time to resurrect Sacco and Vanzetti once again.

When Upton Sinclair published *Boston* in 1928, the novelist's reputation for political activism was already well established. He joined the Socialist Party in 1902 and wrote for the socialist weekly *Appeal to Reason*. After observing the horrid working conditions of Chicago slaughterhouses, Sinclair produced *The Jungle* (1905), earning political acclaim and financial success. Sinclair's novels following *The*

Jungle continued to raise themes of class and politics. *The Industrial Republic* (1907) envisions America's conversion to socialism under the direction of William Randolph Hearst, while *The Moneychangers* (1908) exposes the financial crimes of J. P. Morgan through a thinly veiled "fictionalized" account. Sinclair picketed the New York City offices of John D. Rockefeller, whom he blamed for the bloody suppression of the Ludlow, Colorado, coal strike in 1914. He also denounced Rockefeller in the muckraking novel *King Coal* (1917). During the 1920s, the prolific Sinclair published seventeen books. In his so-called "Dead Hand" series, Sinclair produced a half-dozen nonfiction polemical works depicting how capitalism was undermining American democracy. The author also continued to address political and social issues in his fiction. *Oil!* (1927) focused upon the California petroleum industry and the Teapot Dome scandal, while in *Boston* he turned his attention to the Sacco and Vanzetti case.[9]

In his preface to *Boston*, Sinclair explains that he was attempting to write "a contemporary historical novel" with both historical and fictional characters. For his novel, Sinclair carefully read the trial record and interviewed key participants in the case, including defense attorneys Lee Swanson and Fred Moore as well as defendant Bartolomeo Vanzetti. While clearly sympathetic to the cause of the working class and to Sacco and Vanzetti, Sinclair does introduce a degree of ambiguity in the book. He writes, "I wish to make clear that I have not written a brief for the Sacco-Vanzetti defense. I have tried to be a historian.... My book will not satisfy either side completely; both have expressed dissent — which I take to mean that I have done my job."[10] As a socialist, Sinclair was clearly uncomfortable with elements of anarchism, which he perceived to be advocating violence.

The plot for *Boston* is somewhat contrived, and Sinclair was not a great stylist; his novel of over 700 pages could have used some editing. Nevertheless, one can learn a great deal about the Sacco-Vanzetti case by reading this massive volume. The protagonists of *Boston* are sixty-year-old Cornelia Thornwell and her college-aged granddaughter, Betty Alvin. They are members of the wealthy and prestigious New

England Thornwell family, but the two women turn their backs upon an upper-class upbringing to embrace the cause of the working-class immigrants. This dialectic is at the heart of Sinclair's novel.

Boston ends with the executions of Sacco and Vanzetti. Sinclair concludes his lengthy novel by stating, "To a hundred million groping, and ten times as many still in slumber, the names of Sacco and Vanzetti would be the eternal symbols of a dream, identical with civilization itself, of a human society in which wealth belongs to the laborers."[11] In the final analysis, Sinclair seemed to maintain some doubts and suspicions about anarchism and the innocence of Sacco and Vanzetti, but he was convinced that the Italian immigrants had not received a fair trial. He also believed that revolutionaries and the working class were driven to violence by the oppression of the ruling class.[12]

Woody Guthrie expressed similar opinions about class in his cycle of songs on Sacco and Vanzetti, written in the post-World War II years of 1946–1947. However, Woody's defense of the Italian anarchists was unambiguous. Seeking to expand upon the historical songs Woody recorded for *Struggle*, Moe Asch lent Woody several pamphlets he had saved about the trial and execution of Sacco and Vanzetti. According to biographer Peter Goldsmith, "Having lived through the events as a young adult, Asch, like many leftists, held to them as one of the most unambiguous instances of government persecution of the Left."[13] After examining Asch's material, Woody appeared enthusiastic about the project, writing the record producer that "there is plenty here for a good album" and suggesting "there is a ballad about Sacco, one about Vanzetti, one about the scene of the holdup and killing, one about the arrest and phoney trial, one about all of the screwy witnesses and one about a general shot of the whole thing, the whole story."[14]

Woody was certainly taking this assignment seriously, dedicating a lengthy notebook entry to the martyred anarchists. Observing that this was the first entry in the book, Woody pledged, "I have read the pamphlets about you and my mind is not a blank. I will prove this to you by filling this book with your story, the case, and your frame up." Woody promised Sacco and Vanzetti, "I am going to write your history all over again, because the history of you two men is the pure and perfect reflection of the whole movement of Labor." Recognizing that because of his rural origins in Oklahoma and Texas, some might find him an odd choice to write the story of two Italian anarchists residing on the East Coast, Woody sought to build a union bridge between Oklahoma and Italy. Woody wrote, "You are Italian and I am from Oklahoma, but I have left out from Oklahoma to do some bigger job, just like you left your native house and home back in Italy." Woody believed his migrants from Oklahoma were similar to the immigrants from Italy who were forced to leave their homes and seek a new promised land. Woody concluded, "I saw the same vision that you did and all of us dust bowl families saw your same vision. It is the one big union we all saw. It seems just as bright over your Italy as over the prairies and flatlands of my dust bowl."[15]

Thus, Woody sought to forge an alliance between immigrants from Southern and Eastern Europe and the white working class, which would expand to include black Americans and other racial minorities. It is the type of working-class alliance that eluded progressives and the Democratic Party in the 2016 elections. Woody, who had chronicled the trials and tribulations of the Oklahoma migrants in *Dust Bowl Ballads*, then proceeded to describe the challenges confronting the Italian migrants when they arrived in the alien atmosphere of New York City. Admiring the courage of the immigrants, Woody wrote, "You walked in like you owned this East Seaboard and like you were a free breathing human just down from the hills. You saw in your eyes the brick and the stove, the iron, the concrete, the garbage and people and the smell in your nose was like the death of manure in the place of the perfume you thought you would smell." Woody went on to relate that the challenges confronting migrants in the slums were far greater than they had envisioned. He described what it was like to "pay fifteen cents to sleep on your cot in a room where a hundred men were living on bad alcohol and vomiting up their food, all using the same toilet in the dark. You slept with your clothes on, shoes and all and had to listen to the wild howls and groans till the sun came back through your window again." Woody, however, refused to conclude his message to the Italian anarchists on a negative note, believing that the union of dust bowl migrants and immigrants could end the capitalist exploitation of the people. He asserted, "I can feel your life in me, and the life I feel is not a separate life for each one of us as much as one big life that you gave to all of the people everywhere. You paid your price, your full price, to give a deeper sound and taste to all of us that have seen Labor move. You helped us to see the workers in their right fight and to know free from fear and doubt that the union and the plan will win out over the syphilis and the nightmare of monopoly rule."[16]

Despite his moving tribute to the memory of Sacco and Vanzetti, Woody struggled with the project. But he did not want to give up the assignment, returning to his notebook in the summer of 1946 with the comment, "Sacco could not speak the English language very plain, and neither could Vanzetti. But they lived such lives that the rest of us will read, recite, and sing their words as long as we live. We will tell their story as long as we draw a breath."[17] Asch also maintained his interest in the Sacco and Vanzetti commission, agreeing to advance Woody funds in the fall of 1946 so that the musician might travel to Boston and observe the environment in which the Italian anarchists lived and died. Nevertheless, Asch was concerned with Woody's drinking and erratic behavior. He dispatched Cisco Houston to keep an eye on Woody. The two men spent several weeks in New England, retracing the steps of Sacco and Vanzetti. They were somewhat stymied by having to rely upon public transportation, and it is difficult to envision Woody and Cisco traveling together without some alcohol for stimulation.[18]

After the New England journey, Woody returned to New York where he worked on the Sacco and Vanzetti material. He was, however, dissatisfied with the quality of his product, writing to Asch that he believed it would be necessary to temporarily delay what Woody considered to be "the most important dozen songs I have ever worked on." He was not happy with his research trip to Boston; without an automobile the whole experience felt rushed, and Woody "did not get to go to all of the spots and places so plainly mentioned in the pamphlets and books. . . ." Woody concluded, "I just cant make up these songs till

I've set my foot on every spot related to the Sacco and Vanzetti story and case. I won't let this be one of those hit or miss affairs. I just cant. I wouldn't for no kind of money." By the end of the letter, Woody's usually neat handwriting deteriorated into a scribble — he was intoxicated and asserted that he planned to be "drunk for a long time,"[19] and he refused to write these songs while he was drunk. This was just the type of undisciplined behavior with which Asch was growing impatient.

Although Woody was disappointed with his effort on what he believed to be an important cycle of songs, he did record eleven songs. Asch eventually released these songs in 1960 along with "Sacco's Letter to His Son," in which Pete Seeger put Sacco's words to music. Although somewhat less enthusiastic than he had been with the release of the *Struggle* album, Asch insisted that Woody was "the ideal choice" to document the ordeal of Sacco and Vanzetti. *Ballads of Sacco & Vanzetti* was re-released by Smithsonian/Folkways Recordings in 1996. Antony Seeger, Curator of the Folkways Collection, praised Woody's Sacco and Vanzetti cycle of songs for their continuing historical and cultural relevance. In his 1996 liner notes to the album, Seeger observed, "We are releasing this historic album for several reasons. In 1995 it is clear that the Sacco and Vanzetti case continues to be relevant today when conflicts continue over immigration and union organizing. More importantly, this album contains some powerful songs by one of the best songwriters of the 20th century. Both Woody's daughter Nora and his son Arlo said some of their favorite songs by their father are on this album, and Woody himself referred to it in a letter as 'my most important project.'" In conclusion, Seeger remarked, "Woody Guthrie's songs about the trial of Sacco and Vanzetti continue to document some of the large and enduring conflicts within this nation and demonstrate the enduring ability of songwriters to capture the essence of an event and transform it into poetry communicated with emotion."[20]

While many of Woody's admirers, along with political critics, have panned *Ballads of Sacco & Vanzetti*, a closer examination of Woody's lyrics and music lends support to the commentary by Folkways Curator Seeger and suggests that the folk singer had not lost his ability to communicate the history and lives of working-class people. In "The Flood and the Storm," Woody places the story of Sacco and Vanzetti within the broader historical context of the post-World War I Red Scare and the fears of the ruling class that the spirit of the Russian Revolution might sweep through the world. Thus, Sacco and Vanzetti were agents of change who spread the idea of a workers' revolution on the streets of Boston. For this, they were framed and executed, but their martyrdom inspired common people around the globe and "caused the rich man to pull his hair and cry."[21]

This larger historical perspective is less important for "Two Good Men" and "I Just Want to Sing Your Name," in which Woody extols the Italian immigrants more as workers than as political symbols. Sacco and Vanzetti are portrayed as men who came to America in search of freedom and economic opportunity. Sacco was an excellent shoe-cutter with a wife and three children to support. Vanzetti was an unmarried fish peddler who was something of an intellectual and was always reading and speaking to fellow workers about their rights. Their efforts to improve the lot of their families and fellow workers led the state of Massachusetts to silence them, and Woody laments for "two good men a long time gone."[22]

The details of the case — as a political conspiracy to frame Sacco and Vanzetti — are examined in "Suassos Lane," "You Souls of Boston," and "Red Wine." Woody's background research on the case is evident in his familiarity with discrepancies in the testimony of prosecution witnesses, in the ballistic tests of weapons, and in the supporting evidence for the alibis of Sacco and Vanzetti on the day of the South Braintree robbery and murders. Woody asserts that Judge Webster Thayer wanted to convict the two good Italian men because they were anarchists who fled to Mexico rather than be drafted into a capitalist war where they would have to murder their fellow workers. Thus, the judge failed to accept the confessions of gangsters from the Morelli gang that they were responsible for the crimes committed in South Braintree. Woody's contempt for Judge Thayer is apparent in "Old Judge Thayer," which employs a folk technique of having animals represent humans and comment upon the action. In the conclusion of the song, the animals gather and decide that Thayer is a threat to all innocent life.[23]

The more articulate of the two defendants, Vanzetti, who demonstrated some mastery of the English language, is the subject of two songs, "Vanzetti's Rock" and "Vanzetti's Letter." In "Vanzetti's Rock," Woody claims that through his music he will assure that the story of the Italian men's sacrifices for the working class will be kept alive, just like Plymouth Rock commemorates the Pilgrims. Sacco and Vanzetti were on death row for nearly seven years as their appeals wound through the court system, and "Vanzetti's Letter" is based upon the anarchist's appeal to Massachusetts Governor Alvan Fuller. While denouncing Thayer and the manipulation of evidence in support of the state, Vanzetti refused to ask for a pardon and insisted that he and Sacco were innocent of any crime, concluding, "A pardon you've given to criminals who've broken the laws of our land; We do not ask for pardon, sir, because we are innocent men."[24]

The request was, of course, denied, and the two men were executed on August 23, 1927. The upbeat tempo tune "Root Hog and Die" conveys the urgency of protesters who are attempting to reach Boston before the two Italian immigrants are put to death. Woody's protagonist explains that Judge Thayer has ordered the death of Sacco and Vanzetti because they sought to help the working man, and he has "got to get to Boston 'fore sundown tonight." Despite street protests in Boston and around the world, the executions were carried out as scheduled. Woody concludes the collection with one of his most powerful songs "We Welcome to Heaven," in which he demonstrates his faith that a heavenly reward awaits not those who acquiesce to oppression but rather those who fight for social justice in the contemporary world. Welcoming Sacco and Vanzetti to heaven, Woody's narrator notes the travails of the struggling workers, proclaiming, "If you work for wages, you support the rich capitalist; if you don't work, you're a lumpen to them."[25]

Woody's discontent with capitalism led to the musician's association with the Communist Party, which he perceived as an organization that was at least willing to fight for racial equality and to combat the profit system. Woody, however, was never a totally doctrinaire follower of party orthodoxy. Thus, the philosophical differences which led the communists to denounce anarchists simply did not appear on Woody's radar screen. Even as the party line hardened, the folk singer continued to espouse the solidarity of the Popular Front in which all of those on the political left could march under the banner of union solidarity.

Ballads of Sacco & Vanzetti demonstrate Woody's commitment to working-class protest and his concept of union during a terrible political time when he was increasingly angry with the state of the world. In a 1947 journal entry marking the twentieth anniversary of the Sacco-Vanzetti executions, Woody lamented, "No matter how much my U.S.A. did do, in one hour, or in one year, or in our good two hundred. I hurt and I smile when I say that if we'd not let our crooks mess up so much and if we had not got to be so bad afraid of our cowards, and beat down and killed out so much by our robbers that hate labor unions, we could now be ten times farther on down my good road and feeding and housing and clothing ten times more of us than we are during this early summer morning of the Twenty Third Day of August of this rough year called 1947. My wheels and my plows and my trucks and my planes and my ships just don't move the way they'd ought to move."[26] As Woody's voice was silenced by disease and his hopes for political reform were contained by repression, *Ballads of Sacco & Vanzetti* was forgotten. However, as a new decade dawned and young people were rediscovering folk music in 1960, Asch released Woody's songs of Sacco and Vanzetti, keeping the story of the two Italian anarchists alive and well in an era more conducive to political dissent.

Nevertheless, Hollywood, the nation's most powerful manufacturer of dreams, remained reluctant to address the legacy of American radicalism embraced by Woody Guthrie — as exemplified by the conservative approach of Ashby's *Bound for Glory*. Thus, it was largely left to international cinema to reflect the spirit of rebellion flowing through the United States, Latin America, Europe, Asia, and Africa as world revolution seemed imminent. International and American film audiences in 1971 were treated to Italian filmmaker Giuliano Montaldo's *Sacco and Vanzetti*. Montaldo's film strongly championed the innocence of Sacco and Vanzetti within the historical context of the post-World War I Red Scare oppression, with overtures to the political activism of the 1960s. Montaldo learned his cinematic techniques under the tutelage of radical filmmaker Gillo Pontecorvo. He directed the second unit for Pontecorvo's revolutionary masterpiece *The Battle of Algiers* (1966).

Although the film achieved only limited release in the United States, *Sacco and Vanzetti* generally earned praise from American film critics. Roger Ebert of the *Chicago Sun Times* described *Sacco and Vanzetti* as one of the best films of 1971. Acknowledging that it is easy for a filmmaker to become bogged down in the details of a courtroom drama, Ebert praised Montaldo for maintaining the audience's focus upon the big picture of "how law can be used as a blunt instrument of politics." Vincent Canby of the *New York Times* was less enthusiastic than Ebert, but he was generally favorable in his treatment of the picture. Canby asserts that some might discount *Sacco and Vanzetti* as yet another anti-American foreign art film, but the critic concludes that "because the film calls our attention to a terrible chapter in American history, it can't be easily dismissed." A more complex investigation of the film's politics is presented by Richard Porton's *Film and the Anarchist Imagination*. Porton suggests that by concentrating upon the courtroom drama and questions of guilt and innocence, the anarchist politics of Sacco and Vanzetti are obscured in Montaldo's film. Porton credits the Italian filmmaker with depicting the anti-radicalism of Attorney General A. Mitchell Palmer as well as the historical context that led to the Red Scare and the arrests of Sacco and Vanzetti; however, he argues that the film "shrinks from confronting the anarchists' belief in violence and the propaganda of the deed."[27]

The radical politics of Sacco and Vanzetti were acknowledged in Peter Miller's 2007 documentary film *Sacco and Vanzetti*. In his film the director argues that the Italian immigrants were persecuted and prosecuted for their ethnicity and anarchist ideas within a xenophobic political atmosphere. Miller perceives disturbing parallels between the political environment that led to the fates of Sacco and Vanzetti and contemporary immigration restrictions and the limitations placed upon civil liberties in the wake of the 9/11 terrorist attacks. He asserts, "The case clearly has urgent lessons to offer Americans nearly eighty years after its tragic conclusion. As in the Red Scare of Sacco and Vanzetti's time, present-day Americans have allowed fear and jingoism to erode our civil liberties, scapegoat immigrants, and compromise our judicial system." A nice touch is to conclude the film with Arlo Guthrie performing his father's song "Red Wine" from *Ballads of Sacco & Vanzetti*, which Arlo insists was one of his father's favorite compositions. Miller's film, which was also recognized by the Erik Barnouw Film Award Committee of the Organization of American Historians, was praised by film critics, who emphasized the contemporary parallels with the Sacco-Vanzetti story. J. Hoberman of the *Village Voice* concluded his positive review by noting, "It scarcely needs be said how much the case has to do with contempt for foreigners, legal injustice, and xenophobic terror."[28]

The Presidential election of 2016, in which Donald Trump triumphed on a platform of opposing immigration and refugees, makes the story of Sacco and Vanzetti even more relevant. American voters have seemingly abandoned the notion of America being a beacon for freedom. Lisa McGirr examines the legacy of the Sacco and Vanzetti case in an article for the *Journal of American History*. She suggests, "It was the location of the trial in the United States as a world power that above all explains the case's resonance." McGirr emphasizes that Americans and the global community are often frustrated by the gap between the rhetoric of the United States as a beacon for liberty and the realities of inequality and injustice in the land of the free and the home of the brave. The historian concludes her analysis of global protests against the executions of Sacco and Vanzetti by asserting, "Despite the deaf ears of United States officials to the international outcry, its legitimacy was obvious to millions of citizens of the world. A country claiming global influence — partly based on universal values of democracy and freedom — is the rightful subject of international criticism when free institutions and democratic values appear to fail. In a world ever more shaped by the United States, that holds true as much today as it did in the 1920s."[29]

It is the universal themes of justice, equality, and democracy that elicited the attention of Upton Sinclair, Woody Guthrie, Giuliano Montaldo, and Peter Miller. The travails of Sacco and Vanzetti will continue to resonate within popular culture, as long as people are motivated by the struggle for economic and political democracy and against injustice in the world. Thus, Woody's *Ballads of Sacco & Vanzetti* remain valuable because they help keep the story of the Italian immigrants alive in a nation where demagogues periodically employ xenophobic fears to scapegoat immigrants and refugees. Rather than pitting a white working-class against minorities and immigrants by creating or emphasizing political, racial, ethnic, and religious divisions, Woody proposed a policy of inclusion and justice for all workers and common people. Long live Sacco and Vanzetti and the "commonism" of Woody Guthrie.

Chapter Fifteen

Woody's Children: Arlo Guthrie, Bob Dylan, and Bruce Springsteen

The music contained in albums such as *Dust Bowl Ballads*, *Struggle*, and *Ballads of Sacco & Vanzetti* helped shape my political and social consciousness, reconnecting me to the difficulties my parents endured during the Great Depression and World War II, establishing a foundation for my education into the history of the American working class, and presenting a model of social activism for me to follow. However, I was not introduced to this protest music in my non-musical home. Not only did my family not make music, but we did not even own a record player — although my mother did listen to country music and baseball on the local radio station. In fact, never having been exposed to recorded music, I amused my first-grade teacher (we had no public kindergarten where I went to school) when I assumed that artists such as Elvis Presley simply showed up at the Childress radio station to perform their songs. But as a teenager I purchased a record player and brought rock and roll into the household, much to my father's chagrin. I even bought a used electric guitar and a small amplifier, but I lacked the talent to become a guitar hero. Nevertheless, the records did begin to change my life as I listened to the music of the Beatles, Rolling Stones, Bob Dylan, and the Doors.

I did not initially own any albums by Woody. His work was introduced to me through his interpreters, such as Bob Dylan, Tom Paxton, Phil Ochs, Pete Seeger, Arlo Guthrie, Ramblin' Jack Elliott, and later Bruce Springsteen. These artists educated me on the powerful political messages contained in Woody's songs; in school I had only been exposed to sanitized versions of "This Land Is Your Land," which failed to include his radical fifth and sixth verses challenging private property. While Woody was hospitalized during the 1950s, the singer was de-radicalized. Robert Santelli notes, "For some teachers in American schools 'This Land Is Your Land' was the perfect musical counterpoint to the evil Communist empire." Woody's song became the anthem for American exceptionalism during the Cold War because "the redwood forests stood strong and mighty, just like America."[1]

However, American bombs falling upon poor villagers in Vietnam and police dogs being used against protesting black children convinced many young people in the 1960s that the reality of America was not quite so simple. Woody's interpreters made it their mission to assure that his broader critique of American capitalism and his championing of "commonism" were made available to all his listeners and admirers. Thus, Woody's legacy has been kept alive by a plethora of musicians, sometimes referred to as "Woody's children." All of these artists deserve attention for their efforts to keep Woody's music and memory alive and relevant, but I will concentrate my attention upon three artists whose recordings have encouraged me to become more engaged in my search for Woody Guthrie. In addition, I have had the pleasure to see Arlo Guthrie, Bob Dylan, and Bruce Springsteen in concert on several occasions.

Woody, thus, may be perceived as part of a music protest legacy that resonates with and celebrates the working class and exemplifies the role played by indigenous radicalism in American politics and culture. Woody would likely be delighted at his inclusion in Bryan Garman's study, *A Race of Singers: Whitman's Working Class Hero from Guthrie to Springsteen* — although in his journals Woody often suggested that his appreciation for the language of the people surpassed the more flowery rhetoric of Whitman.[2] In a similar vein, Wayne Hampton describes Woody as a guerrilla minstrel whose approach to music and politics fits well with Joe Hill, John Lennon, and Bob Dylan. In accounting for the continuing relevance of Woody's music so many years after the folk singer's death, Hampton concludes, "Woody Guthrie was not just a musician for the sake of the music. He was a thoroughgoing mind guerrilla. He saw his music as a political tool, a weapon in the class struggle. His purpose as a singer and songwriter was not to preserve the old songs for posterity; his mission was to sing out in protest against the injustices of the world and to rally the people behind revolutionary change. To him, a singing people was a powerful revolutionary strategy and force. Moreover, his vision of the future was crouched in a musical metaphor. He saw a singing people and a singing world in which one people would live together in harmony."[3]

The first interpreter of this message that I was able to observe in concert was Woody's son, Arlo. Arlo Guthrie was born July 10, 1947, in Coney Island, only five months after the death of Stackabones. Woody fled memories of Cathy for the West Coast, where he visited friends and performed his Columbia River ballads at a Seattle convention for the National Association of Rural Electric Cooperatives. He cancelled engagements, however, as the birth of his second child with Marjorie drew near. He told the *People's Daily World*, "If I can get back in time to catch him right early maybe I can talk him (or her) into taking up the bones, tambourines, silver spoons, or to travel with us and knock off my rhythms on my oatmeal box."[4] Despite the pressures of replacing Cathy in his father's affections and attempting to follow in Woody's footsteps as a musician, Arlo accepted the challenge and was able to forge a successful musical career of his own.

Arlo's birth was followed in short order by the arrivals of Joady Ben Guthrie — named after Steinbeck's Tom Joad — on December 25, 1948, and Nora Lee Guthrie on January 2, 1950. While Marjorie worked as a dance teacher, Woody stayed home with the three young children. His moods during this period from 1947 to 1950 varied wildly, as Woody's journals well attest. He loved the children and doted upon them, composing numerous children's songs on daily activities, such as bathing as with "Cleano." Nevertheless, he often seemed bored, and his journals are filled with numerous song topics and project ideas he garnered from the newspaper headlines. His relationship with Marjorie was in trouble, and Woody's behavior was often quite erratic. He wrote intimate letters to other women and often disappeared for days at a time. Woody was also not much of a disciplinarian, and he often allowed the young children to do as they pleased. He believed that learning by experience was the best way for the children to learn, and he usually left a considerable mess for Marjorie to clean up after she returned home from work. And at times, Woody could evidently be quite cruel. Joe Klein relates a story told by radio personality John Henry Faulk about an incident that occurred when he was visiting Woody in 1949. They were walking along the beach when Arlo started crying, and Woody was frustrated when he could not get the boy to stop wailing. As an incredulous Faulk looked on, Woody grabbed a handful of sand and shoved it into Arlo's mouth. Faulk interceded to stop the abuse, "and Woody, stung and embarrassed, tried his best to comfort his son."[5]

In his meditations on his father, Arlo does not usually choose to dwell upon such negative memories. Instead, he recalls his father buying him an expensive guitar when he was only eight years of age and while the Guthrie family was strapped for cash. But Arlo's recollections of his father are limited. He observed in 1965 that his father was hospitalized when Arlo was only six years of age. Arlo could remember only a few things about living with his father, such as "walking on Coney Island, the sounds of his typewriter, and fragments like that." Of course, Arlo recounted that his siblings, Joady and Nora, had less interaction with their famous father at home. Most of their time with Woody "was visiting him in the hospital on weekends, or bringing him home for weekends. And that went on for 15 years."[6]

As a young boy, Arlo was often embarrassed by his ailing father's difficulties walking, which made him look like a stumbling drunk. Nevertheless, Marjorie insisted that Arlo try to connect with his father. Despite being remarried and eschewing the nightclub scene, Marjorie made sure that an underage Arlo was able to see Lead Belly, Ramblin' Jack Elliott, and Cisco Houston perform on stage. Arlo's biographer Hank Reineke asserts that Marjorie "was, in her own way, helping her eldest understand not only who his absentee father was but what Woody represented to many people. In a sense, by trying to get Arlo to understand who Woody was she was helping her son come to terms with who he was." Despite this difficult balancing act, Marjorie believed she succeeded in making the connection. She told *Newsweek* that Arlo and Woody "had a spiritual link. They listened to music even when Woody couldn't talk anymore. There was that common bond."[7]

In addition, Arlo loved playing the guitar and harmonica much more than he enjoyed school. He attended the progressive Woodward School in Brooklyn for the first eight years of his education and graduated in 1968 from the Stockbridge School in Massachusetts. Arlo was also briefly enrolled at Rocky Mountain College in Billings, Montana, but, like many youth in the 1960s, Arlo grew restive with formal education. Instead, he began to make his mark on the music and emerging counterculture scene with his recording "Alice's Restaurant Massacre," a talking blues number that resonated with listeners despite being eighteen minutes and thirty-four seconds long. "Alice's Restaurant" relates the story of Arlo's arrest on Thanksgiving Day 1965 for illegally dumping garbage, from the home of his friends Ray and Alice Brock, onto private property after he had discovered that the local landfill was closed for the holidays. Alice Brock, who was featured in the song, was a former librarian at the Stockbridge School with whom Arlo had formed a friendship.

This brief brush with the law, supposedly based on actual events, ended up being fortunate for Arlo. Because of his criminal record for littering, Arlo was found unfit for military service when he was ordered to report for induction. Thus, "Alice's Restaurant" lampoons the arbitrary nature of the decisions made by the authorities in charge of the Vietnam War, much like Joseph Heller's *Catch-22* (1955) ridicules the decisions made by military leaders in World

War II. Counterculture radio host Bob Foss (of New York City station WBAI) continually played a tape recording of "Alice's Restaurant" on his *Radio Unnamable* program in 1967. After this, Arlo earned his first recording contract, and the song became a staple on college and counterculture radio stations.[8] "Alice's Restaurant," which was hugely popular among the nation's youth, was followed by a film, also called *Alice's Restaurant,* starring Arlo as himself. The film was directed by Arthur Penn, who had been a favorite of the counterculture crowd since the release of his 1967 film, *Bonnie and Clyde.* In this film, Arlo Guthrie's ability to bridge the protests of the 1930s and the dissent of the 1960s was demonstrated by several scenes featuring Arlo interacting with his hospitalized father. Woody, who was deceased by the time the film was made, was played by Joseph Boley. Arlo tends to downplay the anti-Vietnam War politics in both the song and film. He perceived his work as a general critique of stupidity by authority figures. Director Arthur Penn, however, viewed the film as part of the counterculture movement within the political milieu of the 1960s. Penn insisted, "I wanted to show that the U.S. is a country paralyzed by fear, that people were afraid of losing all they hold dear to them. It's the new generation that's trying to save everything." The filmmaker, however, also recognized the limitations of the counterculture, noting that the characters in *Alice's Restaurant* were white and failed to represent the working class and minorities. Thus, *Alice's Restaurant* was a "bourgeois film." Commenting upon the film's ending, when Alice (Patt Quinn) stands alone and stares blankly into the distance, Penn revealed that he intended to portray the inevitable passing of the counterculture. He asserted, "In fact, that last image of Alice on the church steps is intended to freeze time, to say that this paradise doesn't exist anymore, it can only endure in memory."[9]

The film resonated with audiences and grossed over six million dollars in the United States, making it the twenty-first highest grossing film of 1969 and earning Penn an Academy Award nomination for Best Director.[10] *Alice's Restaurant,* both the recording and the film, made Arlo a significant counterculture figure. In 1969, he appeared at the Woodstock Musical Festival, performing his song "Coming into

Los Angeles," which was featured in Michael Wadleigh's documentary film of the iconic concert. While Woody's voice was silenced by disease, the folk-protest music tradition that Woody embraced was kept alive by his son.

The counterculture, as Arthur Penn suggested, faded, but the same cannot be said for Arlo Guthrie. He continues to record, sing, and entertain audiences into his seventh decade. Arlo has enjoyed commercial and critical success, with singles such as "City of New Orleans" and albums such as *Amigos* (1976), while entertaining countless audiences with the hilarious "Motorcycle Song." In 1991, Arlo purchased the church in Great Barrington, Massachusetts, which had served as a home for Alice and Ray Brock. He converted it into the Guthrie Center, which provides health, cultural, and social services for the community. Arlo has also kept his father's legacy alive by performing Woody's songs in concert with Pete Seeger and Ramblin' Jack Elliott. In addition, he has passed the Guthrie musical torch to his own children. He plays and performs a Guthrie Family Values Tour with his son Abe, his grandson Krishna, and his daughters Sarah Lee and Cathy. Arlo's biographer Hank Reineke concludes, "It's possible that Guthrie will be best remembered not for his impressive recorded legacy, but for his engaging stage presence, his considerable musical skills, and his abilities as a raconteur in the manner of Will Rogers and Woody Guthrie. Perhaps Arlo's most important contribution has been his capacity to encourage concertgoers around the world to 'keep the dream alive' by existing and acting, in his father's terminology, as 'Hoping Machines.'"[11]

Reineke's observations certainly re-enforce my experience attending perhaps a half dozen Arlo performances over the years. In fact, one of my great joys in life has been introducing my children to the magic of Arlo's show persona; regardless of their preference for other musical genres, they were delighted with Arlo's stories and performance. It is a family legacy which I am proud to have given my children. In my personal search for Woody Guthrie, I have been most moved by Arlo's performances of his father's songs, such as "Deportees," "Pretty Boy Floyd," "1913 Massacre," and, of course, "This

Land Is Your Land." Of special significance to me was the opportunity to see and hear Arlo present many of his father's songs in Okemah at a concert celebrating Woody's centennial. I felt inspired at this concert to maintain the struggle for a more egalitarian America and world, which Woody exemplified in his life and music. It seemed that I was in Woody's union place where I was part of a larger movement for social change.

It is interesting, nevertheless, to note that while Woody was part of an indigenous, American radicalism, Arlo's politics are far more eclectic. For example, Arlo surprised many of his admirers in 2008 by endorsing Republican Ron Paul for the Presidency — revealing a more libertarian slant to Arlo's world view. By 2016, Arlo asserted that he was an independent who had left the Republican Party. He admired Bernie Sanders but could not completely endorse his socialist platform. Of Donald Trump: Arlo found it a good thing that the wealthy businessman was not dependent upon contributions from corporations, but he concluded "that doesn't mean he has the best interests of everybody in mind." In fact, Arlo expressed frustration over both major political parties, observing that he had more faith in the people coming together to make change on the local level than he did in the plans of leaders. He also argued, "That was the main message my father had for the people he wrote for: Take yourself seriously. You count. And when I see people in positions of authority trying to silence the voice of others, I get pissed off." Seeking to conclude his interview on a positive note, Arlo expressed his faith in the younger generation and harkened back to his own youth in the 1960s. He proclaimed, "You have to understand that what changed in the '60s was not the result of most people doing anything. It wasn't even a whole lot of people. It was a critical mass. As messengers of ideas we have to remember: You don't need to convince everybody. You don't need to convince a lot of people, just enough people. When you have enough people to move the people forward, it will move."[12]

This more evolutionary and somewhat ambiguous perception of change, however, lacks the emotional appeal and utopian vision of Woody's one big union and "commonism." Yet if Arlo has his doubts regarding Woody's politics, they are not apparent in the folk singer's stage persona, which is still able to kindle the fires that burned through his father's music. A similar evolution may be found in the work of perhaps Woody's greatest interpreter, Bob Dylan. The young man from Minnesota burst upon the New York City music scene like the reincarnation of Woody Guthrie with his knowledge of folk music and his ability to create powerful imagery of a changing world. Like Woody, Dylan often employed the news of the day to create powerful ballads, such as "The Lonesome Death of Hattie Carroll," "Only a Pawn in Their Game," and "Ballad of Hollis Brown." Dylan's "The Times They Are A-Changin'" and "Blowing in the Wind" became anthems for the 1960s counterculture and protest movement. Despite his admiration for Woody, Dylan chafed at being placed in the straitjacket of becoming the New Left's prophet and voice of a generation or being the Old Left's heir to the political protest tradition of Woody Guthrie and folk music. Dylan entertained civil rights workers and black sharecroppers in Mississippi during the early days of the Civil Rights Movement and performed at the August 1963 March on Washington, D.C., which was highlighted by Martin Luther King Jr.'s "I Have a Dream" speech. Dylan the artist, however, rebelled against becoming a political spokesman. This was evident when he lashed out at bourgeois liberals in 1963 when he received the Tom Paine Award from the Emergency Civil Liberties Committee. A more public event that exhibited his break from the folk movement was his appearance at the Newport Folk Festival on the evening of July 25, 1965. Here, Dylan and his band launched into an amplified version of "Like a Rolling Stone." Many in the audience loudly made their disappointment with Dylan heard. Although the story is likely apocryphal, a distraught Pete Seeger reportedly fetched an axe to destroy the electric cables to the amplifiers and guitars. Proclaimed a Judas, Dylan's response was to play the new music louder when he issued the innovative rock double-album *Blonde on Blonde* (1966).[13]

Many on the political left were shocked by Dylan's abandonment of the folk protest tradition, but as Mike Marqusee suggests in *Wicked Messenger*, the evolution of Dylan's music in the mid-1960s was more complicated. Seeking to combine the personal and the political, Dylan was an artist attempting to reconcile the aesthetic and political — an odyssey that would eventually garner the poet/musician the Nobel Prize for Literature in 2016. Dylan recognized that the world is full of injustice which the righteous must challenge, but that the world is also full of beautiful and surprising things, which must be expressed aesthetically — not so different from Woody Guthrie in the 1930s. Marqusee concludes that Dylan's work during the 1960s, the era in which both he and Dylan grew up, should not be viewed as "transparent reflections of the times but as expressive objects reflected by an individual in response to those times." And like Woody's music of the 1930s and 1940s, Dylan's compositions of the 1960s resonate beyond the time in which they were created. In summarizing Dylan's work in the 1960s, Marqusee writes, "It still exudes the spirit and the pain of human liberation. It still asks demanding questions of anyone who wants to change society — or just survive within it as a free human being. 'There must be some way out of here.' Dylan may never have found it, but that doesn't mean he can't help the rest of us on the journey."[14]

Dylan began his journey as Robert Allen Zimmerman on May 24, 1941, in Duluth, Minnesota. When Bob was five, his middle-class Jewish family moved to Hibbing, Minnesota. Exhibiting a passion for music, young Bob learned to play the piano, harmonica, and guitar. He formed several bands during his high school years and was especially influenced by Elvis Presley, Hank Williams, and Little Richard. After graduation from Hibbing High School in June 1959, Bob, at the insistence of his father, agreed to attend the University of Minnesota. However, he devoted little attention to his studies and spent most of his time playing guitar in Dinkytown — the Bohemian section of Minneapolis near the university. Hoping that young Bob might outgrow his musical infatuation, Bob's father reluctantly agreed to allow his son to follow his musical dreams to New York City.[15]

Seeking to establish a new identity, Robert Zimmerman changed his name to Bob Dylan. His name selection, according to several biographers, was influenced by the musician's admiration for the Welsh poet Dylan Thomas. After an arduous journey hitchhiking from Minneapolis, Dylan arrived in Greenwich Village in January 1961 — a rather similar odyssey to that of Woody Guthrie twenty years earlier. The new migrant to New York City sang for food and depended upon new friends for shelter. He became a regular performer at Gerde's Folk City on West Fourth Street, where he was noticed by show business manager Roy Silver. Silver was able to attain a contract for Dylan with John Hammond of Columbia Records, and his first album *Bob Dylan* was released in March 1962. Meanwhile, Dylan reached out to Woody Guthrie's family as the young singer was a great admirer of Woody's music and his somewhat autobiographical *Bound for Glory*, which Dylan read in high school. The middle-class young man was rather envious of Woody's authenticity and working-class background, and Dylan often embellished his own life story with tales that better reflected Woody's biography.

Arlo Guthrie offers an amusing account of how the scraggly young musician introduced himself to the Guthrie family. In early 1961 when the Guthrie children were at home with a babysitter, there was a knock at the family's apartment door. According to Arlo, "The door opened to reveal a rag-a-muffin sort of character, nineteen years old, with wild, crazy hair standing out from under a corduroy cap. He introduced himself as Bob Dylan, telling the family that he had just rambled in from the West and had come looking for Woody." The babysitter, Nora, and Joady were somewhat frightened by the strange young man, but Arlo was fascinated. He invited Dylan into the home, and they discussed Woody, while Dylan gave young Arlo some harmonica lessons. After an uncomfortable hour, the babysitter convinced Dylan to leave and come back when Marjorie was home. Nora and Joady were relieved, while Arlo found the uninvited guest captivating.[16] And eventually Dylan would become a regular visitor to the Guthrie home and to Woody's hospital room, entertaining the ailing folk singer with Dylan's renditions of Woody's songs.

Dylan's early infatuation with Woody is described in some detail in Dylan's acclaimed memoir, *Chronicles Volume One*. Dylan provides a different take on his initial meeting with Arlo. He insists that he was already visiting Woody in the hospital, and that he was dispatched by Woody to the Guthrie home to fetch some of the folk singer's lyrics, which had not been set to music. Dylan maintains that these are the lyrics that Billy Bragg and Wilco later used to fashion the *Mermaid Avenue* albums. Whether one accepts this claim or not, Dylan's description of his hospital visits with Woody are quite moving. He would take a bus from the Port Authority in New York City and then ride an hour-and-a-half to Greystone Hospital in Morristown, New Jersey. This was followed by a half-mile walk up a hill to the hospital, "a gloomy and threatening granite building — looked like a medieval fortress." Dylan would bring Woody cigarettes and then play any requests from the folk singer — often songs from *Dust Bowl Ballads* which Dylan knew quite well. Dylan lamented, "Woody was not celebrated at this place, and it was a strange environment to meet anybody; least of all the true voice of the American spirit." Noting wailing in the hallways, Dylan described the hospital as devoid of hope, concluding, "The scene was frightful, but Woody Guthrie was oblivious to all of it."[17]

The pilgrimage to New Jersey was Dylan's mission to find the man whose music changed his life. In *Chronicles*, Dylan writes that after hearing Woody's music, he also wanted to sing the songs of the Oklahoma folk singer: "It was like I had been in the dark and someone had turned on the main switch of a lightening conductor." Capturing Woody's spirit, Dylan wrote, "Guthrie divides the world between those who work and those who don't and is interested in the liberation of the human race and wants to create a world worth living in." Describing the impact of Woody's music upon his psyche, Dylan declared, "Woody made each word count. He painted with words. That along with his stylized type singing, the way he phrased, the dusty cowpoke deadpan but amazingly serious and melodic sense of delivery was like a buzz-saw in my brain and I tried to emulate it any way I could. A lot of folks might have thought of Woody's songs as backdated, but not me. I felt they were totally in the moment, current and even forecasted things to come. I felt anything but like the young punk folk singer who had just begun out of nowhere six months previously. I felt more like I had instantly risen up from a noncommissioned volunteer to an honorable knight — stripe and gold stars."[18]

On his first album, Dylan penned a talking blues homage to his hero, entitled "Song to Woody." In the composition, Dylan acknowledged Woody's dream of creating a new and better world out of the troubled one we have inherited. Dylan concludes that he cannot sing enough about Woody's struggles, "Cause there's not many men that done the things that you've done."[19] Dylan, however, eventually recognized that he had to be his own man, and Ramblin' Jack Elliott had already provided a better impression of Woody than the Minnesota folk singer. Asserting his independence from his hero and the folk movement, Dylan closes *Chronicles* with a bold assertion about striking out on his own in the mid-1960s. He proclaims, "The folk music scene had been like a paradise that I had to leave, like Adam had to leave the garden. It was just too perfect. In a few years' time a shit storm would be unleashed. Things would begin to burn. Bras, draft cards, American flags, bridges, too — everybody would be dreaming of getting it on. . . . The road out would be treacherous, and I didn't know where it would lead but I followed it anyway. It was a strange world ahead that would unfold, a thunderhead of a world with jagged lightening edges. Many got it wrong and never did get it right. I went straight into it. It was wide open. One thing for sure, not only was it not run by God, but it wasn't run by the devil either."[20]

Dylan scholars and biographers have devoted considerable attention to the artist's decision to abandon the folk scene of Woody Guthrie and blaze a new path of personal expression. Perhaps the key to understanding Dylan's evolution as an artist is the concept of change — that one who is not busy being born is busy dying. Dylan scholar John Hughes finds "becoming" to be the central trope to comprehending the rock poet. Writing in an academic fashion, Hughes states, "Dylan's art is essentially temporal and conflictual in its configurations. It projects a sensibility in motion between a discarded past and an unresolved future. . . . Freedom for Dylan is inseparable from an emancipating attitude of rejection in which the self is deducted from its social conditions. Autonomy is felt on the pulse and through the veins, as the self is introduced, now without prescriptions, into its innate capacity to renew itself, and to join itself, potentially to different possibilities of truth and expression."[21]

This rather academic description of Dylan's adaptability is also addressed in popular culture through filmmaker Todd Haynes's innovative biopic of the artist, *I'm Not There* (2007). In the film, Haynes presents Dylan in seven personas portrayed by six actors, reflecting different facets of the rock poet's life and career. The influence of Woody Guthrie on Dylan is presented through a young black character named Woody Guthrie, played by Marcus Carl Franklin. The depiction was controversial, but Haynes's approach was defended by Richard Porton in his review of *I'm Not There* for *Cineaste*. Porton argues, "Since Dylan's first folk efforts are thoroughly indebted to Guthrie, it's not inappropriate that a child is cast as the young Dylan goin' on the road as a virtual Woody clone. And given that Guthrie was the catalyst that eventually led the young Dylan to explore then little-known crevices of American musical history — particularly African-American blues — it's audacious, but not outrageous, for 'Woody' to be portrayed by a black child. By all accounts, Dylan was captivated by Guthrie's rebellious spirit and endlessly intrigued by romantic accounts of jumping boxcars and ramblin' round (all of which is captured in the movie as a pint size Woody sings up a storm throughout the American countryside)." Nevertheless, Dylan's decision to move beyond the folk tradition of Woody led many of Dylan's early fans to denounce him as a Judas who had betrayed Woody. Porton concludes, "Yet the mainstream left's assumption that Dylan would automatically assume Guthrie's mantle and become an obedient mouthpiece resulted in a myriad of generational and cultural conflicts and misunderstandings."[22] It is also difficult to imagine Woody being upset by this casting; he was a proud champion of the African-American blues tradition, enjoyed playing with Lead Belly, and actively opposed Jim Crow as domestic fascism.

While an admirer of Woody and the folk tradition, the young Dylan was concerned about being burdened and limited by the past. For example, in a 1963 radio interview with Studs Terkel (an oral historian of the American working class), Dylan observed that while both the 1930s and 1960s were periods of dissent, there were essential differences between the eras and generations. Dylan explained, "Maybe it's just the time, now is the time maybe you have to belong to yourself. I think maybe in the 1930s, from talking with Woody and Pete Seeger and some other people I know, it seems like everything back then was good and bad and black and white and whatever, you only had one or two. When you stand on one side and you know people are either for you or against you, with you or behind you or whatever you have. Nowadays it's just, I don't know how it got that way but it doesn't seem so simple. There are more than two sides, it's not black and white anymore."[23] Thus, Dylan seemed to be rejecting the Old Left of Woody Guthrie, which focused upon issues of labor politics and the Communist Party, in favor of a more complex and evolving presentism. Rebellion was present in both "Which Side Are You On?" and Dylan's "I Ain't Gonna Work on Maggie's Farm No More," but the protest was more personal than collectivist for Dylan.

Nevertheless, historian Sean Wilentz insists that the music, history, and traditions of America are well embodied in the continuing body of Dylan's work. Wilentz perceives Dylan in his music and writing as something of an American historian, drawing upon an almost encyclopedic knowledge of the nation's musical traditions to create a rich tapestry of the American nation. Rather than viewing Dylan as an artist who abandoned the politics of Woody Guthrie, Wilentz begins his book *Bob Dylan in America* with an in-depth investigation of how the Popular Front of the 1930s, to which Woody ascribed, has influenced Dylan, music, and popular culture. Praising Dylan's memoir *Chronicles* for its honesty, Wilentz writes that as a young artist Dylan "felt destiny looking straight at him and nobody else, but who also entered a universe of archaic yet living American archetypes from which, he says, all his songs sprang." Thus, Wilentz concludes that while Guthrie's influence remains an important element of Dylan's work, it was unfair to expect the rock poet to be a political guru or the voice of his generation. Wilentz writes, "Indeed, it missed the whole point he was laying out in his songs, which was that the songs themselves were what mattered, their words and images alone. We in the audiences were asking him to be a leader and more, but Dylan was slipping the yoke. He certainly enjoyed the fame and fortune that had headed his way. But beyond a certain level of acceptance all he really wanted to do was be a friend, if possible, and an artist writing and singing his songs."[24] The search for poetic meaning, of course, eventually led to Dylan's 2016 Nobel Prize for Literature. Writing before that award was bestowed, biographer Ian Bell argues that Dylan was a product of the American experience and was "shaped as a writer by blues and folk." In his musical journey, Dylan discovered that "the old songs had the resonance of poetry." Bell concludes, "His poetry lives because it breathes. In that it achieves the condition to which all poetry, the descendant of song, aspires."[25]

Thus, for some Dylan has abandoned the political for the personal by failing to write a protest song against the Vietnam War and seemingly condemning the counterculture by releasing the country-influenced *John Wesley Harding* in 1969. But in many ways, this is a false dichotomy as the personal and political overlap. Listening to Dylan today, as I am doing now, evokes images of Woody Guthrie as well as giving me guideposts for the journey of my own life. Until his voice was silenced by illness, Woody remained a fierce opponent of capitalism and a proponent of "commonism." It was impossible, nevertheless, to separate his personal odyssey from Oklahoma and Texas to California and then to New York from Woody's political development. Cathy's death and the rise of McCarthyism both formed Woody's view of the post-World War II world. Dylan's evolution as an artist moved well beyond Guthrie, but Dylan demonstrated considerable insight into Woody when playing for a Guthrie family benefit following the folk singer's death. Dylan elected to perform the obscure "Dear Mrs. Roosevelt," celebrating the New Deal legacy of Franklin D. Roosevelt in the best Popular Front tradition.

The last modern interpreter of Woody to be examined here is Bruce Springsteen, an artist of working-class roots who discovered Woody a little later in his career. Springsteen was born on September 23, 1949, and raised in Freehold, New Jersey. His ancestors were

Irish and Italian immigrants who struggled to make ends meet. Bruce's father, Doug, was a working-class man who labored as a bus driver, millworker, and prison guard. He also endured long periods of unemployment amid mental health issues. The cornerstone of the family was Adele, Bruce's mother, who served as a secretary for an insurance company. It was his mother who helped Bruce purchase his first, eighteen-dollar guitar, which was really beyond the family budget. Although he adored his mother, Bruce found it difficult to forge a relationship with his father, who was not supportive of his son's musical passions. In his autobiography, Springsteen offers a psychological interpretation of his father, observing, "He saw in me too much of his real self. My pop was built like a bull, always in work clothes, he was strong and physically formidable. Toward the end of his life, he fought back from death many times. Inside, however, beyond his rage, he harbored a gentleness, timidity, shyness and a dreamy insecurity. These were all the things I wore on the outside and the reflection of these qualities in his boy repelled him."[26] Springsteen, however, was able to enjoy a reconciliation with his father before he died.

    Attempting to deal with an unsupportive father was certainly a key part of both Springsteen's and Dylan's youth. Arlo Guthrie, on the other hand, has always had to live under his father's shadow. And, of course, Woody Guthrie was often a source of disappointment to his conservative father. While acknowledging Charley Guthrie's opposition to the Socialist Party, Woody failed to confront his father's apparent Klan membership or his participation in an Okemah lynching. In his autobiographical writings about his father, Woody lacks some of Springsteen's honesty. In my search for Woody Guthrie, I have been able to relate to these father/son conflicts. I believe that my father loved me and, in his own way, was proud of me, but he never understood my attraction to books and an academic life. Religion is also an important common theme, and Woody's emphasis upon Jesus fits into my upbringing. Dylan's religious heritage is Judaism, although he went through a major Christian phase in his life and music during the 1970s. Dylan's Jesus, however, seemed more intent upon apocalyptic punishment of nonbelievers than the progressive working-class carpenter embraced by Woody. Springsteen, on the other hand, was brought up Catholic. Although today he rejects much of Catholicism, Springsteen recognizes that it is almost impossible to escape the influence of a religious upbringing — a conclusion with which I concur. I can also identify with Springsteen's impoverished youth, where the pennies from every purchase were carefully counted.

Springsteen, like both Woody and Dylan, expressed little interest in formal education. The difference is that Woody and Dylan were both widely read, and it is probably not a stretch to consider Woody a working-class intellectual. Instead, Springsteen's life was focused upon music, and much of his early musical education came through commercial radio. Thus, Woody Guthrie was not really on young Springsteen's radar screen. His musical heroes were Elvis Presley and the Beatles. Springsteen's ability to concentrate on pursuing a musical career in the late 1960s was also because of a medical deferment; he suffered a concussion during a motorcycle accident, which exempted him from military service in Vietnam. Taking advantage of this opportunity, Springsteen formed the E Street Band and began playing at Asbury Park along the Jersey Shore. In conjunction with the release of his third album *Born to Run* (1975), Springsteen appeared on the covers of both *Time* and *Newsweek* magazines. Working-class themes were featured on the albums *Darkness on the Edge of Town* (1978), *The River* (1980), and *Nebraska* (1982), but Springsteen hit the big time with *Born in the USA* (1984), which featured seven hit singles. This success, however, bothered Springsteen because many listeners and politicians interpreted his music as a patriotic endorsement of the Vietnam War and American exceptionalism — a conclusion which the songwriter's work with Vietnam veterans did not support. A more introspective Springsteen would find his way to Woody Guthrie with the 1995 release of *The Ghost of Tom Joad* in which the musician criticized the growing economic gap between rich and poor in America fostered by the policies of the Reagan administration.[27]

Although he had shown little interest in history during school, Springsteen later expanded his reading to include Henry Steele Commager's *A Pocket History of the United States*, Howard Zinn's *A*

People's History of the United States, and Joe Klein's *Woody Guthrie: A Life*. He began to perceive himself as an actor on the historical stage. Springsteen relates, "What happened here was, in some infinitesimally small way, my responsibility. This was my place, my moment, my opportunity for my voice, no matter how faint, to be heard."[28] Discovering Woody, whom he described as Dylan's predecessor, Springsteen asserts, "I immersed myself and found the subtle writing, raw honesty, humor and empathy that's made his music eternal. In his stories of depression-era Okies and migrant workers, he revealed the folks trapped on the fringes of American life. His writing wasn't soapbox rambling but finely wrought personal portraits of American lives, told with toughness, wit, and common wisdom."[29]

Springsteen's critique of Ronald Reagan's America was also influenced by Dale Maharidge's *Journey to Nowhere: The Saga of the New Underclass* (1985). Maharidge comes from a family of steelworkers in Youngstown, Ohio, and chronicles the impact of globalization upon America's Midwestern industrial heartland. Maharidge laments, "Homelessness was once news, but the dispossessed have been accepted as a part of modern society, so much so that movies feature them as a routine urban backdrop. In the early 1980s, the most elaborate camps of the dispossessed were made of cardboard and plastic — now there are permanent shantytowns.... The terms 'recession' and 'recovery' have been rendered meaningless. Job loss has spread to white collar workers as companies slim down to pretty themselves up for Wall Street. Meanwhile, more wealthy people are living behind walled enclaves, separate from everybody else."[30] The conditions described by Maharidge in the early 1980s have only exacerbated as we have moved into the twenty-first century and have culminated in the election of Donald Trump — a billionaire who claims to be the messiah of the working class.

With the acoustic *Ghost of Tom Joad* album, Springsteen sought to address the plight of a working class that was threatened by automation and globalization without resorting to the demagoguery of blaming recent immigrants and people of color for lost jobs. The twelve songs range from the ballad "Youngstown," describing deindustrialization in the heartland, to the title track, featuring a narrator living under a bridge and waiting for the return of Steinbeck's and Guthrie's Tom Joad — establishing a link between the depression era and contemporary America in the 1980s and 1990s. Although sales were not equal to those of his rock albums, such as *Born in the USA*, *The Ghost of Tom Joad* enjoyed positive reviews from music critics and academics. Writing for *Rolling Stone*, Mikal Gilmore describes Springsteen's album as "a collection of dark tales about dark men who are cut off from the purposes of their own hearts and the prospects of their own lives. On this album almost none of the characters get out with both their bodies and spirits intact, and the few who do are usually left with only frightful, desolate prayers as their solace." Gilmore concludes his review with the observation, "By climbing into their hearts and minds, Springsteen has given voice to people who rarely have one in their culture. And giving voice to people who are typically denied expression in our other arts and media has always been one of rock & roll's most important virtues. As we move into the rough times and badlands that lie ahead, such acts will count for more than ever before."[31] In a commentary for the *Journal of American Folklore*, academic Paul Fischer echoes similar sentiments. He also links Steinbeck, Guthrie, and Springsteen by asserting that nearly fifty years after his initial appearance, "Tom Joad rejoins American life through song to bear witness for the poor who live amidst great wealth." Lauding Springsteen for his social conscience, Fischer argues that with *The Ghost of Tom Joad*, the songwriter "has set insights against a hauntingly quiet musical backdrop, raising his words in stark relief, as if whispering secrets in listeners' ears. On this disc rock and folk music can be seen as complementary, not oppositional forces, for social change."[32]

Describing the album for his autobiography, Springsteen acknowledges his debts to Steinbeck, Woody, and filmmaker John Ford. He also explains that he wanted to expand their focus by telling the stories of migrants from places such as Mexico. In terms of the album's style, Springsteen wrote, "The music was minimal, the melodies uncomplicated; the austere rhythms and arrangements defined who these people were and how they expressed themselves. They traveled light; they were lean, direct in their expression, yet with most of what they had to say left in the silence between words. They were transient and led hard, complicated lives, half of which had been left behind in another world, in another country." Yet Springsteen was concerned that *The Ghost of Tom Joad* might convey a sense of despair. For example, he considered having his protagonist in "Galveston Bay" commit an act of violence. Instead, Springsteen's character "refuses to add to the violence in the world around him. With great difficulty and against his own grain, he transcends his circumstances. He finds the strength and grace to save himself and the part of the world he touches."[33] In the best tradition of Woody, Springsteen rejects the romantic outlaw propaganda of the deed in favor of more collectivist action on behalf of the community or Woody's "commonism."

Numerous scholars of the protest tradition in American popular music find evidence of indigenous radicalism, which they trace from Woody to Dylan and then to Springsteen, although the latter two musicians lack Woody's radical credentials. For example, historian Jim Cullen argues that Springsteen draws upon what the scholar terms the republican tradition in American art and culture, which is exemplified by the values of simplicity, mobility, and hope. Cullen traces this tradition back to Walt Whitman, whom he characterizes as "a representative democrat, depicting ordinary people in ordinary language while finding the music, drama, and beauty of their lives. . . . Whitman was a master of distilling the popular culture of his time and demonstrating its expressive possibilities in a society struggling to realize both freedom and equality in life and art." While Woody was an admirer of Whitman, he nonetheless believed that his poetry was too flowery and that the language of *Dust Bowl Ballads* better captured the common people. Cullen also downplayed the radicalism exhibited by Woody in his art and life by concluding that the most important attribute of Woody's dust bowl migrants "is not their sense of anger or disillusionment, but rather the tenaciousness with which they hold on to their dreams."[34] The more rebellious and radical elements of Woody's art and politics, however, are better recognized by Larry David Smith's book on Dylan and Springsteen, which employs the term "American Song" to characterize their work. Emphasizing the extent to which both Dylan and Springsteen are influenced by Woody's work, Smith argues, "Woody Guthrie may well be the father of rock music and its rebellious messages that challenge the status quo through individual initiative and personal resolve."[35]

Smith's depiction of Woody as a rebel better reflects the reality of his politics, which some prefer to bury under the veil of consensus. Woody as the messenger of the struggles common people face under unfettered capitalism is exemplified in Bryan K. Garman's argument that Springsteen embodied Woody's tradition of the hurt song. According to Garman, "Written in working-class language, hurt songs express the collective pain, suffering, and injustices working people have historically suffered and articulate their hopes and dreams for a less oppressive future."[36] Garman also credits Woody with providing an example of interracial collective action against the forces of greed and oppression, which influences Springsteen's work. Because of their family histories and personal experiences, Woody and Springsteen emphasize issues of class, but both moved their definition beyond the white working class. Garman concludes, "By embracing the hurt song and its history, Springsteen reclaims popular music as a cultural space in which class relations are both taken seriously and historicized. He places his work in the context of a recognizable cultural and political tradition which affords his characters dignity and opens possibilities for social change."[37]

In addition to albums such as *Nebraska* and *The Ghost of Tom Joad*, Woody's influence upon Springsteen is apparent in the rock star's cover versions of "This Land Is Your Land" in concert — although he was inconsistent in performing the more radical verses questioning private property. Garman notes that while Springsteen sometimes emphasized the aesthetics of the song in his concert introductions, he also recognized the political impact of "This Land Is Your Land." He explains that he covered Guthrie's song "because that is what is needed right now.... I sing the song to let people know that America belongs to everybody who lives there: the blacks, Chicanos,

Indians, Chinese, and the whites. . . ."[38] Rock critic and Springsteen biographer Dave Marsh also observes that in bringing Woody's music to European concert audiences, Springsteen was spreading a message of ambiguity regarding the reality of the American dream. Speaking before a large crowd in Paris, Springsteen introduced "This Land Is Your Land" by asserting, "This is an old song about an old dream. It's hard to think what to say about this song, because it's sung a whole lot in the States and it's been misinterpreted a whole lot. It was written as a fighting song and it was written, I feel, as a question everybody has to ask themselves about the land they live in, every day."[39] Marsh, however, concludes that Springsteen is not a political radical in the tradition of Woody Guthrie. Noting that Woody wrote "This Land Is Your Land" in response to Irving Berlin's "God Bless America," Marsh asserts, "Springsteen's interpretation of what the song was about was smack dab in the middle between Woody Guthrie, who wrote as a Marxist disillusioned with the America of fable, and Irving Berlin, who wrote as a man who had seen his every dream fulfilled and in one lifetime moved from the hellish pits of New York's Lower East Side to Beekman Place, the shortest, most exclusive street uptown."[40]

Nevertheless, Springsteen's political activism has increased in recent years moving from working with Vietnam veterans to supporting liberal Democratic candidates, such as John Kerry, Barack Obama, and Hillary Clinton. He has also made it clear that he has major concerns about the Trump Presidency. In an interview with comedian and podcaster Mark Maron, Springsteen expressed reservations about "un-American" tendencies in the policies endorsed by Donald Trump. While acknowledging real economic concerns among many working-class voters who support Trump, Springsteen was, nonetheless, outspoken about the xenophobic tone of Trump's campaign. He proclaimed, "When you let that genie out of the bottle — bigotry, racism, intolerance ... they don't go back in the bottle that easily, if they go back at all. Whether it's a rise in hate crimes, people feeling they have license to speak and behave in ways that previously were considered un-American and are un-American. That is what he's appealing to. My fears are that those things find a place in ordinary, civil society."[41]

Springsteen's continuing political engagement and class consciousness place him in the protest tradition embodied by Woody, while Arlo Guthrie and Bob Dylan have grown more apolitical. And we are apparently going to continue hearing from Springsteen. Even at age seventy, the high energy level he displays in long concert performances shows no signs of dissipating. The recordings and performances of Arlo, Dylan, and Springsteen were crucial in guiding my search for Woody Guthrie. As we enter an uncertain political future, dominated by demagoguery and xenophobia targeting immigrants and people of color, it is more imperative than ever for the nation to keep Woody's music alive.

Conclusion

Woody Guthrie and Our Times

The search for Woody Guthrie has taken me from the dusty plains of Oklahoma and the Texas Panhandle to the fields of California and finally to the sidewalks of New York. This voyage has taught me a great deal about Woody, myself, and America. My journey has not produced a eureka moment, but I have learned to look both backward and forward, to never lose faith in the people, and to maintain the courage to fight for progressive ideas of equality and social justice despite the powerful forces arrayed against you. My examination of Woody's music along with his voluminous journals and correspondence has convinced me, in agreement with Woody's biographer Will Kaufman, that to understand Woody it is imperative to recognize that he is part of an essential indigenous American radicalism. This radicalism is often omitted from the nation's history books, but it continues to influence citizens who are engaged in the struggle for social justice. Nora Guthrie, on the other hand, tends to de-emphasize Woody's radicalism in favor of her father's all-encompassing sense of love and compassion. And Woody's capacity for love did allow him to move beyond the racial prejudices of his upbringing to embrace all people in what he termed "commonism." However, he had little patience for corrupt politicians and selfish capitalists who sought to prevent the working people of America and the world from achieving their well-deserved pastures of plenty. Thus, it is difficult to imagine Woody having much tolerance for the divisive politics of Donald Trump — and it is worth remembering that Woody registered his opposition to the segregated housing policies of Trump's father in New York City. But Woody would have empathy for many of Trump's white working-class voters from the de-industrialized American heartland, who have suffered so much economically in recent decades. Woody, however, would have little use for divisive politics that seek to place blame upon immigrants and people of color rather than on the corporate interests responsible for the increasing class inequality in America. Woody would instead advocate for an inclusive working-class alliance of the common people of all colors and backgrounds in support of a progressive social and economic agenda and in opposition to the greedy designs of corporate millionaires and billionaires.

Before concluding upon the lessons Woody's life and work offer to the continuing struggle for progressive ideas in Trump's America, I would like to take a few minutes of self-indulgence to consider what my search for Woody has taught me about my own life. Most importantly, Woody's experience has reminded me how much I should appreciate the sacrifices my parents made to assure that my brother and I had food on the table, clothes on our backs, and a roof over our heads. I must confess that growing up I was often embarrassed by their lack of sophistication and education, and as I grew older their religious and racial intolerance often antagonized me. I was pleased that my father was a union member and often voted for liberal Democrats who sought to expand the social safety net of progressive government programs, such as Social Security and Medicare. Yet he never wanted to raise his voice against social or economic inequality for fear that he might lose his job and we would wind up living under a bridge. Nevertheless, neither my father nor his generation were without courage. As a boy, my father sacrificed his education to become a laborer and to contribute his share to the feeding of his family. Despite his lack of education and skills, he and my mother were able to secure a tiny home of their own and send their two boys off to college — although that would not have happened without student loans and an expansion of federal assistance to higher education.

My parents also made sacrifices during the Second World War. My father joined the Army and was sent to Europe, where he joined people like Woody Guthrie in the struggle against fascism. Thus, it angers me a great deal today when I see young, well-dressed neo-Nazis in the nation's capital, marching through the streets and preaching racial intolerance while extending their hands in a fascist salute to hail the victory of Donald Trump. This is the type of intolerance my father and hundreds of thousands of common Americans fought against in World War II. It must make Woody symbolically roll over in his grave — although he was cremated, and his ashes were scattered near his beloved Coney Island home.

My parents were the common people who built America and defended the country from an external fascist threat. Yet they received little financial return, but they believed that their efforts would grant them a heavenly paradise. While the search for Woody has contributed to a greater appreciation for my parents' labors, I have struggled with their religious views after becoming an atheist. This was probably the greatest disappointment for my mother, who was otherwise quite proud of my educational achievements. I find myself subscribing to the Marxist notion that religion was created by the upper class to maintain a sense of control over the masses. Don't protest working and economic conditions in this life, and your reward will be, as Joe Hill cynically remarked, pie in the sky when you die (that's a lie). Adopting the policy of Hill's IWW, I perceived the capitalist class as manipulating my parents to accept their economic position in this life in exchange for a better one in the next world. I rejected this teaching and in the 1960s embraced an activism that sought to help the plight of the poor in their daily lives. Yet Woody was able to accommodate both Marx and Jesus into his thinking.

Woody viewed Jesus as the prince of peace and a working-class carpenter who would drive the money changers (capitalists) out of the temple and assure a more equitable distribution of the earth's resources. Thus, Woody incorporated Jesus and Christianity into this struggle for progressive change and the creation of a more just world — an approach that resonated with many working-class people.

Despite the many disappointments in his life, Woody never abandoned his belief in Jesus as a champion of "commonism." He would probably be quite disillusioned with contemporary mega-churches and their ministers, who shun the social gospel and celebrate the gospel of wealth. Nevertheless, the Christian socialist movement, which I could never convince my family to embrace, persists into the twenty-first century and provides a model for many working-class families.

Although there was certainly a spiritual element to the upheaval of the 1960s, I was more attracted to the secularism of SDS and Tom Hayden's *Port Huron Statement*. Much like Woody's belief that the struggle against fascism would usher in a better world and the one big union, I believed in the "Greening of America" and the "Dawning of the Age of Aquarius." My expectations proved to be naïve and unrealistic. In reaction to the progressive 1960s, which did suffer from its excesses, conservatives obtained power with the election of Ronald Reagan in 1980. The cultural wars of the 1960s continue to rage even after the election of a black President, and the Presidency of Donald Trump appears to threaten progressive causes of social, racial, and economic equality as much as did that of Ronald Reagan. As the proud parent of a transgender son, I am concerned about discrimination against the LGBTQ community under the guise of religious liberty. As I am approaching age seventy, I fear Congressional Republican attacks upon the safety nets of Social Security and Medicare — programs which were beneficial to my hard-working parents during their final years. In addition, the bellicose rhetoric of President Trump makes me, and others, apprehensive about the possibility of nuclear proliferation and global conflict. Climate change deniers have been placed in control of government agencies that were established to protect the environment; our dependence upon fossil fuel has expanded, endangering the future of life on this planet and constituting a far greater danger to the lives of our children and grandchildren than terrorism.

Despite these serious threats, I am convinced that the country today is a far better one than the America of 1949, into which I was born. When I was in high school, it was common behavior to publicly denigrate people of color and ridicule individuals for their sexual orientation. With the Civil Rights Movement, we have made tremendous racial progress, and we have more recently extended legal protections to the LGBTQ community. But these changes are not accepted by all Americans; many want to see the nation return to a past "greatness" for which they are nostalgic but which was based upon discrimination. Thus, there is considerable work for progressives today, but it is no time for despair. Throughout American history, periods of progress have often been followed by periods of reactionary politics; it seems as if for every two steps forward there is often a large step backwards. Donald Trump's sexism and association with right-wing racial hate groups, along with his contempt for such concepts as political correctness, seem to presage a return to the white America of the 1950s — before the sexual revolution and Civil Rights Movement of the 1960s. This effort to take America back to the 1950s returns us to Woody Guthrie, raising the question — with apologies to Christian evangelicals — "what would Woody do?"

An examination of Woody's life and work demonstrates that he would hardly tolerate such reactionary politics without voicing his dissent and opposition. Woody challenged the discrimination that migrants from Oklahoma and Texas confronted when they were forced off their farms and faced hostility in California. He advocated public power for the people and embraced the labor movement. Despite being raised in a racist environment, he rallied to the cause of racial equality and fought against Jim Crow and the Klan. Woody also enlisted in the international fight against fascism. He believed, as his letters to Railroad Pete and Marjorie indicate, that the hardships people endured during the war would result in a world free from capitalist exploitation. The postwar world did not usher in the millennium Woody had imagined. He was disappointed and discouraged by the Cold War, HUAC, and McCarthyism, but he refused to abandon the struggle for a better world. And Woody kept up the fight during difficult times in his personal life. By the 1950s he was suffering from Huntington's disease, his behavior was sometimes erratic, and his marriage to the beloved Marjorie collapsed. But the greatest tragedy of his life was the death of four-year-old Cathy in a fire only days after her birthday. In his letters to an unborn Cathy (whom he then called Railroad Pete), Woody demonstrated how he poured his hopes and dreams for the postwar era into the child. Following her birth, Woody celebrated Cathy for her intelligence and compassion. He composed children's songs for her and was her primary caregiver while Marjorie was working. Woody believed that children should be encouraged to learn through experience, and he placed few restrictions upon the child. Cathy symbolized the new world for which Woody had struggled during the war. In letters following her death, Woody praised Cathy's progressive spirit at school and in the home. He also noted that in her final hours, she never complained; she only expressed concern for her grieving parents and friends. Despite this crushing loss — which continued the tragic Guthrie family history of family members being killed or injured in fires — Woody maintained his efforts to forge that better world represented by Cathy.

Politically, Woody placed a great deal of faith in the union movement. In fact, he was entertaining striking workers when Cathy's accident occurred. Combining his devotion to racial equality and organized labor, Woody believed the union idea would be the means for realizing Preacher Casy's "one big soul" and the folk singer's concept of "commomism." Before World War II, Woody fought to organize farmworkers in California and supported industrial unionism by the CIO among auto workers, electrical workers, and steelworkers. During the war, Woody joined the Merchant Marine and NMU. He perceived the global conflict as a struggle between the greed of fascism and the common humanity of the union idea. After the war's conclusion, Woody believed that he might witness the triumph of union solidarity. The postwar environment, however, did not prove hospitable to organized labor. Seeking to roll back the gains made by unions during the New Deal and World War II, big business and reactionary politicians discredited labor leaders by preying upon the American public's fears of the Cold War, Soviet Russia, and communism. Amid the climate of McCarthyism, the FBI and Congressional Committees, such as HUAC, violated the civil liberties of American citizens; labor leaders who supported reforms, racial unity, and collectivist solutions to the nation's economic concerns were dismissed as communists. Labor's gains were curtailed by repressive legislation, such as the Taft-Hartley Act, and labor leaders with radical agendas were purged. At the same time, the union movement abandoned Woody's dream of forging a more egalitarian society in favor of the bread and butter unionism of pensions, wages, hours, and better working conditions for their members.

Today, union membership continues to decline in the United States, while the right to work movement gains traction and undermines labor organization. Only about ten percent of workers are still organized, and unions fail to countervail big business. This erosion of labor's influence, exacerbated during the 1980s under the Reagan Presidency, has left American workers with little means to combat the forces of globalization and automation. These have lain waste to the industrial heartland of the United States. As a result, many desperate voters placed their trust in the demagoguery of Donald Trump, who has consistently opposed organized labor. In fact, Woody was an early critic of Fred Trump, the Donald's father, for supporting and implementing segregated housing. Donald Trump has never disavowed this family business practice. For progressives seeking to check the power of Trump and his billionaire allies, it is time to promote the organization of American workers and reawaken Woody's union ideas. It will not be easy — almost no cause worthy of the struggle is easily realized. Woody committed himself to the union idea during the dark days of McCarthyism, and progressives today should follow his example rather than curse the darkness.

Woody was discouraged by the political climate in postwar America and personal tragedies he endured, but the folk singer remained in the fray until he was sidelined by illness. He enlisted his guitar and song writing abilities in the struggle against the KKK, supported organizing efforts by the CIO among Southern textile workers, and campaigned for the 1948 Progressive Party candidacy of Henry A. Wallace. For these activities, Woody was denounced as a communist, but such accusations did not deter the musician from fighting for his ideas of a more egalitarian society based upon the union idea and "commonism." Much time and energy have been wasted debating whether Woody was a member of the Communist Party. Labels did not matter much to Woody. He often supported the communists because in the 1930s and 1940s the party backed workers' rights and battled against racism and fascism. He refused to be intimidated by the red-baiters and never denounced the party. Failing health prevented Woody from suffering the indignities of the blacklist, which were visited upon many of his associates, such as Seeger. Nevertheless, Woody is still often condemned as an apologist for Stalinism. This allowed critics to discount the causes for which both Woody and the Communist Party often struggled. In fact, when I informed one of my former students that I was completing a book on Woody Guthrie, he quickly replied that he would not read the volume because Woody was a communist. Of course, such a knee-jerk reaction makes it possible to simply disregard the common humanity for which Woody was fighting in the postwar world and for which progressives today continue to struggle.

Woody also recognized that the concept of "commonism" was part of a larger historical movement to assure that the principles enunciated in the Declaration of Independence were bestowed upon all Americans. The folk singer was part of an indigenous, American radicalism, which was reflected in his music. Woody celebrated the courage of black abolitionists, such as Harriet Tubman, who fought against slavery. He also recognized the bravery of Southern whites, such as Stetson Kennedy, who challenged the Klan and Jim Crow. The contributions of women to forging a more just society were eloquently addressed in the classic labor anthem, "Union Maid." The first Red Scare following World War I sought to obliterate America's radical history in a wave of jingoistic patriotism by painting groups such as the IWW and Socialist Party as un-American. Thus, the fact that the Socialist Party had considerable appeal in Oklahoma and the American heartland is little known today, but Woody labored to keep this more radical past alive with compositions such as "1913 Massacre" and "Ludlow Massacre," which commemorate American workers — many of them immigrants fighting against capitalistic big business to feed their families. It is a legacy of struggle that deserves an honored place in the nation's history classrooms.

In his *Ballads of Sacco & Vanzetti*, Woody also told a story of discrimination against immigrants, which is often forgotten today but which remains extremely relevant in an era when immigration is blamed for terrorism and economic decline. In a beautiful introduction to his songs on the Italian immigrants, Woody relates Sacco's and Vanzetti's experiences as immigrants to the migrant experience of the dust bowl refugees who fled Oklahoma and Texas in search of new opportunities, only to find intolerance and repression. Instead, Woody believes that America should be a land that celebrates diversity and welcomes immigrants into the community. This inclusive vision is also the message of Woody's most famous composition, "This Land Is Your Land." Woody's radicalism is also apparent in the anti-imperialist themes of his Korean War song cycle. Woody's voice of protest was silenced by disease before a widespread discontent with the Vietnam War was manifest in American society. As many historians have noted, however, the origins of the Vietnam conflict may be found in the Korean War and in early years of the Cold War, which Woody was not afraid to question. Thus, Woody served as a historian of the indigenous, American radicalism that has played a significant, but often ignored, role in the American past. As a historian, Woody reminds progressive citizens of a radical tradition upon which they might draw in the contemporary fight for social justice. Woody provides us with examples of a usable past.

Woody dared to challenge the post-World War II anticommunist atmosphere and the assumption that American society was fundamentally sound and that problems such as racism would be solved by an ever-expanding capitalist pie. Woody was, accordingly, an outsider in the conservative atmosphere of postwar America. In addition to embracing America's radical past and refusing to denounce the Communist Party, Woody may be perceived as demonstrating a "queer" sensibility, which further separated him from 1950s society and conventions. Although he was often guilty of objectifying women, Woody also questioned the conformity of middle-class life in suburbia against which many women of the 1950s rebelled. Instead of fitting in as the "organization man" or "the man in the gray flannel suit," Woody chafed under social conventions. Although he loved his children and celebrated their creativity, Woody was often irresponsible; he frequently deserted the family and sought other women as sexual partners. His sexually explicit letters got Woody into trouble with the law, and his sexual dalliances eventually led to divorce from Marjorie and to marriage with a woman half his age. Some of his obsession with sexuality was likely attributable to the onset of Huntington's disease, but Woody was also something of a sexual libertine. He took great pride in challenging the conventional, puritanical attitudes of Americans toward sexual freedom of expression. Thus, he resented authority figures who attempted to dictate how he was supposed to express himself sexually. It was simply a matter of individual freedom.

Woody, however, was reluctant to extend similar notions of freedom to same-sex relationships, which he often denounced. Homosexuality in the 1950s — employing the language of the time — was regarded as a threat to the American family and to national security. Homosexuals were seen as being "soft" on communism and as threats to security because they could be blackmailed by Soviet agents. The psychiatric community characterized homosexuality as a mental disorder, and homosexuals were forced out of the public eye and into the closet and an underground culture. Queer became a popular pejorative term for describing the homosexual community, but it is a word that the LGBTQ community today has re-appropriated with a sense of pride. Recognizing that he was himself often outside of the norm of American suburban values in the 1950s, Woody referred to himself as queer. He was a political radical, sexual libertine, vagabond, musician, and outsider who questioned conventional values. It does not seem a stretch to argue that the queer, nonconformist Woody might have evolved in his thinking toward the LGBTQ community, just as he rejected the prejudices of his youth in favor of supporting racial equality and opposing the intolerance of the Klan. I have traveled a similar path after being brought up in an atmosphere of homophobia and racism. As an outsider with a love of humanity who was open to change and modernity, Woody, I believe, would accept my transgender son.

In conclusion, my search for Woody Guthrie, often guided by musicians Arlo Guthrie, Bob Dylan, and Bruce Springsteen, has helped me better understand myself and the world in which I live. I share a similar background with Woody: I also grew up in the Texas Panhandle and was raised by a conservative fundamentalist Christian family. Like Woody, I fled the rural environment for a more urban lifestyle and embraced an indigenous, radical, political philosophy that was often at odds with the traditional values of my family. While today I feel at home in a city and university environment, much like Woody I have never been able to escape the Texas Panhandle. I have a copy of Dorothea Lange's classic photograph "Tractored Out in Childress" on my office wall. The photograph is a stark depiction of an abandoned shack/home amid a barren landscape of dust. It reminds me of the economic difficulties my parents had to surmount in this harsh environment. I find a sense of pride in my parents' achievements, and I often feel like an outsider around more privileged peers who do not quite understand what it is like to grow up poor or to struggle to attain the necessities of life such as food, shelter, clothing, health care, and education. Yet it is this outsider status that has often provided me with the motivation to pursue my education and teaching career. It has also helped me cultivate a vision of a better world in which all people have equal access to the world's resources. This dream is the same as Woody's one big union or "commonism," which efforts to de-radicalize the singer and activist have never quite succeeded in erasing.

In making this journey through the past, I hope that I have been fair to my parents, who sacrificed so much for my brother and me. While I have challenged some of their assumptions and prejudices, I have no doubt of their love for me. It is also my hope that I have not offended my brother, whose values and politics are more conservative than my own. This introspective voyage could not have been undertaken without the support of my family. They have listened patiently to stories about Childress and even accompanied me on trips to Pampa and Okemah. Woody's musical tradition may not fit with their contemporary tastes, but they certainly know a great deal about Woody and his values. They also represent the better world to which Woody dedicated his life. I must also acknowledge my debt to my mentor at West Texas State University, Professor Pete Petersen, who inspired my study of history and helped me discover Woody and an indigenous, American radical tradition.

My final expression of gratitude is, of course, reserved for Woody Guthrie. His amazing life and music have illuminated my way on this voyage of self-discovery. My quest was guided by archivist Hillel Arnold, whose labors on behalf of my research are much appreciated. After an intensive investigation of Woody's songs, correspondence, and notebooks, which are found in the Woody Guthrie Archives, I believe that Woody's allegiance to indigenous, American radicalism is essential to understanding the man and his influence. Nora Guthrie, however, tends to downplay the radicalism in favor of Woody's tremendous capacity for love. I would argue that the two motivations are related. Woody was no scholar of Marx or dialectical materialism, but he was willing to support aspects of communism if they helped the people whom he loved and perceived to be exploited by capitalist interests. Woody's legacy for today is the idea of an interracial alliance of working people struggling together to improve their lives and achieve the dream of "commonism" and one big union. It is a noble undertaking and a legacy of which Woody and his family can be quite proud. Thank you, Woody Guthrie. So long, it's been good to know you!

Notes

Introduction

1. Joe Klein, *Woody Guthrie: A Life* (New York: Alfred A. Knopf, 1980); Ed Cray, *Ramblin' Man: The Life and Times of Woody Guthrie* (New York: W. W. Norton & Company, 2004); and Will Kaufman, *Woody Guthrie: American Radical* (Urbana: University of Illinois Press, 2011), xxv.
2. Nora Guthrie, phone interview with author, May 19, 2010.

Chapter One

1. Jack Newfield, "American Radicalism," *Nation* 277 (July 21/28, 2003): 13; and Steve Earle, "Woody Guthrie," *Nation* 277 (July 21/28, 2003): 30–32.
2. Woody Guthrie, 1941, Woody Guthrie Archives (hereafter cited as WGA), Manuscript Series 1, Box 1, Folder 3.2, New York City, New York (now located in Tulsa, Oklahoma).
3. Bryan K. Garman, *A Race of Singers: Walt Whitman's Working-Class Hero from Guthrie to Springsteen* (Chapel Hill: The University of North Carolina Press, 2000), 69–70.
4. Robert Santelli, *This Land Is Your Land: Woody Guthrie and the Journey of an American Folk Song* (Philadelphia: Running Press, 2012), 181–82.
5. Cray, *Ramblin' Man*, xxii.
6. Santelli, *This Land Is Your Land*, 71.
7. Dave Marsh, *Bruce Springsteen: Two Hearts, The Definitive Biography, 1972–2003* (New York: Routledge, 2004), 278–79.
8. Mark Allan Jackson, *Prophet Singer: The Voice and Vision of Woody Guthrie* (Jackson: University Press of Mississippi, 2007), 45.
9. Cray, *Ramblin' Man*, 317–18, 310, and 323.

10. For background information on Leventhal, see Peter Appleborne, "He Caught Folk on the Rise and Held On," *New York Times*, November 26, 1998.
11. Joseph McBride, "Song for Woody," *Film Comment* 12 (November–December 1976): 26.
12. For background information on Hal Ashby, see Nick Dawson, *Being Hal Ashby: Life of a Hollywood Rebel* (Lexington: University Press of Kentucky, 2011); Christopher Beach, *The Films of Hal Ashby* (Detroit: Wayne State University Press, 2009); James R. Davidson, *Hal Ashby and the Making of Harold and Maude* (Jefferson, North Carolina: McFarland, 2016); and Nick Dawson, ed., *Hal Ashby Interviews* (Jackson: University of Mississippi Press, 2010).
13. McBride, "Song for Woody," 27.
14. Larry Salvato and Dennis Schaefer, "Hal Ashby Interview," *Millimeter* 4 (October 1976), reprinted in *Hal Ashby Interviews*, Dawson, 42.
15. McBride, "Song for Woody," 28.
16. Ed Robbin, *Woody Guthrie and Me* (Berkeley, California: Lancaster-Miller Publications, 1979), 81.
17. Roger Ebert, "*Bound for Glory*," March 9, 1977, www.rogerebert.com.
18. David Sterritt, "That Special Okie Southwest Flavor, That Humor," *Christian Science Monitor*, February 4, 1977.
19. Aljean Harmetz, "Gambling on a Film about the Great Depression," *New York Times*, December 5, 1976.
20. McBride, "Song for Woody," 38.
21. Jeff Green, "*Bound for Glory*," *Cineaste* 8 (Summer 1977): 36–37.
22. *Bound for Glory*, directed by Hal Ashby (1976; Hollywood, California: MGM Home Entertainment, 2000), DVD.
23. For *Rocky* see Tom O'Brien, *The Screening of America: Movies and Values from Rocky to Rain Man* (New York: Bloomsbury Academic, 2016); Larry Powell, *The Films of John Avildson: Rocky, The Karate Kid and Other Underdogs* (Jefferson, North Carolina: McFarland, 2013); and Victoria A. Elmwood, "'Just Some Bum from the Neighborhood': The Resolution of Post-Civil Rights Tension and Heavyweight Public Sphere Discourse in *Rocky*," in Ron Briley, Michael K. Schoenecke, and Deborah Carmichael, eds., *All Stars and Movie Stars:*

Sports in Film History (Lexington: University Press of Kentucky, 2008), 172–98.

24. Vincent Canby, "*Bound for Glory*," *New York Times*, December 6, 1976; and Richard Schickel, "*Bound for Glory*," *Time* 108 (December 20, 1976): 62.
25. Judith Crist, "*Bound for Glory*," *Saturday Review* 40 (December 11, 1976): 78; McBride, "Song for Woody," 26; David Sterritt, "*Bound for Glory*," *Christian Science Monitor*, December 30, 1976; Frank Rich, "*Bound for Glory*," *New York Post*, December 6, 1976; and John Simon, "*Bound for Glory*," *New York Magazine*, December 6, 1976.
26. Stanley Kauffmann, "Poor Folk," *New Republic* 175 (November 27, 1976): 18 and 40.
27. Pauline Kael, "Affirmation," *New Yorker*, December 13, 1976, 148–152.
28. Green, "*Bound for Glory*," 36–37.
29. Robbin, *Woody Guthrie and Me*, 83–84.
30. Roxanne Dunbar-Ortiz, "One or Two Things I Know about Us: 'Okies' in American Culture," *Radical History Review* 59 (Spring 1994): 32.

Chapter Two

A version of this chapter was originally published as "'Woody Sez': Woody Guthrie, The *People's Daily World*, and Indigenous Radicalism," *California History* 84 (Fall 2006): 30–43.

1. Charles J. Shindo, *Dust Bowl Migrants in the American Imagination* (Lawrence: University Press of Kansas, 1997), 169.
2. Darryl Holter and William Deverell, eds., *Woody Guthrie L. A. 1937 to 1941* (Los Angeles: Angel City Press, 2015), 47.
3. Nora Guthrie, phone interview with author, May 19, 2010.
4. James R. Green, *Grass Roots Socialism: Radical Movements in the Southwest, 1895–1943* (Baton Rouge: Louisiana State University Press, 1978), 173.
5. Harry Menig, "Woody Guthrie: The Oklahoma Years, 1912–1929," in *An Oklahoma I Had Never Known Before: Alternative Views of Oklahoma*

History, ed. Davis D. Joyce (Norman: University of Oklahoma Press, 1994), 162–90.

6. Quoted in Cray, *Ramblin' Man*, 79.
7. Woody Guthrie to Mary Ann Guthrie, February 5, 1937, WGA, Correspondence Series 1, Box 1, Folder 29.
8. For the IWW see Joyce Kornbluh, ed., *Rebel Voices: An IWW Anthology* (Ann Arbor: University of Michigan Press, 1964); Melvyn Dubofsky, *We Shall Be All: A History of the Industrial Workers of the World* (Urbana: University of Illinois Press, 1988); and Woody Guthrie, "Joe Hillstrom," in *American Folksong: Woody Guthrie*, ed. Moses Asch (New York: Oak Publications, 1961), 22–23.
9. Quoted in Cray, *Ramblin' Man*, 130–31.
10. Woody Guthrie, "Tom Mooney is Free," in *Hard Hitting Songs for Hard-Hit People*, eds. Woody Guthrie, Alan Lomax, and Pete Seeger (New York: Oak Publications, 1967), 356; and Robbin, *Woody Guthrie and Me*, 30–33.
11. Dorothy Ray Healey and Maurice Isserman, *California Red: A Life in the American Communist Party* (Urbana: University of Illinois Press, 1979); Dave Marsh and Harold Leventhal, eds., *Pastures of Plenty: Woody Guthrie: The Unpublished Writings of an American Folk Hero* (New York: Harper Perennial, 1992), 163; Woody Guthrie, *Woody Sez* (New York: Grosset and Dunlap, 1975); Paul Richards, "*People's Daily World*," in *Encyclopedia of the American Left*, Marie Jo Buhle, Paul Buhle, and Dan Georgakas (Urbana: University of Illinois Press, 1992), 573–74; and Woody Guthrie, "Woody Sez," *People's Daily World* (hereafter cited as *PDW*), June 17, 1939.
12. Woody Guthrie, "Woody Sez: A New Columnist Introduces Himself," *PDW*, May 12, 1939.
13. Woody Guthrie, "Woody Sez," *PDW*, May 18, 1939; and Woody Guthrie, "Woody Sez," *PDW*, May 19, 1939.
14. Woody Guthrie, "Woody Sez: Migratious Workers Take Lots of Abuse," *PDW*, May 23, 1939.
15. Woody Guthrie, "Woody Sez: House," *PDW*, May 31, 1939; and Woody Guthrie, "Woody Sez," *PDW*, June 1, 1939.
16. Woody Guthrie, "Woody Sez," *PDW*, June 3, 1939.

17. Woody Guthrie, "Woody Sez," *PDW*, June 6, 1939; and Woody Guthrie, "Woody Sez," *PDW*, June 19, 1939.
18. Woody Guthrie, "Woody Sez," *PDW*, June 23, 1939.
19. Woody Guthrie, "Woody Sez," *PDW*, June 24, 1939; and Woody Guthrie, "Woody Sez," *PDW*, June 28, 1939.
20. Woody Guthrie, "Woody Sez," *PDW*, July 7, 1939; Woody Guthrie, "Woody Sez," *PDW*, July 12, 1939; and Woody Guthrie, "Woody Sez," *PDW*, August 11, 1939.
21. Woody Guthrie, "Woody Sez," *PDW*, July 17, 1939; and for James Leech see Harvey Klehr, *The Heyday of American Communism: The Depression Decade* (New York: Basic Books, 1984), 463.
22. Woody Guthrie, "Woody Sez," *PDW*, August 3, 1939; Woody Guthrie, "Woody Sez," *PDW*, August 4, 1939; and Charles P. Larrowe, *Harry Bridges: The Rise and Fall of Radical Labor in the United States* (Westport, Connecticut: Lawrence Hill & Co., 1977).
23. Woody Guthrie, "Woody Sez," *PDW*, July 31, 1939.
24. Woody Guthrie, "Woody Sez," *PDW*, September 6, 1939.
25. Woody Guthrie, "Woody Sez," *PDW*, August 15, 1939.
26. Woody Guthrie, "Woody Sez," *PDW*, September 12, 1939. For the American Communist Party during the Second World War, see Klehr, *The Heyday of American Communism*; Fraser M. Ottanelli, *The Communist Party of the United States from the Depression to World War II* (New Brunswick, New Jersey: Rutgers University Press, 1991); and Maurice Isserman, *Which Side Were You On?: The American Communist Party During the Second World War* (Urbana: University of Illinois Press, 1993).
27. Woody Guthrie, "Woody Sez," *PDW*, September 15, 1939.
28. Woody Guthrie, "Woody Sez," *PDW*, September 22, 1939; Woody Guthrie, "Woody Sez," *PDW*, September 26, 1939; Woody Guthrie, "Woody Sez," *PDW*, October 6, 1939; and Maurice Isserman, *Which Side Were You On? The American Communist Party During the Second World War.*
29. Woody Guthrie, "Woody Sez," *PDW*, November 22, 1939; and Woody Guthrie, "Woody Sez," *PDW*, November 30, 1939.
30. Woody Guthrie, "Woody Sez," November 30, 1939.

31. Woody Guthrie, "Woody Sez," *PDW*, December 1, 1939.
32. Nora Guthrie, phone interview with author, May 19, 2010.
33. Cray, *Ramblin' Man*, 138–40; and Ronald D. Cohen, "Woody the Red?," in *Hard Travelin': The Life and Legacy of Woody Guthrie*, eds. Robert Santelli and Emily Davidson (Hanover, New Hampshire: Wesleyan University Press, 1999), 150; and Klein, *Guthrie*, 113–35.
34. Marsh and Leventhal, *Pastures of Plenty*, 35.
35. Woody Guthrie, 1939, WGA, Notebook Series 1, Number 89.
36. Aaron J. Leonard, "Newly Released FBI Files Expose Red-Baiting of Woody Guthrie," Truthout, August 14, 2018, www.truthout.org.
37. "Woody Guthrie: One Hundredth Birthday of a Communist," *Oklahoma Constitution*, May 7, 2012, http://www.oklahomaconstitution.com.
38. David R. Shumway, "Your Land: The Lost Legacy of Woody Guthrie," in *Hard Travelin'*, eds. Santelli and Davidson, 157.

Chapter Three

1. Nora Guthrie, telephone interview with author, May 19, 2010.
2. Cray, *Ramblin' Man*, 162–65.
3. Santelli, *This Land Is Your Land*, 71–84. For "God Bless America," see Sheryl Kaskowitz, *God Bless America: The Surprising History of an Iconic Song* (New York: Oxford University Press, 2013), 57.
4. Pete Seeger quoted in Cray, *Ramblin' Man*, 160.
5. John Steinbeck, "Foreword," in *Hard Hitting Songs*, Guthrie, Lomax, and Seeger, 8–9.
6. John Szwed, *Alan Lomax: The Man Who Recorded the World* (New York: Penguin Books, 2011), 157–61.
7. For background information on Pete Seeger, see David Dunaway, *How Can I Keep from Singing? The Ballad of Pete Seeger* (New York: McGraw-Hill, 1981); and Alan W. Winkler, *"To Everything There Is a Season": Pete Seeger and the Power of Song* (New York: Oxford University Press, 2009).
8. "Woody, Our New Columnist," *Daily Worker*, April 2, 1940; and Mike Quinn, "Double Check," *Daily Worker*, April 25, 1940.
9. Woody Guthrie, "Woody Sez," *Daily Worker*, April 4, 1940.
10. Woody Guthrie, "Woody Sez," *Daily Worker*, April 8, 1940.

11. Woody Guthrie, "Woody Sez," *Daily Worker*, April 13, 1940.
12. On the election of 1940, see Susan Dunn, *1940: FDR, Lindbergh, Hitler — the Election Amid the Storm* (New Haven, Connecticut: Yale University Press, 2013); and Richard Moe, *Roosevelt's Second Act: The Election of 1940 and the Politics of War* (New York: Oxford University Press, 2013).
13. Woody Guthrie, "Woody's Artist Friend Paints Lynch Scene," *Daily Worker*, April 21, 1940.
14. Woody Guthrie, "Woody Sez Most Here by Accident," *Daily Worker*, May 2, 1940.
15. Woody Guthrie, "Woody Sez that Okies Haven't Given Up Fight," *Daily Worker*, April 23, 1940. For the Farm Securities Administration, see Shindo, *Dust Bowl Migrants in the American Imagination*; and Sidney Baldwin, *Poverty and Politics: The Rise and Decline of the Farm Security Administration* (Chapel Hill: University of North Carolina Press, 1968).
16. Woody Guthrie, "Woody Says Okie Film Not Doing Well in Oklahoma," *Daily Worker*, May 7, 1940. For John Ford, see Tay Gallagher, *John Ford: The Man and his Films* (Berkeley: University of California Press, 1986).
17. Woody Guthrie, "Old Dust Storm Can't Get Me, Declares Woody," *Daily Worker*, May 11, 1940.
18. Woody Guthrie, "Woody Leaves New York But Not His Column," *Daily Worker*, May 22, 1940.
19. Woody Guthrie, "Woody Says 20 Rooms Too Many for Four Persons," *Daily Worker*, May 24, 1940; Woody Guthrie, "Dentist Wants $5 for Tooth Woody Left Behind," *Daily Worker*, May 25, 1940; and Woody Guthrie, "Woody Confesses He Hasn't Shaved Since Leaving N.Y.," *Daily Worker*, May 30, 1940.
20. Woody Guthrie, "Woody Says Love and KKK Don't Go Together," *Daily Worker*, May 31, 1940.
21. For the Woody-Seeger trip, see Cray, *Ramblin' Man*, 185–190; and Klein, *Guthrie*, 160–64.
22. Kaufman, *Guthrie: American Radical*, 48; and Woody Guthrie, "Union Maid," WGA, Song Series 1, Box 13, Folder 13.

23. Woody Guthrie, "Woody Describes One of Those Joad Camps," *Daily Worker*, June 7, 1940.
24. Woody Guthrie, "1,000 People Eat in Town the Day Woody Arrives," *Daily Worker*, June 6, 1940; and Woody Guthrie, "Woody Asks About the U.S. Constitution," *Daily Worker*, June 15, 1940.
25. Woody Guthrie, "Woody Declares He's Got No Yen to Go Enlistin'," *Daily Worker*, June 13, 1940; and Woody Guthrie, "Woody and Okie Preacher Talk About the War," *Daily Worker*, June 2, 1940.
26. Quoted in Winkler, *"To Everything There Is a Season,"* 22–23.
27. Woody Guthrie, "Woody's Been Moving As Fast as WPA Cuts," *Daily Worker*, June 20, 1940.
28. Woody Guthrie, "Woody Says Demos Don't Speak for 'Okies,'" *Daily Worker*, June 27, 1940; Woody Guthrie, "Demos Braying for Big Vote, Woody Finds," *Daily Worker*, July 9, 1940; and Woody Guthrie, "Woody Asserts It's Time for New, New Deal," *Daily Worker*, July 13, 1940.
29. Woody Guthrie, "Dies Aim Is To Keep You from Righting Wrongs," *Daily Worker*, July 15, 1940.
30. Woody Guthrie, "World Is Full of Refugees, Thinks Woody," *Daily Worker*, July 31, 1940.
31. Woody Guthrie, "Woody Describes Possible Results of Conscription," *Daily Worker*, August 16, 1940; and Woody Guthrie, "Woody Convinced That the Yanks Are Not Coming," *Daily Worker*, August 24, 1940.
32. Woody Guthrie, "Woody Asks More Old-Fashioned Get-Togethers," *Daily Worker*, September 17, 1940; Woody Guthrie, "Woody Says Same Crowd Puts Out Voting Buttons," *Daily Worker*, September 3, 1940; and Woody Guthrie, "Take It Easy, Says Woody, But Take It," *Daily Worker*, September 24, 1940.
33. Woody Guthrie, "Woody Says He's Took Down with Publicity," *Daily Worker*, October 7, 1940; and Woody Guthrie, "Woody Says Memo Book Tells Him Where to Go," *Daily Worker*, October 18, 1940.
34. Woody Guthrie, "Dig Up the Real Folk Material Says Woody," *Daily Worker*, November 4, 1940; Guthrie to Lomax, quoted in Cray, *Ramblin' Man*, 189; and Klein, *Guthrie*, 171.
35. Szwed, *Alan Lomax*, 165–67; Cray, *Ramblin' Man*, 198–99; and Kaufman, *Guthrie: American Radical*, 52.

36. Woody Guthrie, *Bound for Glory* (New York: E. P. Dutton & Company, 1943), 399.
37. Woody Guthrie, "I'm Always on the Go," December 16, 1940, WGA, Notebook One.
38. Robert Coles, *Privileged Ones: The Well-Off and Rich in America*, vol. 5, *Children of Crisis* (New York: Little, Brown, 1977).

Chapter Four

1. Greg Vandy with Daniel Person, *26 Songs in 30 Days: Woody Guthrie's Columbia River Songs and the Planned Promised Land in the Pacific Northwest* (Seattle: Sasquatch Books, 2016), xiv.
2. Woody Guthrie to Elizabeth and Harold Ambellan, June 10, 1941, WGA, Correspondence Series 1, Box 1, Folder 3.
3. Shindo, *Dust Bowl Migrants in the American Imagination*, 169; and Peter La Chapelle, *Proud to Be an Okie: Cultural Politics, Country Music, and Migration to Southern California* (Berkeley: University of California Press, 2007).
4. Robbin, *Woody Guthrie and Me*, 58–62 and 88–89.
5. Woody Guthrie to Almanac Singers, March 1941, WGA, Correspondence Series 1, Box 1, Folder 3. The Almanac Singers were a group founded by Woody, Millard Lampell, Lee Hays, and Pete Seeger.
6. Woody Guthrie to Almanac Singers, March 1941, in *Pastures of Plenty*, Marsh and Leventhal, 51.
7. Woody Guthrie to Almanac Singers, March 1941, WGA, Correspondence Series 1, Box 1, Folder 3.
8. Szwed, *Alan Lomax*, 175.
9. Cray, *Ramblin' Man*, 208–9; and Marsh and Leventhal, *Pastures of Plenty*, 26.
10. For background information on the BPA, see Vandy, *26 Songs in 30 Days*, 86–83; and Mark Pedelty, "Woody Guthrie and the Columbia River: Propaganda, Art, and Irony," *Popular Music and Society* 31 (July 2008): 329–55.
11. For Pare Lorentz, see Robert L. Snyder, *Pare Lorentz and the Documentary Film* (Norman: University of Oklahoma Press, 1968);

and Pare Lorentz, *FDR's Moviemaker: Memoirs and Scripts* (Reno: University of Nevada Press, 1992).

12. Vandy, *26 Songs in 30 Days*, 44–45.
13. Pedelty, "Woody Guthrie and the Columbia River," 339.
14. Vandy, *26 Songs in 30 Days*, 101–2.
15. Ibid., 120–23.
16. Brad Knickerbocker, "Saving an Icon of the Pacific Northwest," *Christian Science Monitor*, January 30, 1997; Brad Cain, "Judge Orders Endangered Salmon Plan," *Seattle Times*, October 1, 2005; and R. C. Wissmar and S. D. Craig, "Factors Affecting Habitat Selection by a Small Spawning Chart Population, Bull Trout: Implications for Recovery of an Endangered Species," *Fisheries Management and Ecology* 11 (February 2004): 23–31.
17. Pedelty, "Woody Guthrie and the Columbia River," 333.
18. Ibid., 334.
19. Vandy, *26 Songs in 30 Days*, 109–10.
20. Woody Guthrie to Millard Lampell, September 9, 1941, WGA, Correspondence Series 1, Box 1, Folder 39.
21. Pedelty, "Woody Guthrie and the Columbia River," 334.
22. Asch, *American Folksong*, 44.
23. Richard Nate, "'Pastures of Plenty,' Woody Guthrie and the New Deal," in *The Life, Music and Thought of Woody Guthrie: A Critical Approach*, ed. John S. Partington (Burlington, Vermont: Ashgate Publishing Company, 2011), 3.
24. Richard Lowitt, *The New Deal and the West* (Norman: University of Oklahoma Press, 1984).
25. Will Kaufman, *Woody Guthrie's Modern World Blues* (Norman: University of Oklahoma Press, 2017), 23.
26. Arlo Guthrie quoted in Vandy, *26 Songs in 30 Days*, 98.
27. Vandy, *26 Songs in 30 Days*, 89.
28. Elia Kazan, *A Life* (New York: Alfred A. Knopf, 1988), 596–601.
29. Woody Guthrie to Almanac Singers, July 8, 1941, WGA, Correspondence Series 1, Box 1, Folder 3.

30. Woody Guthrie to Almanac Singers, n.d., WGA, Correspondence Series 1, Box 1, Folder 3.

Chapter Five

1. Robert Kennedy, *To Seek a Newer World* (New York: Doubleday and Company, 1967).
2. Pete Seeger, *"Where Have All the Flowers Gone": A Singer's Stories, Songs, Seeds, Robberies* (Bethlehem, Pennsylvania: Sing Out Corporation, 1993), 19.
3. Michael Denning, *The Cultural Front: The Laboring of American Culture in the Twentieth Century* (New York: Verso, 1997), 6–7. For the CIO, see Robert H. Zieger, *The CIO, 1935–1950* (Chapel Hill: University of North Carolina Press, 1997).
4. Woody Guthrie, "With the NMU Boys in Cleveland," 1941, WGA, Manuscripts Series 1, Box 1, Folder 10.
5. Woody Guthrie, "Union Show Troup," 1941, WGA, Manuscripts Series 1, Box 1, Folder 12.
6. Ibid.
7. Ibid.
8. Woody Guthrie, "Woody Says," n.d., WGA, Manuscript Series 1, Box 1, Folder 13.
9. Klein, *Guthrie*, 207.
10. Robbie Lieberman, *"My Song Is My Weapon": People's Songs, American Communism, and the Politics of Culture, 1930–50* (Urbana: University of Illinois Press, 1989), 57.
11. Bess Lomax Hawes, *Sing It Pretty* (Urbana: University of Illinois Press, 2008), 43.
12. Doris Willens, *Lonesome Travelin': The Life of Lee Hays* (Lincoln: University of Nebraska Press, 1993), 69.
13. Cray, *Ramblin' Man*, 242–54.
14. Klein, *Guthrie*, 237.
15. Kaufman, *Guthrie: American Radical*, 91–92.

16. Quoted in Klein, *Guthrie*, 270.
17. Woody Guthrie to Mama and Pete, November 17, 1942, WGA, Correspondence Series 1, Box 1, Folder 44.
18. Ibid.
19. Woody Guthrie to Mama and Pete, December 9, 1942, WGA, Correspondence Series 1, Box 1, Folder 44.
20. Woody Guthrie to Marjorie Greenblatt Mazia, "Talking Blues," n.d., WGA, Correspondence Series 1, Box 1, Folder 44.
21. Ibid.
22. Woody Guthrie to Pete and Little Mama, January 16, 1943, WGA, Correspondence Series 1, Box 1, Folder 45.
23. Ibid.
24. For the letters to Railroad Pete, many of them written on a desktop calendar that does not corresponded to when they were written, see WGA, Notebooks Series 1, Number 10; and Marsh and Leventhal, *Pastures of Plenty*, 95–112.
25. Ibid.
26. For Woody's Merchant Marine experience, see Jim Longhi, *Woody, Cisco, and Me: Seamen Three in the Merchant Marine* (Urbana: University of Illinois Press, 1997).
27. Woody Guthrie to Pete Seeger, October 30, 1943, WGA, Correspondence Series 1, Box 3, Folder 23.
28. Woody Guthrie to Marjorie Mazia Greenblatt, 1944, WGA, Correspondence Series 1, Box 1, Folder 51.
29. Woody Guthrie to *Daily Worker*, November 26, 1943, WGA, Manuscript Series 1, Box 4, Folder 5.
30. Ibid.
31. Woody Guthrie to *Daily Worker*, August 30, 1944, WGA, Manuscript Series 1, Box 4, Folder 9.

Chapter Six

1. Woody Guthrie to Marjorie Greenblatt Mazia, May 19, 1945, Correspondence Series 1, Box 2, Folder 1, WGA.

2. Woody Guthrie to Beth and Harold Ambellan, October 18, 1945, Correspondence Series 1, Box 1, Folder 1, WGA.
3. Woody Guthrie to Marjorie Greenblatt Mazia, August 1, 1945, WGA, Correspondence Series 1, Box 2, Folder 6.
4. Ibid. For revisionist scholarship on the atomic bomb, see Gar Alperovitz, *Atomic Diplomacy: Hiroshima and Potsdam* (New York: Vintage, 1965); Alperovitz, *The Decision to Use the Bomb* (New York: Random House, 1997); Ronald Takaki, *Hiroshima: Why America Dropped the Bomb* (New York: Back Bay Books, 1995); and Paul Ham, *Hiroshima and Nagasaki: The Real Story of the Atomic Bombings and Their Aftermath* (New York: Thomas Dunne Books, 2014).
5. Woody Guthrie to Marjorie Greenblatt Mazia, October 14, 1945, WGA, Correspondence Series 1, Box 2, Folder 6.
6. Woody Guthrie to Marjorie Greenblatt Mazia, November 5, 1945, WGA, Correspondence Series 1, Box 2, Folder 11.
7. Cray, *Ramblin' Man*, 288–92; and Klein, *Guthrie*, 292–304.
8. Quoted in Winkler, "*To Everything There Is a Season*," 40.
9. Woody Guthrie, "People's Songs and Its People," March 19, 1946, WGA, Manuscripts 1, Box 4.
10. Ibid.
11. Woody Guthrie, March 23, 1946, quoted in Marsh and Leventhal, *Pastures of Plenty*, 173–75.
12. Ibid.
13. William Chafe, *The Unfinished Journey: America Since World War II* (1986; repr. New York: Oxford University Press, 2015), 73–74.
14. For the labor movement in World War II and its aftermath, see Nelson Lichtenstein, *Labor's War at Home: The CIO in World War II* (Philadelphia: Temple University Press, 2008); Timothy J. Minchin, *Fighting Against the Odds: A History of Southern Labor Since World War II* (Gainesville: University Press of Florida, 2006); Philip Dray, *There Is Power in a Union: The Epic Story of Labor in America* (New York: Anchor, 2011); and Melvyn Dubofsky, *Labor in America: A History* (New York: Wiley, 2010).

15. Lieberman, "*My Song Is My Weapon*," 113.
16. Woody Guthrie to Moe Asch, 1945, Correspondence Series 1, Box 1, Folder 6; and Woody Guthrie to *Daily Worker*, August 30, 1944, WGA, Manuscripts 1, Box 4, Folder 9.
17. Woody Guthrie to Moe Asch, July 15, 1946, WGA, Correspondence Series 1, Box 1, Folder 6.
18. Quoted in Marsh and Leventhal, *Pastures of Plenty*, 164.
19. Woody Guthrie, "Cathy Ann Guthrie," n.d., WGA, Manuscripts 1, Box 4, Folder 59.
20. Woody Guthrie to Pete and Toshi Seeger, February 27, 1947, WGA, Correspondence Series 1, Box 3, Folder 24.
21. Woody Guthrie, "The Life of Our Little Four Year Old Daughter, Cathy Ann," June 29, 1947, WGA, Manuscripts 1, Box 4, Folder 56.2.
22. For Woody's troubling times in the late 1940s and early 1950s, see Cray, *Ramblin' Man*, 320–53.
23. Statement by President Harry S. Truman, June 27, 1950, Harry Truman Library and Museum, www.trumanlibrary.org. For the Korean War, see Clay Blair, *The Forgotten War: America in Korea, 1950–1953* (New York: Times Books, 1987); Bruce Cumings, *The Origins of the Korean War*, 2 vols. (Princeton, New Jersey: Princeton University Press, 1981); Dorothy Foot, *The Wrong War: American Policy and the Dimensions of the Korean Conflict, 1950–1953* (Ithaca, New York: Cornell University Press, 1985); David Halberstam, *The Coldest Winter: America and the Korean War* (New York: Hyperion, 2007); and Joseph C. Goulden, *Korea: The Untold Story of the War* (New York: Times Books, 1982).
24. Steve Casey, *Selling the Korean War: Propaganda, Politics, and Public Opinion in the United States, 1950–1953* (New York: Oxford University Press, 2008), 367; and Robin Brooks, "Domestic Violence and American Wars: A Historical Interpretation," in *Violence in America: Politics, Rebellion, Reform*, vol. 2, ed. Ted Robert Gurr (New York: Sage, 1994), 183–84.
25. Larry Ceplair and Steven Englund, *The Inquisition in Hollywood: Politics in the Film Community, 1930–1960* (Berkeley: University

of California Press, 1979); and Winkler, "*To Everything There Is a Season*," 64–65.

26. Woody Guthrie to Harry Truman, July 31, 1949, WGA, Correspondence Series 1, Box 3, Folder 27.
27. For Woody and the atomic bomb, see Pedelty, "Guthrie and the Columbia River," 346–347; Woody Guthrie, "Freedom's Fire," September 26, 1945, WGA, Song Texts, Box 1, Folder 1; and Woody Guthrie, "One Thing the Atom Can't Do," April 9, 1946, WGA, Notebook Series 1, Number 2.
28. Woody Guthrie, "Why Is It?", n.d., WGA, Notebook Series 1, Number 64.
29. Woody Guthrie, "Thirty 8th Parallel," March 19, 1951, WGA, Notebook Series 1, Number 64; and Woody Guthrie, "Jeep in the Mud," November 1952, WGA, Notebook Series 1, Number 65.
30. Woody Guthrie, "Korea Send Me Home Blues," December 1952, WGA, Notebook Series 1, Number 64; Woody Guthrie, "Korean Quicksands," April 1951, WGA, Notebook Series 1, Number 64; Woody Guthrie, "Korea Bye Bye," November 1952, WGA, Notebook Series 1, Number 64; and Woody Guthrie, "I Don't Want Korea," November 1952, WGA, Notebook Series 1, Number 64.
31. Woody Guthrie, "Korean Beauty," December 1952, WGA, Notebook Series 1, Number 64; Woody Guthrie, "Korean Girly," April 1951, WGA, Notebook Series 1, Number 64; Woody Guthrie, "Korean Boogey," December 1952, WGA, Notebook Series 1, Number 64; Woody Guthrie, "Korea I Love You," November 1952, WGA, Notebook Series 1, Number 64; and Woody Guthrie, "Korea and Me," November 1952, WGA, Notebook Series 1, Number 64.
32. Woody Guthrie, "Mr. Sickyman Ree," November 1952, WGA, Notebook Series 1, Number 64; Woody Guthrie, "Korea Mackarter," November 1952, WGA, Notebook Series 1, Number 64; Woody Guthrie, "Han River Blood," December 1952, WGA, Notebook Series 1, Number 64; and Woody Guthrie, "Han River Mud," n.d., WGA, Notebook Series 1, Number 64.
33. Charles J. Hanley, Sang-Hun Choe, and Martha Mendoza, *The Bridge at No Gun Rio* (New York: Henry Holt and Company, 2001), 94.
34. Woody Guthrie, April 1953, WGA, Notebook Series 2, Book 3.

35. Chafe, *Unfinished Journey*, 247–55.
36. Arnold A. Offner, *Another Such Victory: President Truman and the Cold War, 1945–1953* (Stanford, California: Stanford University Press, 2002), 470.
37. Nora Guthrie, telephone interview with author, May 19, 2010.

Chapter Seven

A version of this chapter was originally published as "Woody Guthrie and the Christian Left: Jesus and 'Commonism,'" *Journal of Texas Music History* 7 (2007): 2–14.

1. Joyce Kornbluh, *Rebel Voices: An IWW Anthology*; Franklin Rosemont, *Joe Hill and the IWW & the Making of a Revolutionary Workingclass Counterculture* (Oakland, California: PM Press, 2015); and William Adler, *The Man Who Never Died: The Life, Times, and Legacy of Joe Hill, American Labor Icon* (New York: Bloomsbury, 2012).
2. Kevin M. Kruse, *One Nation Under God: How Corporate America Invented Christian America* (New York: Basic Books, 2013).
3. Paul Krugman, "No Surrender," *New York Times*, November 5, 2004; Thomas Frank, *What's the Matter with Kansas? How Conservatives Won the Heart of America* (New York: Henry Holt, 2004); and Kevin Phillips, *American Theocracy: The Peril of Radical Religion, Oil, and Borrowed Money in the 21st Century* (New York: Viking Press, 2006).
4. Jim Wallis, *The Soul of Politics: A Practical and Prophetic Vision for Change* (New York: The New Press, 1997), xxiv; and Jim Wallis, *God's Politics: Why the Right Gets It Wrong and the Left Doesn't Get It* (New York: Harper Collins, 2005).
5. John C. Cost, *Christian Socialism: An Informal History* (Mary Knoll, New York: Orbis Books, 1988); and James A. Drombrowski, *The Early Days of Christian Socialism in America* (New York: Octagon Books, 1977).
6. Jim Bissett, *Agrarian Socialism in America: Marx, Jefferson, and Jesus in the Oklahoma Countryside, 1904–1920* (Norman: University of Oklahoma Press, 1999), 97.

7. Stephen Prothero, *American Jesus: How the Son of God Became a National Icon* (New York: Farrar, Straus and Giroux, 2003), 7.
8. Klein, *Guthrie*, 61.
9. Bissett, *Agrarian Socialism in America*, 99.
10. Guthrie, *Bound for Glory*, 333–34.
11. Woody Guthrie, "Woody Sez," *PDW*, July 12, 1939; and Woody Guthrie, "Woody Sez," *PDW*, December 5, 1939.
12. Woody Guthrie, "Woody Sez," *PDW*, October 27, 1939.
13. Woody Guthrie, "Jesus Christ Was a Man," in *Hard Hitting Songs*, eds. Lomax, Guthrie, and Seeger, 8–9; and Woody Guthrie, "Pretty Boy Floyd," Library of Congress Recordings, March 21, 22, and April 26, 1940 in *Woody Guthrie: American Radical Patriot*, ed. Bill Nowlin (New York: Rounder, 2013), 86–87.
14. Woody Guthrie, "Jesus Christ for President," in *Pastures of Plenty*, Marsh and Leventhal, 43.
15. Woody Guthrie, "This Morning I Am Born Again," in *Pastures of Plenty*, Marsh and Leventhal, 141.
16. Klein, *Guthrie*, 340; and Woody Guthrie to Marjorie Guthrie, October 4, 1956, WGA, Correspondence Series 1, Box 3, Folder 10.
17. Klein, *Guthrie*, 408; and Woody Guthrie to Mary Jo Edgmon, September 4, 1956, WGA, Correspondence Series 1, Box 1, Folder 14.
18. Wallis, *God's Politics*, 19.

Chapter Eight

1. E. J. Hobsbawm, *Primitive Rebels: Studies in Archaic Forms of Social Movements in the 19th and 20th Centuries* (New York: W. W. Norton & Company, 1965), 5.
2. For the social bandits of the depression era, see Bryan Burrough, *Public Enemies: America's Greatest Crime Wave and the Birth of the FBI, 1933–34* (New York: Penguin, 2005); Jeff Guinn, *Go Down Together: The True Untold Story of Bonnie and Clyde* (New York: Simon and Schuster, 2010); and Elliott J. Gorn, *Dillinger's Wild Ride: The Year That Made America's Public Enemy Number One* (New York: Oxford University Press, 2009).

3. Lomax, Guthrie, and Seeger, *Hard Hitting Songs*, 232.
4. Jackson, *Prophet Singer*, 169.
5. Richard Slotkin, *Regeneration through Violence: The Mythology of the American Frontier, 1600–1860* (Middletown, Connecticut: Wesleyan University Press, 1973), 5.
6. For background information on Pretty Boy Floyd, see Michael Wallis, *"Pretty Boy": The Life and Times of Charles Arthur Floyd* (New York: St. Martin's Press, 1993); and Jeffrey S. King, *The Life & Death of Pretty Boy Floyd* (Kent, Ohio: Kent State University Press, 1998).
7. Woody Guthrie, "Pretty Boy Floyd," n.d., WGA, Notebook Series 1, Number 4; Guthrie, "Pretty Boy Floyd," in *Hard Hitting Songs*, 114–15; and Guthrie, Library of Congress Recordings, 82–83. Excerpted lyrics from "Pretty Boy Floyd" by Wood Gurthrie ©Woody Guthrie Publications, Inc. All rights reserved. Used by Permission.
8. Guthrie, "Pretty Boy Floyd," in *Hard Hitting Songs*, 114–115.
9. Woody Guthrie, "The Dalton Boys," March 7, 1939, WGA, Notebook Series 1, Number 4; and Nancy B. Samuelson, *The Dalton Gang Story: Lawmen to Outlaws* (Eastford, Connecticut: Shooting Star Press, 1992).
10. Glenn Shirley, *Belle Starr and Her Times: The Literature, the Facts and the Legends* (Norman: University of Oklahoma Press, 1982); and Woody Guthrie, "Belle Starr," in *American Folksong*, Asch, 28.
11. Robert M. Utley, *Wanted: The Outlaw Lives of Billy the Kid & Ned Kelly* (New Haven, Connecticut: Yale University Press, 2015), 208–9; Woody Guthrie, "Billy the Kid," in *American Folksong*, Asch, 29; and Jackson, *Prophet Singer*, 176–77.
12. Lomax, Guthrie, and Seeger, *Hard Hitting Songs*, 18.
13. Woody Guthrie, "Jesse James and His Gang," n.d., WGA, Notebook Series 1, Number 4; and Woody Guthrie, "Jesse James and His Boys," in *Hard Hitting Songs*, eds. Lomax, Guthrie, and Seeger, 112–13.
14. Guthrie, Library of Congress Recordings, 84–85.
15. Woody Guthrie, "Woody Sez," *PDW*, October 10, 1939.
16. T. J. Stiles, *Jesse James: Last Rebel of the Civil War* (New York: Alfred A. Knopf, 2002), 5–6.
17. Guthrie, "Jesus Christ Was a Man," 336–37.

18. Guthrie, "This Morning I Am Born Again," 141.
19. Woody Guthrie, "Tom Joad," in *Hard Hitting Songs*, eds. Lomax, Guthrie, Seeger, 236–38.
20. Zoe Trodd, "Star Symbols: John Steinbeck in the American Protest Tradition," *The Steinbeck Review* 5 (Fall 2008): 29.
21. Bryant Simon and William Deverell, "Come Back, Tom Joad: Thoughts on a California Dreamer," *California History* 79 (Winter, 2000/2001): 184.
22. Paul D. Fischer, "Review of *The Ghost of Tom Joad* by Bruce Springsteen," *The Journal of American Folklore*, 110 (Spring 1997): 211.
23. Simon and Deverell, "Come Back, Tom Joad: Thoughts on a California Dreamer," 191; and Rick Wartzman, *Obscene in the Extreme: The Burning and Banning of John Steinbeck's The Grapes of Wrath* (New York: Public Affairs, 2008).

Chapter Nine

1. For a good brief discussion of the post-World War II union movement, see Philip Dray, *There is Power in a Union*, 485–546.
2. Jefferson Cowie, *Stayin' Alive: The 1970s and the Last Days of the Working Class* (New York: The New Press, 2010), 368–69; and Joseph McCartin, *Collision Course: Ronald Reagan, the Air Traffic Controllers, and the Strike that Changed America* (New York: Oxford University Press, 2013).
3. Jackson, *Prophet Singer*, 252.
4. Quoted in Asch, *American Folksong*, 4.
5. Lomax, Guthrie, and Seeger, *Hard Hitting Songs*, 17.
6. Nora Guthrie, phone interview with author, May 19, 2010; and Lomax, Guthrie, and Seeger, *Hard Hitting Songs*, 281.
7. Woody Guthrie, "Final Call," February 12, 1939, WGA, Song Texts, Box 1, Folder 9.
8. Woody Guthrie, March 1941, WGA, Song Texts, Box 1, Folder 9.
9. Woody Guthrie, "When You're Down and Out," 1944, WGA, Song Texts, Box 4, Folder 30.

10. Woody Guthrie to Ed Robbin, 1941, quoted in Robbin, *Woody Guthrie and Me*, 149.
11. Zieger, *The CIO*, 1–2.
12. Woody Guthrie to Pat Lyon, August 9, 1942, WGA, Correspondence Series 1, Box 1, Folder 41.
13. Woody Guthrie, "Union Show Troup," 1942, WGA, Manuscripts Series 1, Box 1, Folder 12.
14. Ibid.
15. Ibid.
16. Woody Guthrie, "War Songs & Work Songs," 1942, WGA, Manuscripts Series 1, Box 3, Folder 22.
17. Woody Guthrie to *Daily Worker* Staff, November 26, 1944, WGA, Manuscripts Series 1, Box 4, Folder 1.
18. Woody Guthrie to *Daily Worker*, August 30, 1944, WGA, Manuscripts Series 1, Box 4, Folder 9.
19. Woody Guthrie, "Union Labor or Slave Labor," 1944, WGA, Manuscripts Series 1, Box 4, Folder 16. For the 1944 political campaign see Jay Wink, *1944: FDR and The Year that Changed History* (New York: Simon & Schuster, 2015).
20. Woody Guthrie, "WNEW," December 3, 1944, WGA, Manuscripts Series 1, Box 4, Folder 14.
21. Guthrie, "This Morning I Am Born Again," 141.
22. Woody Guthrie to Duncan Emrich, March 29, 1946, WGA, Correspondence Series 1, Box 1, Folder 15.
23. Jackson, *Prophet Singer*, 248–49.
24. Zieger, *The CIO*, 239.
25. Woody Guthrie to People's Songs, June 29, 1947, WGA, Correspondence Series 1, Box 4, Folder 2.5.
26. Woody Guthrie, "Wallace Day," n.d., WGA, Song Texts, Box 1, Folder 30, WGA.
27. For Henry Wallace and the election of 1948, see David Pretrusza, *1948: Harry Truman's Improbable Victory and the Year that Transformed America* (New York: Union Square Press, 2011); Thomas W. Devine, *Henry Wallace's 1948 Presidential Campaign and the Future of Postwar Liberalism* (Chapel Hill: The University of North Carolina Press, 2015);

and John C. Culver and John Hyde, *American Dreamer: A Life of Henry Wallace* (New York: W. W. Norton & Company, 2000).
28. Woody Guthrie to Aliza Greenblatt, March 20, 1949, WGA, Correspondence Series 1, Folder 24.

Chapter Ten

1. Guthrie, *Bound for Glory*, 35.
2. Ibid., 246.
3. Ibid., 292–93.
4. Jackson, *Prophet Singer*, 137.
5. Jimmie Lewis Franklin, *The Blacks in Oklahoma* (Norman: University of Oklahoma Press, 1980), 21–24.
6. James S. Hirsch, *Riot and Remembrance: The Tulsa Race War and Its Legacy* (Boston: Houghton Mifflin Company, 1992), 6.
7. Seth Archer, "Reading the Riot Acts," *Southwest Review*, 91 (Winter 2006): 500–516.
8. Woody Guthrie, "Don't Kill My Baby and My Son," in *Hard Hitting Songs*, eds. Lomax, Guthrie, and Seeger, 334–35.
9. Jackson, *Prophet Singer*, 137.
10. Guthrie, 1937, WGA, Notebook Series 1, Number 2.
11. Quoted in Kaufman, *Woody Guthrie: American Radical*, 149–50.
12. Klehr, *Heyday of American Communism*, ix and 324–28.
13. Woody Guthrie, "Hallelujah, I'm a Ku Klux," in *Hard Hitting Songs*, eds. Lomax, Guthrie, and Seeger, 340–41.
14. Woody Guthrie, "War Songs and Work Songs," n.d., WGA, Notebook Series 1, Number 3.
15. Woody Guthrie, "World Hope," n.d., WGA, Manuscript Series 1, Box 3, Folder 23.
16. Woody Guthrie, "Postage Stamp," July 19, 1944, WGA, Manuscript Series 1, Box 4, Folder 6.
17. Woody Guthrie, "Negro History," March 1947, WGA, Notebook Series 1, Number 58.
18. For Lead Belly see Kip Lornell and Charles Wolfe, *The Life and Legend of Leadbelly* (New York: Da Capo Press, 1999).

19. John Szwed, *Alan Lomax*, 158–59.
20. Woody Guthrie, "Leadbelly," April 16, 1944, WGA, Manuscript Series 1, Box 4, Folder 3; and "Midnight Special," March 4, 1947, WGA, Manuscript Series 1, Box 4, Folder 51.
21. Woody Guthrie to Marjorie Mazia Greenblatt, May 19, 1945, WGA, Correspondence Series 1, Box 2, Folder 1.
22. Longhi, *Woody, Cisco, and Me*, 227–31.
23. Jackson, *Prophet Singer*, 248–49.
24. Will Kaufman, "Woody Guthrie, 'Old Man Trump,' and a Real Estate Empire's Racist Foundations," *The Conversation*, January 26, 2016, www.theconversation.com; and Woody Guthrie, "Beach Haven Race Hate," 1954, WGA, Notebook Series 1, Number 64:2, p. 73.
25. Woody Guthrie to Moe Asch, August 15, 1946, WGA, Correspondence Series 1, Box 1, Folder 6; and Woody Guthrie, "The Ballad of Isaac Woodard," August 16, 1946, WGA, Correspondence Series 1, Box 1, Folder 6.
26. For a discussion of Guthrie's compositions "The Killing of the Ferguson Brothers," "Buoy Bells from Trenton," and "The Ballad of Rosa Lee Ingram," see Kaufman, *Woody Guthrie: American Radical*, 355–58.
27. Woody Guthrie, "Ballad of Harriet Tubman," April 11, 1953, WGA, Notebook Series 2, Number 1; Jackson, *Prophet Singer*, 197–99; and Milton C. Sernett, *Harriet Tubman: Myth, Memory, and History* (Durham, North Carolina: Duke University Press, 2007).
28. Woody Guthrie, "Peekskill," n.d., WGA, Notebook Series 2, Book 7; Woody Guthrie, "My Thirty Thousand," n.d., WGA, Song Series 1, Box 1, Folder 18; and Lee Hays and Robert S. Koppelman, ed., *Sing Out, Warning! Sing Out, Love: The Writings of Lee Hays* (Amherst: University of Massachusetts Press, 2004), 97. For Paul Robeson see Martin Duberman, *Paul Robeson* (New York: Knopf, 1989); Paul Robeson Jr., *Paul Robeson: The Undiscovered Quest for Freedom, 1939–1976* (New York: Wiley, 2010); and Gerald Horne, *Paul Robeson: The Artist as Revolutionary* (New York: Pluto Press, 2016).
29. Jorge Arevalo Mateus, "*Beluthahatchee Blues*: An Interview with Stetson Kennedy," in *Radicalism in the South Since Reconstruction*,

eds. Chris Green, Rachel Rubin, and James Smethurst (New York: Palgrave, 2006), 213.

30. For Stetson Kennedy, see Edward A. Hatfield, "Stetson Kennedy (1916–2011)," *New Georgia Encyclopedia*, August 14, 2009, www.georgiaencyclopedia.org; Stetson Kennedy, *The Klan Unmasked* (1954; repr. Tuscaloosa: University of Alabama Press, 2011); and Stetson Kennedy, *Jim Crow Guide to the U.S.A.* (1959; repr. Tuscaloosa: University of Alabama Press, 2011).
31. Woody Guthrie to Stetson Kennedy, April 21, 1945, WGA, Correspondence Series 1, Box 1, Folder 32.
32. Cray, *Ramblin' Man*, 344.
33. Woody Guthrie to Moe Asch, August 26, 1953, WGA, Correspondence Series 1, Box 1, Folder 9.
34. Woody Guthrie, "Genocide," 1952, WGA, Notebook Series 2, Number 3.
35. Woody Guthrie, "Pistol Packer," 1953, WGA, Notebook Series 2, Number 3; "Hold On," 1953, WGA, Notebook Series 2, Number 1; "Belutchahatchee Blues," 1953, WGA, Notebook Series 2, Number 1; "Peace Town," 1953, WGA, Notebook Series 2, Number 1; "Choppin Axe Blues," 1953, WGA, Notebook Series 1, Number 2; and "Seeds of Man," 1953, WGA, Notebook Series 2, Number 9.
36. Woody Guthrie, "Harriet Tubman," April 11, 1953, WGA, Notebook Series 2, Number 1.
37. Mateus, "Interview with Stetson Kennedy," 223.
38. Woody Guthrie, "Will Rogers Highway," March 1940, WGA, Notebook Series 1, Number 4.
39. Woody Guthrie, "The Chinese and the Japs," 1938, WGA, Notebook Series 1, Number 4; and "The Nazis and the Japs," n.d., WGA, Notebook Series 1, Number 3.
40. John Dower, *War Without Mercy: Race and Power in the Pacific War* (New York: Pantheon, 1987).
41. Guthrie, *Bound for Glory*, 354–55.
42. Carey McWilliams, *Factories in the Field: The Story of Migratory Farm Labor in California* (1939; repr. Berkeley: University of California Press, 2000); and Klein, *Guthrie*, 349.
43. Kaufman, *Woody Guthrie: American Radical*, 165.

Chapter Eleven

1. Woody Guthrie, 1941, WGA, Manuscript Series 1, Box 1, Folder 14.2.
2. Woody Guthrie, "She Came Along to Me," Woody Guthrie Publications, 1942, www.woodyguthrie.org; and Billy Bragg and Wilco, *Mermaid Avenue*, vol. 1, Nonesuch Records, 1998, compact disc. Excerpted lyrics from "She Came Along to Me" Words by Woody Guthrie, Music by Billy Bragg © Copyright Woody Guthrie, Publications, Inc. All rights reserved. Used by Permission.
3. For background information on Aunt Molly Jackson, see Shelly Romalis, *Pistol Packing Mama: Aunt Molly Jackson and the Politics of Folksong* (Urbana: University of Illinois Press, 1998); and John W. Hevener, *Which Side Are You On?: The Harlan County Coal Miners, 1931–39* (Urbana: University of Illinois Press, 1992).
4. Woody Guthrie, "Hell Bursts Loose in Kentucky," in *Hard Hitting Songs*, eds. Lomax, Guthrie, and Seeger, 139–40.
5. Woody Guthrie, "The Story of Sara Ogan," in *Hard Hitting Songs*, eds. Lomax, Guthrie, and Seeger, 154–55.
6. Woody Guthrie, "Union Maid # 1," n.d., WGA, Song Series 1, Box 3, Folder 28.
7. Woody Guthrie, "Miss Pavlachenko," November 10, 1942, WGA, Notebook Series 1, Number 3.
8. Woody Guthrie, "Wimmens Hats," February 24, 1940, WGA, Notebook Series 1, Number 4.
9. Woody Guthrie to Marjorie Greenblatt Mazia, "Talking Blues," 1942, WGA, Correspondence Series 1, Folder 44.
10. Woody Guthrie to Marjorie Mazia Greenblatt, November 17, 1942, WGA, Correspondence Series 1, Box 1, Folder 44.
11. Woody Guthrie to Marjorie Greenblatt Mazia, December 9, 1942, WGA, Correspondence Series 1, Box 1, Folder 44; and Woody Guthrie to Marjorie Greenblatt Mazia, 1942, WGA, Correspondence Series 1, Box 1, Folder 44.
12. Wood Guthrie to Railroad Pete, January 1943, WGA, Notebook Series 1, Number 10.

13. Woody Guthrie, "Union Home," April 4, 1944, WGA, Notebook Series 1, Number 26.
14. Woody Guthrie to Marjorie Greenblatt Guthrie, December 1, 1945, WGA, Correspondence Series 1, Box 2, Folder 11.
15. For the sexual relationship between Marjorie and Woody see Klein, *Guthrie*, 299–301.
16. Woody Guthrie to Marjorie Greenblatt Guthrie, May 9, 1947, WGA, Correspondence Series 1, Box 2, Folder 12.
17. Woody Guthrie to Marjorie Greenblatt Guthrie, May 16, 1947, WGA, Correspondence Series 1, Box 2, Folder 12.
18. Woody Guthrie, "Marjorie," August 9, 1947, WGA, Notebook Series 1, Number 57.
19. Woody Guthrie, "Whores and Wives," August 6, 1947, WGA, Notebook Series 1, Number 54.
20. Woody Guthrie, "Union Love Juice," August 10, 1947, WGA, Notebook Series 1, Number 57.
21. Cray, *Ramblin' Man*, 318–19.
22. Woody Guthrie, "Ranian's Finbow and Me," 1947, WGA, Manuscript Series 1, Box 4, Folder 60.
23. Ibid.
24. Cray, *Ramblin' Man*, 118–20.
25. Woody Guthrie, diary entry, November 8, 1947, WGA, Notebook Series 1, Number 62.
26. Woody Guthrie, diary entry, November 10, 1947, WGA, Notebook Series 1, Number 62.
27. Woody Guthrie, diary entry, October 1949, WGA, Notebook Series 1, Book 71.
28. Woody Guthrie, diary entry, October 19, 1947, WGA, Notebook Series 1, Box 52.
29. Woody Guthrie, "I Cant Love My Wife No More," December 1952, WGA, Notebook Series 1, Number 74.
30. Klein, *Guthrie*, 358–59.
31. Woody Guthrie to Moe Asch, August 24, 1953 and December 12, 1953, WGA, Correspondence Series 1, Box 1, Folder 9.

32. Guthrie, *Bound for Glory*, 381.
33. Arthur Falek, "Observations on Patient and Family Coping with Huntington's Disease," *Omega: An International Journal for the Study of Dying, Death, Bereavement, Suicide, and Other Lethal Behaviors* 10, no. 1 (1979): 36.
34. Woody Guthrie, "Whitman, Sandberg & Pushkin," August 5, 1947, WGA, Notebook Series 1, Number 54.
35. Woody Guthrie, "Both of You," October 17, 1947, WGA, Notebook Series 1, Number 52. For Walt Whitman see David Reynolds, *Walt Whitman's America: A Cultural Biography* (New York: Vintage, 1996); Justin Kaplan, *Walt Whitman: A Life* (New York: Perennial, 2003); and Justin Martin, *Rebel Souls: Walt Whitman and America's First Bohemians* (New York: Da Capo Press, 2014).
36. Woody Guthrie, "My Big Mixed Race," WGA, Notebook Series 1, Book 2.
37. Woody Guthrie, "Baby Knocker," April 1953, WGA, Notebook Series 2, Book 1.
38. Woody Guthrie to Marjorie Greenblatt Guthrie, December 1956, WGA, Correspondence Series 1, Folder 11.
39. K. A. Cuordileone, *Manhood and American Political Culture in the Cold War* (New York: Routledge, 2005), xx–xxi; and David K. Johnson, *The Lavender Scare: The Cold War Persecution of Gays and Lesbians in the Federal Government* (Chicago: University of Chicago Press, 2006), 2–3.
40. Woody Guthrie, diary entry, August 23, 1947, WGA, Notebook Series 1, Number 52.
41. Marsh and Leventhal, *Pastures of Plenty*, 234.

Chapter Twelve

1. Dayton Duncan and Ken Burns, *The Dust Bowl: An Illustrated History* (San Francisco: Chronicle Books, 2012), 90–91. For an excellent oral history of the dust bowl, see Timothy Egan, *The Worst Hard Time: The Untold Story of Those Who Survived the Great American Dust Bowl* (Boston: Houghton Mifflin, 2005).

2. Donald Worster, *Dust Bowl: The Southern Plains in the 1930s* (New York: Oxford University Press, 1979), 4–5. Also see Paul Bonnefield, *The Dust Bowl: Men, Dust, and Depression* (Albuquerque: University of New Mexico Press, 1979).
3. Shindo, *Dust Bowl Migrants*, 168–69.
4. Brad Lookingbill, "Dusty Apocalypse and Socialist Salvation," *Chronicles of Oklahoma* 74 (Winter 1994): 396–413 is an example of scholarship that credits Woody's dust bowl experience as fostering his radical political perspective.
5. Szwed, *Alan Lomax*, 160–64.
6. For an analysis of critical reaction in 1940 to *Dust Bowl Ballads*, see Klein, *Guthrie*, 163–64.
7. Ibid., 159.
8. Woody Guthrie, *Dust Bowl Ballads*, Buddha Records, 2000, compact disc (originally release 1940).
9. Anthony Decurtis, "*Dust Bowl Ballads*," *Rolling Stone*, 2000, www.rollingstone.com.
10. Woody Guthrie, "Liner Notes," in *Dust Bowl Ballads*, Buddha Records, 2000, compact disc.
11. Ibid.
12. Worster, *Dust Bowl*, 49.
13. Woody Guthrie, Liner Notes, *Dust Bowl Ballads*.
14. Woody Guthrie, "The Okie Section," in *Hard Hitting Songs*, eds. Lomax, Guthrie, and Seeger, 213.
15. Woody Guthrie, "Dust Bowl Refugee," in *Hard Hitting Songs*, eds. Lomax, Guthrie, and Seeger, 224.
16. Woody Guthrie, "Dust Storm Disaster," and "Dust Cain't Kill Me," in *Hard Hitting Songs*, eds. Lomax, Guthrie, and Seeger, 218–20.
17. Woody Guthrie, "Vigilante Man," in *Hard Hitting Songs*, eds. Lomax, Guthrie, and Seeger, 234–35.
18. Woody Guthrie, "I'm Goin' Down That Road Feeling Bad," in *Hard Hitting Songs*, eds. Lomax, Guthrie, and Seeger, 215–16.
19. Guthrie, "When the Great Dust Storm Struck," Library of Congress Recordings, in *American Radical Patriot*, Nowlin, 71.

20. Woody Guthrie, "So Long, It's Been Good to Know You," Library of Congress Recordings, in *American Radical Patriot*, Nowlin, 72–73.
21. Neil Larry Shumsky, "Dust, Disease, Death and Deity: Constructing and Deconstructing the Dust Bowl," *The Journal of American Culture* 38 (September 2015): 229–31; and Paul Boyer, *When Time Shall Be No More: Prophecy Belief in Modern American Culture* (Cambridge, Massachusetts: Harvard University Press, 1992).
22. Woody Guthrie, "Dust Bowl Pneumonia Blues," Library of Congress Recordings, in *American Radical Patriot*, Nowlin, 112–13.
23. Worster, *Dust Bowl*, 20–21.
24. Woody Guthrie, "Talking Dust Bowl," Library of Congress Recordings, in *American Radical Patriot*, Nowlin, 74–75.
25. Woody Guthrie, "Do Re Mi," Library of Congress Recordings, in *American Radical Patriot*, Nowlin, 75–76.
26. Woody Guthrie, "I Ain't Got No Home in the World Anymore," Library of Congress Recordings, in *American Radical Patriot*, Nowlin, 89.
27. Klein, *Guthrie*, 117–118. For the Carter Family, see Mark Zwonitzer with Charles Hirschberg, *Will You Miss Me When I'm Gone? The Carter Family and Their Legacy in American Music* (New York: Simon & Schuster, 2004); and Beth Harrington, *The Winding Stream: An Oral History of the Carter and Cash Family* (Georgetown, Massachusetts: PFP, 2014).
28. Wartzman, *Obscene in the Extreme*, 6–7; and Kaufman, *Woody Guthrie: American Radical*, 25.
29. Woody Guthrie, "Going Down That Road Feeling Bad," Library of Congress Recordings, in *American Radical Patriot*, Nowlin, 103–104; and Guthrie, "Pretty Boy Floyd," Library of Congress Recordings, 83–84.
30. Nancy Isenberg, *White Trash: The 400-Year Untold History of Class in America* (New York: Viking Press, 2016).
31. Jeff Morgan, "Hard Travelin': Constructing Woody Guthrie's Dust Bowl Legacy," in *The Life, Music and Thought of Woody Guthrie*, ed. Partington, 99–113; and Jerome Rodnitzsky, *Minstrels of the Dawn: The Folk Singer as a Cultural* Hero (New York: Nelson-Hall, 1976), 43–44.

32. Woody Guthrie, "Hard Time on the Farm," in *Hard Hitting Songs*, eds. Lomax, Guthrie, and Seeger, 27.
33. Woody Guthrie, "Seven Cent Cotton and Forty Cent Meat," in *Hard Hitting Songs*, eds. Lomax, Guthrie, and Seeger, 38–39.
34. Woody Guthrie to Lee Hays, February 25, 1941, WGA, Correspondence Series 1, Box 1, Folder 31.
35. Ibid.
36. Woody Guthrie to Eugene Saxton, June 14, 1942, WGA, Correspondence Series 1, Box 3, Folder 21.

Chapter Thirteen

1. Moses Asch, "Liner Notes," in *Struggle*, Woody Guthrie, Folkways Records, 1976, compact disc.
2. Wayne Hampton, *Guerrilla Minstrels: John Lennon, Joe Hill, Woody Guthrie, and Bob Dylan* (Knoxville: The University of Tennessee Press, 1986), 146–47.
3. Alan Lomax quoted in Jon Pareles, "Moses Asch, Who Founded Folkways Records, Dies at 81," *New York Times*, October 21, 1986. For additional background on Asch see Peter D. Goldsmith, *Making People's Music: Moe Asch and Folkways Records*; and Tony Olmstead, *Folkways Records: Moses Asch and His Encyclopedia of Song* (New York: Routledge, 2003).
4. Woody Guthrie to Moe Asch and Marian Distler, summer 1945, WGA, Correspondence Series 1, Box 1, Folder 6.
5. Woody Guthrie, "Don't Lie to Me," 1945, WGA, Manuscript Series 1, Box 4, Folder 22.2.
6. Woody Guthrie to Marian Distler, July 10, 1945, WGA, Correspondence Series 1, Box 1, Folder 6.
7. Woody Guthrie to Charlotte Strauss, December 6, 1945, Charlotte Strauss Collection, WGA, Accession #2008-242.3.
8. Woody Guthrie to Moe Asch, September 9, 1945, WGA, Correspondence Series 1, Box 1, Folder 6.

9. Carey McWilliams, *Ill Fares the Land: Migrants and Migratory Labor in California* (Boston: Little, Brown and Company, 1942); and Woody Guthrie to Moe Asch, June 21, 1946, WGA, Correspondence Series 1, Box 1, Folder 6.
10. Woody Guthrie to Moe Asch, August 1, 1946, WGA, Correspondence Series 1, Box 1, Folder 6.
11. Woody Guthrie to Moe Asch, July 15, 1946, WGA, Correspondence Series 1, Box 1, Folder 6.
12. Ibid.
13. Woody Guthrie to Moe Asch, August 15, 1946, WGA, Correspondence Series 1, Box 1, Folder 6.
14. Goldsmith, *Making People's Music*, 182–83.
15. Klein, *Guthrie*, 314–15.
16. Woody Guthrie to Moe Asch, June 24, 1947, WGA, Correspondence Series 1, Box 1, Folder 8.
17. Woody Guthrie to Moe Asch and Marian Distler, April 22, 1947, WGA, Correspondence Series 1, Box 1, Folder 8.
18. Woody Guthrie to Moe Asch, December 2, 1950, WGA, Correspondence Series, 1, Box 1, Folder 9.
19. Thomas G. Andrews, *Killing for Coal: America's Deadliest Labor War* (Cambridge, Massachusetts: Harvard University Press, 2008), 290.
20. Archie Green, *Only a Miner: Studies in Recorded Coal-Mining Songs* (Urbana: University of Illinois Press, 1972); Robert V. Wells, *Life Flows On in Endless Song: Folk Songs and American History* (Urbana: University of Illinois Press, 2009), 92–93; U.S. Department of Labor, Mine Safety, and Health Administration, "Mining Industry Accident, Injuries, Employment, and Production," accessed August 15, 2012, www.msha.gov/ACCIN3/BOTCL.HTM; Robert Bartley and David Kenney, *Death Underground: The Centralia and West Frankfurt Mine Disasters* (Carbondale: Southern Illinois University Press, 2006); and Woody Guthrie, "The Dying Miner" and "Waiting at the Gate," *Struggle*, Folkways Records, 1976, compact disc.
21. Woody Guthrie, "Silicosis is Killin' Me," in *Hard Hitting Songs*, eds. Lomax, Guthrie, and Seeger, 134; and Woody Guthrie, "Union Burying Ground," *Struggle*, Folkways Records, 1976, compact disc.

22. Woody Guthrie, "Get Along Little Doggies," *Struggle*, Folkways Records, 1976, compact disc. For the reality of the cattle drives and the cowboy life see J. Marvin Hunter, ed., *The Trail Drivers of Texas: Interesting Sketches of Early Cowboys* (1920; repr. Austin: University of Texas Press, 1992); Philip Ashton Rollins, *The Cowboy: An Unconventional History of Civilization on the Old-Time Cattle Range* (Norman: University of Oklahoma Press, 1997); and Patrick Dearen, *Saddling Up Anyway: The Dangerous Lives of Old-Time Cowboys* (Dallas, Texas: Taylor Trade Publishing, 2006).
23. Woody Guthrie, "The Buffalo Skinners," in *Hard Hitting Songs*, eds. Lomax, Guthrie, and Seeger, 100.
24. Woody Guthrie, "A Dollar Down, A Dollar a Week," *Struggle*, Folkways Records, 1976, compact disc.
25. Woody Guthrie, "Leadbelly," n.d., WGA, Manuscript Series 1, Box 4, Folder 5.
26. Woody Guthrie, "Slip Knot," "Lost John," and "Struggle Blues," *Struggle*, Folkways Records, 1976, compact disc.
27. Melvyn Dubofosky, *We Shall Be All: A History of the Industrial Workers of the World*, 16.
28. Woody Guthrie, "A Tribute to Mother Bloor," *Daily Worker*, June 22, 1941.
29. Ella Reeve Bloor, *We Are Many* (New York: International Publishers, 1940), 118–38.
30. Bloor, *We Are Many*, 124; Daniel Wolff, *Grown-Up Anger: The Connected Mysteries of Bob Dylan, Woody Guthrie, and the Calumet Massacre of 1913* (New York: Harper Collins, 2017); and Woody Guthrie, "1913 Massacre," *Struggle*, Folkways Records, 1976, compact disc.
31. *1913 Massacre*, directed by Ken Ross and Louis Galdieri, (2011; Brooklyn, NY: Dreamland Pictures, 2012), DVD.
32. Ibid.
33. Bloor, *We Are Many*, 132.
34. Andrews, *Killing for Coal*, 15.
35. Scott Martelle, *Blood Passion: The Ludlow Massacre and Class War in the American West* (New Brunswick, New Jersey: Rutgers University Press, 2007), 5–6.

36. Woody Guthrie, "Ludlow Massacre," *Struggle*, Folkways Records, 1976, compact disc.

Chapter Fourteen

A version of this chapter was originally published as "The Legend of Sacco and Vanzetti: Keeping the Story Alive in Literature, Song, and Film," *Studies in Popular Culture* 31 (Spring 2009): 101–21

1. Hampton, *Guerrilla Minstrels*, 124; Klein, *Guthrie*, 313–15; and Cray, *Ramblin' Man*, 299–300.
2. Kenneth Roberts, *Why Europe Leaves Home* (New York: Bobbs-Merrill Company, 1922), 113–14.
3. For studies of the Sacco-Vanzetti case see, Paul Avrich, *Sacco and Vanzetti: The Anarchist Background* (Princeton, New Jersey: Princeton University Press, 1991); Herbert B. Ehrmann, *The Case That Will Not Die: Commonwealth vs. Sacco and Vanzetti* (Boston: Little, Brown, 1969); David Felix, *Protest: Sacco-Vanzetti and the Intellectuals* (Bloomington: Indiana University Press, 1965); Roberta Strauss Feurlicht, *Justice Crucified: The Story of Sacco and Vanzetti* (New York: McGraw Hill, 1977); Felix Frankfurter, *The Case of Sacco and Vanzetti: A Critical Analysis for Lawyers and Laymen* (Boston: Little, Brown, 1927); Francis Russell, *Sacco and Vanzetti: The Case Remembered* (New York: Harper & Row, 1986); David E. Kaiser, *Postmortem: New Evidence in the Case of Sacco and Vanzetti* (Amherst: University of Massachusetts Press, 1983); and Bruce Watson, *Sacco and Vanzetti: The Men, the Murders, and the Judgment of Mankind* (New York: Viking Press, 2007).
4. The proclamation is reprinted in Upton Sinclair, *Boston: A Documentary Novel of the Sacco-Vanzetti Case* (1928; repr. Cambridge, Massachusetts: Robert Bentley, 1978), 797–99.
5. For an overview of the Sacco-Vanzetti case in popular culture, see Jerome H. Dalamater and Mary Anne Trasciatti, eds., *Representing Sacco and Vanzetti* (New York: Palgrave, 2005).

6. LeRoy Ashby, *With Amusement for All: A History of American Popular Culture Since 1830* (Lexington: The University Press of Kentucky, 2006), 512.
7. Avrich, *Sacco and Vanzetti*, 56–57.
8. Mary Beth Norton, David M. Katzman, Paul D. Escott, Howard Chudacoff, Thomas Paterson, and William M. Tuttle Jr., *A People and a Nation: A History of the United States* (Boston: Houghton Mifflin Company 1998), 707; and Howard Zinn, "Introduction," in *Boston*, Sinclair, xii–xiii.
9. For background information on Upton Sinclair, see *The Autobiography of Upton Sinclair* (New York: Harcourt, Brace & World, 1962); Greg Mitchell, *The Campaign of the Century: Upton Sinclair's Race for Governor of California and the Birth of Media Politics* (New York: Random House, 1992); Anthony Arthur, *Radical Innocent: Upton Sinclair* (New York: Random House, 2006); and Lauren Coodley, *Upton Sinclair: California Socialist, Celebrity Intellectual* (Lincoln: University of Nebraska Press, 2013).
10. Sinclair, *Boston*, xxxvi.
11. Ibid., 755.
12. Canadian Broadcasting System, "Novelist's Book about Murder Trial Called into Question," January 28, 2006, www.cbc.ca; Jean O. Pasco "Smoking Gun," *Los Angeles Times*, December 24, 2005; and Kevin Mattson, "The Smoking Gun that Wasn't," *Chronicle of Higher Education*, March 2, 2006.
13. Goldsmith, *Making People's Music*, 182.
14. Woody Guthrie to Moe Asch, January 2, 1946, quoted in Goldsmith, *Making People's Music*, 183.
15. Woody Guthrie, March 4, 1946, WGA, Notebook Series 1, Number 52.
16. Ibid.
17. Woody Guthrie, summer 1946, WGA, Notebook Series 1, Number 52.
18. Goldsmith, *Making People's Music*, 184–85.
19. Woody Guthrie to Moe Asch and Marian Distler, November 4, 1946, WGA, Correspondence Series 1, Box 1, Folder 6.

20. Moe Asch, "Introduction," in *Ballads of Sacco & Vanzetti*, Woody Guthrie, Smithsonian/Folkways Records, 1996, compact disc (originally released 1960); and Anthony Seeger, "Curator's Foreword," in *Ballads of Sacco & Vanzetti*, Woody Guthrie, Smithsonian/Folkways Records, 1996, compact disc (originally released 1960).
21. Woody Guthrie, "The Flood and the Storm," *Ballads of Sacco & Vanzetti*, Smithsonian/Folkways Records, 1996, compact disc (originally released 1960).
22. Woody Guthrie, "Two Good Men," and "I Just Want to Sing Your Name," *Ballads of Sacco & Vanzetti*, Smithsonian/Folkways Records, 1996, compact disc (originally released 1960).
23. Woody Guthrie, "Suassos Lane," "You Souls of Boston," "Red Wine," and "Old Judge Thayer," *Ballads of Sacco & Vanzetti*, Smithsonian/Folkways Records, 1996, compact disc (originally released 1960). In fact, the amount of detail on the trial provided in these songs reminds one of Bob Dylan's "The Ballad of the Hurricane" (1976) regarding the conviction of boxer Rubin "Hurricane" Carter for murder.
24. Woody Guthrie, "Vanzetti's Rock" and "Vanzetti's Letter," *Ballads of Sacco & Vanzetti*, Smithsonian/Folkways Records, 1996, compact disc (originally released 1960).
25. Woody Guthrie, "Root Hog and Die" and "We Welcome to Heaven," *Ballads of Sacco & Vanzetti*, Smithsonian/Folkways Records, 1996, compact disc (originally released 1960).
26. Woody Guthrie, August 3, 1947, WGA, Notebook Series 1, Number 52.
27. Joan Mellen, "*Sacco and Vanzetti* and *Joe Hill*," *Film Quarterly* 25 (Spring 1972): 48–53; Roger Ebert, "*Sacco and Vanzetti*," *Chicago Sun Times*, November 1, 1971; Vincent Canby, "A Moving *Sacco and Vanzetti*," *New York Times*, October 7, 1971; and Richard Porton, *Film and the Anarchist Imagination* (New York: Verso 1999), 62–66.
28. Annie Anderson, "The Lessons of *Sacco and Vanzetti*," *In These Times*, March 27, 2007, www.inthesetimes.com; Matt Zoller Seitz, "From Immigration to Anarchy," *New York Times*, March 29, 2007; Michael Wilmington, "*Sacco and Vanzetti*," *Chicago Tribune*, May 17, 2007; and J. Hoberman, "*Sacco and Vanzetti*," *Village Voice*, March 28, 2007.

29. Lisa McGirr, "The Passion of Sacco and Vanzetti: A Global History," *Journal of American History* 93 (March 2007): 1115.

Chapter Fifteen

1. Santelli, *"This Land Is Your Land,"* 181–82.
2. Garman, *A Race of Singers*; and Woody Guthrie, "Whitman, Sandberg, and Pushkin," August 5, 1947, WGA, Notebook Series 1, Number 54.
3. Hampton, *Guerrilla Minstrels*, 147.
4. Woody Guthrie, "New People's Songster on the Way," *People's Daily World*, June 3, 1947.
5. Klein, *Guthrie*, 351.
6. Karl Dallas, "Guthrie JNR: Living in the Shadow of Legend," *Melody Maker*, July 10, 1965.
7. Hank Reineke, *Arlo Guthrie: The Warner/Reprise Years* (Lanham, Maryland: Scarecrow Press, 2012), 14; and Paul D. Zimmerman, "Alice's Restaurant's Children," *Newsweek*, September 29, 1969, 10.
8. Mark Fisher, *Something In the Air: Radio, Rock, and the Revolution That Shaped a Generation* (New York: Random House, 2007), 136.
9. Michael Chaiken and Paul Cronin, eds., *Arthur Penn Interviews* (Jackson: University Press of Mississippi, 2008), 65; and Gary Crowdus and Richard Porton, "The Importance of a Singular Guiding Vision: An Interview with Arthur Penn," *Cineaste* 20 (December 1993): 4–16.
10. *"Alice's Restaurant,"* 1969, Internet Movie Data Base, www.imdb.com.
11. Reineke, *Arlo Guthrie*, 248–49.
12. Deborah Solomon, "Questions for Arlo Guthrie: Just Folk," *New York Times*, July 26, 2009; and Andrew Kirell "Arlo Guthrie on Stupid Politicians and 50 Years of Thanksgiving Classic 'Alice's Restaurant,'" *The Daily Beast*, November 26, 2015, www.thedailybeast.com.
13. Elijah Wood, *Dylan Goes Electric: Newport, Seeger, Dylan, and the Night that Split the 1960s* (New York: Dey Street Books, 1965).
14. Mike Marqusee, *Wicked Messenger: Bob Dylan and the 1960s* (New York: South End Press, 2005), 3 and 335.

15. The literature on Dylan is quite extensive. The following books are in my library and provide considerable insight into the musician's life and work. Sean Wilentz, *Bob Dylan in America* (New York: Anchor, 2011); Robert Shelton, *No Direction Home: The Life and Music of Bob Dylan* (1998; repr. Winona, Minnesota: Hal Leonard Corporation, 2011); Howard Sounes, *Down the Highway: The Life of Bob Dylan* (New York: Grove Press, 2011); Ian Bell, *Once Upon a Time: The Lives of Bob Dylan* (New York: Pegasus, 2014); Ian Bell, *Time Out of Mind: The Lives of Bob Dylan* (New York: Pegasus, 2015); David Hajdu, *Positively 4th Street: The Lives and Times of Joan Baez, Bob Dylan, Mimi Baez Farina, and Richard Farina* (New York: Picador, 2011); and John Hughes, *Invisible Now: Bob Dylan in the 1960s* (Burlington, Vermont: Ashgate, 2013).
16. Reineke, *Arlo Guthrie*, 15; and Arlo Guthrie, "Foreword," in *Early Dylan*, Barry Feinstein, Daniel Kramer, and Jim Marshall (Boston: Little, Brown and Company, 1999), 5.
17. Bob Dylan, *Chronicles Volume One* (New York: Simon & Schuster, 2004), 98–100.
18. Ibid., 244–47.
19. Bob Dylan, "Song to Woody," in *Lyrics, 1962–1968*, Bob Dylan (New York: Alfred A. Knopf, 1998), 6.
20. Dylan, *Chronicles*, 292–93.
21. Hughes, *Invisible Now: Bob Dylan in the 1960s*, xv.
22. Richard Porton, "*I'm Not There*," *Cineaste* 33 (Winter 2007): 56–57.
23. "Radio Interview with Studs Terkel," May 1963, in *Bob Dylan: The Essential Interviews*, ed. Jonathan Colt (New York: Wenner Books, 2006), 5–12.
24. Wilentz, *Dylan in America*, 297 and 103.
25. Bell, *Once Upon a Time: The Lives of Bob Dylan*, 561–62.
26. Bruce Springsteen, *Born to Run* (New York: Simon & Schuster, 2016), 29.
27. For a solid biographical overview of Springsteen's life, see Peter Ames Carlin, *Bruce* (New York: Simon & Schuster, 2012).
28. Springsteen, *Born to Run*, 291.

29. Ibid., 292.
30. Dale Maharidge, *Journey to Nowhere: The Saga of the New Underclass* (New York: Hyperion, 1985), 191.
31. Mikal Gilmore, "*The Ghost of Tom Joad*: Year-End Album Review," *Rolling Stone*, December 28, 1995/January 11, 1996," in *Rolling Stone, Bruce Springsteen: The Rolling Stone Files* (New York: Hyperion, 1996), 341–42.
32. Fischer, "The Ghost and Mr. Springsteen," 208–11.
33. Springsteen, *Born to Run*, 400–405.
34. Jim Cullen, *Born in the U.S.A.: Bruce Springsteen and the American Tradition* (Middletown, Connecticut: Wesleyan University Press, 1999), 28–30 and 44.
35. Larry David Smith, *Bob Dylan, Bruce Springsteen, and American Song* (Westport, Connecticut: Praeger, 2002), xxi.
36. Bryan K. Garman, "The Ghost of History: Bruce Springsteen, Woody Guthrie, and the Hurt Song," in *Racing in the Street: The Bruce Springsteen Reader*, ed. June Skinner Sawyers (New York: Penguin Books, 2004), 222.
37. Ibid.
38. Ibid., 224.
39. Dave Marsh, *Bruce Springsteen, Two Hearts*, 279.
40. Ibid., 278.
41. Cole Oelbyck, "Bruce Springsteen Says Trump Is Actually Appealing to Un-American Tendencies," *Huffington Post*, January 3, 2017, http://www.huffingtonpost.com.

Bibliography

Adler, William. *The Man Who Never Died: The Life, Times, and Legacy of Joe Hill, American Labor Icon.* New York: Bloomsbury, 2012.

"Alice's Restaurant." 1969. Internet Movie Data Base. www.imdb.com.

Alperovitz, Gar. *Atomic Diplomacy: Hiroshima and Potsdam.* New York: Random House, 1997.

———. *The Decision to Use the Bomb.* New York: Random House, 1997.

Anderson, Annie. "The Lessons of Sacco and Vanzetti." *In These Times,* March 27, 2007. www.inthesetimes.com.

Andrews, Thomas G. *Killing for Coal: America's Deadliest Labor War.* Cambridge, Massachusetts: Harvard University Press, 2008.

Appleborne, Peter. "He Caught Folk on the Rise and Held On." *New York Times,* November 26, 1998.

Archer, Seth. "Reading the Riot Acts." *Southwest Review* 91 (Winter 2006): 500–516.

Arthur, Anthony. *Radical Innocent: Upton Sinclair.* New York: Random House, 2006.

Asch, Moses, ed. *American Folksong: Woody Guthrie.* New York: Oak Publications, 1961.

Ashby, LeRoy. *With Amusement for All: A History of American Popular Culture Since 1830.* Lexington: The University Press of Kentucky, 2006.

Avrich, Paul. *Sacco and Vanzetti: The Anarchist Background.* Princeton, New Jersey: Princeton University Press, 1991.

Baldwin, Sidney. *Poverty and Politics: The Rise and Decline of the Farm Security Administration.* Chapel Hill: University of North Carolina Press, 1968.

Bartley, Robert and David Kenney. *Death Underground: The Centralia and West Frankfurt Mine Disasters.* Carbondale: Southern Illinois University Press, 2006.

Beach, Christopher. *The Films of Hal Ashby*. Detroit: Wayne State University Press, 2009.

Bell, Ian. *Once Upon a Time: The Lives of Bob Dylan*. New York: Pegasus, 2014.

——. *Time Out of Mind: The Lives of Bob Dylan*. New York: Pegasus, 2015.

Bissett, Jim. *Agrarian Socialism in America: Marx, Jefferson, and Jesus in the Oklahoma Countryside, 1914–1920*. Norman: University of Oklahoma Press, 1999.

Blair, Clay. *The Forgotten War: America in Korea, 1950–1953*. New York: Times Books, 1987.

Bloor, Ella Reeve. *We Are Many*. New York: International Publishers, 1940.

Bonnefield, Paul. *The Dust Bowl: Men, Dust, and Depression*. Albuquerque: University of New Mexico Press, 1979.

Bound for Glory. Directed by Hal Ashby. Hollywood, California: MGM Home Entertainment, 2000. DVD.

Boyer, Paul. *When Time Shall Be No More: Prophecy Belief in Modern American Culture*. Cambridge, Massachusetts: Harvard University Press, 1992.

Bragg, Billy and Wilco. *Mermaid Avenue*, vol. 1. Nonesuch Records, 2012, compact disc.

Briley, Ron. "The Legend of Sacco and Vanzetti: Keeping the Story Alive in Literature, Song, and Film." *Studies in Popular Culture* 31 (Spring 2009): 101–21.

——. "Woody Guthrie and the Christian Left: Jesus and 'Commonism.'" *Journal of Texas Music History* 7 (2007): 2–14.

——. "'Woody Sez': Woody Guthrie, The *People's Daily World,* and Indigenous Radicalism." *California History* 84 (Fall 2006): 30–43.

Brooks, Robin. "Domestic Violence and American Wars: A Historical Interpretation." In *Violence in America: Politics, Rebellion, Reform*, vol. 2., edited by Ted Robert Gurr. New York: Sage, 1994.

Burrough, Bryan. *Public Enemies: America's Greatest Crime Wave and the Birth of the FBI, 1933–34*. New York: Penguin, 2005.

Cain, Brad. "Judge Right to Demand New Salmon Plan." *Seattle Times*, October 5, 2005.

Canadian Broadcasting System. "Sinclair's Book about Murder Trial Called into Question." January 28, 2006. www.cbc.ca.
Canby, Vincent. *"Bound for Glory." New York Times,* December 6, 1976.
———. "A Moving Sacco and Vanzetti." *New York Times,* October 7, 1971.
Carlin, Peter Ames. *Bruce.* New York: Simon & Schubert, 2012.
Casey, Steve. *Selling the Korean War: Propaganda, Politics, and Public Opinion in the United States, 1950–1953.* New York: Oxford University Press, 2008.
Ceplair, Larry and Steven Englund. *The Inquisition in Hollywood: Politics in the Film Community, 1930–1960.* Berkeley: University of California Press, 1979.
Chafe, William. *The Unfinished Journey: America Since World War II.* New York: Oxford University Press, 2015. First published 1986.
Chaiken, Michael and Paul Cronin, eds. *Arthur Penn Interviews.* Jackson: University Press of Mississippi, 2008.
Cohen, Ronald D. "Woody the Red?" In *Hard Travelin': The Life and Legacy of Woody Guthrie,* edited by Robert Santelli and Emily Davidson. Hanover, New Hampshire: Wesleyan University Press, 1999.
Coles, Robert. *Privileged Ones: The Well-Off and Rich in America.* Vol 5, *Children in Crisis.* New York: Little, Brown, 1977.
Coodley, Lauren. *Upton Sinclair: California Socialist, Celebrity, Intellectual.* Lincoln: University of Nebraska Press, 2013.
Cost, John C. *Christian Socialism: An Informal History.* Mary Knoll, New York: Orbis Books, 1988.
Cowie, Jefferson. *Stayin' Alive: The 1970s and the Last Days of the Working Class.* New York: The New Press, 2010.
Cray, Ed. *Ramblin' Man: The Life and Times of Woody Guthrie.* New York: W. W. Norton & Company, 2004.
Crist, Judith. *"Bound for Glory." Saturday Review* 40 (December 11, 1976): 78.
Crowdus, Gary and Richard Porton. "The Importance of a Singular Guiding Vision: An Interview with Arthur Penn." *Cineaste* 20 (December 1993): 4–16.
Cullen, Jim. *Born in the U.S.A.: Bruce Springsteen and the American Tradition.* Middletown, Connecticut: Wesleyan University Press, 1999.

Culver, John C. and John Hyde. *American Dreamer: A Life of Henry Wallace.* New York: W. W. Norton & Company, 2000.

Cumings, Bruce. *The Origins of the Korean War,* 2 vols. Princeton, New Jersey: Princeton University Press, 1981.

Cuordileone, K. A. *Manhood and American Political Culture in the Cold War.* New York: Routledge, 2005.

Dallas, Karl. "Guthrie JNR: Living in the Shadow of Legend." *Melody Maker,* July 10, 1965.

Davidson, James R. *Hal Ashby and the Making of Harold and Maude.* Jefferson, North Carolina: McFarland, 2016.

Dawson, Nick. *Being Hal Ashby: Life of a Hollywood Rebel.* Lexington: University Press of Kentucky, 2011.

——, ed. *Hal Ashby Interviews.* Jackson: University of Mississippi Press, 2010.

Dearen, Patrick. *Saddling Up Anyway: The Dangerous Lives of Old-Time Cowboys.* Dallas, Texas: Taylor Trade Publishing, 2006.

DeCurtis, Anthony. *"Dust Bowl Ballads." Rolling Stone,* 2000. www.rollingstone.com.

Delamater, Jerome H. and Mary Anne Trasciatti, eds. *Representing Sacco and Vanzetti.* New York: Palgrave, 2005.

Denning, Michael. *The Cultural Front: The Laboring of American Culture in the Twentieth Century.* New York: Verso, 1997.

Devine, Thomas W. *Henry Wallace's 1948 Presidential Campaign and the Future of Postwar Liberalism.* Chapel Hill: The University of North Carolina Press, 2015.

Dower, John. *War Without Mercy: Race and Power in the Pacific War.* New York: Pantheon, 1987.

Dray, Philip. *There Is Power in a Union: The Epic Story of Labor in America.* New York: Anchor, 2011.

Drombrowski, James A. *The Early Days of Christian Socialism in America.* New York: Octagon Books, 1977.

Duberman, Martin. *Paul Robeson.* New York: Alfred A. Knopf, 1989.

Dubofsky, Melvyn. *Labor in America: A History.* New York: Wiley, 2010.

——. *We Shall Be All: A History of the Industrial Workers of the World.* Urbana: University of Illinois Press, 1988.

Dunaway, David. *How Can I Keep from Singing? The Ballad of Pete Seeger.* New York: McGraw-Hill, 1981.

Dunbar-Ortiz, Roxanne. "One or Two Things I know about Us: 'Okies' in American Culture." *Radical History Review* 59 (Spring 1994): 5–33.

Duncan, Dayton and Ken Burns. *The Dust Bowl: An Illustrated History.* San Francisco: Chronicle Books, 2012.

Dunn, Susan. *1940: FDR, Lindbergh, Hitler—the Election Amid the Storm.* New Haven, Connecticut: Yale University Press, 2013.

Dylan, Bob. *Chronicles Volume One.* New York: Simon & Schuster, 2004.

———. *Lyrics, 1962–1968.* New York: Alfred A. Knopf, 1998.

Earle, Steve. "Woody Guthrie." *Nation* 277 (July 21/28, 2003): 30–32.

Ebert, Roger. "*Bound for Glory.*" March 9, 1977. www.rogerebert.com.

———. "Sacco and Vanzetti." *Chicago Sun Times,* November 1, 1971.

Egan, Timothy. *The Worst Hard Time: The Untold Story of Those Who Survived the Great American Dust Bowl.* Boston: Houghton Mifflin, 2005.

Ehrmann, Herbert B. *The Case That Will Not Die: Commonwealth vs. Sacco and Vanzetti.* Boston: Little, Brown, 1969.

Elmwood, Victoria A. "'Just Some Bum from the Neighborhood': The Resolution of Post-Civil Rights Tension and Heavyweight Public Sphere Discourse in *Rocky.*" In *All Stars and Movie Stars: Sports in Film History*, edited by Ron Briley, Michael K. Schoenecke, and Deborah Carmichael. Lexington: University Press of Kentucky, 2008.

Falck, Arthur. "Observations on Patient and Family Coping with Huntington's Disease." *Omega: An International Journal for the Study of Dying, Death, Bereavement, Suicide, and Other Lethal Behaviors* 10:1 (1979): 20–36.

Feinstein, Barry, Daniel Kramer, and Jim Marshall. *Early Dylan.* Boston: Little, Brown and Company, 1999.

Felix, David. *Protest: Sacco-Vanzetti and the Intellectuals.* Bloomington: Indiana University Press, 1965.

Feurlicht, Roberta Strauss. *Justice Crucified: The Story of Sacco and Vanzetti.* New York: McGraw Hill, 1977.

Fischer, Paul D. "Review of *The Ghost of Tom Joad* by Bruce Springsteen." *The Journal of American Folklore* 110 (Spring 1997): 208–11.

Fisher, Mark. *Something in the Air: Radio, Rock, and the Revolution that Shaped a Generation.* New York: Random House, 2007.

Foot, Dorothy. *The Wrong War: American Policy and the Dimensions of the Korean Conflict, 1950–1953.* Ithaca, New York: Cornell University Press, 1985.

Frank, Thomas. *What's the Matter with Kansas? How Conservatives Won the Heart of America.* New York: Henry Holt, 2004.

Frankfurter, Felix. *The Case of Sacco and Vanzetti: A Critical Analysis for Lawyers and Laymen.* Boston: Little, Brown, 1927.

Franklin, Jimmie Lewis. *The Blacks in Oklahoma.* Norman: University of Oklahoma Press, 1980.

Gallagher, Tay. *John Ford: The Man and His Films.* Berkeley: University of California Press, 1986.

Garman, Bryan K. "The Ghost of History: Bruce Springsteen, Woody Guthrie, and the Hurt Song." In *Racing in the Street: The Bruce Springsteen Reader*, edited by June Skinner Sawyers. New York: Penguin Books, 2004.

———. *A Race of Singers: Walt Whitman's Working-Class Hero from Guthrie to Springsteen.* Chapel Hill: University of North Carolina Press, 2000.

Gilmore, Mikal. *"The Ghost of Tom Joad:* Year-End Album Review." *Rolling Stone,* December 28, 1995/January 11, 1996. In *Rolling Stone. Bruce Springsteen: The Rolling Stone Files,* edited by the Rolling Stone editors. New York: Hyperion, 1996.

Goldsmith, Peter. *Making People's Music: Moe Asch and Folkways Records.* Washington, DC: Smithsonian Press, 1998.

Gorn, Elliott J. *Dillinger's Wild Ride: The Year That Made America's Public Enemy Number One.* New York: Oxford University Press, 2009.

Goulden, Joseph C. *Korea: The Untold Story of the War.* New York: Times Books, 1982.

Green, Archie. *Only a Miner: Studies in Recorded Coal-Mining Songs.* Urbana: University of Illinois Press, 2009.

Green, James R. *Grass Roots Socialism: Radical Movements in the Southwest, 1895–1943.* Baton Rouge: Louisiana State University Press, 1978.

Green, Jeff. *"Bound for Glory." Cineaste,* 8 (Summer 1977): 36–37.

Guinn, Jeff. *Go Down Together: The True Untold Story of Bonnie and Clyde.* New York: Simon and Schuster, 2010.
Guthrie, Nora. Telephone interview with author. May 19, 2011.
Guthrie, Woody. *Ballads of Sacco & Vanzetti.* Smithsonian/Folkways Records, 1996, compact disc. Originally released in 1960.
———. *Bound for Glory.* New York: E. P. Dutton & Company, 1943.
———. *Dust Bowl Ballads.* Buddha Records, 2000, compact disc. originally released in 1940.
———. *Struggle.* Folkways Records, 1976, compact disc.
———. *Woody Sez.* New York: Grossett & Dunlap, 1973.
———. "Woody Sez." *Daily Worker,* 1941.
———. "Woody Sez." *People's Daily World,* 1939–1940.
Guthrie, Woody, Alan Lomax, and Pete Seeger, eds. *Hard Hitting Songs for Hard-Hit People.* New York: Oak Publications, 1967.
Hajdu, David. *Positively 4th Street: The Lives and Times of Joan Baez, Bob Dylan, Mimi Baez Farina, and Richard Farina.* New York: Picador, 2011.
Halberstam, David. *The Coldest Winter: America and the Korean War.* New York: Hyperion, 2007.
Ham, Paul. *Hiroshima and Nagasaki: The Real Story of the Atomic Bombings and Their Aftermath.* New York: Thomas Dunne Books, 2014.
Hampton, Wayne. *Guerrilla Minstrels: John Lennon, Joe Hill, Woody Guthrie, and Bob Dylan.* Knoxville: The University of Tennessee Press, 1986.
Hanley, Charles J., Sang-Hun Choe, and Martha Mendoza. *The Bridge at No Gun Rio: A Hidden Nightmare from the Korean War*. New York: Henry-Holt, 2001.
Harmetz, Aljean. "Gambling on a Film about the Great Depression." *New York Times,* December 5, 1976.
Harrington, Beth. *The Winding Stream: An Oral History of the Carter and Cash Family.* Georgetown, Massachusetts: PFP, 2014.
Hatfield, Edward A. "Stetson Kennedy (1916–2011)." *New Georgia Encyclopedia,* August 14, 2009. www.georgiaencyclopedia.org.
Hawes, Beth Lomax. *Sing It Pretty.* Urbana: University of Illinois Press, 2008.

Hays, Lee and Robert S. Koppelman, eds. *Sing Out, Warning! Sing Out, Love: The Writings of Lee Hays*. Amherst: University of Massachusetts Press, 2004.

Healy, Dorothy Ray and Maurice Isserman. *California Red: A Life in the American Communist Party*. Urbana: University of Illinois Press, 1979.

Hevener, John W. *Which Side Are You On? The Harlan Country Coal Miners, 1931–39*. Urbana: University of Illinois Press, 1992.

Hirsch, James S. *Riot and Remembrance: The Tulsa Race War and Its Legacy*. Boston: Houghton Mifflin Company, 1992.

Hirshberg, Charles. *Will You Miss Me When I'm Gone? The Carter Family and Their Legacy in American Music*. New York: Simon & Schuster, 2004.

Hoberman, J. "Sacco and Vanzetti." *Village Voice*, March 28, 2007.

Hobsbawm, E. J. *Primitive Rebels: Studies in Archaic Forms of Social Movements in the 19th and 20th Centuries*. New York: W. W. Norton & Company, 1965.

Holter, Darryl and William Deverell, eds. *Woody Guthrie L.A. 1937 to 1941*. Los Angeles: Angel City Press, 2015.

Horne, Gerald. *Paul Robeson: The Artist as Revolutionary*. New York: Pluto Press, 2016.

Hughes, John. *Invisible Now: Bob Dylan in the 1960s*. Burlington, Vermont: Ashgate, 2013.

Hunter, Marvin, ed. *The Trail Drivers of Texas: Interesting Sketches of Early Cowboys*. Austin: University of Texas Press, 1992. First published 1920.

Isenberg, Nancy. *White Trash: The 400-Year Untold History of Class in America*. New York: Viking Press, 2016.

Isserman, Maurice. *Which Side Were You On? The American Communist Party During the Second World War*. Urbana: University of Illinois Press, 1993.

Jackson, Mark Allan. *Prophet Singer: The Voice and Vision of Woody Guthrie*. Jackson: University Press of Mississippi, 2007.

Johnson, David K. *The Lavender Scare: The Cold War Persecution of Gays and Lesbians in the Federal Government.* Chicago: University of Chicago Press, 2006.

Kael, Pauline. "Affirmation." *New Yorker* 52 (December 13, 1976): 148–52.

Kaiser, David E. *Postmortem: New Evidence in the Case of Sacco and Vanzetti.* Amherst: University of Massachusetts Press, 1983.

Kaplan, Justin. *Walt Whitman: A Life.* New York: Perennial, 2001.

Kaskowitz, Sheryl. *God Bless America: The Surprising History of an Iconic Song.* New York: Oxford University Press, 2013.

Kauffmann, Stanley. "Poor Folk." *New Republic* 175 (November 27, 1976): 18 and 40.

Kaufman, Will. *Woody Guthrie: American Radical.* Urbana: University of Illinois Press, 2011.

———. "Woody Guthrie, 'Old Man Trump,' and a Real Estate Empire's Racist Foundation." *The Conversation,* January 26, 2016. www.theconversation.com.

———. *Woody Guthrie's Modern World Blues.* Norman: University of Oklahoma Press, 2017.

Kazan, Elia. *A Life.* New York: Alfred A. Knopf, 1988.

Kennedy, Robert. *To Seek a Better World.* New York: Doubleday and Company, 1967.

Kennedy, Stetson. *Jim Crow Guide to the U.S.A.* Tuscaloosa: University of Alabama Press, 2011. First published 1959.

———. *The Klan Unmasked.* Tuscaloosa: University of Alabama Press, 2011. First published 1954.

King, Jeffrey S. *The Life & Death of Pretty Boy Floyd.* Kent, Ohio: Kent State University Press, 1998.

Kirell, Andrew. "Arlo Guthrie on Stupid Politicians and 50 years of Thanksgiving Classic 'Alice's Restaurant.'" *The Daily Beast,* November 26, 2015. www.thedailybeast.com.

Klehr, Harvey. *The Heyday of American Communism: The Depression Decade.* New York: Basic Books, 1984.

Klein, Joe. *Woody Guthrie: A Life*. New York: Alfred A. Knopf, 1980.

Knickerbocker, Brad. "Saving an Icon of the Pacific Northwest." *Christian Science Monitor,* January 30, 1997.

Kornbluh, Joyce, ed. *Rebel Voices: An IWW Anthology*. Ann Arbor: University of Michigan Press, 1964.

Krause, Kevin M. *One Nation Under God: How Corporate America Invented Christian America.* New York: Basic Books, 2013.

Krugman, Paul. "No Surrender." *New York Times,* November 5, 2004.

La Chapelle, Peter. *Proud to Be an Okie: Cultural Politics, Country Music, and Migration to Southern California.* Berkeley: University of California Press, 2007.

Larrowe, Charles P. *Harry Bridges: The Rise and Fall of Radical Labor in the United States.* Westport, Connecticut: Lawrence Hill & Co., 1977.

Leonard, Aaron J. "Newly Released FBI Files Expose Red-Baiting of Woody Guthrie." *Truthout,* August 14, 2018. www.truthout.org.

Lichtenstein, Nelson. *Labor's War at Home: The CIO in World War II.* Philadelphia: Temple University Press, 2008.

Lieberman, Robbie. *"My Song Is My Weapon": People's Songs, American Communism, and the Politics of Culture.* Urbana: University of Illinois Press, 2008.

Longhi, Jim. *Woody, Cisco, and Me: Seamen Three in the Merchant Marine.* Urbana: University of Illinois Press, 1997.

Lookingbill, Brad. "Dusty Apocalypse and Socialist Salvation." *Chronicles of Oklahoma* 74 (Winter 1994): 396-413.

Lorentz, Pare. *FDR's Moviemaker: Memoirs and Scripts.* Reno: University of Nevada Press, 1992.

Lornell, Kip and Charles Wolfe. *The Life and Legend of Leadbelly.* New York: Da Capo Press, 1999.

Lowitt, Richard. *The New Deal and the West.* Norman: University of Oklahoma Press, 1984.

Maharidge, Dale. *Journey to Nowhere: The Saga of the New Underclass.* New York: Hyperion, 1985.

Marqusee, Mike. *Wicked Messenger: Bob Dylan and the 1960s.* New York: South End Press, 2005.

Marsh, Dave. *Bruce Springsteen: Two Hearts, The Definitive Biography, 1972–2003*. New York: Routledge, 2004.

Marsh, Dave and Harold Leventhal, eds. *Pastures of Plenty: Woody Guthrie: The Unpublished Writings of an American Folk Hero*. New York: Harper Perennial, 1992.

Martelle, Scott. *Blood Passion: The Ludlow Massacre and Class War in the American West*. New Brunswick, New Jersey: Rutgers University Press, 2007.

Martin, Justin. *Rebel Souls: Walt Whitman and America's First Bohemians*. New York: Da Capo Press, 2014.

Mateus, Jorge Arvealo. "Beluhahatchee Blues: An Interview with Stetson Kennedy." In *Radicalism in the South Since Reconstruction*, by Chris Green, Rachel Rubin, and James Smethurst. New York: Palgrave, 2006.

Mattson, Kevin. "The Smoking Gun that Wasn't." *Chronicle of Higher Education*, March 2, 2006.

McBride, Joseph. "Song for Woody." *Film Comment* 12 (November/December, 1976): 26–28.

McCartin, Joseph. *Collision Course: Ronald Reagan, the Air Traffic Controllers, and the Strike that Changed America*. New York: Oxford University Press, 2013.

McGirr, Lisa. "The Passion of Sacco and Vanzetti: A Global History." *Journal of American History* 93 (March 2007): 1085–115.

McWilliams, Carey. *Factories in the Field: The Story of Migratory Farm Labor in California*. Berkeley: University of California Press, 2000. First published 1939.

———. *Ill Fares the Land: Migrants and Migratory Labor in California*. Boston: Little, Brown and Company, 1942.

Mellen, Joan. "*Sacco and Vanzetti* and *Joe Hill*." *Film Quarterly* 25 (Spring 1972): 48–53.

Menig, Harry. "Woody Guthrie: The Oklahoma Years, 1912–1929." In *An Oklahoma I Had Never Known Before: Alternative Views of Oklahoma History*, edited by Davis D. Joyce. Norman: University of Oklahoma Press, 1994.

Minchin, Timothy J. *Fighting Against the Odds: A History of Southern Labor Since World War II*. Gainesville: University Press of Florida, 2006.

Mitchell, Greg. *The Campaign of the Century: Upton Sinclair's Race for Governor of California and the Birth of Media Politics*. New York: Random House, 1992.

Moe, Richard. *Roosevelt's Second Act: The Election of 1940 and the Politics of War*. New York: Oxford University Press, 2013.

Morgan, Jeff. "Hard Travelin': Constructing Woody Guthrie's Dust Bowl Legacy." In *The Life, Music and Thought of Woody Guthrie: A Critical Approach*, edited by John S. Partington. Burlington, Vermont: Ashgate Publishing Company, 2011.

Nate, Richard. "'Pastures of Plenty,' Woody Guthrie and the New Deal." In *The Life, Music and Thought of Woody Guthrie: A Critical Approach*, edited by John S. Partington. Burlington, Vermont: Ashgate Publishing Company, 2011.

"New People's Songster on the Way." *People's Daily World*, June 3, 1947.

Newfield, Jack. "American Radicalism." *Nation* 277 (July 21/28, 2003): 13.

1913 Massacre. Directed by Ken Ross and Louis Galdieri. Brooklyn, New York: Dreamland Pictures, 2012. DVD.

Norton, Mary Beth, David M. Katzman, Paul D. Escott, Howard Chudacoff, Thomas Paterson, and William M. Tuttle Jr. *A People and a Nation: A History of the United States*. Boston: Houghton Mifflin Company, 1998.

Nowlin, Bill, ed. *Woody Guthrie: Radial American Patriot*. New York: Rounder, 2013.

O'Brien, Tom. *The Screening of America: Movies and Values from Rocky to Rain Man*. New York: Bloomsbury Academic, 2016.

Oelbyck, Cole. "Bruce Springsteen Says Trump Is Actually Appealing to Un-American Tendencies." *Huffington Post,* January 3, 2017. www.huffingtonpost.com.

Offner, Arnold A. *Another Such Victory: President Truman and the Cold War, 1945–1953*. Stanford, California: Stanford University Press, 2002.

Olmstead, Tony. *Folkways Records: Moses Asch and His Encyclopedia of Song*. New York: Routledge, 2003.

Ottanelli, Fraser M. *The Communist Party of the United States from the Depression to World War II.* New Brunswick, New Jersey: Rutgers University Press, 1991.

Pareles, Jon. "Moses Asch, Who Founded Folkways Records, Dies at 81." *New York Times,* October 21, 1986.

Pasco, Jean O. "Smoking Gun." *Los Angeles Times,* December 24, 2005.

Pedelty, Mark. "Woody Guthrie and the Columbia River: Propaganda, Art, and Irony." *Popular Music and Society* 31 (July 2008): 329–55.

Phillips, Kevin. *American Theocracy: The Peril of Radical Religion, Oil, and Borrowed Money in the 21st Century.* New York: Viking Press, 2006.

Porton, Richard. *Film and the Anarchist Imagination.* New York: Verso, 1999.

———. "I'm Not There." *Cineaste* 33 (Winter 2007): 56–57.

Powell, Larry. *The Films of John Avildson: Rocky, The Karate Kid, and Other Underdogs.* Jefferson, North Carolina: McFarland, 2013.

Pretrusza, David. *1948: Harry Truman's Improbable Victory and the Year that Transformed America.* New York: Union Square Press, 2011.

Prothero, Stephen. *American Jesus: How the Son of God Became a National Icon.* New York: Farrar, Straus and Giroux, 2003.

Quinn, Mike. "Double Check." *Daily Worker,* April 25, 1940.

"Radio Interview with Studs Terkel." May 1961. In *Bob Dylan: The Essential Interviews,* edited by Jonathan Colt. New York: Wenner Books, 2006.

Reineke, Hank. *Arlo Guthrie: The Warner/Reprise Years.* Lanham, Maryland: Scarecrow Press, 2012.

Reynolds, David. *Walt Whitman's America: A Cultural Biography.* New York: Vintage, 1996.

Rich, Frank. "*Bound for Glory.*" *New York Post,* December 6, 1976.

Richards, Paul. "*People's Daily World.*" In *Encyclopedia of the American Left,* edited by Marie Jo Buhle, Paul Buhle, and Dan Georgakas. Urbana: University of Illinois Press, 1992.

Robbin, Ed. *Woody Guthrie and Me.* Berkeley, California: Lancaster-Miller Publications, 1979.

Roberts, Kenneth. *Why Europe Leaves Home.* New York: Bobbs-Merrill Company, 1922.

Robeson, Paul Jr. *Paul Robeson: The Undiscovered Quest for Freedom, 1939–1976*. New York: Wiley, 2010.

Rodnitzsky, Jerome. *Minstrels of the Dawn: The Folk Singer as a Cultural Hero*. New York: Nelson-Hall, 1976.

Rollins, Philip Ashton. *The Cowboy: An Unconventional History of Civilization on the Old-Time Cattle Range*. Norman: University of Oklahoma Press, 1997.

Romalis, Shelly. *Pistol Packing Mama: Aunt Molly Jackson and the Politics of Folksong*. Urbana: University of Illinois Press, 1992.

Rosemont, Franklin. *Joe Hill and the IWW & the Making of a Revolutionary Workingclass Counterculture*. Oakland, California: PM Press, 2015.

Russell, Francis. *Sacco and Vanzetti: The Case Remembered*. New York: Harper & Row, 1986.

Samuelson, Nancy B. *The Dalton Gang Story: Lawmen to Outlaws*. Eastford, Connecticut: Shooting Star Press, 1992.

Santelli, Robert. *This Land Is Your Land: Woody Guthrie and the Journey of an American Folk Song*. Philadelphia: Running Press, 2012.

Schickel, Richard. "Bound for Glory." *Time* 108 (December 20, 1976): 78.

Seeger, Pete. *"Where Have All the Flowers Gone": A Singer's Stories, Songs, Seeds, Robberies*. Bethlehem, Pennsylvania: Sing Out Corporation, 1993.

Seitz, Matt Zoller. "From Immigration to Anarchy." *New York Times*, March 29, 2007.

Sernett, Milton C. *Harriet Tubman: Myth, Memory, and History*. Durham, North Carolina: Duke University Press, 2007.

Shelton, Robert. *No Direction Home: The Life and Music of Bob Dylan*. Winona, Minnesota: Hal Leonard Corporation, 2011. First published 1998.

Shindo, Charles J. *Dust Bowl Migrants in the American Imagination*. Lawrence: University Press of Kentucky, 1997.

Shirley, Glenn. *Belle Starr and Her Times: The Literature, the Facts and the Legends*. Norman: University of Oklahoma Press, 1982.

Shumsky, Neil Larry. "Dust, Disease, Death and Deity: Constructing and Deconstructing the Dust Bowl." *The Journal of American Culture* 38 (September 2015): 218–31.

Shumway. David R. "Your Land, The Lost Legacy of Woody Guthrie." In *Hard Travelin': The Life and Legacy of Woody Guthrie*, edited by Robert Santelli and Emily Davidson. Hanover, New Hampshire: Wesleyan University Press, 1999.

Simon, Bryant and William Deverell. "Come Back, Tom Joad: Thoughts on a California Dreamer." *California History* 79 (Winter 2000/2001): 180–91.

Simon, John. *"Bound for Glory." New York Magazine,* December 6, 1976.

Sinclair, Upton. *Boston: A Documentary Novel of the Sacco-Vanzetti Case.* Cambridge, Massachusetts: Robert Bentley, 1978. First published 1928.

———. *The Autobiography of Upton Sinclair.* New York: Harcourt, Brace & World, 1962.

Slotkin, Richard. *Regeneration through Violence: The Mythology of the American Frontier, 1600–1860.* Middletown, Connecticut: Wesleyan University Press, 1973.

Smith, Larry David. *Bob Dylan, Bruce Springsteen, and American Song.* Westport, Connecticut: Praeger, 2002.

Snyder, Robert L. *Pare Lorentz and the Documentary Film.* Norman: University of Oklahoma Press, 1968.

Solomon, Deborah. "Questions for Arlo Guthrie: Just Folk." *New York Times,* July 26, 2009.

Sounes, Howard. *Down the Highway: The Life of Bob Dylan.* New York: Grove Press, 2011.

Springsteen, Bruce. *Born to Run.* New York: Simon & Schuster, 2016.

Sterritt, David. *"Bound for Glory." Christian Science Monitor,* December 30, 1976.

———. "The Special Okie Southwest Flavor, That Humor." *Christian Science Monitor,* February 4, 1977.

Stiles, T. J. *Jesse James: Last Rebel of the Civil War.* New York: Alfred A. Knopf, 2002.

Szwed, John. *Alan Lomax: The Man Who Recorded the World.* New York: Penguin Books, 2011.

Takaki, Ronald. *Hiroshima: Why America Dropped the Bomb.* New York: Back Bay Books, 1995.

Trodd, Zoe. "Star Symbols: John Steinbeck in the American Populist Tradition." *The Steinbeck Review* 5 (Fall 2008): 10–37.

Truman, President Harry S., statement by. Harry Truman Library and Museum, June 27, 1950. www.trumanlibrary.org.

U.S. Department of Labor, Mine Safety, and Health Administration. "Mining Industry Accident, Injuries, Employment, and Production." www.msha.gov.

Utley, Robert M. *Wanted: The Outlaw Lives of Billy the Kid & Ned Kelly*. New Haven, Connecticut: Yale University Press, 2015.

Vandy, Greg with Daniel Person. *26 Songs in 30 Days: Woody Guthrie's Columbia River Songs and the Planned Promised Land in the Pacific Northwest*. Seattle, Washington: Sasquatch Books, 2016.

Wallis, Jim. *God's Politics: Why the Right Gets It Wrong and the Left Doesn't Get It*. New York: Harper Collins, 2005.

——. *The Soul of Politics: A Practical and Prophetic Vision for Change*. New York: The New Press, 1997.

Wallis, Michael. *"Pretty Boy": The Life and Times of Charles Arthur Floyd*. New York: St. Martin's Press, 1993.

Wartzman, Rick. *Obscene in the Extreme: The Burning and Banning of John Steinbeck's The Grapes of Wrath*. New York: Public Affairs, 2008.

Watson, Bruce. *Sacco and Vanzetti: The Men, the Murders, and the Judgment of Mankind*. New York: Viking Press, 2007.

Wells, Robert V. *Life Flows On in Endless Song: Folk Songs and American History*. Urbana: University of Illinois Press, 2009.

Wilentz, Sean. *Bob Dylan in America*. New York: Anchor, 2011.

Willens, Doris. *Lonesome Travelin': The Life of Lee Hays*. Lincoln: University of Nebraska Press, 1993.

Wilmington, Michael. "Sacco and Vanzetti." *Chicago Tribune*, May 17, 2007.

Wink, Jay. *1944: FDR and The Year that Changed History*. New York: Simon & Schuster, 2015.

Winkler, Alan W. *"To Everything There Is a Season:" Pete Seeger and the Power of Song*. New York: Oxford University Press, 2009.

Wissmar, R. C. and S. D. Craig. "Factors Affecting Habitat Selection by a Small Spawning Chart Population, Bull Trout: Implications for

Recovery of an Endangered Species." *Fisheries Management and Ecology* 11 (February 2004): 23–31.

Wolff, Daniel. *Grown-Up Anger: The Connected Mysteries of Bob Dylan, Woody Guthrie, and the Calumet Massacre of 1913*. New York: Harper Collins, 2017.

Wood, Elijah. *Dylan Goes Electric: Newport, Seeger, Dylan, and the Night that Split the 1960s*. New York: Dey Street Books, 1965.

Woody Guthrie Archives (WGA). New York City. Now located in Tulsa, Oklahoma.

"Woody Guthrie: One Hundredth Birthday of a Communist." *Oklahoma Constitution*, May 7, 2012. www.oklahomaconstitution.com.

"Woody Our New Columnist." *Daily Worker*, April 2, 1940.

Worster, Donald. *Dust Bowl: The Southern Plains in the 1930s*. New York: Oxford University Press, 1979.

Zieger, Robert H. *The CIO, 1935–1950*. Chapel Hill: University of North Carolina Press, 1997.

Zimmerman, Paul D. "Alice's Restaurant's Children." *Newsweek*, September 29, 1969, 10.

Index

Page numbers in **boldface** refer to illustrations.

abortion, 214–15
AFL (American Federation of Labor), 92, **151**, 165, 172, 186. *See also* unions
"Against the Law," 176
Alice's Restaurant (film), 280
"Alice's Restaurant Massacre" (Arlo Guthrie), 279–80
Almanac Singers, 3, 17–18, 80, 87–88, 92–97, 99, 170–73
American dream, 10, 21, 111, 163, 168, 232, 297. *See also* social mobility
American Federation of Labor (AFL), 92, **151**, 165, 172, 186. *See also* unions
American Legion, 192–93
anarchism, 260, 261–62, 263, 270, 271. *See also* politics
antifascism: and Almanac Singers, 95; and artists, 187; and the big union idea, 186–88; and *Bound for Glory* (Guthrie), 182; during the Great Depression, 10; and *Mother* (Gorky), 102; and Popular Front, 54; post–World War II, 102, 105, 107, 109; and Roosevelt, 51; during World War II, 3, 16, 172. *See also* fascism; politics
archives, 12–14, 62, 176, 200, 310
Arnold, Hillel, 310
art, 99
artists, 173, 187, 243
Asch, Moe, 19, 61, 219, 220, 237–40, 242, 245, 264, 266–67
Ashby, Hal, 24, 28–29, 32
atomic bomb, 107, 110–11, 122, 126, 197
Audioslave, 4

Balboa, Rocky, 24, 37. See also *Rocky* (film)
"Ballad of Harriet Tubman, The," 192
"Ballad of Hollis Brown" (Dylan), 283
"Ballad of Rosa Lee Ingram, The," 192
"Ballad of the Big Ben," 242
"Ballad of the Red Socks," 242
Ballads from the Dust Bowl, 246
Ballads of Sacco and Vanzetti, 19, 220, 258–73, 307
banditry, social, 50, 174, 232. *See also* outlaws; rebels, primitive
bankers, 50, 63, 132, 171, 229. *See also* capitalism
Beluthahatchee, Florida, 193–95, 198, 212, 250

367

Beluthahatchee Blues (cycle), 193, 195–96, 250
"Beluthahatchee Blues" (song), 195–96
Berardelli, Alessandro, 260
Berger, Annette, 112
Berlin, Irving, 24, 25–26, 60–61, 297
bicentennial, 15, 24, 36, 37, 237, 238. *See also* 1970s; patriotism
"Biggest Thing That Man Has Ever Done," 78, 84, 85–86
Billy Bragg and Wilco, 4, 193, 194, 202, 286
Billy the Kid, 159
biographies, 13–14
Black Lives Matter, 179
blacklist, 4, 27, 120–22, 175, 306. *See also* Cold War; Hollywood; HUAC; McCarthyism; Red Scare
"Blinding of Isaac Woodard, The," 191, 245
"Bloody Poll Tax Chain," 244
Bloor, Ella Reeves, 251
"Blowin' Down the Road," 18, 231–32
"Blowing in the Wind" (Dylan), 283
blues music, 178, 188, 189, 193, 240, 250, 288, 290
Blumofe, Robert F., 28
Boley, Joseph, 280
Bonneville Power Administration (BPA), 3, 16, 75, 77, 81–88, 246. *See also* Columbia River songs
Born in the USA (Springsteen), 292
Born to Run (Springsteen), 292
Boston (Sinclair), 262–64
Bound for Glory (film): according to Robbin, 39–40; awards, 36, 37; chronology, 33–36; cinematography, 31, 36–37, 39; depiction of Guthrie and his family, 30, 33; de-radicalization of Guthrie, 15, 23–24, 37–41, 238, 270; and Guthrie's politics, 31–32, 37–41; historical context, 30–31; idea and script, 27–28; music in, 32; and nostalgia, 164; possible actors for, 29–30; poster from, **146**; and religion, 34; reviews, 36–41. See also *Bound for Glory* (Guthrie)
Bound for Glory (Guthrie), 13, 27, 74, 135, 181–82, 197. See also *Bound for Glory* (film)
BPA (Bonneville Power Administration), 3, 16, 75, 77, 81–88, 246. *See also* Columbia River songs
Bragg, Billy, 4, 193, 194, 202, 286
Bridges, Harry, 52
Briley, F. C., 5, 14, 75, 166, 200, 235, 291, 300–301
Briley, Ron: career, 11–13; and "communism," 22–23; in the cotton fields, 8, 39; and dust storms, 33, 235–36; education, 8–11; evolution of, 216; and feminism, 201; his family, 1, 5–8, 19, 200–201, 300–301, 309–10; his inspiration, 1, 4–5, 20, 110, 259, 300–303, 309–10; and music, 4–8, 12, 275–76; in 1960s, 9, 23, 107, 127; and the outlaw tradition, 155–56; in Pampa, Texas, **143–45**; and politics, 10–11, 23; and race,

368 *Index*

180–81, 198; and religion, 129–30, 140–41; and research, 12–14; and *Struggle*, 239; and unions, 166–67
Brock, Alice and Ray, 279, 281
Browder, Earl, 116–17
Browne, Jackson, 13
Buehler, Elmer, 83, 85
"Buffalo Skinners," 237, 248–49
Bule, Osark (*Bound for Glory* film), 34
"Buoy Bells from Trenton," 191–92
Burke, Frank, 25, 35, 46, 56

California: and *Bound for Glory* (film), 15, 24, 28, 34, 39; and *Bound for Glory* (Guthrie), 135; and *Dust Bowl Ballads*, 219; and Mexican laborers, 197–98, 243; and migrants, 79, 171, 196, 222, 224–27, 230–31, 249, 303; move to, 2–3, 33, 43, 134, 231; and *People's Daily World*, 16, 24, 47–58, 135, 249; and race, 185; return to, 60, 80–81; and unions, 169, 170, 304
Calumet, Michigan, 251–53
capitalism: and the American dream, 10, 232; and anarchism, 262; and artists, 243; and atomic diplomacy, 122–23; and "commonism," 23–24, 232; and communism, 116–17; crisis of, 51, 153, 185–86; critique of, 3, 15–16, 63, 70, 122–24, 234–35, 238, 243–44, 269; and the cult of Jesus, 136, 138, 301; and the dust bowl, 221, 226; exploitation of working class, 10, 266, 301, 310; and greed, 21, 119, 123, 221, 238; and homosexuality, 215; inequities of, 46; and labor, 186, 250–55; and migrants, 43–44; and music, 71; and the outlaw tradition, 153–64; and race, 307; and "This Land Is Your Land," 25; and unionism, 166; and war, 53, 55, 64–65, 98. *See also* corporations; imperialism
Carradine, David, 30
cattle drives, 248
censorship, 14, 25, 200, 210
Centralia, Illinois, 247–48, 253
Cherokees, 196
children, 25, 52, 61, 117, 199, 245, 278, 304. *See also* family
Childress, Texas, 5–8, 89, 180–81
China, 111
"Chinese and the Japs, The," 197
"Chopping Axe Blues," 196
Christianity, 7, 14, 17, 44, 57, 130, 131–41, 194, 269, 301–2. *See also* Jesus of Nazareth; religion
Church of Christ, 44, 134. *See also* Jesus of Nazareth; religion
CIO (Congress for Industrial Organization): and the Almanac Singers, 171–72; and communism, 115; Dixie campaign, 176–77; and fascism, 94–95, 172–73; and Jim Crow, 172–73; and Kennedy, Stetson, 193–94; and race, 186; and textile workers, 176; and unions, 170; and World War II, 92–93. *See also* unions

Index 369

"City of New Orleans" (Arlo Guthrie), 281
civil liberties, 262, 272, 283, 304. *See also* freedom; social justice
Civil Rights Movement, 4, 7, 18, 155, 178, 238, 283, 303. *See also* race
class: and capitalism, 186; consciousness, 44, 48–49, 155, 237, 298; and health care, 50–51; and the hurt song, 296; oppression, 50, 264; and race, 183, 239; and religion, 301; and struggle, 238; in Tulsa, 183. *See also* common people; social justice; *Struggle*; working class
"Cleano," 278
Clemence, Annie, 251, 252
climate change, 302. *See also* environment; global warming
Cold War, 17, 109, 115, 126–27, 165–66, 192–93, 215, 304. *See also* HUAC; McCarthyism; Red Scare
collective action, 171, 249–50, 295. *See also* unions
collective bargaining, 175. *See also* unions
Colorado Fuel and Iron Company, 253
Columbia: America's Greatest Power Stream, The, (film), 82–84
Columbia River songs, 78, 83–86, 246. *See also* Bonneville Power Administration (BPA)
"Coming into Los Angeles" (Arlo Guthrie), 280–81
common people: and the Almanac Singers, 93, 99; and the American dream, 21, 111; and the Briley family, 301; and capitalism, 70; and communism, 116; and *Dust Bowl Ballads*, 234, 295; and fascism, 103; and Guthrie, 28, 83; and the HUAC, 116; and Native Americans, 85; natural instincts of, 99; and the outlaw tradition, 17, 154, 162; and public power, 77, 87; and religion, 132, 136, 137, 231; and *Struggle*, 19; struggle of, 13, 296; today, 4, 224, 300; and violence, 171; and World War II, 91, 106. *See also* "commonism"; migrants (dust bowl); *Struggle*; unions; working class
"commonism": according to Guthrie, Nora, 14, 56; allegiance to, 17, 306, 309; and *Bound for Glory* (film), 24; and the BPA, 87; and the Briley family, 22–23; and capitalism, 23–24, 232; and communism, 14, 22, 104–5, 127, 132–40; dream of, 107, 310; elements of, 57; and fascism, 215–16; and individual freedom, 212–13; and individualism, 154–55; and Jesus of Nazareth, 135–40; and New York City, 74–75; and one big union, 178, 282, 309, 310; and popular culture, 111; and populism, 58; and the profit system, 71, 107; and race, 189, 238; and Sacco and Vanzetti, 272; today, 20; and unions, 168–69, 304–7; and violence, 154, 162; and women, 111, 204. *See also* politics; working class

370　*Index*

communism: and *Bound for Glory* (film), 24, 28, 32, 34, 38; and CIO, 115; and "commonism," 14, 22, 104–5, 127, 132–40; and equality, 56; and Guthrie, 72, 81–82, 94, 115, 138, 305–6; and homosexuality, 215, 308; and Jesus of Nazareth, 132–40; and Jim Crow, 23; and Korea, 120–21; and labor movement, 114–17; as a possible path, 53; and race, 138–39, 188; and socialism, 44; and "This Land Is Your Land," 25; and unions, 172. *See also* Communist Party; Marxism; politics

Communist Party: and the Almanac Singers, 95–97; and Bloor, 251; and *Bound for Glory* (film), 15; during the Great Depression, 185–86; and Guthrie, 14, 22, 47, 52, 56, 81–82, 104, 117, 269–70, 305–6; and the Ku Klux Klan, 186; national convention, 69; and the Nazi-Soviet Non-aggression Pact, 25; in Oklahoma, 67; and People's Songs, 116; and the profit system, 269–70; and segregation, 186; and social banditry, 162; and the Soviet Union, 53; and Wallace, 177; and World War II, 175. *See also* communism; politics; Popular Front

Congress for Industrial Organization (CIO). *See* CIO (Congress for Industrial Organization)

conservativism, 130, 139, 302. *See also* politics

coperialist, 64

Cornell, Katharine, 73

corporations, 10, 49, 131, 172, 224, 239, 250, 254, 300. *See also* capitalism

Cox, Ronny, 34

creditors, 50, 51, 249. *See also* capitalism

Crissman, Mary Ruth, 120, 209–10, 211, 213

Crissman, Maxine (Lefty Lou), 35, 46, 120, 210

Cumbuka, Ju-Tu, 33

Cunningham, Sis, 92

Daily Worker columns, 60, 63–75, 106–7, 116

"Dalton Boys, The," 158

dams, 78, 82, 84, 86. *See also* Bonneville Power Administration (BPA)

"Dance Around My Atomic Fire," 122

Darkness on the Edge of Town (Springsteen), 292

"Dear Mrs. Roosevelt," 290

Debs, Eugene, 133

"Deep in the Mud," 123

Democratic Party, 2, 69, 130, 265. *See also* politics

"Deportees," 197–98, 281

Dewey, Thomas, 175, 177

Dillon, Melinda, 33, 34

dissent: and the 1960s, 270, 280, 289; and Guthrie's ideal, 303; history of, 10; post–World War I, 257; post–World War II, 112, 120, 121, 211,

Index 371

dissent (*continued*)
    239. *See also* protests; radicalism; reform
"Do Re Mi," 18, 223, 230–31
Documentary Struggle album, 244–45. See also *Struggle*
"Dollar Down, A Dollar a Week, A," 237, 249
"Don't Kill My Baby and My Son," 184, 244
"Don't Lie to Me," 240–41
dust bowl, 2, 78, 220–36. *See also* farmers; migrants (dust bowl)
Dust Bowl Ballads, 18, 59, 62, 219–36, 249, 286, 295
"Dust Bowl Pneumonia Blues," 229
"Dust Bowl Refugee," 226
"Dust Can't Kill Me," 227
"Dust Storm Disaster," 220
"Dusty Old Dust," 18, 45, 223
"Dying Miner, The," 237, 247
Dylan, Bob, 4, 283–90, 295–96, 308

economics, 130–31, 171, 221, 302. *See also* capitalism; communism
Edgmon, Mary Jo, 139
electricity. *See* Bonneville Power Administration (BPA)
elitism, 58, 75–76, 84, 99, 133, 140. *See also* class
Elliott, Ramblin' Jack, 287
Emrich, Duncan, 176
environment, 16, 84, 85, 86, 221, 233, 239. *See also* climate change; global warming

equality: and communism, 56; economic, 171, 302; gender, 18, 200–202, 206, 208, 212, 215–16; and Guthrie's vision, 168; and Jesus of Nazareth, 53–54, 136, 165, 176; and 1960s counterculture, 107; post-World War II, 115; and race, 139, 178, 182, 185–86, 190, 193; and unions, 168. *See also* LGBTQ community; social justice; women
escapism, 111, 121. *See also* popular culture
Everly Brothers, 7

faith healing, 129, 134, 140. *See also* religion
family: after Cathy Ann's death, 119–20; in *Bound for Glory* (film), 31–32, 33, 35; desertion of, 3, 18, 120, 200, 207, 308; married life, 2–4, 45, 75, 91, 101, 125, 193, 195, 278; and miscegenation laws, 214; and other women, 18, 112, 200, 207, 209, 213, 241, 278, 308; parents, 1, 2, 6, 44–45, 181; and politics, 204; traditional, 101–2, 201, 204, 206, 209, 210, 213, 309; and unions, 206, 212. *See also* Mazia, Marjorie Greenblatt; sexuality
farmers, 232–34. *See also* dust bowl
fascism: and the Almanac Singers, 92–97; and the CIO, 172–73; and "commonism," 215–16; and greed, 91, 94, 98, 100–101, 103, 107, 168, 173, 187–88, 304; and Guthrie's

personal dreams, 97–107; Japanese, 197; and Jim Crow, 241; and the Ku Klux Klan, 178; and love, 205–6; and nativism, 65; in the South, 194; and *Struggle*, 240; and Trump, 301; and unions, 170, 173, 219, 304. *See also* antifascism; Hitler, Adolf; neo-Nazis; politics

Federal Bureau of Investigation (FBI), 57, 115, 121, 126, 156–57, 175, 239, 261, 304

Federal Housing Authority, 191. *See also* race

feminism, 201. *See also* gender equality; women

"Final Call," 170

Finian's Rainbow (1947), 209

"Flood and the Storm, The," 268

Floyd, Charles Arthur. *See* Pretty Boy Floyd

folk song, 62, 86, 88, 96, 113, 115, 154, 174, 176, 240, 277. *See also* music

Folkways Records, 19, 84, 237, 240, 267

Food, Tobacco, and Allied Workers (FTA), 176–77, 190. *See also* unions

Ford, John, 221–22, 224

Foster, William, 116

Franklin, Marcus Carl, 288

free speech, 88, 121. *See also* civil liberties; freedom

freedom, 53, 88, 121, 187–88, 211, 262, 308. *See also* civil liberties

"Freedom's Fire," 122

FTA (Food, Tobacco, and Allied Workers), 176–77, 190. *See also* unions

Fuller, Alvan, 269

Galleani, Luigi, 261

"Galveston Bay" (Springsteen), 295

Geer, Will, 60, 73, 234

gender equality, 18, 200–202, 206, 208, 212, 215–16. *See also* LGBTQ community; women

General Motors, 121, 176

"Genocide," 195

"Germans and the Japs, The," 197

"Get Along Little Doggies," 237, 248

Getchell, Robert, 28

Ghost of Tom Joad, The (Springsteen), 292–95

"Ghost of Tom Joad, The" (Springsteen), 4, 163–64

global warming, 220. *See also* climate change; environment

"God Bless America" (Berlin), 24, 25–26, 60–61, 297

"Going Down the Road Feeling Bad," 231–32. *See also* "Blowin' Down the Road"

"Goodbye Centralia," 247. *See also* Centralia, Illinois

government: and anarchism, 260, 261–62, 263, 270, 271; and climate change, 302; and the Columbia River songs, 16, 78, 82, 84–85; and the Communist Party, 52; and corporations, 239; and farmers, 234;

Index 373

government (*continued*)
and the FBI, 57, 122; Guthrie's ideal, 53, 71, 105; and immigration, 257; and Native Americans, 248–49; and outlaws, 155, 156; propaganda, 38, 84–85, 271, 295; suppressing dissent, 44, 121, 211, 215, 264; and unions, 172. *See also* New Deal; politics

grafters, 49, 52, 61, 139. *See also* law enforcement; legal system; politics

Grand Coulee Dam, 86. *See also* Bonneville Power Administration (BPA); Columbia River songs

"Grand Coulee Dam," 3, 78

Grapes of Wrath (film), 27, 31, 66, 162, 227

Grapes of Wrath (Steinbeck), 27, 52, 162, 231. *See also* Steinbeck, John

Great Depression, 10, 49, 153, 160, 165, 185–86, 221, 235–36

"Great Dust Storm, The" 223, 226–27

greed: and capitalism, 21, 119, 123, 221, 238; vs. "commonism," 44, 243; and corporations, 224, 239, 254, 300; and crops, 233; and the dust bowl, 221; and fascism, 91, 94, 98, 100–101, 103, 107, 168, 173, 187–88, 304; and migrants, 227; and "1913 Massacre," 252; and outlaws, 159; and poverty, 21; and power, 136; and the profit system, 21; and racism, 187–88, 224; vs. love, 98, 102, 208

Guthrie, Arlo: as actor, 30; and *Ballads of Sacco & Vanzetti*, 267, 272; and the Columbia River songs, 86; and Dylan, 285; as Guthrie's interpreter, 277–82, 308; his family, 3, 119, 277–79, 281; his politics, 282–83; letters to, 211–12; and Leventhal, 27; and "1913 Massacre," 252; and "This Land Is Your Land," 4

Guthrie, Cathy Ann, 3, 16–17, 45, 91, 98, 103, 109–10, 118–19, 177, 206, 303–4. *See also* Railroad Pete

Guthrie, Charley, 1, 6, 44–45, 65, 139, 184, 244, 250, 291

Guthrie, Clara, 2

Guthrie, Claude, 184

Guthrie, Jerry P., 134

Guthrie, Joady Ben, 119, 277, 285

Guthrie, Marjorie Greenblatt Mazia. *See* Mazia, Marjorie Greenblatt

Guthrie, Mary Ann (niece), 46

Guthrie, Mary Jennings, 2, 3, 33, 60, 68, 72–75, 79–81, 88, 101, 204

Guthrie, Nora (mother), 2, 45

Guthrie, Nora Lee (daughter), 14, 15, 56, 119, 217, 267, 277, 285, 299

Guthrie, Woody, **147, 149**

Guthrie Center, 281

Guthrie Children's Trust, 4, 27

Guthrie Family Values Tour, 281

"Han River Mud," 125

"Han River Woman," 125

"Hang Knot," 237, 250

Hard Hitting Songs for Hard-Hit People, 62, 80, 159, 169, 202, 226, 232–33

Harris Drug Store, **143–45**
Hatch Act, 81–82
Hawes, Baldwin "Butch," 92
Hawes, Bess Lomax, 92, 96
Hawes, Pete, 92
Hayden, Tom, 302
Hays, Lee, 92, 96–97, 114, 193, 233–34
health, 4, 27, 109, 123, 178, 216, 270, 278–79. *See also* Huntington's disease
health care, 50–51
Hearst, William Randolph, 52, 263
Hill, Joe, 46, 130
Hitler, Adolf, 94–95, 173, 174, 175, 182, 187–88, 197. *See also* fascism
"Hold On," 195
Hollywood, 15, 27, 31, 93, 121, 173, 270. *See also* blacklist; *Bound for Glory* (film); McCarthyism
homosexuality, 215–16, 308
Honor the Poets (Asch), 243
Hoover, J. Edgar, 175
Hoovervilles, 31, 34, 61, 67. *See also* migrants (dust bowl)
House Un-American Activities Committee (HUAC), 52, 70, 115, 116–17, 121, 126, 239, 304. *See also* McCarthyism; Red Scare
Houston, Cisco, 92, 103, 106, 174, 190, 197, 240, 250, 266
Howell, Terrence, 185
HUAC (House Un-American Activities Committee), 52, 70, 115, 116–17, 121, 126, 239, 304. *See also* McCarthyism; Red Scare

Huntington's disease, 2, 3–4, 17, 108, 112, 120, 200, 213, 303, 308. *See also* health

"I Ain't Going to Be Treated This Way," 227
"I Ain't Gonna Work on Maggie's Farm No More" (Dylan), 289
"I Ain't Got No Home in the World Anymore," 231
"I Don't Want Korea," 123
"I Just Want to Sing Your Name," 268
I'm Not There (Haynes), 288
immigrants, 220, 251, 255, 257–59, 265–66, 307
immigration, 65, 257, 258, 267, 272, 307
imperialism, 17, 64, 98, 120, 122–23, 156, 307. *See also* capitalism
Indigenous peoples, 84. *See also* Native Americans; race
individualism, 15, 24, 34, 130, 154–55, 158, 162, 174, 212–13, 249
Industrial Workers of the World (IWW), 10, 23, 46, 130, 169, 246, 250, 301, 306. *See also* unions
Ingram, Rosa Lee, 192
intellectualism, 102, 222, 292
internment camps, 197
isolationism, 71. *See also* politics
Italian Hall (Calumet, Michigan), 251–52
Ives, Burl, 243
IWW (Industrial Workers of the World), 10, 23, 46, 130, 169, 246, 250, 301, 306. *See also* unions

Index 375

Jackson, Aunt Molly, 62, 202–3
James, Frank, 160–61
James, Jesse, 159–62
Japan, 111, 197
"Jeep in the Mud," 123
Jeffersonianism, 14, 22, 57, 232. *See also* politics
Jennings, Mary. *See* Guthrie, Mary Jennings
Jesse James (film), 160–61
"Jesse James and His Boys," 160
"Jesus Christ for President," 137–38
"Jesus Christ Was a Man," 137, 161–62
Jesus of Nazareth: and bankers, 132; and capitalism, 136, 138, 301; and "commonism," 17, 22, 132–40; and communism, 132–40; Dylan's, 291–92; and equality, 53–54, 136, 165, 176; and Guthrie, 135–40; and Jesse James, 161–62; and Marx, 22; and outlaws, 137–38, 141, 161–62; and politics, 139; as social reformer, 130; and socialism, 133–40; and unions, 138, 176; and the working class, 132; and World War II, 137. *See also* Christianity
Jews, 65
Jim Crow: and blacklists, 122; and the CIO, 92, 172–73; and communism, 23, 185–86; and the *Daily Worker*, 63; and fascism, 240–41; in Florida, 195; and Guthrie's growth, 33–34; and *Struggle*, 250; and unionism, 170. *See also* race; segregation
Joad, Tom, 4, 154, 162–64, 246, 294

Johnson, Luther (*Bound for Glory* film), 34, 35
Jungle, The (Sinclair), 262

Kael, Pauline, 38–39
Kahn, Stephen, 81, 82–83
Kai-shek, Chiang, 111
Kansas City Massacre, 156
Kazan, Elia, 87
Kennedy, Stetson, 193–195
"Killing of the Ferguson Brothers, The," 191
"Korea and Me," 124
"Korea Bye Bye," 123
"Korea I Love You," 124
"Korea I'm Alone," 123
"Korea Korea," 125
"Korea Mackarter," 125
"Korea Send Me Home," 123
"Korean Baby Goodbye," 124
"Korean Beauty," 124
"Korean Blues," 123
"Korean Boggyhole Blues," 123
"Korean Boogey," 124
"Korean Girly," 124
"Korean Quicksands," 123
"Korean Quickstep," 123
"Korean Waltz," 124
Korean War, 17, 109, 120–27. *See also* war
Korean War songs, 307
"Korean War Tank," 123
Kristofferson, Kris, 13
Ku Klux Klan: and the Briley family, 6–7; CIO's opposition to, 186;

Communist Party's opposition to, 186; during the 1920s, 257; and fascism, 178; and Guthrie, Charley, 6, 291; and Guthrie's columns, 66–67; Guthrie's opposition to, 195, 198; and Hitler, 187–88; and Jesse James, 161; and Kennedy, Stetson, 193–95; in Oklahoma, 183–84; and the Peekskill riots, 192. *See also* race

labor: black, 241; and capitalism, 186, 250–55; and cowboys, 248–49; exploitation of, 155, 249; and folk music, 115; and McCarthyism, 114–17; Mexican, 197–98, 243; and miners, 202, 246–47, 251–55; organized, 18, 165, 166, 239, 305; and Sacco and Vanzetti, 265, 268; and World War II, 18, 98, 165, 167. *See also* unions; working class
Lampell, Millard, 92, 95
Lang, Pearl, 209, 213
Lange, Dorothea, 221–22, 309
law enforcement, 50, 173, 179, 191, 227, 251, 253. *See also* legal system
Lead Belly, 62, 73, 178, 188–89, 198, 240, 250
Ledbetter, Huddie William. *See* Lead Belly
Leech, John, 52
Lefty Lou (Maxine Crissman), 35, 46, 120, 210
legal system, 17, 50, 154, 159, 211, 260, 261, 271, 272. *See also* law enforcement

Lehne, John, 35
Lerner, Irving, 27
Leventhal, Harold, 27–28, 30
LGBTQ community, 198, 216, 302, 303, 308
Light, The, 46–47
"Like a Rolling Stone" (Dylan), 283
Lincoln, Abraham, 169, 245–46
Lomax, Alan, 3, 18, 59, 62, 81, 188–89, 219, 222, 228–31, 240
Lomax, John, 188
Lomax Hawes, Bess, 92, 96
"Lonesome Death of Hattie Carroll, The" (Dylan), 283
"Long and Lonesome Chain Around My Leg," 244
Longhi, Jim, 103, 106, 174, 190
"Lost John," 237, 250
love, 98, 99, 124, 170, 205–6, 213, 217, 299, 310. *See also* sexuality
"Low Down Thieves," 249
loyalty oaths, 81–82. *See also* Cold War; HUAC; McCarthyism; Red Scare
Loyalty Review Board, 176
Ludlow, Colorado, 251, 253–55, 263
"Ludlow Massacre," 19, 219, 237, 250, 253–55, 306–7
lynching, 65, 183–84, 192, 244, 250, 291

MacArthur, Gen. Douglas, 125
Major League Baseball, 186
Marshall, Anneke Van Kirk, 3, 120, 123, 193, 195, 212
Marx, Karl, 22, 48, 51, 63, 132, 310

Marxism, 17, 22, 58, 70, 99, 130, 133, 297, 301. *See also* communism
materialism, 44, 111. *See also* popular culture
Matusow, Harvey, 121
Mazia, Marjorie Greenblatt: and Arlo Guthrie, 279; and *Bound for Glory* (film), 30; care for Guthrie, 4, 120, 200, 212, 279; and Korean War songs, 125; love letters to, 199, 204–6; marriage to, 3, 4, 16, 91–92, 103, 107, 110, 211–12; politics and letters to, 98–102, 105–6, 110–12, 205–6; sexuality and letters to, 105–6, 112, 207–11, 213
McCarthyism, 4, 109, 114–17, 165–66, 170, 304. *See also* blacklist; Cold War; HUAC; Red Scare
McKenzie, Eulys, 134
media, 52. *See also* publicity; radio
Memphis Sue (*Bound for Glory* film), 34, 35
Merchant Marine, 3, 93, 103–7, 165, 170, 174–75, 190, 206
Merchant Marine Three, 190
Meriwether, Annie Mae, 67, 203
Mermaid Avenue (Billy Bragg and Wilco), 4
migrants (dust bowl): after the Pacific Northwest, 88–89; and bankers, 171; in *Bound for Glory* (film), 33–34; and capitalism, 43–44; and *Dust Bowl Ballads*, 220–36; exploitation of, 3, 47–49, 230–31, 249; federal camps for, 234; Guthrie's migration, 45–46; Hoovervilles, 31, 34, 61, 67; and immigrants, 255, 265–66, 307; and music, 79; and the New Deal, 87–88; in "Pastures of Plenty," 86; treatment of, 46; virtues of, 51–52; while in New York City, 64, 65–66; and the Will Rogers Highway, 196. *See also* dust bowl; labor; working class
migrants, Mexican, 294
miners, 202, 246–47, 251–55
"Miner's Kids and Wives," 247
miscegenation laws, 214. *See also* race
"Miss Pavlachenko," 203
modernism (modernity), 44, 86
Mooney, Tom, 47
Morello, Tom, 4, 13
Morgan, J. P., 263
Mother (Gorky), 102
"Motorcycle Song" (Arlo Guthrie), 281
movies, 27, 64, 111, 160, 293. *See also* popular culture
"Mr. Sickyman Ree," 125
music: the blues, 178, 188, 189, 193, 240, 250, 288, 290; and Briley, Ron, 4–5, 7–8, 12, 275–76; children's, 25, 61, 117, 199, 245, 278, 304; and Christian fundamentalism, 7–8; Columbia River songs, 78, 83–86, 246; contemporary, 4, 19; and dust bowl migrants, 79, 87–88; and elements of irony, 85–86; folk music tradition, 26; and Guthrie's family, 7–8; and Guthrie's interpreters, 276; and Guthrie's vision, 188; and the

hurt song, 296; Korean War songs, 109, 123–25; outlaw ballads, 156–63; performances, 61–62, 190, 245, 277, 281; and politics, 238, 245; and the profit system, 71; and protest songs, 62, 123, 137, 238; and race, 178, 189; and radicalism, 18, 22, 295–96, 307, 310; and the truth, 61; and unions, 106–7; while in Pacific Northwest, 78, 83. *See also* folk song
"My Big Mixed Race," 214
"My Thirty Thousand," 193

Nash, Gerald D., 11
Nash, Graham, 13
National Labor Relations Board, 175. *See also* unions
National Maritime Union (NMU), 93, 165, 173, 175, 304. *See also* unions
Native Americans, 16, 85, 196, 248. *See also* Indigenous peoples; race
nativism, 65. *See also* fascism; politics
Nazis, 88, 92. *See also* fascism; Hitler, Adolf; neo-Nazis
Nazi-Soviet Non-aggression Pact, 25, 51, 54, 56
Nebraska (Springsteen), 292
Nelson family, 183–84
neo-Nazis, 180, 194, 301. *See also* fascism; Nazis; race
New Deal, 3, 69–71, 77, 78, 86, 87, 130, 138, 225–26, 247. *See also* Bonneville Power Administration (BPA); government
New York City, 3, 58, 60–75, 88–89

Nightwatchman, 4
1970s: bicentennial, 15, 24, 36, 37, 237, 238; fight for social justice, 238–39; and Guthrie's music, 232; working class, 167–68. *See also Bound for Glory* (film)
1960s: and Arlo Guthrie, 279, 282; and *Ballads of Sacco & Vanzetti*, 19, 270; and Briley, Ron, 9, 23, 107, 127; counterculture, 107, 280, 283, 302; and dissent, 270, 280, 289; and Dylan, 284, 287, 289; and Guthrie's interpreters, 276; and Guthrie's music, 4, 126; and the outlaw tradition, 155; and *Sacco and Vanzetti* (Montaldo), 262, 271; and Springsteen, 292
"1913 Massacre," 19, 219, 237, 250–53, 281, 306–7
Nixon, Richard, 168
NMU (National Maritime Union), 93, 165, 173, 175, 304. *See also* unions

Ogan, Sara, 203
Okemah, Oklahoma: in *Bound for Glory* (film), 33; in *Bound for Glory* (Guthrie), 181–82; early life in, 2; and Jessie James, 160; lynching, 65, 183–84, 244, 250, 291; photographs, **148, 150–52**; Woodyfest, 4, 282. *See also* Oklahoma
Okies, 65, 87–88, 226–27, 231, 234. *See also* migrants (dust bowl); Oklahoma

Index 379

Oklahoma, 44–45, 66–68, 133, 183–84, 225–26. *See also* Okemah, Oklahoma
"Old Judge Thayer," 268–69. *See also* Thayer, Webster
one big union: and "commonism," 178, 282, 309, 310; Guthrie's vision of, 55, 107, 114, 174, 176, 203, 238, 309, 310; and his family, 204; and Jesus of Nazareth, 170; and Lincoln, 169; post-World War II, 239; and race, 186, 189, 241; and Sacco and Vanzetti, 265. *See also* unions
"One Thing the Atom Can't Do," 122
"Only Pawn in Their Game" (Dylan), 283
Oregon. *See* Bonneville Power Administration (BPA)
outlaws, 17, 50, 137–38, 141, 154, 173–74, 179, 249, 295. *See also* banditry, social; rebels, primitive

Palmer, A. Mitchell, 261
Palmer Raids, 257
Pampa, Texas, 2, 33, 45, 68, **143–45**, 182, 225, 228
Parmenter, Frederick A., 260
"Pastures of Plenty," 3, 78, 84, 86, 87
patriotism, 44, 78, 122, 238, 306. *See also* bicentennial; radicalism
Paul, Ron, 282
"Pauline" (*Bound for Glory* film), 35
Pavlachenko, Luidmilla, 203
"Peace Town," 196
Peekskill riots, 192–93

Peekskill Songs, 193
People's Daily World, 16, 24, 47–58, 135, 249. *See also* "Woody Sez" columns
People's Songs, 112–16, 177. *See also* unions
People's Utility Districts, 78, 82. *See also* Bonneville Power Administration
Petersen, Peter, 9, 310
Phelps Dodge workers, 177. *See also* unions
picket lines, 166. *See also* strikes; unions
"Pistol Packer," 195
Plessy v. Ferguson, 241. *See also* segregation
politics: and the Almanac Singers, 92–97; and Arlo Guthrie, 282–83; and *Bound for Glory* (film), 24–25, 31–32, 37–41; and the BPA, 81, 84–88; and Briley, Ron, 10–11, 23; and the Briley family, 6, 23; conservativism, 130, 139, 302; Democratic Party, 2, 69, 130, 265; and *Dust Bowl Ballads*, 223; and Dylan, 283–84, 287–90; eclectic, 22; and elitism, 75–76; of fear, 115; and Guthrie's columns, 53–56, 75; and Guthrie's sophistication, 154; of identity, 216; and Jesse James, 161; and Jesus of Nazareth, 139; and lynching, 184; and Marxism, 22, 58, 70, 99; and migrants, 79; and music, 238, 245; nativism, 65; in New York City, 63–75; and the obscenity charge,

210; and patriotism, 44, 78, 122, 238, 306; and the personal sphere, 98, 119, 123, 201, 204–6, 210, 213, 284, 290; populism, 14–15, 22, 57–58, 133, 232; post-World War II, 116–17, 177–78; radical critique of, 60; and radio sponsors, 72–75; Republican Party, 130–31, 175, 282; and sexual freedom, 105–6, 213–14; and Springsteen, 297–98; and women, 201–2, 204; and the working class, 167–68; and World War II, 98. *See also* anarchism; communism; fascism; government; Korean War; progressivism; radicalism

popular culture, 87, 111, 160, 260–61, 262, 295. *See also* escapism; materialism; movies

Popular Front, 51, 53, 64, 69, 137–38, 163, 270, 289. *See also* Communist Party

populism, 14–15, 22, 57–58, 133, 232. *See also* politics

poverty, 19, 21, 26, 44, 67–68, 70, 194. *See also* class

"Preacher and the Slave, The" (Hill), 130

Presley, Elvis, 7

Pretty Boy Floyd, 156–58

"Pretty Boy Floyd," 156–58, 174, 223, 232, 237, 249, 281

primitive rebels. *See* rebels, primitive

prison-industrial complex system, 179

private property, 25, 26. *See also* capitalism

profit system: and "commonism," 71, 107; and the Communist Party, 269–70; critique of, 221; and family, 101; and greed, 21; and the Okies, 65, 67; and the outlaw tradition, 158, 159; and popular culture, 111; and unions, 219; and war, 55, 69

progressivism: and Briley, Ron, 201, 239, 259, 299, 302; and "commonism," 14; and *Dust Bowl Ballads*, 223; and folk music, 96, 113; and gender, 200, 202, 215–16; and Guthrie's ideal, 4, 13, 40, 41, 118–19, 224, 300, 303–8, 310; and labor, 115, 305; and race, 188; and the Red Scare, 122; and religion, 130–32, 140–41, 301; and *Struggle*, 219, 239; today, 303, 305, 306, 307. *See also* politics; reform

propaganda, 38, 84–85, 271, 295. *See also* government

protests: and Dylan, 283, 289; history of, 10, 163–64, 276; intolerance for, 121; and Sacco and Vanzetti, 269, 272; songs, 62, 123, 137, 238; and Springsteen, 298. *See also* dissent; radicalism; reform

public power. *See* Bonneville Power Administration

publicity, 72. *See also* media

Pushkin, Aleksander, 213–14, 223

Quaid, Randy, 34

queer sensibility, 216, 307, 308

Quinn, Patt, 280

Index 381

race: and blackface, 182–83; in *Bound for Glory* (film), 33; and Briley, Ron, 180–81; and the Briley family, 6–7; and class, 183, 239; and "communism," 189, 238; and communism, 138–39, 188; and *Documentary Struggle* album, 244–45; and freedom, 187; and greed, 187–88, 224; and Guthrie, Charley, 6; and Guthrie's columns, 66–67; and Guthrie's growth, 18, 250, 303; and Guthrie's prejudices, 185; and Hitler, 174; and labor, 197–98, 241, 243; and lynching, 65, 183–84, 192, 244, 250, 291; and miscegenation laws, 214; and music, 178, 189; and Native Americans, 85; and neo-Nazis, 180, 194, 301; and the one big union, 186–88, 241, 306; and socialism, 45; in the South, 193–95; today, 179–80; and unions, 67; while in New York City, 64; and Woodard, Isaac, 191; and the working class, 168; and World War II, 103, 197; and xenophobia, 259. *See also* Civil Rights Movement; class; equality; Jim Crow; Ku Klux Klan; neo-Nazis; segregation; social justice

radicalism: and *Bound for Glory* (film), 24, 27, 32, 39–40, 270; commitment to, 75; and Dylan, 295; and efforts to alter capitalism, 46; and Guthrie's columns, 58, 60, 64; and Guthrie's music, 18, 22, 295–96, 307, 310; and Guthrie's travels, 46; history of, 10, 14, 23, 44, 276, 295, 299, 306–7, 310; and patriotism, 44; and Sacco and Vanzetti, 262, 271; and Springsteen, 295; and *Struggle*, 237; and "This Land Is Your Land," 4, 15, 276, 307; and violence, 154. *See also* dissent; politics; protests; reform

radio, 35, 46, 59, 60, 72–75, 79, 185, 204

Rage Against the Machine, 4

Railroad Pete, 16–17, 91, 97–98, 102–3, 107, 206. *See also* Guthrie, Cathy Ann

railroads, 33–34, 241

Raver, Paul J., 81

Ray, Nick, 73

Reagan, Ronald, 167, 168, 239, 292, 293, 302, 305

rebels, primitive, 17, 153–62. *See also* banditry, social; outlaws

red-baiting, 45, 52. *See also* Cold War; HUAC; McCarthyism; Red Scare

Red Scare: and the Almanac Singers, 96; and labor movement, 114–17; and Lerner, 27; and Leventhal, 28; and the Loyalty Review Board, 176; and the obscenity charge, 210; and organized labor, 18; post-World War I, 122, 220, 257, 260, 268, 271, 306. *See also* Cold War; HUAC; McCarthyism

"Red Wine," 268, 272

reform, 3, 109, 115, 130, 167, 222, 238, 239, 270, 304. *See also* dissent; progressivism; protests; radicalism; unions religion: in *Bound for Glory* (film), 34; and Briley, Ron, 301; and the Briley family, 7–8, 129–30, 140–41; and Christian social justice, 131–132, 139–140, 269; and the common people, 132, 136, 137, 231; and the dust bowl, 228–29; and economics, 130–31; and faith healing, 129, 134, 140; organized, 17, 53, 138; and progressives, 130–32, 140–41, 301; and radicalism, 44; and segregation, 140; and speaking in tongues, 129, 134, 140; and unions, 170. *See also* Christianity

Republican Party, 130–31, 175, 282. *See also* politics

Rhee, Syngman, 125

River, The (Springsteen), 292

Robbin, Ed, 24, 31, 39–40, 47, 79

Robeson, Paul, 192–93

Robinson, Earl, 62

Rockefeller, John D., 263

Rocky (film), 15, 36. *See also* Balboa, Rocky

Rogers, Will, 196

"Roll On, Columbia," 3, 78, 84, 85

Roosevelt, Franklin, 51, 53, 63, 64, 69–71, 92, 175, 197

"Root Hog and Die," 269

Rosenberg, Julius and Ethel, 126

Rosenman, Leonard, 32

Russo, Mario, 177

Sacco, Nicola, 257, 260, 267. *See also* Sacco and Vanzetti

Sacco and Vanzetti (Miller), 271–72

Sacco and Vanzetti (Montaldo), 262, 271

Sacco and Vanzetti, 117, 220, 245, 253, 257–73

Salcedo, Andrea, 261

Sandberg, Carl, 213–14, 223

Sanders, Bernie, 282

Sandia Prep (Albuquerque, New Mexico), 11

"Scottsboro Boys," 186

Scottsboro Sharecroppers Union, 186. *See also* unions

SDS (Students for a Democratic Society), 10, 155. *See also* politics

Seeds of Man (novel), 184

"Seeds of Man," 196

Seeger, Antony, 267–68

Seeger, Pete: and Dylan, 283; and Folkways Records, 240; and Guthrie, 3, 62; letter to, 104–5; 1940 road trip, 66–69; and the Peekskill riots, 193; and People's Songs, 112–14; and Sacco, 266; and "This Land Is Your Land," 4, 26; "Waist Deep in the Big Muddy," 123; and the Weavers, 121. *See also* Almanac Singers

segregation: and Briley, Ron, 180; and the Communist Party, 186; and the FTA strike, 176, 190; and the military, 189–90, 240–41; in Oklahoma, 182–83; and religion, 140; and Trump, Fred, 191, 300, 305. *See also* Jim Crow; race

Index 383

"Seven Cent Cotton and Forty Cent Meat," 233
sexuality: and Guthrie's other women, 18, 112, 200, 207, 209, 213, 241, 278, 308; and homosexuality, 215–16; and Korean War songs, 123, 124; and letters to Crissman, 120; and letters to Marjorie, 105–6, 112, 207–11, 213; and LGBTQ community, 198, 216, 302, 303, 308; and marching songs, 240; and obscenity charge, 120, 200, 209–10, 211; and obsession, 200, 208–10, 213, 216; and politics, 105–6, 213–14; and sexual freedom, 209–11, 213–14, 215, 307–8. *See also* Huntington's disease; love; women
Sharecroppers Union, 67, 203. *See also* unions
Shaw Family, 220–21, 229
"She Came Along to Me," 201–2
Sinclair, Upton, 262–64
Snedeger, Slim (*Bound for Glory* film), 33
"So Long, It's Been Good to Know You," 228
social banditry, 153–62. *See also* outlaws
social justice: 1970s, 238–39; Christian, 131–32, 139–40, 269; fight for, 2, 5, 13, 19, 209, 249, 269, 299, 307; today, 302–3. *See also* civil liberties; class; gender equality; Jesus of Nazareth; race; reform; religion
social mobility, 10, 232, 238. *See also* American dream

socialism, 7, 14, 17, 44–45, 57, 85, 87, 133–40, 169, 302. *See also* Jesus of Nazareth; politics; Socialist Party
Socialist Party, 2, 44–45, 133, 169, 251, 257, 262, 306. *See also* socialism; social justice
"Soldiers in the Dust," 234
"Solidarity Forever," 115
"Song to Woody" (Dylan), 287
Soviet Union, 88, 92, 105–6, 173. *See also* communism; Communist Party
speaking in tongues, 129, 134, 140. *See also* religion
Springsteen, Bruce, 4, 26–27, 163–64, 290–98, 308
Stackabones. *See* Guthrie, Cathy Ann
Starr, Belle, 158–59
Steinbeck, John, 62, 163, 221–22, 224. *See also* Grapes of Wrath (Steinbeck)
Stern, Arthur, 92
"Stetson Kennedy," 194
Strauss, Charlotte, 241
Strickland, Gail, 35
strikes, 167, 171–72, 176–77, 231, 251–55, 262. *See also* picket lines; unions
Struggle, 18, 219, 236–55
"Struggle Blues," 237, 250
Students for a Democratic Society (SDS), 10, 155. *See also* politics
"Suassos Lane," 268

Taft-Hartley Act, 115, 239. *See also* unions

"Talking Dust Bowl Blues," 223
technology, 85. *See also* Bonneville Power Administration
Ten Songs by Woody Guthrie, 240–41
Terry, Sonny, 189, 250
Thayer, Webster, 260, 268. *See also* Sacco and Vanzetti
"They Laid Jesus Christ in His Grave," 137, 161–62
"Thirty 8th Parallel," 123
"This Land Is Your Land": and Arlo Guthrie, 281–82; in *Bound for Glory* (film), 24, 25, 35; and collective action, 250; composition of, 59; de-radicalization of, 4, 15, 276, 307; and "God Bless America" (Berlin), 24, 25–26, 60–61; and Springsteen, 296–97
"This Morning I Am Born Again," 138, 162, 176
"This World Is Not My Home" (hymn), 231
"Three Sisters," 242
Thurmond, Strom, 177
"Times They Are A-Changing, The" (Dylan), 283
"Tom Joad," 12, 27, 162–64, 223
Trenton Six, 192
Truman, Harry, 120, 126, 175–76
Trump, Donald: according to Guthrie, Arlo, 282; and fascism, 301; and Guthrie's progressive vision, 224, 239, 259, 299–300, 302; and hate groups, 303; his father, 191, 300, 305; and Nazi marchers, 180, 301; and the Republican Party, 130, 131; and Springsteen, 297; and the working class, 131, 168, 293, 305; and xenophobic rhetoric, 258, 272, 297
Trump, Fred, 191, 300, 305
Tubman, Harriet, 192, 196
Tulsa, Oklahoma, 183
"Two Good Men," 268

"Union Boys," 174
"Union Burying Ground," 237, 247, 248
"Union Love Juice," 208–9
"Union Maid," 67, 170, 203, 212, 306
unions: and the Almanac Singers, 17–18, 92–97, 173; and artists, 173; and black music, 189; in *Bound for Glory* (film), 34, 35; and Bridges, 52; and California, 169, 170, 304; and collective action, 162, 249–250; collective bargaining, 175; and "commonism," 168–69; and communism, 172; contemporary, 267; and the cult of Jesus, 138, 176; and equality, 168; and family, 206, 212; and farmers, 233–34; and fascism, 170, 173, 219; and Guthrie's ideal, 168, 169–70, 304–7; and the Korean War, 121; and the Merchant Marine, 174; and miners, 246–48, 251–55; and the New Deal, 138; and the NMU, 93, 165; and the outlaw tradition, 173–74; picket lines, 166; postwar, 114; and poverty, 194; and the profit system, 219; and race, 67, 190; and Reagan, 167–68; and

unions (*continued*)
    religion, 170; and Robeson, 192; and the Sharecroppers Union, 67, 203; songs, 106–7; strikes, 167, 171–72, 176–77, 231, 251–55, 262; and *Struggle*, 241–42, 246–48; today, 305; and Tom Joad, 163; and violence, 170–71, 246, 251–55; and women, 67, 93, 168, 173, 202–4, 209; and the working class, 55–56. *See also* labor; one big union; reform
United Auto Workers, 121. *See also* unions
United Mine Workers, 246, 253. *See also* miners; unions
U.S. Army, 110–12, 189–90, 240–41, 242
utility companies, 50. *See also* Bonneville Power Administration

Vanzetti, Bartolomeo, 257, 260. *See also* Sacco and Vanzetti
"Vanzetti's Letter," 269
"Vanzetti's Rock," 269
"VD Gunner," 242
Veterans of Foreign Wars, 192–93
Vietnam War, 9, 39, 123–24, 126–27, 155, 279–80, 290, 292, 307. *See also* war
"Vigilante Man," 34, 223, 227
violence: and anarchism, 263; in Calumet, Michigan, 251–53; and "commonism," 154, 162; and fighting racism, 195–196; and "Galveston Bay" (Springsteen), 295; Kansas City Massacre, 156; in Ludlow, Colorado, 251, 253–55, 263; lynching, 65, 183–84, 192, 244, 250, 291; and the outlaw tradition, 155–56; Peekskill riots, 192–93; and Sacco and Vanzetti, 261; in Tulsa, Oklahoma, 183; and unions, 170–71, 246, 251–55; vs. collective action, 171
Von Fritsch, Gunther, 81, 82–83

Wagner Act, 175. *See also* unions
"Waist Deep in the Big Muddy" (Seeger), 123
"Waiting at the Gate," 237, 247
Wall Street, 49, 51, 74, 123, 125, 293. *See also* capitalism
Wallace, Henry, 116, 122, 175, 177, 305
"Wallace Day," 177
war: and capitalism, 53, 55, 64–65, 98; and the CIO, 92; Korean War, 17, 109, 120–27; love not war, 124; military preparedness, 78; and the Nazi invasion of Soviet Union, 88; opposition to, 68, 69–72, 78–79, 135; and the profit system, 55, 69; and unions, 114; Veterans of Foreign Wars, 192–93; Vietnam War, 9, 39, 123–24, 126–27, 155, 279–80, 290, 292, 307. *See also* World War I; World War II
"War Songs & Work Songs," 174, 187
Washington, D.C., 176
"We Welcome to Heaven," 269

Weavers, 121. *See also* blacklist
West Texas State University, 9, 10, 181, 310
Western Federation of Miners, 246, 251. *See also* miners; unions
Wetherald, Robert P., 219, 222
Wexler, Haskell, 24, 31, 36–37, 39
"What Kind of Bomb," 242
"When You're Down and Out," 171
"Which Side Are You On?" (Dylan), 289
White, Josh, 92, 243
Whitman, Walt, 213–14, 223, 276–77, 295
"Why Do They Stand in the Rain," 93
"Why Is it?," 123
Wilco, 4, 193, 194, 202, 286
Wilkie, Wendell, 71
"Will Rogers Highway," 196
women: and abortion, 214–215; in *Bound for Glory* (film), 35; and "commonism," 111, 204; and feminism, 201; and gender roles, 18, 105–6, 200–202, 204, 206, 208, 212; and the Korea songs, 125; and politics, 201–2, 204; and popular culture, 111; and unions, 67, 93, 168, 173, 202–4, 209. *See also* family; gender equality; sexuality
Wood, Bob and Ida, 67, 69
Woodard, Isaac, 191
Woodstock Music Festival, 280–81. *See also* music
Woodward, Isaac, 245
Woody Guthrie Archives, 12–14

Woody Guthrie Folk Music Center, **143–45**
"Woody Sez" columns, 16, 47–58, 60, 63–75, 116, 135–40, 160–61, 249
Woodyfest, 4, 13, **150–52**. *See also* music
Workers Alliance, 68
working class: and the Briley family, 22; exploitation of, 10, 266, 301, 310; and Guthrie's ideal, 300; and the hurt song, 296; and Jesus of Nazareth, 132; in 1970s, 167–68; and race, 168; and religion, 130–31, 301–2; and Springsteen, 293–98; and Trump, 131, 168, 293, 305; and the "Woody Sez" columns, 48–49. *See also* class; common people; labor; migrants (dust bowl); *Struggle*; unions
World War I: and farming, 221, 233; Red Scare, 122, 220, 257, 260, 268, 271, 306; and socialism, 44, 169
World War II: and the Almanac Singers, 92–97; as capitalist conflict, 53, 55; and the CIO, 172–73; and Guthrie's Jesus, 137; and labor, 18, 98, 165, 167; and politics, 98; postwar disillusionment, 219–20; service during, 3, 103–7, 110–12. *See also* antifascism; fascism; HUAC; McCarthyism; Red Scare; war
writings: album notes, 224–26; and Guthrie's agricultural roots, 232–34; letter to Hays, 233–34;

writings (*continued*)
　letters to other women, 112, 120, 200, 207, 209–10, 211, 213, 241–42, 278, 308; in 1947, 210; other projects, 119, 123. See also *Bound for Glory* (Guthrie); "Woody Sez" columns

xenophobia, 19, 168, 220, 257–58, 262, 271–73

"You Are the People's Army," 244
"You Got to Walk That Lonesome Valley," 242
"You Gotta Go Down and Join the Union," 190
"You Souls of Boston," 268
"Your Ku Klux Klan," 195

Zimmerman, Robert Allen. *See* Dylan, Bob

www.ingramcontent.com/pod-product-compliance
Lightning Source LLC
Chambersburg PA
CBHW030441090526
44586CB00044B/452